William Miller, PhD, MLS
Rita M. Pellen, MLS
Editors

Evolving
Internet Reference Resources

Evolving Internet Reference Resources has been co-published simultaneously as *Journal of Library Administration*, Volume 43, Numbers 3/4 2005 and Volume 44, Numbers 1/2 2006.

*Pre-publication
REVIEWS,
COMMENTARIES,
EVALUATIONS . . .*

"**F**inding information on the Web is easy. Finding QUALITY information on the Web is quite another story. Mixed in with all the commercial come-ons, political rants, and adult content are some very good information sources. THIS NEW BOOK WILL HELP READERS SEPARATE THE GOOD FROM THE MEDIOCRE (OR WORSE). Each of the chapters points to some of the best academic resources on the Web, providing researchers with evaluative Webliographies of quality information. Each contribution will help guide researchers to relevant information and will also help librarians build stronger pathfinders and subject guides."

David Tyckoson, MLS
*Director of Public Services
Henry Madden Library
California State University–Fresno*

More pre-publication
REVIEWS, COMMENTARIES, EVALUATIONS . . .

"The contributors have performed two REALLY USEFUL services. The first was to create an annotated list of essential Web sites (both open-access and proprietary) in over twenty academic subject areas ranging from art to engineering to Latin-American studies. The second was to add value by framing their annotated lists within the context of how research is conducted in the field as well as within each field's major print resources. This book is a good tool for reference and collection development librarians, but don't hide your copy in the back room. STUDENTS AND RE-SEARCHERS WILL BENEFIT AS MUCH AS LIBRARIANS."

Donald A Barclay, MLIS, MA
Assistant University Librarian
for Public Services
University of California, Merced

The Haworth Information Press®
An Imprint of The Haworth Press, Inc.

Evolving
Internet Reference Resources

Evolving Internet Reference Resources has been co-published simultaneously as *Journal of Library Administration*, Volume 43, Numbers 3/4 2005 and Volume 44, Numbers 1/2 2006.

Monographic Separates from the *Journal of Library Administration*™

For additional information on these and other Haworth Press titles, including descriptions, tables of contents, reviews, and prices, use the QuickSearch catalog at http://www.HaworthPress.com.

Evolving Internet Reference Resources, edited by William Miller, PhD, MLS, and Rita M. Pellen, MLS (Vol. 43, No. 3/4, 2005 and Vol. 44, No. 1/2, 2006). *This book surveys the availability of online information, both free and subscription-based, in a wide variety of subject areas, including law, psychology, health and medicine, engineering, Latin American studies, and more.*

Portals and Libraries, edited by Sarah C. Michalak, MLS (Vol. 43, No. 1/2, 2005). *An examination of the organization of Web-based and other electronic information resources with a review of different types of portals, attached services, and how to make the best use of them.*

Licensing in Libraries: Practical and Ethical Aspects, edited by Karen Rupp-Serrano, MLS, MPA (Vol. 42, No. 3/4, 2005). *Presents state-of-the-art information on licensing issues, including contract management, end-user education, copyright, e-books, consortial licensing software, legalities, and much more.*

Collection Management and Strategic Access to Digital Resources: The New Challenges for Research Libraries, edited by Sul H. Lee (Vol. 42, No. 2, 2005). *Examines how libraries can make the best use of digital materials, maintain a balance between print and electronic resources, and respond to electronic information.*

The Eleventh Off-Campus Library Services Conference, edited by Patrick B. Mahoney, MBA, MLS (Vol. 41, No. 1/2/3/4, 2004). *Examines–and offers solutions to–the problems faced by librarians servicing faculty and students who do not have access to a traditional library.*

Libraries Act on Their LibQUAL+™ *Findings: From Data to Action*, edited by Fred M. Heath, EdD, Martha Kyrillidou, MEd, MLS, and Consuella A. Askew, MLS (Vol. 40, No. 3/4, 2004). *Focuses on the value of LibQUAL+*™ *data to help librarians provide better services for users.*

The Changing Landscape for Electronic Resources: Content, Access, Delivery, and Legal Issues, edited by Yem S. Fong, MLS, and Suzanne M. Ward, MA (Vol. 40, No. 1/2, 2004). *Focuses on various aspects of electronic resources for libraries, including statewide resource-sharing initiatives, licensing issues, open source software, standards, and scholarly publishing.*

Improved Access to Information: Portals, Content Selection, and Digital Information, edited by Sul H. Lee (Vol. 39, No. 4, 2003). *Examines how improved electronic resources can allow libraries to provide an increasing amount of digital information to an ever-expanding patron base.*

Digital Images and Art Libraries in the Twenty-First Century, edited by Susan Wyngaard, MLS (Vol. 39, No. 2/3, 2003). *Provides an in-depth look at the technology that art librarians must understand in order to work effectively in today's digital environment.*

The Twenty-First Century Art Librarian, edited by Terrie L. Wilson, MLS (Vol. 39, No. 1, 2003). *"A MUST-READ addition to every art, architecture, museum, and visual resources library bookshelf." (Betty Jo Irvine, PhD, Fine Arts Librarian, Indiana University)*

The Strategic Stewardship of Cultural Resources: To Preserve and Protect, edited by Andrea T. Merrill, BA (Vol. 38, No. 1/2/3/4, 2003). *Leading library, museum, and archival professionals share their expertise on a wide variety of preservation and security issues.*

Distance Learning Library Services: The Tenth Off-Campus Library Services Conference, edited by Patrick B. Mahoney (Vol. 37, No. 1/2/3/4, 2002). *Explores the pitfalls of providing information services to distance students and suggests ways to avoid them.*

Electronic Resources and Collection Development, edited by Sul H. Lee (Vol. 36, No. 3, 2002). *Shows how electronic resources have impacted traditional collection development policies and practices.*

Information Literacy Programs: Successes and Challenges, edited by Patricia Durisin, MLIS (Vol. 36, No. 1/2, 2002). *Examines Web-based collaboration, teamwork with academic and administrative colleagues, evidence-based librarianship, and active learning strategies in library instruction programs.*

Evaluating the Twenty-First Century Library: The Association of Research Libraries New Measures Initiative, 1997-2001, edited by Donald L. DeWitt, PhD (Vol. 35, No. 4, 2001). *This collection of articles (thirteen of which previously appeared in ARL's bimonthly newsletter/ report on research issues and actions) examines the Association of Research Libraries' "new measures" initiative.*

Impact of Digital Technology on Library Collections and Resource Sharing, edited by Sul H. Lee (Vol. 35, No. 3, 2001). *Shows how digital resources have changed the traditional academic library.*

Libraries and Electronic Resources: New Partnerships, New Practices, New Perspectives, edited by Pamela L. Higgins (Vol. 35, No. 1/2, 2001). *An essential guide to the Internet's impact on electronic resources management past, present, and future.*

Diversity Now: People, Collections, and Services in Academic Libraries, edited by Teresa Y. Neely, PhD, and Kuang-Hwei (Janet) Lee-Smeltzer, MS, MSLIS (Vol. 33, No. 1/2/3/4, 2001). *Examines multicultural trends in academic libraries' staff and users, types of collections, and services offered.*

Leadership in the Library and Information Science Professions: Theory and Practice, edited by Mark D. Winston, MLS, PhD (Vol. 32, No. 3/4, 2001). *Offers fresh ideas for developing and using leadership skills, including recruiting potential leaders, staff training and development, issues of gender and ethnic diversity, and budget strategies for success.*

Off-Campus Library Services, edited by Ann Marie Casey (Vol. 31, No. 3/4, 2001 and Vol. 32, No. 1/2, 2001). *This informative volume examines various aspects of off-campus, or distance learning. It explores training issues for library staff, Web site development, changing roles for librarians, the uses of conferencing software, library support for Web-based courses, library agreements and how to successfully negotiate them, and much more!*

Research Collections and Digital Information, edited by Sul H. Lee (Vol. 31, No. 2, 2000). *Offers new strategies for collecting, organizing, and accessing library materials in the digital age.*

Academic Research on the Internet: Options for Scholars and Libraries, edited by Helen Laurence, MLS, EdD, and William Miller, MLS, PhD (Vol. 30, No. 1/2/3/4, 2000). *"Emphasizes quality over quantity. . . . Presents the reader with the best research-oriented Web sites in the field. A state-of-the-art review of academic use of the Internet as well as a guide to the best Internet sites and services. . . . A useful addition for any academic library." (David A. Tyckoson, MLS, Head of Reference, California State University, Fresno)*

Management for Research Libraries Cooperation, edited by Sul H. Lee (Vol. 29. No. 3/4, 2000). *Delivers sound advice, models, and strategies for increasing sharing between institutions to maximize the amount of printed and electronic research material you can make available in your library while keeping costs under control.*

Integration in the Library Organization, edited by Christine E. Thompson, PhD (Vol. 29, No. 2, 1999). *Provides librarians with the necessary tools to help libraries balance and integrate public and technical services and to improve the capability of libraries to offer patrons quality services and large amounts of information.*

Library Training for Staff and Customers, edited by Sara Ramser Beck, MLS, MBA (Vol. 29, No. 1, 1999). *This comprehensive book is designed to assist library professionals involved in presenting or planning training for library staff members and customers. You will explore ideas for effective general reference training, training on automated systems, training in specialized subjects such as African American history and biography, and training for areas such as patents and trademarks, and business subjects.* Library Training for Staff and Customers *answers numerous training questions and is an excellent guide for planning staff development.*

Evolving
Internet Reference Resources

William Miller
Rita M. Pellen
Editors

Evolving Internet Reference Resources has been co-published simultaneously as *Journal of Library Administration*, Volume 43, Numbers 3/4 2005 and Volume 44, Numbers 1/2 2006.

The Haworth Information Press®
An Imprint of The Haworth Press, Inc.

New York • London • Victoria (AU)
www.HaworthPress.com

Published by

The Haworth Information Press®, 10 Alice Street, Binghamton, NY 13904-1580 USA

The Haworth Information Press® is an imprint of The Haworth Press, Inc., 10 Alice Street, Binghamton, NY 13904-1580 USA.

Evolving Internet Reference Resources has been co-published simultaneously as *Journal of Library Administration*™, Volume 43, Numbers 3/4 2005 and Volume 44, Numbers 1/2 2006.

The development, preparation, and publication of this work has been undertaken with great care. However, the publisher, employees, editors, and agents of The Haworth Press and all imprints of The Haworth Press, Inc., including The Haworth Medical Press® and Pharmaceutical Products Press®, are not responsible for any errors contained herein or for consequences that may ensue from use of materials or information contained in this work. Opinions expressed by the author(s) are not necessarily those of The Haworth Press, Inc. With regard to case studies, identities and circumstances of individuals discussed herein have been changed to protect confidentiality. Any resemblance to actual persons, living or dead, is entirely coincidental.

Cover design by Wendy Arakawa.

Library of Congress Cataloging-in-Publication Data

Evolving Internet reference resources / William Miller, Rita M. Pellen, editors.
    p. cm.
    Co-published simultaneously as Journal of library administration, v. 43, nos. 3/4, 2005 and v. 44, nos. 1/2, 2006.
    Includes bibliographical references and index.
    ISBN-13: 978-0-7890-3024-5 (alk. paper)
    ISBN-10: 0-7890-3024-1 (alk. paper)
    ISBN-13: 978-0-7890-3025-2 (pbk. : alk. paper)
    ISBN-10: 0-7890-3025-X (pbk. : alk. paper)
    1. Internet in library reference services. 2. Electronic reference sources. 3. Scholarly Web sites.
I. Miller, William, 1947- II. Pellen, Rita M. III. Journal of library administration.

Z711.47 .E97 2006
025.5'24–dc22

2005014525

Indexing, Abstracting & Website/Internet Coverage

This section provides you with a list of major indexing & abstracting services and other tools for bibliographic access. That is to say, each service began covering this periodical during the year noted in the right column. Most Websites which are listed below have indicated that they will either post, disseminate, compile, archive, cite or alert their own Website users with research-based content from this work. (This list is as current as the copyright date of this publication.)

(continued)

(continued)

(continued)

Special Bibliographic Notes related to special journal issues (separates) and indexing/abstracting:

- indexing/abstracting services in this list will also cover material in any "separate" that is co-published simultaneously with Haworth's special thematic journal issue or DocuSerial. Indexing/abstracting usually covers material at the article/chapter level.
- monographic co-editions are intended for either non-subscribers or libraries which intend to purchase a second copy for their circulating collections.
- monographic co-editions are reported to all jobbers/wholesalers/approval plans. The source journal is listed as the "series" to assist the prevention of duplicate purchasing in the same manner utilized for books-in-series.
- to facilitate user/access services all indexing/abstracting services are encouraged to utilize the co-indexing entry note indicated at the bottom of the first page of each article/chapter/contribution.
- this is intended to assist a library user of any reference tool (whether print, electronic, online, or CD-ROM) to locate the monographic version if the library has purchased this version but not a subscription to the source journal.
- individual articles/chapters in any Haworth publication are also available through the Haworth Document Delivery Service (HDDS).

Evolving
Internet Reference Resources

CONTENTS

ABOUT THE EDITORS

William Miller, PhD, MLS, is Director of Libraries at Florida Atlantic University in Boca Raton. He formerly served as Head of Reference at Michigan State University in East Lansing, and as Associate Dean of Libraries at Bowling Green State University in Ohio. Dr. Miller is past President of the Association of College and Research Libraries, has served as Chair of the *Choice* magazine editorial board, and is a contributing editor of *Library Issues*. He was named Instruction Librarian of the Year in 2004 by the Association of College and Research Libraries Instruction Section.

Rita M. Pellen, MLS, is Associate Director of Libraries at Florida Atlantic University in Boca Raton. She was formerly Assistant Director of Public Services and Head of the Reference Department at Florida Atlantic. In 1993, Ms. Pellen received the Gabor Exemplary Employee Award in recognition for outstanding service to FAU, and in 1997, the "Literati Club Award for Excellence" for the outstanding paper presented in *The Bottom Line*. She has served on committees in LAMA, ACRL, and ALCTS, as well as the Southeast Florida Library Information Network, SEFLIN, a multi-type library cooperative in South Florida. Honor society memberships include Beta Phi Mu and Phi Kappa Phi.

Introduction:
Conducting Research Online:
A Survey of the Information Map

William Miller

This volume is in many ways a successor to *Academic Research on the Internet: Options for Scholars and Libraries*, which I edited with Helen Laurence for The Haworth Press, Inc. in 1999 (and which was co-published as Volume 30 of *Journal of Library Administration* (no. 1-4, 2000)). In some ways, the world has changed greatly in the intervening five or six years. At that time, the most widely-known search engines were Northern Light, Snap, AltaVista, HotBot, and Lycos. Google did not yet exist, Yahoo had not proliferated, blogs were yet to be born, and we did not imagine that scholars, at any rate, would attempt to conduct all of their research via the Internet, except in the most limited of circumstances. Accordingly, that book covered the printed as well as online sources in a wide variety of fields. This volume, on the other hand, covers only online resources, and illustrates that in certain fields, it is possible now to conduct much of one's work online on a regular basis, although many of the sources one might want are not free of charge. As usual, therefore, libraries continue to be the avenue for research, as it moves online, for the vast majority of students and scholars, many of whom will not even understand that the materials available to them are available only because their library is paying the subscription cost.

[Haworth co-indexing entry note]: "Introduction: Conducting Research Online: A Survey of the Information Map." Miller, William. Co-published simultaneously in *Journal of Library Administration* (The Haworth Information Press, an imprint of The Haworth Press, Inc.) Vol. 43, No. 3/4, 2005, pp. 1-7; and: *Evolving Internet Reference Resources* (ed: William Miller, and Rita M. Pellen) The Haworth Information Press, an imprint of The Haworth Press, Inc., 2006, pp. 1-7. Single or multiple copies of this article are available for a fee from The Haworth Document Delivery Service [1-800-HAWORTH, 9:00 a.m. - 5:00 p.m. (EST). E-mail address: docdelivery@haworthpress.com].

Available online at http://www.haworthpress.com/web/JLA
doi:10.1300/J111v43n03_01

The relative paucity of resources in 1999 did not inhibit the tendency of students to assume that all knowledge was already available online, and to assume that whatever they could find online for free was good enough for whatever they had to do. These assumptions have not changed, and constitute a major problem for instructors. Much of what is on the Web could have been created by *Saturday Night Live*'s Brian Fellow, the idiotic nature program host described this way at the start of every TV episode featuring him:

> Brian Fellow is not an accredited zoologist, nor does he hold an advanced degree in any of the environmental sciences. He is simply an enthusiastic young man with a sixth grade education and an abiding love for all of God's creatures . . . share his love tonight on Brian Fellow's Safari Planet!

There is much more available on the Internet now than there was five years ago, but much of it seems to have been created by Brian Fellow. Students use such materials at their intellectual peril, but they do persist in using whatever pops up first and is handiest. Moreover, the usual search result of 10,000 hits, in no particular order, generated by popular Web search engines will not help novice researchers very much. Hence, the Webliographic essays presented here should be of value to the novice, if directed to them, as well as to more mature researchers who have a difficult time, quite understandably, in keeping up with new developments in this rapidly growing Web universe.

Part I of the monograph concentrates on the Humanities and Social Sciences. Roberto C. Ferrari, one of only two "repeat authors" from my earlier volume, concentrated on art and architecture in general in that work, but in his article here, "Researching Art(ists) on the Internet," he concentrates on biographical sources and the significant developments in the availability of images on the Web which have arisen in the past several years. Julie Roberson, in "Removing the Boundaries: Composition and Rhetoric Internet Resources from Classical Greece to the Present Day," discusses the ways in which Internet resources are "transforming the theory and practice of rhetoric and composition today," as well as "providing new modes of expression." In a related piece, Debora Richey and Mona Kratzert's "'I Too Dislike It': The Evolving Presence of Poetry on the Internet" discusses the enormous burgeoning of both primary and secondary materials relating to poetry on the Internet, and the ways in which poetry itself is being transformed by this widespread availability. Rebecca S. Albitz's piece "From Celluloid to Digital: Electronic Resources for Film Studies" surveys the large variety of free Web sites but concludes that "their veracity can be suspect." She recommends using commercial sites for more reliable information.

Paul A. Frisch, in "Popular Web-Based Reference Sources for United States History," discusses how to cope with the almost overwhelming volume of material in this area on the Web, and explores strategies for librarians to categorize this material and point their users to metasites, directories, and other resources which could facilitate organized inquiry. Wade R. Kotter, in "Evolving Internet Reference in Anthropology: What Our Patrons Want and How We Can Help Them Find It," takes the interesting approach of categorizing "eight of the most common categories of reference questions in this extraordinarily broad and diverse discipline," such as finding information about recent discoveries or finding information about specific archeological sites and ancient cultures, and shows the reader some of the best resources for dealing with these major areas. Many of these resources, such as eHRAF, are not free, but are nevertheless crucial in providing the quality of information the serious inquirer will need to have.

In "Exploring LGBTQ Online Resources," Ellen Greenblatt evaluates a variety of resources in the area of lesbian, gay, bisexual, and transgender studies, and points to the trend in which commercial publishers have been acquiring some of the best resources in this field, resources which were formerly available without charge online. A similar trend exists in the field of women's studies, as pointed out by Cindy Ingold in her article "Women and Gender Studies Internet Reference Resources: A Critical Overview." She states that "there has been a steady growth of online databases including indexing and abstracting services, full-text databases, and digitized collections." Many of these, from publishers such as Alexander Street Press, will be affordable only at larger libraries.

Several articles, included here, explore geographical area studies. Lisa Klopfer, in "Internet Reference Sources for Asian Studies," states that "the Internet has actually broadened and enlivened this field," and is providing information that has not been available previously in printed form, such as mapping data. Molly Molloy's "The Internet in Latin America: Development and Reference Sources," explores the development of Internet resources in Latin America, both public domain and subscription-based, and discusses the potential of online resources to enhance social activism and level the economic and social disparities in that region.

Two articles describe new approaches to the creation of Internet-accessible information by librarians. In "Creating a Web Resource: African American Kentuckian Profiles," Reinette F. Jones describes an interesting project undertaken by reference librarians at the University of Kentucky, to create their own online reference tool to supplement the scarcity of printed information regarding Black Kentuckians. Melissa Laning, Catherine Lavallée-Welch, and Margo Smith discuss the history of librarian-created Weblogs and their value as professional development tools in "Frontiers of Effort: Librarians and Professional Development Blogs."

In "Psyched About Psychology Internet Resources," Alice J. Perez provides an overview of both free and proprietary resources in the field of psychology, such as databases, encyclopedias, dictionaries, megasites, yearbooks, and research guides which reference staff can use to help the public. Her piece reveals the wide variety of resources now available in this popular field. Linda Marie Golian-Lui provides a similar overview of education in her article, "Internet Resources for Education Reference." Golian-Lui highlights commercial databases, government and educational association Web sites, and specialty Web pages in her piece.

Ellen M. Krupar and Nicole J. Auer discuss online resources about the world's largest industry—tourism—in "Avoiding Accidental Tourism: Reference Resources for Travel Research." They point out that most people are familiar only with booking Web sites, but that there is a whole wealth of information beyond them. In "Finding Your Future: College and Career Information on the Internet," Kara J. Gust and Holly A. Flynn survey the state of Internet-accessible information in free and proprietary college and career resources. Gust and Flynn point to many resources on testing, and state that online versions of college guides "provide great additional benefits such as customizable searches, personal accounts and portals, and automated search engines that match preferences to majors and careers."

John Hickok, in "ESL (English as a Second Language) Web Sites: Resources for Library Administrators, Librarians, and ESL Library Users," emphasizes the resources available to those who teach English to speakers of other languages. At least 37 million people speak a language other than English at home, and these resources would be useful to that population as well. Yvonne J. Chandler's very extensive review of online legal resources, in "Accessing Legal and Regulatory Information in Internet Resources and Documents," shows how far the Internet age has come, in terms of the quantity and quality of legal and governmental information that is now accessible online. The difference in length between Chandler's earlier piece in *Academic Research on the Internet* (she is the other "repeat" author) and her article here underscores the growth of electronic resources, in all areas. Here, she emphasizes two factors causing this growth: the U.S. government's determined effort to increase such resources, and the development of RSS technology, which serves customized information directly to users.

Brenda G. Mathenia, in "A Guide to Online Map and Mapping Resources," shows that the Internet has created not only widespread availability but also new kinds of information such as interactive mapping, not possible with traditional printed maps. New mapping sites allow people to correlate socio-economic, historical, and physical data to create their own personalized maps. In "Searching of Our Surroundings: Looking at the Environment from the Internet," Ola C. Riley surveys Web sites in five major categories: portals, government sites, special environmental issues, general environmental sites, and databases. As might be expected, government agency Web sites are an important component here, though private agencies such as the National Resources Defense Council also make important contributions.

Government Web sites are also an important component of the wealth of information available online regarding agriculture, as documented in Kathy Fescemyer's "Using the Internet to Find Information on Agriculture's Hot Topics." University-based sites are also important, of course. Fescemyer focuses on describing sites for general information, statistics, agricultural economics, plant sciences, food sciences, and animal and veterinary sciences. Another piece focuses on the area of health, where the available online resources are, of course, enormous. In "Health and Medical Resources: Information for the Consumer," Caryl Gray surveys a wide range of comprehensive sites, directories, portals, governmental and association sites, and sites that deal with drug information, alternative medicine, nutrition and food safety, and other health issues.

In "A Virtual Reference Shelf for Nursing Students and Faculty: Selected Sources," Eleanor Lomax and Susan K. Setterlund declare that it is now reasonable for those who study nursing to have a virtual reference shelf equivalent to that which formerly existed only in paper, and they systematically show how a variety of online resources can be put together to constitute this electronic reference shelf. In addition to things like CINAHL and Books@Ovid, they cover the fields of research and grants, education and careers, organizations, discussion forums and e-mail lists, dictionaries, encyclopedias, drugs and pharmacology, handbooks and manuals, laboratory and diagnostic tests, statistical sources, and the history of nursing.

The hard sciences are represented in this volume by two pieces. Michael Knee surveys the field of computer science in "Internet Reference Sources for Computing and Computer Science: A Selected Guide." He covers bibliographic databases, bibliographies, dictionaries, encyclopedias, directories and guides, book reviews, and finding aids for technical reports. He covers both fee-based and free resources at a variety of skill levels, from general user to faculty and professionals. Finally, in "Web-Based Reference Sources for Engineering," Thomas W. Conkling surveys the online availability of numerical data resources, formulas, conversion factors, materials property data, information on components and parts, and information on vendors and their products. He states that "companies, publishers, and government agencies have digitized large quantities of data in the last several years and are making it available on the Web in either free or subscription-based modes."

Taken as a whole, several clear themes emerge from an analysis of the articles collected here. Obviously, there is considerably more information available online now than there was several years ago, but this increase comes at a cost, including all the dangers inherent in slipshod or untrustworthy material being purveyed, either free or for a fee. Now that we have inherited a wide-ranging universe of electronic information, much of it divorced from the traditional editing and editorial functions, we find our chief reliance to be on information produced by government agencies, independent associations, and academic institutions—as well as the more traditional products of commercial publishers in the online realm.

Researchers can now commonly find much of what they need electronically. It is also the case that much high quality information is available free of charge. On the other hand, the online world has not overturned the commercial model, and does not appear likely to do so; the tendency of commercial publishers to take over databases that began as volunteer efforts, for instance, in the areas of Women's Studies and Gay, Lesbian, and Bisexual Studies, is noteworthy in this regard.

Internet resources are certainly more ubiquitous and accessible now than print materials, and that is of considerable importance, but they are most important when they add value, enabling researchers to do things they could not do with traditional printed resources, such as interactive mapping, creation of new literary genres, or full-text searching for terms. It may be that the open-source movement, Wikipedia-like self-correcting strategies, and new, as-yet-unknown developments will change the map of online resources considerably in future years, and further increase the possibility that they could constitute essentially all that is needed in most fields. However, that time has not yet come upon us, and there is no particular indication that it ever will. Meanwhile, however, we are all coming to depend more and more on online resources for at least some of our work, and in many cases a considerable portion of it.

Researching Art(ists) on the Internet

Roberto C. Ferrari

SUMMARY. This article addresses some of the important Internet reference sources currently available for researching art and artists. The most common art reference question is usually biographical in nature, but art- and artist-related questions don't stop there. Reference questions can be about specific works of art, looking for images, and so on. Fortunately, the Internet has become an excellent place to track down the answers to these and many other art reference questions. *[Article copies available for a fee from The Haworth Document Delivery Service: 1-800-HAWORTH. E-mail address: <docdelivery@haworthpress.com> Website: <http://www.HaworthPress.com> © 2005 by The Haworth Press, Inc. All rights reserved.]*

KEYWORDS. Art information, art history research, art Web sites, digital images

"I need information on the artist Pablo Picasso."
"I'm writing my thesis on the critical history of Michelangelo's *Creation of Adam* since the nineteenth century."

Roberto C. Ferrari is Associate University Librarian, Florida Atlantic University, S. E. Wimberly Library, 777 Glades Road, Boca Raton, FL 33431 (E-mail: rferrari@fau.edu).

[Haworth co-indexing entry note]: "Researching Art(ists) on the Internet." Ferrari, Roberto C. Co-published simultaneously in *Journal of Library Administration* (The Haworth Information Press, an imprint of The Haworth Press, Inc.) Vol. 43, No. 3/4, 2005, pp. 9-25; and: *Evolving Internet Reference Resources* (ed: William Miller, and Rita M. Pellen) The Haworth Information Press, an imprint of The Haworth Press, Inc., 2006, pp. 9-25. Single or multiple copies of this article are available for a fee from The Haworth Document Delivery Service [1-800-HAWORTH, 9:00 a.m. - 5:00 p.m. (EST). E-mail address: docdelivery@haworthpress.com].

Available online at http://www.haworthpress.com/web/JLA
© 2005 by The Haworth Press, Inc. All rights reserved.
doi:10.1300/J111v43n03_02

9

"Can you help me find images of bamboo in Asian art?"

These are samples of the many different types of reference questions an art librarian or art information specialist may receive on a given day. The art librarian might easily answer the first question by consulting her/his library OPAC. But what if the person needs an exhaustive bibliography? And what of the other questions? They may not be so easily answered using an OPAC. More detailed research is needed in order to help the person find out what s/he wants to know. Traditional print sources that might answer these questions have existed for most of the twentieth century, but over the past decade, the Internet has made accessing the answers to these questions faster, easier, and more up-to-date. But traditionally art researchers have been hesitant to use the Internet for their research.

Art researchers typically work with materials based on creativity (e.g., paintings and sculptures), and then with the age, medium, and/or theories related to that creative process. In other words, they work first with a three-dimensional creative object and then apply ideas to it. Art researchers need to "see" the work which they are discussing, and thus often visit museums or galleries or private collections in order to "do" their primary research. When personal visits are not possible, they rely on illustrated monographs, from catalogues raisonnes to "coffee table books," journal articles, and slides or photographs to provide the visual images they need for study.[1] This reliance on site visits and print materials might seem to negate the use of the Internet as a research tool. This assumption, however, is a mistake. Over the past few years, the Internet–specifically the World Wide Web–has become a major arena for visual imagery and art resources that before one could only find in print. It is now the job of the art librarian to know how to stand in the middle of that arena and strategically manipulate all of the art resources that surround her/him.

A recent informal survey on ARLIS-L, the discussion list for ARLIS/NA, the Art Libraries Society of North America, gleaned a few interesting, although not necessarily surprising, results.[2] Over two-thirds of the respondents identified that the most common type of art question they answered was biographical in nature. Other frequent questions related to researching a specific work of art or finding images.[3] This informal survey also produced an interesting list of some of the most common Internet-based resources consulted by art librarians in order to assist people with these reference questions.[4] Those most frequently used, and other important Internet-based sources, are discussed in this article, within the framework of the type of materials or research often sought by the researcher. These include both fee-based databases and free Web sites, and are divided into four sections: Books, Articles, Internet Subject Directories, and Images. It is not my intention to create an exhaustive list of art information sources, but rather to provide the reader with some of the best Internet-based resources for answering common art(ist)-related reference questions. All resources were available as of December 1, 2004.

BOOKS

There should be no hesitation on the part of every art librarian to use her/his own library OPAC to look for books on art and artists. Arguably, the most common art biographical questions will relate to artists who are more well known. As a result, it stands to reason that most libraries will have at least one or two books on these individuals or at least the movements with which s/he may be associated.

But every librarian knows that one's own OPAC may not be enough to help a researcher. Online databases such as OCLC's WorldCat <http://www.oclc.org/worldcat/> have expanded the scope of book research. By consulting WorldCat after one's own OPAC, a researcher has opened up to her/himself an entire country, if not a world, of library holdings. Yet, WorldCat can be overwhelming, with its contents of the thousands of libraries' holdings resulting in an awesome number of hits. For instance, the inexperienced lay person might perform a simple keyword search on "pablo picasso" and s/he would be presented with an intimidating 6,630 hits. Because WorldCat is also a fee-based product, it is possible the researcher might not have ready access to the product. As a result, the librarian should not rule out the possibility that free Web databases might be helpful.

The OPACs of large art museum libraries may prove to be extremely helpful to the researcher. Like most OPACs, these are free to the public and allow the researcher to see information specific to the discipline and topic at hand. In addition, art museum libraries will often carry smaller works such as exhibition pamphlets or brochures produced by local museums or galleries. Most university and public libraries often discard these items because they are easily lost, stolen, or damaged, and/or the content may not be considered cost-effective for cataloging purposes. Yet, these small publications might turn out to be some, if not all, the information available on a particular artist or her/his work. Often these works are housed in artist files or vertical files in these museums' libraries. Art museum libraries also actively collect non-English publications in an attempt to collect all print resources on the artists, cultures, and movements represented in their museum collections. Because of the narrow focus of their discipline, they attempt to collect exhaustively materials from around the world to provide the art researcher with an inclusive amount of material.

Among the most comprehensive art museum libraries are those located at the Metropolitan Museum of Art. The largest is the Thomas J. Watson Library <http://library.metmuseum.org>, with its free online OPAC, Watsonline, containing the holdings of this library and others at the Met. Watsonline provides researchers with over 500,000 volumes of art-related information encompassing works and artists represented in their collection, from the ancient Greeks to international artists of the modern period. For book research in the twentieth and twenty-first century areas, one should also consult DADABASE, the OPAC for the Museum of Modern Art Library, Archives, and Study Centers <http://library.moma.org>. The title of the OPAC is a pun on the early twentieth-century Dada anti-art movement and thus illustrates the focus of MOMA's museum and library collection: world art produced from 1880 to the present. The MOMA Library also houses one of the largest collections of artists' books throughout the world, also available for searching in DADABASE. Both Watsonline and DADABASE allow the researcher to perform basic keyword and more advanced searching, such as including a vast number of non-English publications. Both museum libraries are open to all qualified researchers.

Alternatives to using museum library OPACs might be commercial online Web sites, such as Amazon <http://www.amazon.com>, Barnes & Noble <http://www.bn.com>, or even Alibris <http://www.alibris.com> for out-of-print books, to assist a researcher in creating a comprehensive resource of books on an artist or art movement. However, much like the problems associated with WorldCat, these sources are not specific to the art discipline and will generate thousands of superfluous hits. The online catalogs for art book dealers might prove more beneficial, especially if the art historian is seeking to purchase materials for her/his own library and some of this material is obscure or long out of print. Two such vendors are Ars Libri and Worldwide Books. Ars Libri <http://www.arslibri.com> was founded in 1976 and "maintains the largest stock in America of rare and out-of-print books on art." Their holdings encompass all areas of art history with holdings ranging from reference books to artists' books. Worldwide Books <http://www.worldwide.com>, in turn, provides a similar service, although they specialize in exhibition catalogs published around the world. Both companies regularly publish print catalogs of their materials for sale, and offer through their Web sites online searching of their catalogs and full capabilities of online purchasing.

One cannot end the discussion of books without mentioning the impact of electronic books on the art researcher. As in many disciplines, the availability of electronic books through companies such as netLibrary and from publishers themselves has provided an advantage for a researcher looking for information in a quick and easy way. Keyword searching in full-text books has in many ways replaced browsing through print indexes, as it arguably provides more results for what a researcher is seeking. Electronic books have their drawbacks, however, most dealing with the attempt to literally "read" a book online. The greatest successes of the electronic book seem to be in the creation of online encyclopedias out of what was formerly only available in print.

When the Grove *Dictionary of Art* premiered in print in 1996, it was a monumental project welcomed by the art world. One reviewer called it "an astounding feat" (Doumato 23). The 34 volumes of the print edition of the *Dictionary of Art* include 41,000 articles on worldwide topics ranging from prehistory through art of the 1990s in every visual medium. There were 6,802 contributors from 120 countries, 15,000 visual reproductions, 300,000 bibliographic citations, and an index of over 720,000 terms. The encyclopedia served both the art historian and general public by providing high quality, comprehensive, scholarly information. While some entries on less-known artists are brief, other entries are over 200 pages in length.

As more information went online, so too did the *Dictionary of Art* as a subscription-based product under the name *Grove Art Online* <http://www.groveart.com>. The online version premiered in November 1998, with all of the print content transformed into keyword-searchable text. Since that time, more content has been added and bibliographies have been updated to reflect recent additions of artists and new research in the field. The visual images that were reproduced in the print version are not included online because Grove did not have copyright permission to reproduce them in another format. Therefore, they made digital images of works of art available first through an agreement with *The Bridgeman Art Library* and by creating external links from articles to digital art collections on the Internet. Since that time, they have expanded digital image content through an agreement with *Art Resource* and through their own art image links program, creating a comprehensive textual and visual electronic book for both the novice and advanced art researcher. The Internet version of this important art reference source demonstrates the power of online information for visual arts research.

ARTICLES

After books, librarians typically assist patrons in searching for journal and magazine articles to assist the researcher with her/his project. Journal and magazine articles can work as a supplement to monographic sources, but often in the case of more obscure artists or subjects, articles may provide the exact information a researcher needs. Like all disciplines, the field of art and art history has advanced in journal research with the implementation of online indexes and databases. Print indexes have always forced individuals to search volume after volume to ensure that they gather all of their information. Electronic access allows for much easier searching. The recent developments of full-text articles, retrospective indexing, and digital images, essential for the field of art, have made article research now easier than ever. The art periodical databases discussed here are all fee-based and available with a subscription to their parent database company.

The leading periodical database for the discipline of art is the *Art Index*. Published in print format since 1929, the H. W. Wilson *Art Index* has been the most popular source for the indexing of articles, book and exhibition reviews, and visual reproductions of works of art in art journals, museum bulletins, and other art-related resources published primarily in English but also in other European languages as well. Topics include traditional art history, architecture, and museology, as well as video and television. In online format, the Art Index <http://www.hwwilson.com/Databases/artindex.htm> provides citation information dating from September 1984 to the present. The enhanced *Art Abstracts* version provides the same citations but adds a 50-300 word abstract.

In 1999, the Art Index added a new component called *Art Full Text* and currently provides full text access to 129 journals going back for some to 1997. Articles appear both in HTML and/or PDF formats, with PDF versions including the images as they appeared in print, an important component of the art research process.[5] Also added in 1999 was *Art Index Retrospective: 1929-1984*. This enhanced component includes all of the data found in the original print volumes of that time period, with indexing terms updated to reflect current vocabulary usage. This added feature allows for easier cross-searching in both the current and retrospective databases. Databases such as Art Index Retrospective have been a boon to the humanities because they have made what was once considered obscure material easier to find.

Another such retrospective historical database is the *Index to Nineteenth Century American Art Periodicals* <http://www.rlg.org/en/page. php?Page_ID=11161>. Although seemingly restrictive in its scope, it remains an essential resource for those doing historical art research. Compiled by Mary Morris Schmidt and originally published in 1999 by Sound View Press in two volumes, the database is also available as part of the Eureka suite of services produced by the Research Libraries Group. Eureka is arguably favored by many art libraries because many of the databases are geared towards humanities research, such as the *Avery Index to Architectural Periodicals, Bibliography of the History of Art (BHA)*, and *SCIPIO: Art and Rare Book Sales Catalogs*.

The Index to Nineteenth Century American Art Periodicals indexes the entire contents of 42 American art journals that were published from approximately 1840 through 1907. Despite its indexing of just American periodicals, the database includes numerous articles relating to European and non-Western art and artists as well. For instance, a keyword search on Michelangelo Buonarroti produced nearly 60 hits. One of the highlights of this database is the indexing not only of articles but also of the pictures and advertisements found in the journals, providing a comprehensive database of nineteenth century cultural life.

A companion resource for the Art Index is *ARTbibliographies Modern*, a database that provides "information on modern and contemporary arts dating from the late 19th century onwards, and including photography since its invention" <http://www.csa.com/csa/factsheets/ artbm.shtml>. Although there is some crossing of journal coverage with the Wilson index, ARTbibliographies Modern also includes books, essays, exhibition catalogs, and dissertations, with coverage dating back to the 1960s. Because of its focus specifically related to modern and contemporary art history, it provides a broader range of information in its content and addresses media not typically seen in traditional resources, including performance art, body art, artists' books, and so on. This database is an excellent reference source for the researcher focusing on work in these areas.

Both ARTbibliographies Modern and a companion resource, the *Design and Applied Arts Index*, are available through CSA. In contrast to the aforementioned art-related indexes, the Design and Applied Arts Index does not focus on traditional art historical media <http://www. csa.com/csa/factsheets/daai.shtml>. Rather, it provides references from over 500 design and craft journals from 1973 to the present. Subject coverage for this database includes information related to crafts such as jewelry design, glassmaking, and goldsmithing, and industrial design areas as diverse as vehicle and furniture design. Unique to the database are the inclusion of an Education Directory, providing information on universities and colleges throughout the world that provide courses and programs in design and craft subjects, and a Periodicals Directory, with full publisher's information and the ability to produce lists of periodicals in the craft and design disciplines.

INTERNET SUBJECT DIRECTORIES

After books and articles, a reference librarian may turn to the Web in order to help a patron with her/his art research project. The hesitancy about using potentially questionable information on Web sites is compounded by the problem of not knowing where or how to begin to search for art information on the Web. Typing "cubism" into the Google search engine <http://www.google.com> generates 529,000 hits, and "creation of adam michelangelo" gives you 45,800 hits. While in all likelihood some of the top hits may be useful, how does a researcher know for sure if they are reliable sites? How useful are the 529,000 Web sites going to be for the student asking for more information about Picasso and the Cubist art movement? And will the student really want to browse through that many Web sites? These questions are not restrictive to the art field, but hold true for almost any research topic imaginable. Internet search engines, while useful, are not always the best way to find high quality Web sites on the Internet. Often Internet subject directories are a better alternative, perhaps more so for the art discipline. Two excellent art Internet subject directories are those designed by Christopher Witcombe and Alan Liu.

Art History Resources on the Web <http://witcombe.sbc.edu/ ARTHLinks.html> is one of the most comprehensive Internet subject directories for art history. The Web site was created in October 1995 by Christopher Witcombe, Professor of Art History at Sweet Briar College, to accompany one of the most frequently used textbooks for introductory art history courses, *Gardiner's Art Through the Ages*. He uses the prehistoric Venus of Willendorf figure as a logo on each page, providing consistency as one literally travels through the history of Western and non-Western art using his category links. He also provides specialized areas such as Research Resources (including Image Finders,

Research and Methodology, etc.) and Museums and Galleries (arranged by country). He links to major Web sites and specific related pages within these sites. The series of links on each page occasionally seem scattered and are not always well organized, but the pages are updated on a regular basis. Despite the fact that Witcombe does not cite criteria for selecting links, *Art History Resources on the Web* is one of the most comprehensive Web site directories for art history.

Perhaps one of the most famous Web site directories for the humanities has been the Voice of the Shuttle <http://vos.ucsb.edu/index.asp>. Created by Alan Liu, a professor in the English Department at the University of California, Santa Barbara, this site has been a long-standing Web site directory since it premiered on the Internet in 1995. The site takes its name from the ancient Greek myth of Philomela, who despite having had her tongue cut out, was able to tell her story by weaving a narrative tapestry, her "voice" becoming the "shuttle" of the loom. Over the years, Voice of the Shuttle has developed in its design and look, starting originally as static Web pages and transforming into an SQL database with pages of links. One can perform keyword searching on the entire site, or browse through specific subject pages. Web pages of links for art include sections on Art (Modern and Contemporary), Art History, Photography, and other interdisciplinary related pages. The Art page includes links arranged by categories such as Art Theory & Politics and Art Therapy. The Art History page is arranged geographically, and then branches into discipline-related sections such as Course Syllabi & Teaching Resources. Once arranged by the section, each page has an alphabetical list of links to Web pages, almost all of which are briefly annotated. Both Liu's and Witcombe's Internet subject directory pages have the advantage of organizing comprehensive art information by discipline or subject, allowing for a researcher to browse more efficiently than by randomly selecting links from Google.

IMAGES

As discussed earlier, the visual creative object is the primary focus of the art researcher. In order to assess, discuss, and investigate the visual creative object, s/he must see it. Short of visiting museums in person, the art researcher must utilize picture resources to see these visual works of art. Books and articles traditionally have provided the dominant way to see these items, but the Web has made digital images one of the most exciting developments in art research. Digital image databases for art have been mentioned already, specifically The Bridgeman Art Library and Art Resource, both of which are available through a subscription to Grove Art Online.[6] But these aren't the only fee-based digital image databases. The newest addition to the digital art image world is *ARTstor*, which may become the leader in the world of digital images.

ARTstor is a non-profit entity initiated by The Andrew W. Mellon Foundation <http://www.artstor.org>. It premiered in July 2004 with its "Charter Collection" of approximately 300,000 digital images with basic cataloging data for each image. By Summer 2006, they expect to add an additional 200,000 images to the database. While not directly tied to JSTOR, another Mellon project, ARTstor has been compared to its sister database with the foundation of providing digitized content to non-profit educational institutions for scholarly research and learning purposes. ARTstor's "Charter Collection" of digital images "documents artistic traditions across many times and cultures and embraces architecture, painting, sculpture, photography, decorative arts, and design as well as many other forms of visual culture." This digital "collection of collections" was created through partnerships with museums and individual art historians. Among the impressive digital holdings are "The Art History Survey Collection," approximately 4,000 images drawn from 13 standard art history textbooks for use in introductory art history classes, "The Huntington Archive of Asian Art," with over 12,000 images taken by Asian art historians John and Susan Huntington, and "The Illustrated Bartsch," including more than 50,000 digitized images from 96 published volumes of old master European prints from the fifteenth to the nineteenth centuries. ARTstor has both basic keyword and advanced field searching options. A basic search on "bamboo" in the "Huntington Archive" produced 33 hits, easily satisfying the person looking for examples of bamboo in Asian art.

For the art researcher looking for images by a particular artist or subject in world art, ARTstor is undoubtedly one of the most important Internet sites on which to search, assuming that the researcher needs the images for non-profit educational purposes, such as classroom use and lecture-type presentations. Despite its impressive content, however, ARTstor has had some criticism. ARTstor utilizes its own proprietary software for digital images. While at first this should not seem to be a problem, the difficulty is that the images are incompatible and cannot be used with any other software package, including PowerPoint or Blackboard, two softwares commonly used for digital presentations and teaching purposes. The end-user is forced to use the ARTstor platform online in order to work with any of the images in the database. In Fall

2004, ARTstor announced the creation of an offline image viewer in an attempt to correct this restriction. The viewer is available for downloading from the ARTstor site and requires some practice in its use. However, once mastered, the offline image viewer is a welcome product, allowing the user to download ARTstor images for offline use and to import other personal digital images into the viewer. Having offline capability also allows one to use the images without the need for an Internet connection, which is helpful for classroom and lecture presentations.[7]

Pricing for ARTstor has been a concern. For universities and colleges, pricing is based on Carnegie Classification and includes a one-time Archive Capital Fee (ACF) ranging from $1,000 for community colleges to $40,000 for Research I institutions, and an Annual Access Fee (AAF) of $1,200 to $20,000. For independent schools, pricing is based on FTE, with ACFs ranging from $600 to $8,500 and AAFs ranging from $500 to $4,500.[8] The price for such a product is higher than typically expected for an art database, especially considering that humanities databases historically have cost much less when compared to science databases such as those produced by Elsevier. Smaller schools, with active art and design programs, may not be able to license ARTstor because of their smaller budgets, thus losing out on this important resource.

The ongoing efforts of ARTstor to produce archival quality, high-resolution digital images for educational purposes is impressive. Undoubtedly ARTstor will assert itself over the next few years as the leading image database in the world.[9] However, it is worth noting that for the purposes of the non-art specialist who may not be affiliated with an educational institution but looking for images of famous works of art, there are free resources on the Internet that may provide the images s/he is seeking. Art museums around the world, for instance, have begun digitizing their own collections and putting these images on the Web both to whet the appetite of the art seeker and to satisfy a basic academic need to provide quality information about creativity and art. Two such museums are the aforementioned Metropolitan Museum of Art and the Tate Museums.

The Met Web site <http://www.metmuseum.org> arguably stands as a model for museum Web sites, including for the distribution of digital images. The home page welcomes the visitor with featured artwork of the day. Along with a digital image of the work of art, a descriptive paragraph about the piece and specific item information, such as date and medium, are provided. Under the heading of "Works of Art" the viewer can click on "Permanent Collection" and select one of many different categories from Egyptian art to the Costume Institute. One can browse through approximately 50 highlights from each category, with each image page providing a description of the work as on the home page, plus the ability to see provenance. An added feature is the ability to clearly zoom in on works of art, allowing for details one might not be able to see except in person. *Tate Online* is the official Web site for the Tate Museums <http://www.tate.org.uk>. Their online digital collection includes an impressive 65,000 digital works of British art. One can browse by artist or subject, or perform keyword searches. Each individual work of art appears with a display caption talking more about the work and its artist. One has the ability to change the narrative to "full catalogue" and discover detailed information such as medium, provenance, and exhibition history. Zooming on the image is not possible, but the amount of information and number of digital images available makes the Tate Online site easily comparable in quality to the digital works provided by the Met.

The disadvantage to the non-art specialist using these museum sites, however, is that s/he would need to know to look to these museum sites for works specifically in their collections. If the researcher does not know where works by Pablo Picasso are located around the world, s/he would do well to start with a digital image directory such as *Artcyclopedia: The Fine Art Search Engine* <http://www.artcyclopedia. com>. Active since 1999 and created by John Malyon, an IT entrepreneur based in Calgary, *Artcyclopedia* indexes "over 8,000 famous painters, sculptors and photographers, at art museum sites & image archives worldwide." The criteria for an artist to appear on the Web site is that "if an artist is in an arts museum collection, then he or she is qualified to be listed in our database." While perhaps not the most authoritative way to determine inclusion, Malyon has at least established criteria and provides the researcher with knowledge of the expectations of the site. It also makes *Artcyclopedia* one of the best places to discover where works of art by particular artists are located around the world. One can perform keyword searches by the artist's name, the title of a work of art, or an art museum. The best part of the site is the ability to browse through entries by name, subject, nationality, and so on, giving the novice researcher an excellent way to determine more information about a particular artist and her/his associated media or art movements. Searching for Picasso on the site provides the viewer with a brief biographical entry, information about Cubism, and links to his colleague Georges Braque and other Spanish artists, and direct links to digital images of works by Picasso located in museums around the world. There are nearly 5,500 artists' pages, including both the masters and contemporary artists, and there are also monthly featured artists, museums, art books, and art prints on the site. *Artcyclopedia* undoubtedly ranks as one of the best free indexes for digital images by particular artist and movement, although it is worth noting that there are no digital images on the site itself, with the exception of randomly linked advertisements of posters for sale.

For the researcher who is looking for a Web site that includes digital images, s/he should consider looking at *Mark Harden's Artchive* <http://www.artchive.com/>. This site contains an impressive collection of digitized works of fine art. After following the link to the "Artchive" itself, the visitor has the option of browsing through the links in the main page that are arranged by major art historical movement, or by using the alphabetical list of artists' names and art movements in the left frame. Artists from Altdorfer to Zurbaran are represented. An individual artist page, such as that for Michelangelo, provides a biographical overview on the life and work of the artist, excerpted from an art text, and a list of available digital images. Clicking on the link for *The Creation of Adam* produces a thumbnail image of the work, which in turn leads to the Image Viewer, which allows the researcher's Internet browser to alter the size of the image to fit the screen and/or to zoom in on the work. Harden provides these works to the public under the claim of public domain and fair use for copyrighted works, and also provides stipulations for use of these images, which should be consulted by potential researchers. From the home page one can also visit virtual galleries he has designed and browse through other art information. The one distraction to the Web site is the use of pop-up advertisements that apparently help provide support for Harden's work.

Finally, for the novice researcher and art librarian, one should also consider using *Google's Image Search* <http://images.google.com>. Google credits the site as being "the most comprehensive on the Web, with more than 880 million images indexed and available for viewing." On the help page, Google takes no credit for the quality of the images or the integrity of the sites it indexes, nor does it suggest any form of copyright clearance for the use of these images, thus attempting to protect itself from any use or misuse of images or the discovery of images of an adult nature.[10] Google's Image Search serves one purpose: to index the Web for images based on search criteria entered by the researcher. After performing a search, results are generated in a series of thumbnail images. Clicking on one of these images produces a frames-based page with the same thumbnail at the top and the actual Web site where it appears in the frame below. There is also an Advanced Image Search which allows for natural language Boolean operators and specific image features such as file size, image type, and coloration. Performing a search for "bamboo" produced 193,000 hits; adding "Chinese painting" to it produced 297 results, providing the potential researcher with numerous possible pictures of bamboo in Asian art.

CONCLUSION

Biographical information. Art object research. Images. The list goes on. Art librarians are expected to know the resources to use in order to answer such questions. These are the assignments of art history students, the projects of design students, and the curiosity of people simply needing answers for any reason. The art librarian has served these individuals by answering many of these questions throughout the twentieth century using print sources. The Internet, however, has altered information seeking patterns, providing faster, easier, and more up-to-date ways of finding the information these people seek. Using the Internet resources mentioned in this article, the art librarian will be able to tackle those difficult questions, and help that student or person find out more about Pablo Picasso, trace the critical development of Michelangelo's *Creation of Adam*, or help find images of bamboo in Asian art.

NOTES

1. For more on the researching trends of arts and humanities scholars, see Ron Blazek and Elizabeth Aversa, *The Humanities* (Englewood, CO: Libraries Unlimited, 1994), 2-7.

2. This informal survey was submitted by me on June 30, 2004, with results collated and returned to the list on July 9, 2004. It was not meant to be scientific and should not be considered official in any way. I received responses from 30 librarians and visual resource curators from the following library types: college/university (11), museum (8), art and design school (7), public (2), and specialized research library (2). The survey asked the following three questions: (1) What are your top 3 most consulted Internet-based indexes/databases/bibliographic utilities (e.g., RLIN, Art Index, etc.)?; (2) What are your top 3 most consulted art-related Web sites (e.g., Artcyclopedia.com, Google Images, etc.)? and (3) What type of art-related reference question (e.g., biographical, value of art, picture of . . . , etc.) do you seem to answer most frequently?

3. Individuals responding to this question often answered with more than one response, so the numbers do not accurately reflect the demographics. The number of respondents per type of art research question were as follows: biographical (22), art object research [e.g., specific painting] (12), value of art (10), images [i.e., "Who painted . . . ?" and "I need a picture of . . ."] (8), architectural (7), historic/stylistic [e.g., Renaissance, Impressionism] (4), exhibition information (2), museum information (1), other [e.g., company histories, advertising, etc.] (4). For the purposes of this article, I am focusing on Internet resources that address biographical, art object research, and images. Valuation questions are common especially in public and museum libraries; for more information on resources in this area, see Angela Graven, "Web-based Auction Resources," *Art Documentation* 22 (Fall 2003): 26-30.

4. Respondents to the first two questions regarding the top three resources produced confusing results (which I acknowledge as partially my fault in how I worded the questions), with some citing Web sites as databases, and vice-versa. As a result, I merged the responses into one master list then highlighted whether a particular resource was fully or partially subscription-based. The three most frequently cited resources were: Art Index/Abstracts/Full Text/Art Retrospective (20), Grove Art Online (12), and Google's Image Search (11).

5. For an overview of various aggregators and their inclusions of digital images in art periodical databases, see Alexandra de Luise, "Full Text or Not? All Illustrations or Not?" *Art Documentation* 22 (Fall 2003): 20-25.

6. These two sources are also available to the art researcher without a subscription to the Grove Art Online. The British-based Bridgeman Art Library <http://www.bridgeman.co.uk> offers the viewer the opportunity to license digital images acquired from partnerships with museums worldwide. Art Resource <http://www.artres.com> targets the writer who needs images for her/his publications, in turn acting as the middleman between the writer and the rights and reproductions offices of museums and galleries. Both Web sites offer libraries of digital images with keyword searching and browsing capabilities.

7. Libraries and visual resource centers that have been digitizing their own image collections over the past few years will find of interest that ARTstor has begun a pilot project with ten institutions to host their digital image collections and provide these specialized collections back to the institution using the ARTstor interface. For more on this pilot project and details about the offline image viewer, see *ARTstor Newsletter* 3 (Fall 2004).

8. Museum pricing for ARTstor is more complicated, basing its "size" on a combination of operating budget, library materials budget, number of active serials subscriptions, and FTE of museum and library staff. ACFs range from $600 to $10,000 and AAFs range from $500 to $5,000.

9. It is worth adding mention of AMICO, the Art Museum Image Consortium <http://www.amico.org>, which premiered with its digital image library around the year 2000. Its digital library includes over 100,000 works of art from American museums in partnership with the organization. AMICO made its content available through vendors such as H. W. Wilson and RLG. As of 2004, however, it was reported that AMICO would be ceasing, and there is talk of its content being taken over by ARTstor.

10. Google does provide an automatic filter in the English version of the site, but there is an option for turning off the filter.

WORKS CITED

Alibris.com. <http://www.alibris.com> (accessed November 29, 2004).

Amazon.com. <http://www.amazon.com> (accessed November 29, 2004).

AMICO. <http://www.amico.org> (accessed November 23, 2004).

Ars Libri. <http://www.arslibri.com> (accessed November 20, 2004).

Art Index. New York: H. W. Wilson, 1929- .

Art Resource. <http://www.artres.com> (accessed November 29, 2004).

ARTstor. <http://www.artstor.org> (accessed November 23, 2004).

ARTstor Newsletter 3 (Fall 2004).

Barnes & Noble. <http://www.bn.com> (accessed November 29, 2004).

Blazek, Ron, and Elizabeth Aversa. *The Humanities: A Selective Guide to Information Sources.* Englewood, CO: Libraries Unlimited, 1994.

The Bridgeman Art Library. <http://www.bridgeman.co.uk> (accessed November 29, 2004).

CSA. *ARTbibliographies Modern.* <http://www.csa.com/csa/factsheets/artbm.shtml> (accessed November 22, 2004).

_____. *Design and Applied Arts Index.* <http://www.csa.com/csa/factsheets/daai.shtml> (accessed November 22, 2004).

de Luise, Alexandra. "Full Text or Not? All Illustrations or Not?" *Art Documentation* 22 (Fall 2003): 20-25.

Doumato, Lamia. "Overview." Review of the *Dictionary of Art. Art Documentation* 16 (Spring 1997): 23-24.

Ferrari, Roberto C. E-mail to the ARLIS-L discussion list. June 30, 2004. <http://lsv.uky.edu/cgi-bin/wa.exe?A2=ind0406&L=arlis-l&P=R16145&I=-3>.

_____. E-mail to the ARLIS-L discussion list. July 9, 2004. <http://lsv.uky.edu/cgi-bin/wa.exe?A2=ind0407&L=arlis-l&P=R3244&I=-3>.

Google. <http://www.google.com> (accessed December 28, 2004).

Google's Image Search. <http://images.google.com> (accessed November 26, 2004).

Graven, Angela. "Web-Based Auction Resources: The Sites and How Art Libraries Use Them." *Art Documentation* 22 (Fall 2003): 26-30.

Grove Art Online. <http://www.groveart.com> (accessed November 20, 2004).

H. W. Wilson. *Art Index/Abstracts/Full Text/Art Retrospective.* <http://www.hwwilson.com/Databases/artindex.htm> (accessed November 22, 2004).

Harden, Mark. *Mark Harden's Artchive.* <http://www.artchive.com> (accessed November 26, 2004).

Liu, Alan. *Voice of the Shuttle.* University of California-Santa Barbara. <http://vos.ucsb.edu/index.asp> (accessed November 20, 2004).

Malyon, John. *Artcyclopedia: The Fine Art Search Engine.* http://www.artcyclopedia.com (accessed November 25, 2004).

The Metropolitan Museum of Art. <http://www.metmuseum.org> (accessed November 25, 2004).

The Metropolitan Museum of Art Thomas J. Watson Library. <http://library.metmuseum.org> (accessed November 20, 2004).

Museum of Modern Art Library, Archives, and Study Centers. <http://library.moma.org> (accessed November 20, 2004).

OCLC. WorldCat. <http://www.oclc.org/worldcat/> (accessed December 22, 2004).

Research Libraries Group. *Index to Nineteenth Century American Art Periodicals.* <http://www.rlg.org/en/page.php?Page_ID=11161> (accessed November 22, 2004).

Schmidt, Mary Morris. *Index to Nineteenth Century American Art Periodicals.* Madison, CT: Sound View, 1999.

Tate Museums. *Tate Online.* <http://www.tate.org.uk> (accessed November 25, 2004).

Turner, Jane, ed. *Dictionary of Art.* 34 vols. London: Macmillan, 1996.

Witcombe, Christopher. *Art History Resources on the Web.* Sweet Briar College. <http://witcombe.sbc.edu/ARTHLinks.html> (accessed November 23, 2004).

Worldwide Books. <http://www.worldwide.com> (accessed November 20, 2004).

Removing the Boundaries:
Composition and Rhetoric
Internet Resources from Classical Greece
to the Present Day

Julie Roberson

SUMMARY. Rhetoric is one of the oldest disciplines in the world. Throughout its long history, rhetoric has been applied to speech, writing, and electronic media. Not only is the Internet transforming the theory and practice of rhetoric and composition; it is also providing new modes of expression. This article examines Web sites about rhetoric and composition covering a variety of topics from its origins to new applications using technology. *[Article copies available for a fee from The Haworth Document Delivery Service: 1-800-HAWORTH. E-mail address: <docdelivery@haworthpress.com> Website: <http://www.HaworthPress.com> © 2005 by The Haworth Press, Inc. All rights reserved.]*

KEYWORDS. Rhetoric, composition, speech

No other field of study has been so impacted by the Internet as rhetoric and composition. From practice to theory, the study of rhetoric has

Julie Roberson is Information Services Librarian, King College, Bristol, TN (E-mail: jarobers@king.edu).

[Haworth co-indexing entry note]: "Removing the Boundaries: Composition and Rhetoric Internet Resources from Classical Greece to the Present Day." Roberson, Julie. Co-published simultaneously in *Journal of Library Administration* (The Haworth Information Press, an imprint of The Haworth Press, Inc.) Vol. 43, No. 3/4, 2005, pp. 27-40; and: *Evolving Internet Reference Resources* (ed: William Miller, and Rita M. Pellen) The Haworth Information Press, an imprint of The Haworth Press, Inc., 2006, pp. 27-40. Single or multiple copies of this article are available for a fee from The Haworth Document Delivery Service [1-800-HAWORTH, 9:00 a.m. - 5:00 p.m. (EST). E-mail address: docdelivery@haworthpress.com].

doi:10.1300/J111v43n03_03

not only been applied to this new medium, but is also being transformed by the technology. Among the oldest disciplines in the world, the field of rhetoric has undergone many changes in focus throughout its long history.

The Greek word *rhetorke* refers to the craft of speaking. Rhetoric originally referred to the persuasive use of speech and had its beginnings with the sophistic tradition in Classical Greece. Even at that time, there was some disagreement about the proper place of rhetoric. While philosophers such as Plato and Socrates believed that rhetoric was "more concerned with appearances rather than substance" and could be deceptive, others believed that an understanding of the principles of rhetoric played a key role in having a well-informed citizenry (Petraglia-Bahri).

One of Plato's students, Aristotle, did much to advance the study of rhetoric by developing the three persuasive appeals: logos, pathos, and ethos. The Romans, namely Quintilian and Cicero, took the Greeks' ideas about rhetoric and extended them. One of the most famous Roman rhetoricians, Cicero, augmented many of Aristotle's original theories and ideas about rhetoric to develop the "canons" of rhetoric: invention, arrangement, style, memory, and delivery which are often used today to teach the writing process.

Rhetoric continued to grow during the Medieval and Renaissance era; however, it took on a slightly different application. In *De Doctrina Christiana*, Augustine argued that rhetoric was still necessary to make Biblical teachings successful, and he remodeled rhetoric for the use of Christian purposes (Petraglia-Bahri). Additionally, rhetoric became a cornerstone of what is now known as the liberal arts. Rhetoric, grammar, and logic formed the trivium which along with the quadrivium was the basis of education during the Middle Ages.

During the Renaissance, many rhetoricians hoped to recover older classical texts and codify them according to strict rules about grammar and style. These texts become more prescriptive with long lists of rules to follow in writing (Reynolds). As greater literacy developed around the world, the focus shifted more toward writing than speech. Peter Ramus, an influential French scholar during the Renaissance, began to focus on style, memory, and delivery and emphasized the division of the different composition stages first suggested by Cicero and Aristotle. With the greater emphasis on writing rather than speech, memory and delivery declined as important components of rhetoric. The object of rhetorical study became to "clothe one's ideas in the most elegant dress possible" and rhetoric was viewed as a necessary part of an upper-class education (Reynolds). Instead of being integral to the study of thought and expressions, rhetoric became mere window dressing.

During the late 19th century, rhetoric in the United States became forever linked with composition as Harvard required all freshmen to study basic skills of writing (Petraglia-Bahri). Throughout the early 19th century, composition existed in a service role to literary study and was viewed by literary scholars as an inferior and subordinate field. Freshmen composition was used to introduce students to literary study and as a by-product, problems with grammar or style were addressed (Reynolds). Literary study and writing remained separate until the advent of New Criticism. With New Criticism and its emphasis on literary texts as "complex structures of meaning," the relationship between thought and language was reestablished (Reynolds). Today, rhetoric survives as a discipline of study in many departments of English and composition. New Rhetoric asks questions about how and why something is communicated rather than what is communicated. This has opened the field of rhetoric up to many possibilities and more scholars than ever are contributing to this field.

Rhetoric is also being transformed by another advancement: hypertext. The Internet has made it necessary to develop a rhetoric that can be applied to a new electronic writing space in which old rules no longer apply or at least do not apply in the same way. This change has had both negative and positive effects. For Freshman Writing teachers, the informal, chatty style of e-mail and chat programs has produced students who are unaccustomed to writing formal, thesis-driven essays. Composition teachers have noted that while students are writing longer papers, they are not submitting better written papers (Leibowitz). Technology has also changed the writing and reading process of many students. Since computers encourage quick composing with little more than surface changes and scanning for ideas rather than deep reading and comprehension, composition teachers have new challenges when teaching students to think, read, and write critically.

While the challenges to teaching rhetoric and composition have been compounded by technology, the positive effects of technology are evidenced by the application of rhetorical theories to media other than speech and writing. Many scholars have predicted the death of print and literary studies because of the electronic age. While some believe that this could result in the end of rhetoric, others believe that this is another opportunity for rhetoric to reinvent itself: "Once rhetoricality is understood as the fundamental condition under which any contemporary literary criticism must proceed, the discipline itself will be transformed because its boundaries will be redrawn" (qtd. in Brooke). These boundaries, as Brooke predicted in a 1997 article in *Enculturation*, are in the process of being redrawn and do include multimedia and cyberspace. In his book, *The Rise of the Image, the Fall of the Word*, Mitchell Stephens writes about the suspicion and judgment that classical rhetoricians held towards the new medium of writing. They believed that writing was a lesser form of communication as it would cause people to rely less on their memories and would produce only a "semblance of wisdom not truth, not real judgment" (qtd. in Stephens 23). Likewise, Stephens contends that we are again in the midst of another sea change in communications moving this time from the printed word to images, and he sees great possibility in this new media format. Rhetoric scholars have already begun to apply rhetorical principles to multimedia and hypertext. New fields and specializations such as visual rhetoric, hypertext theory, and cybertheory offer the field of rhetoric and composition yet another chance to apply classical ideas to another new technology that in some ways returns rhetoric yet again to its traditional roots.

The Web sites selected for this article have been chosen to reflect the changes and development throughout the years in the study of rhetoric and composition from the classical era to the present day. Since composition has played such an important role in the development of rhetoric, sites about grammar and style have also been included. Web sites were excluded because of poor design, out-of-date content, or poor connectivity of links. Course Web pages were also excluded because of the sheer number of those types of Web sites unless these sites included information not found anywhere else.

MEGASITES/PORTALS

These Web sites offer a broad range of information about rhetoric and composition including historical overviews, discussions of main principles and theories, and biographies of important rhetoricians and scholars.

Eserver Technical Communications Library
<http://tc.eserver.org/dir/Rhetoric/Theory>

This resource is part of the Technical Communications Eserver Library at Iowa State University and the resources are aimed at professional scientific and technical writers. There is a section of Web sites on rhetoric which includes resources on making presentations, rhetorical theory, risk communication, and visual rhetoric.

Rhetoricians.com
<http://members.fortunecity.com/rhetoric/index.html>

This Web site provides an historical overview of rhetoric and rhetoricians from its beginnings to the modern day. Sections include overview, origins, Plato, Aristotle, Rome, Middle Ages, Renaissance, Enlightenment, and Contemporary. The resources sections contain links to other rhetoric Web sites. Good Web site for anyone who would like to learn more about the major theorists in rhetoric.

Rhetoric Resources at Tech
<http://www.lcc.gatech.edu/gallery/rhetoric/>

Developed as a resource for undergraduate students at Georgia Institute of Technology, this Web site contains an annotated, hypertextual introduction to ideas and key people in composition and rhetoric. Narrative essays include resource links and overviews of history and theory of rhetoric.

Rhetoric Eserver
<http://eserver.org/rhetoric/>

Originally housed at Carnegie Mellon, the Eserver is now at Iowa State University. This page includes resources for classical rhetoric, articles on literacy and education, online journals, writing centers. Some of the links no longer work and need to be updated.

Rhetcomp.com
<http://rhetcomp.com/>

This is one of the most comprehensive Web portals for composition and rhetoric. It contains a list of calls for papers, explanations of the different fields of study within composition and rhetoric, lists of journals, listservs, and discussion boards, moos and owls, organizations, and links to other portals and programs.

CLASSICAL RHETORIC

These Web sites trace the origins of rhetoric and include background and history on influential people and events demonstrating how rhetoric has become the varied and exciting field of study that it is today.

Ancient Rhetoric: An Introduction
<http://www.leeds.ac.uk/classics/resources/rhetoric/index.htm>

This is a course Web site on classical rhetorical theory. It includes introductory papers on rhetorical invention and declamation among others, as well as course notes and outlines which provide overviews and introductions to the topic.

Aristotle's Rhetoric
<http://www.public.iastate.edu/%7Ehoneyl/Rhetoric/>

Maintained by Lee Honeycutt, an associate professor of Rhetoric and Technical Communication at Iowa State University, this site provides an online version of Aristotle's classic Greek work based on the translation by noted scholar W. Rhys Roberts. The online version includes Roberts's original chapter introductions and a Bekker index for those familiar with the referencing system from the Greek text. The advantage of the online version is that it is also keyword searchable, providing easy access for rhetoric scholars.

Classical Rhetoric
<http://web.utk.edu/~gwynne/classical.html>

This site provides a basic outline and overview of classical rhetoric including the history, key figures, and timeline. The information is directed mostly toward the study of oral rhetoric, but it also has applications for understanding techniques of written rhetoric.

Renaissance Rhetoric
<http://www.hf.ntnu.no/engelsk/shakespeare/indrhet.htm>

Another course Web site, the site includes definitions of classical terms, a bibliography, guidelines for reading renaissance texts, and a bibliography of Internet resources for the Renaissance and rhetoric.

Silva Rhetoricae: The Forest of Rhetoric
<http://humanities.byu.edu/rhetoric/silva.htm>

This is an excellent site for gaining a good introduction to the terms and ideas of classical and Renaissance rhetoric. The purpose of the Web site is to help beginners and experts understand both the "trees" of rhetoric–examples, definitions, and specific devices–as well as the "forest"–the purpose and pattern of rhetoric. There is a comprehensive glossary of rhetorical terms and devices. The narrative essays on the history, appeals, and forms of rhetoric are clear and easy to understand as well as useful for the novice or experienced rhetorician.

SPEECH

No article on rhetoric would be complete without a section devoted to speech and oral literacy. These Web sites provide texts of significant speeches as a resource for the scholarly study of rhetoric. The power of the Internet is evident as many of these Web sites contain not only text, but also video and audio files of the speeches themselves.

American Rhetoric
<http://www.americanrhetoric.com/>

This Web site contains a wealth of information on speech and rhetoric in American life including everything from politics to movies. The online speech bank contains over 5,000 full-text and audio and video versions of public speeches, sermons, legal proceedings lectures, and debates. There is also a special section on the rhetoric of 9-11. The Top 100 Speeches area includes the 100 most significant American political speeches. There are also links to speeches from movies, Christian rhetoric, and much more.

DOUGLASS: Archives of American Public Address
<http://douglassarchives.org/>

Named after Frederick Douglass, this site is an electronic archive of American speeches. The purpose of the Web site is to provide a resource for the scholarly study of American rhetorical history. The speeches can be browsed by speaker, title, date, or issue. There is also a keyword-searchable index.

Rhetorica
<http://www.rhetorica.net/>

Rhetorica is a useful site for anyone who would like to better decode the rhetoric and propaganda of politics and journalism. This site provides commentary and analysis on both of these topics including presidential speeches and elections. Rhetorica also contains a blog, a rhetoric primer, and a cultural meter that includes information to analyze rhetorical techniques used by journalists and politicians. There are also many links to media outlets and to critiques of politics and media.

DICTIONARIES/GLOSSARIES

There are many examples of dictionaries and glossaries of rhetorical devices found on the Internet. These are three of the most well-known and best examples. These Web sites demonstrate the emphasis of rhetoric on figures of speech and correct style.

Handbook of Rhetorical Devices
<http://www.virtualsalt.com/rhetoric.htm>

This site contains definitions and examples of over 60 commonly used rhetorical devices such as chiasmus, oxymoron, and hyperbole among others. A short description and examples are included for each entry as well as a self-test. This is a good quick reference to common rhetorical terms.

A Glossary of Rhetorical Terms with Examples
<http://www.uky.edu/ArtsSciences/Classics/rhetoric.html>

From the Classics Department at the University of Kentucky, this is another helpful online dictionary of many rhetorical terms. Each entry includes examples and definitions as well as links to examples in the Perseus Digital Library. Good for anyone looking for succinct definitions of these terms.

Short Handbook on Rhetorical Analysis
<http://www.english.ilstu.edu/wbanks/rhetoric/rhetanalysis.html>

This well-written handbook provides a guide for anyone who would like to be more adept at analyzing rhetorical situations and features of a piece of writing. This guide explains the types of rhetorical appeals, commonplaces or arguments, and rhetorical methods. Includes a selected bibliography also.

BIBLIOGRAPHIES

Rhetoricians and composition teachers, like librarians, are also fond of bibliographies. These bibliographies were created in response to the need for easy access to scholarship about rhetoric and composition. They reflect the changing way technology is being used for accessing information resources. Some of the bibliographies are flat html files that must be browsed while others are searchable by either keyword or subject area.

Bedford Bibliography for Teachers of Writing
<http://www.bedfordbooks.com/bb/contents.html>

This is the online version of the well-respected print resource. There are 704 entries divided into five major headings: resources, history and theory, composing, literacy, and rhetorics of writing, curriculum development, and writing programs. An index of authors is also included.

Bibliography for Rhetoric, Composition, and Communication Research
<http://www.public.iastate.edu/~wsthune/research/>

This is an extensive bibliography with citations on over 7,000 books and articles published in major journals in the composition and rhetoric field. Users can search by topic or browse by author, keyword, or journal. Additionally, the bibliography can be searched online or downloaded and used offline. Although this resource is somewhat dated (it was last updated in 1998), it is still a valuable tool for the composition researcher.

CCCC Bibliography of Composition and Rhetoric 1984-1999
<http://www.ibiblio.org/cccc/links.html>

Sponsored by the Conference on College Composition and Communication, this bibliography indexes periodicals, books, dissertations, and ERIC documents from 1984-1999. Compilation ceased in 1999 when the MLA International Bibliography began including research on teaching with the 2000 edition. Keyword and advanced searching capabilities are included.

Comppile
<http://comppile.tamucc.edu/>

An excellent bibliography of publications in post-secondary composition, rhetoric, ESL and technical writing, this resource covers 71 different journals from 1939 to 1999. It is keyword searchable and freely available.

Computers and Composition Comprehensive Bibliography
<http://www.hu.mtu.edu/%7Ecandc/bib/>

This bibliography covers a narrow range of publications in composition and computers. Included are works cited in *Computers and the Teaching of Writing in American Higher Education* by Gail Hawisher, Paul LeBlanc, Charles Moran, and Cynthia Selfe, past issues of *Computers and Composition*, and each book in *New Directions in Computers and Composition Book Series.*

Composition and Rhetoric Bibliographic Database
<http://www.public.iastate.edu/~honeyl/bib/index.html>

Even though this bibliography is no longer actively maintained, it is still a useful resource. The bibliography includes citations from 10 major composition journals and books. Citations must be downloaded in either EndNote or ReferBib/IX format. Users may download a "viewer" version of EndNote Plus or a demo version of EndNote.

Rebecca Moore Howard's Bibliographies
<http://wrt-howard.syr.edu/bibs.html>

Howard is a noted scholar in composition and rhetoric. The bibliographies on her Web site span a variety of topics in composition from advanced writing to ethnicity to organization to writing program administration. This is a very useful Web site for anyone beginning research in one of these areas.

GRAMMAR

For many years grammar, style, and correctness were the main criteria for creating a well-written essay. There are many guides to grammar and writing freely available online. These sites were included because of their ease of use, design, and widely known reputation.

Guide to Grammar and Writing
<http://webster.commnet.edu/grammar/>

Sponsored by the Capital Community College Foundation, this invaluable resource contains information on word and sentence level grammar, paragraphs, essays, research papers as well as quizzes, FAQs, and other tutorials. This is an excellent reference source for questions about usage and grammar.

HyperGrammar
<http://www.uottawa.ca/academic/arts/writcent/hypergrammar/>

HyperGrammar is an electronic grammar course from the University of Ottawa Writing Center. The course begins with the parts of speech and progresses to writing paragraphs and word choice. Users may move sequentially through the tutorial or follow their own path. This Web site is another excellent reference on grammar and writing.

Jack Lynch Guide to Grammar and Style
<http://andromeda.rutgers.edu/~jlynch/Writing/>

From the same author of Literary Resources Web site, the site includes a miscellaneous collection of grammar rules, style notes, and suggestions for usage. Sections are arranged alphabetically and include further reading suggestions and links to other Web sites.

Paradigm Online Writing Assistant
<http://www.powa.org/>

This online guide helps writers understanding the writing process and gives instruction on each step of the process. Each section includes a narrative explanation and an activity that can be completed.

Strunk's Elements of Style
<http://www.bartleby.com/strunk/>

This is the online text of the classic writing reference. From the Bartleby Web site, the online version contains the complete text of the print version.

VISUAL RHETORIC AND HYPERTEXT

Reflecting the new application of rhetoric to the visual and hypertext medium of the Internet, these Web sites demonstrate how rhetoric is once again being reinvented to be applied to a new medium. Many of these Web sites take advantage of the hypertext medium not only to distribute information, but also to demonstrate the rhetorical features of the Internet.

Enculturation: Special Issue on Visual Rhetoric
<http://enculturation.gmu.edu/3_2/>

This is a special issue on visual rhetoric. It is edited by David Blakslee and Collin Gifford Brooke, both researchers in visual rhetoric. This issue includes essays that examine how the visual functions in the literary. There are photographs and poetry also.

Hypertext Kitchen
<http://www.hypertextkitchen.com/>

This is a good Web site for anyone who wants to keep abreast about what is occurring in the world of hypertext. The Web site provides daily updates of news and announcements, conferences, writing and job opportunities, reviews, and information on Web design.

HyperText.net
<http://www.hypertext.net/default.asp>

This is an online resource for scholars who study the intersections of hypertext with rhetoric, education, literature, or critical theory. The site includes a bibliography and is keyword searchable. The "rhizome" section includes the author's discussion and research on hypertext as it relates to rhetoric, critical theory, and pedagogy.

Technical Communication E-Server: Visual Rhetoric
<http://tc.eserver.org/dir/Visual-Rhetoric>

Part of the Technical Communication E-Server, this site contains an extensive collection of links for visual rhetoric including many on document design, Web page design, and presentation design.

Visual Rhetoric
<http://www.sla.purdue.edu/people/engl/dblakesley/visual/>

This site was originally developed for a course in visual rhetoric. It contains many Web links for studying the various domains of visual rhetoric including film and visual art as well as links to online courses in visual rhetoric, media studies, scholarly resources, and journals.

Visual Rhetoric Portal
<http://www.tc.umn.edu/~prope002/visualRhet.htm>

This site is a gateway to visual rhetoric resources including courses, journals, and conferences. It presents a good overview of available resources for this subject area.

Voice of the Shuttle: Technology of Writing
<http://vos.ucsb.edu/browse.asp?id=2733>

Part of the well-respected Voice of the Shuttle Web site, this section offers a plethora of resources on new media, technology, and writing. Web sites include resources for hypertext research and theory, interface theory, computers and composition, cyberethics, theoretical works on technology and writing, and course syllabi. This site offers an extensive overview of the major issues related to writing and new media.

BIBLIOGRAPHY

Brooke, Collin Gifford. "The Fate of Rhetoric in an Electronic Age." *Enculturation*, 1 no. 1 (1997): <http://enculturation.gmu.edu/1_1/brooke.html>.
Leibowitz, Wendy R. "Technology Transforms Writing and the Teaching of Writing." *The Chronicle of Higher Education*, 26 Nov. 1999. <http://chronicle.com/weekly/v46/i14/14a06701.htm>.

Petraglia-Bahri, Joseph. "A Brief Overview of Rhetoric." Rhetoric Resources at Georgia Tech. <http://www.lcc.gatech.edu/gallery/rhetoric/essay.html>.

Reynolds, Nedra, Bruce Herzberg and Patricia Bizzell. "Bedford Bibliography for Teachers of Writing." Bedford/St. Martins. <http://www.befordstmartins.com/bb/history.html>.

Stephens, Mitchell. *The Rise of the Image, the Fall of the Word.* New York: Oxford University Press, 1998.

"I Too Dislike It":
The Evolving Presence of Poetry
on the Internet

Debora Richey
Mona Kratzert

SUMMARY. The last decade has witnessed an exciting resurgence in poetry, which is due in part to its increasing accessibility on the Internet. The Web provides the text and criticism of well-known poems within the established canon, as well as contemporary experimental verse that often challenges the notions of what a poem can be. This article discusses the development of traditional or academic poetry on the Internet while also covering the new cutting-edge verse that is expanding the genre into new poetic forms, and includes information on Web sites and databases that facilitate access to poems and poetry criticism. *[Article copies available for a fee from The Haworth Document Delivery Service: 1-800-HAWORTH. E-mail address: <docdelivery@haworthpress.com> Website: <http://www.HaworthPress.com> © 2005 by The Haworth Press, Inc. All rights reserved.]*

KEYWORDS. Poetry, electronic poetry, new media poetry, literary research, Internet resources

Debora Richey is Research Librarian (E-mail: drichey@fullerton.edu); and Mona Kratzert is Emerita Librarian (E-mail: mkratzert@fullerton.edu), both at Pollak Library, California State University, Fullerton, 800 North State College Boulevard, Fullerton, CA 92834.

[Haworth co-indexing entry note]: "'I Too Dislike It': The Evolving Presence of Poetry on the Internet." Richey, Debora, and Mona Kratzert. Co-published simultaneously in *Journal of Library Administration* (The Haworth Information Press, an imprint of The Haworth Press, Inc.) Vol. 43, No. 3/4, 2005, pp. 41-54; and: *Evolving Internet Reference Resources* (ed: William Miller, and Rita M. Pellen) The Haworth Information Press, an imprint of The Haworth Press, Inc., 2006, pp. 41-54. Single or multiple copies of this article are available for a fee from The Haworth Document Delivery Service [1-800-HAWORTH, 9:00 a.m. - 5:00 p.m. (EST). E-mail address: docdelivery@haworthpress.com].

41

INTRODUCTION

The past decade has seen an exciting resurgence in poetry which has, in part, left the cloisters of academia and entered popular culture. The primary reason for this phenomenon is the significant change in access to poetry. Desktop publishing, poetry readings, rap, slam, MTV, and, of course, the Internet have all helped demystify poetry and return it to the everyday world. The American Academy of Poets has done much to expose the general public to poetry and to create an egalitarian audience. In 1996, the Academy introduced Annual National Poetry Month, which has enjoyed tremendous success. The poetry information kits, posters, and promotional materials distributed to the public for this event have attracted even more fans to the art. Although Michael Scharf recently bemoaned the small return on published trade books of poetry in an article in *Publishers Weekly*,[1] the industry still publishes over a thousand poetry anthologies each year, along with new verse collections and critical works on poetry. College creative writing programs are also attracting an increasing number of poetry students, both graduate and undergraduate.

Of all the changes in access to poetry, the Internet has had the greatest effect on this poetry renaissance. There is certainly no shortage of poetry Web sites–a Google search for the word poetry pulls up over 27 million–and millions of people now have access to new works as well as long out-of-print poetry books. The proliferation of Internet sites has vastly altered the ways in which poems are disseminated, published, written, and read. The Internet has also proven to be an especially friendly medium for cutting-edge experimental poetry, which is generally not supported by publishing houses or university presses. While the publishing industry and academia once controlled the publication of poetry, the Internet has allowed for the dissemination of wildly innovative verse.

For reference librarians and literary researchers, poetry related resources on the Internet can be viewed as falling into two distinct groups: conventional sites that provide the text and criticism of well-known poems within the established canon, and contemporary experimental sites that often challenge traditional notions of what a poem can be. These types of poetry–the traditional and the experimental–exist in two separate realms on the Internet, and the Web resources used to find one will not find the other. Many reference librarians do not read poetry, and others would agree with the opening lines of Marianne Moore's famous poem "Poetry" ("I too dislike it"), but would still have no difficulty finding celebrated and classical poetry on the Internet. Locating multimedia, interactive, and hypertext poems that rely on computer technology, however, can be problematic. This article discusses the development of traditional or academic poetry on the Internet, but will also cover the new multimedia sites that are expanding the genre into new poetic forms.

TRADITIONAL OR ACADEMIC POETRY ON THE INTERNET

When the Internet became publicly accessible in the 1980s, classic verse and verse collections first appeared in FTP and gopher formats from such sites as *Project Gutenberg* <http://www.gutenberg.net/>. As the World Wide Web evolved, additional archival sites (*Bartleby.com* <http://www.bartleby.com/verse/>, *Poets' Corner* <http://theotherpages. org/poems/>, *The Online Books Page* <http://digital.library.upenn.edu/ books/>) developed, allowing millions of poetry readers access to the most studied and acclaimed collections of poetry. Not only could poetry lovers read electronic versions of published poetry, but also different editions of the same work were readily available for study. The University of Virginia's *Walt Whitman Collection* <http://etext.lib.virginia. edu/whitman/>, for instance, provided seven different versions of *Leaves of Grass* along with an online "side-by-side comparator" for examining multiple editions. For the first time, scholars could view various versions of landmark works without leaving their chairs. More recent developments in poetry collection sites include *The Internet Poetry Archive* <http://www.ibiblio.org/ipa/> with sound and graphics, the extensive *World Poetry Database: World Poetry* <http://www. lingshidao.com/waiwen/index.htm>, and the University of Michigan's *American Verse Project* <http://www.hti.umich.edu/a/amverse/>, that provides electronic versions of American poetry before 1920. In addition, librarians, faculty members, scholars, and poetry fans alike have commenced mounting sites devoted to individual classic and contemporary authors (e.g., *Geoffrey Chaucer* <http://www.courses.fas. harvard.edu/~chaucer/>, *Mr. William Shakespeare and the Internet* <http://shakespeare.palomar.edu/>, *William Blake Archive* <http:// www.blakearchive.org/>, *AllenGinsberg.org* <http://allenginsberg.org/ home.asp>). Scholarly Internet sites have also emerged that gather poetry and poetry criticism by time period, nationality, and genre (e.g., *Poetry and Prose of the Harlem Renaissance* <http://www.nku.edu/ ~diesmanj/poetryindex.html>, *British Women Romantic Poets, 1789-1832*

<http://www.lib.ucdavis.edu/English/BWRP/>, *British Poetry 1780-1910*
<http://etext.lib.virginia.edu/britpo.html>, *Lost Poets of the Great
War* <http://www.emory.edu/ENGLISH/LostPoets/>, *Sonnet Central*
<http://www.sonnets.org>).

Poetry Finders

To facilitate access to the great amount of poetry publicly available
on the Internet, educational and private groups as well as organizations
began to create databases specifically designed to provide quick and
easy access to full-text online poems. *Representative Poetry Online*
<http://eir.library.utoronto.ca/rpo/display/index.cfm>, maintained by the
University of Toronto English Department, is a searchable database of
over 2,900 English language poems by over 400 poets, with many
choices of entry point. These works run from the Old English period
up through the twentieth century. The Academy of American Poets, founded in 1934, offers a "Find-a-Poem" database at its Web site
Poets.org <http://www.poets.org/index.cfm> that contains 1,200 poems searchable by keyword, title, and first line. The database, which is
constantly updated, also includes biographies, photographs, and other
information on more than 450 poets.
Realizing the potential market, commercial database vendors have
come hurrying to the table with facilitated access to poetry through their
online fee-based poetry finder databases. For over a century, *Granger's
Index to Poetry in Collected and Selected Works* has been considered
the definitive source for retrieving poetry in anthologies. In 1999,
Granger's went online as *Granger's World of Poetry–Online* <http://
www.columbiagrangers.org/grangers/> which now provides access to
50,000 full-text poems and more than 400,000 poem citations. Over
32 million users now access the fee-based site through libraries worldwide.
Added to *LitFinder* by Thomson Gale in June 2004, *PoemFinder*
<http://www.poemfinder.com/login.asp> features 125,000 full-text po-
ems, including 25,000 new, copyrighted poems and the complete works
of many poets. Claiming to be the largest, most comprehensive, and
most current database available, *PoemFinder* includes 800,000 poem
citations and excerpts, along with poetry explanations, and subject access to over 10,000 topic headings. It indexes 7,500 periodical issues as
well. There are also scholarly subscription-based sites that cover poetry
niches, such as the *Database of Twentieth-Century African-American
Poetry* <http://www.il.proquest.com/products/pd-product-AfAmPoetry2.

shtml> and *African-American Poetry, 1760-1900* <http://www.il. proquest.com/products/pd-product-AfAmPoetry.shtml>. Both part of the Chadwyck-Healey's *Literature Online (LION)* <http://www.il. proquest.com/products/pd-product-Lion.shtml> (now acquired by Pro-Quest Information & Learning), these databases provide readers with thousands of full-text poems by African American poets.

While poets' biographies and poetry explication can be found throughout the Web and on such sites as *LitLinks* <http://www. bedfordstmartins.com/litlinks/> and the *Internet Public Library Online Literary Criticism Collection* <http://www.ipl.org/div/litcrit/bin/litcrit. crowse.pl$au=OP>, both geared toward high school and undergraduate students, the commercial sites offer the most in-depth research and criticism. Scholarly information on poets and great works of poetry will be found at Thomson Gale's *Literature Resource Center* <http://www. gale.com/LitRC/>, ProQuest's *Literature Online* <http://www.il.proquest. com/products/pd-product-Lion.shtml>, and Facts on File's *Literary Reference Online* <http://www.factsonfile.com>, a new online resource. Researchers will, of course, still need to consult periodical databases (e.g., *MLA International Bibliography, Humanities Abstracts, JSTOR*, etc.) for further poetry criticism.

What all of these Web sites and databases have in common is that they contain full-text poetry almost exclusively in the public domain. There are only a handful of traditional poetry sites–most notably *The Internet Poetry Archive* <http://www.ibiblio.org/ipa> that features seven contemporary poets–which contain up-to-date poetry. While poets such as Robert Pinsky have worked hard to promote electronic poetry, there is still somewhat of a stigma on publishing online, but this bias should end as the Internet becomes an accepted publishing medium by academicians. Until then, researchers need to assume that archival poetry sites will generally include only twentieth century poetry just out of protection of copyright. Readers looking for recently published poetry, including such acclaimed and award-winning collections as Susan Stewart's *Columbarium*, Louise Gluck's *The Seven Ages*, and C. K. Williams's *The Singing*, will still need to consult print volumes.

NONTRADITIONAL POETRY AND THE INTERNET

While formal poetic works, especially those taught in traditional high school and college courses, are plentiful on the Internet, there is also a growing presence of avant-garde electronic verse. These are poems not written for the printed page but rather for the computer screen. Poets use audio, visuals, graphics, animation, gaming, hyperlinks, mathematical algorithms, and other applications to compose their poems. These new forms of poetry challenge readers accustomed to print formats. Instead of a flat printed page, new and unusual effects become a part of an interactive poetic experience as the poem is performed on the computer screen. Letters and words change color, dance around the screen, and fade in and out. Sounds, videos, and other images interpret, enhance, or even distort the poem's language or meaning. Instead of reading a poem from top to bottom on the page, readers can enter or exit a poem at will, click on hyperlinks within the text, or move words around the screen with a mouse. These technological innovations provide contemporary poets with unlimited potential for incorporating digital media into the poetic experience.

There is no accepted term for this cyberbased poetry, and since the 1960s, experimental works have been labeled computer poetry, computer-based poetry, multimedia poetry, cyberpoetry, digital poetry, and electronic or e-poetry.[2] More recently, the phrase "new media poetry" has been used to lump together a variety of digital applications. While traditional poetry relies on academia, publishing houses, and libraries for distribution, e-poetry relies exclusively on the Internet, a trend which has been a boon for avant-garde poets and the Net generation. The Web provides a cheap and quick means of publishing innovative multimedia poetry that would be too costly or impossible to reproduce on the printed page.

Influence of New Technology on Poetry

As the Internet has evolved, so has the technology available to poets. Early and now rudimentary programs such as Travesty have been replaced by Macromedia Flash, JavaScript, HTML, RealAudio, QuickTime, and many others that allow poets the luxury of using an amazing mix of images, sound, animation, typography, and text. These digital applications have led to the development of new genres of poetry, including flash, kinetic, and hypertext poetry. Older genres, such as visual or concrete poetry, which have long been available in print formats, have likewise been enhanced by computer software. Digital changes just in concrete poetry show how new technologies have affected poetry. Coined as a term in the 1950s, concrete or shape poetry, which has been around in concept for hundreds of years, is poetry that relies on the typographical arrangement of words to convey its meaning. A poem that describes a wave, for instance, would be shaped on the page in the form of an actual wave. With new computer technology, that wave could now flow or move on the screen, and with the addition of audio, the sound of waves crashing on a beach can be heard.

The user can easily locate specific examples of these new poetic genres on the Internet by using a search engine, and there are now Web sites that will collect them as well. Examples of flash poetry can be found at *Low Probability of Racoons* <http://www.hphoward.demon.co.uk/poetry/>; visual poetry which relies on the visual presentation as an intrinsic part of the poem at *The Gates of Paradise* <http://www.thegatesofparadise.com/>; hypertext poetry at *Hypertext Poetry and Web Art* <http://www.hphoward.demon.co.uk/poetry/hypelink.htm>; and kinetic poetry at Ken Perlin's *Kinetic Poetry* site <http://mrl.nyu.edu/~perlin/poetry2/>. There are also meta sites and other collections of e-poetry, including the *Electronic Poetry Center* <http://wings.buffalo.edu/epc/>, *Arras: New Media Poetry and Poetics* <http://www.arras.net/web_poetry.htm>, *UbuWeb, Visual, Concrete, Sound* <http://www.ubu.com/>, and *VISPO LANGU(IM)AGE* <http://vispo.com/misc/links.htm>, which serve as good starting points.

Users can also locate critical essays on e-poetry on the Web. The Technology of Writing section of Alan Liu's extensive *Voice of the Shuttle* <http://vos.ucsb.edu/browse.asp?id=2733> presents essays and other information on the different theories behind e-poetry. Peer-reviewed articles on e-poetry and other digitalized forms of fiction will be found at *NMEDIAC: The Journal of New Media and Culture* <http://www.ibiblio.org/nmediac/>. For those interested in the difference between print and electronic poetry, Andrew Strycharski's brief article (*Hypertext Poetry vs. Print Poetry* <http://composition.miami.edu/~strycharski/link02/brodyWeb/page_five.html>) posted on the Internet compares and contrasts a traditional poem and a hypertext poem.

Online Poetry Journals

The transformation of poetry from the traditional to the experimental is reflected in online poetry journals. Most mainstream print poetry journals now have a Web presence even if it is only to promote the publication and to provide subscription and submission information (e.g., *International Poetry Review* <http://www.uncg.edu/rom/IPR/IPRcurrent.htm>, *Southern Poetry Review* <http://www.spr.armstrong.edu/>, *Long Shot* <http://www.longshot.org/>).[3] Other poetry journals, such as *The Kenyon Review* <http://www.kenyonreview.org/>, *Poetry* <http://

poetrymagazine.org/>, *The American Poetry Review* <http://www.aprweb. org/>, and *Poets & Writers* <http://www.pw.org/>, publish some poems, articles, and excerpts while reserving others for their print publications. Rather than just printing the texts of poems, still other online poetry journals have taken some steps toward incorporating some of the Internet's technological capabilities. *The Cortland Review: An Online Literary Magazine in RealAudio* <http://www.cortlandreview.com> pioneered the use of RealAudio by having poets read their works, and journals such as *The Atlantic Online: Fiction & Poetry* <http://www. theatlantic.com/index/fiction> have followed suit.

These online poetry periodicals now seem very staid when compared to outsider journals–*Poems That Go* <http://www.poemsthatgo.com/>, *Mudlark* <http://www.unf.edu/mudlark>, *BeeHive: hypertext/hypermedia literary journal* <http://beehive.temporalimage.com/bee_core/>, *Drunken Boat* <http://www.drunkenboat.com/>, *Born Magazine* <http:// www.bornmag.org>, *Word Circuits: New Media Poetry* <http://www. wordcircuits.com/>, *Riding the Meridian* <http://www.heelstone.com/ meridian/>, *Cauldron and Net* <http://studiocleo.com/cauldron/volume4/ layout2.html>–that exist solely on the Web, taking full advantage of the rich mix of technologies now available to poets. The poems published in these non-mainstream journals, which are limited only by the imaginations of their authors, present a dazzling array of verse that completely alters the way poetry is traditionally read and enjoyed. Readers who visit these contemporary, innovative journals experience dynamic works that capitalize on the interactive experience.

Researching E-Poets and E-Poetry

While finding research information on traditional or academic poetry can be quite easy, locating biographical and literary criticism on experimental poets and poetry can be challenging at best. While a handful of well-known innovative poets and critics, such as Charles Bernstein and Loss Pequeno Glazier, will be covered in fee-based online library resources, including *Academic Search Elite* and the *Literature Resource Center*, for the most part, e-poets–David Knoebel, Peter Howard, John Cayley, David Cammack, Robert Kendall, Aya Karpinska, etc.–are not covered in literary print sources and commercial databases. It is equally difficult to find explication and criticism for poetry published exclusively online. Faculty and students seeking information on cyberbased poets and poetry will need to rely solely on the Internet for their research. The Author section of the *Electronic Poetry Center* <http://

wings.buffalo.edu/epc/>, for example, provides biographical information, criticism, and samples of work from 150 poets. *Electronic Poetry Review* <http://www.poetry.org>, along with poetry, provides essays and interviews with poets. Often, however, researchers will have to piece together information from a number of Web sites, including the poet's own Web site, to get a full picture of an author and his or her works.

The limited availability of information on e-poets and poetry is due to a number of reasons. It takes a while for a poet to establish a reputation, and even longer for an author to be recognized in standard literary reference sources. This delay goes against the very nature of the Web, which has always been based on newness, speed, and instant access. It is also sometimes difficult to determine good online poetry from bad, especially in an environment where any poetry that is disseminated is considered valid. Any would-be bard can now publish poetry on the Internet without commercial restraints, and there are now hundreds of open admission sites. The Web site *Poetry.com* alone boasts that it features the works of 5.1 million poets.[4] These informal self-publishing sites do eliminate barriers that prevent poets or the general public from publishing, but the sheer number of poems disseminated makes it difficult to separate new and exciting poetry from the unimaginative.

In addition, there are no set vocabularies or techniques for evaluating and analyzing experimental poetry. With conventional poetry, critics and researchers have long-established tools and methodologies for evaluating and analyzing the format, words, and language of poetry. With e-poetry, it can be difficult to judge and evaluate words that dance around on a computer screen and poems that meld together words, images, and sound. Computer technology is also in a continual state of change, and poets and readers alike face the possibility of using a tool that may be outmoded in the near future, rendering once cutting-edge poetry obsolete.

CONCLUSION

By bringing poetry to a wider audience than ever before, the Internet has facilitated a renaissance in poetry. Since technology has now enabled literally millions of people around the world to enter a proliferation of online poetry sites, poetry has become popularized despite the scholarly credibility of these poetry sites and of e-poetry in general still being questioned. The greatest advance that the digital age has brought to poetry is a new way of perceiving a poem, and the Internet has thus irrevocably modified poetic form. Reading has been supplemented by other unlimited possibilities of approaching a poem, such as images, animation, audio, typography, and hypertext. While academic and classical Internet poetry will certainly continue as a staple, especially for universities and academic communities, it is the new experimental Web poetry that will alter poetry and poetry publishing in the twenty-first century.

NOTES

1. Michael Scharf, "What does it cost to do poetry?" *Publishers Weekly* (April 12, 2004): 29.

2. Books that discuss the history and development of innovative e-poetry include Loss Pequeno Glazier's *Digital Poetics: The Making of E-Poetics* (Tuscaloosa: University of Alabama Press, 2002), Charles O. Hartman's *Virtual Muse: Experiments in Computer Poetry* (Hammer, NH: University Press of New England, 1996), and Michael Joyce's *Of Two Minds: Hypertext Pedagogy and Poetics* (Ann Arbor: University of Michigan Press, 1995). A good online bibliography is *New Media Poetry, Hypertext, and Experimental Literature Bibliography* <http://mitpress2.mit.edu/e-journals/Leonardo/isast/spec.projects/newmediapoetry.html>.

3. A list of poetry journals that have a Web presence is available at *Poets & Writers, Inc.* <http://www.pw.org/links_pages/Literary_Magazines/>.

4. Other well-known sites that allow people to publish their poems for free include *Poetry Poem* <http://www.poetrypoem.com>, *Web Poetry Corner* <http://www.dreamagic.com/poetry/poetry1.html>, and *PoetryPen.com* <http://poetrypen.com>.

APPENDIX. Web Sites Discussed

African-American Poetry, 1760-1900
<http://www.il.proquest.com/products/pd-product-AfAmPoetry.shtml>

AllenGinsberg.org
<http://allenginsberg.org/home.asp>

The American Poetry Review
<http://www.aprweb.org/>

American Verse Project
<http://www.hti.umich.edu/a/amverse/>

Arras: New Media Poetry and Poetics
<http://www.arras.net/web_poetry.htm>

The Atlantic Online: Fiction & Poetry
<http://www.theatlantic.com/index/fiction>

Bartleby.com: Verse
<http://www.bartleby.com/verse/>

BeeHive: hypertext/hypermedia literary journal
<http://beehive.temporalimage.com/bee_core/>

Born Magazine
<http://www.bornmag.org>

British Poetry 1780-1910
<http://etext.lib.virginia.edu/britpo.html>

British Women Romantic Poets, 1789-1832
<http://www.lib.ucdavis.edu/English/BWRP/>

Cauldron and Net
<http://www.studiocleo.com/cauldron/volume4/layout2.html>

Cortland Review: An Online Literary Magazine in RealAudio
<http://www.cortlandreview.com/>

Database of Twentieth-Century African-American Poetry
<http://www.il.proquest.com/products/pd-product-AfAmPoetry2.shtml>

Drunken Boat
<http://www.drunkenboat.com/>

Electronic Poetry Center
<http://wings.buffalo.edu/epc/>

Electronic Poetry Review
<http://www.poetry.org>

APPENDIX (continued)

The Gates of Paradise
<http://www.thegatesofparadise.com/>

Geoffrey Chaucer Website
<http://www.courses.fas.harvard.edu/~chaucer/>

Granger's World of Poetry–Online
<http://www.columbiagrangers.org/grangers/>

Hypertext Poetry and Web Art
<http://www.hphoward.demon.co.uk/poetry/hypelink.htm>

Hypertext Poetry vs. Print Poetry
<http://composition.miami.edu/~strycharski/link02/brodyWeb/page_five.html>

International Poetry Review
<http://www.uncg.edu/rom/IPR/IPRcurrent.htm>

The Internet Poetry Archive
<http://www.ibiblio.org/ipa/>

Internet Public Library Online Literary Criticism Collection
<http://www.ipl.org/div/litcrit/bin/litcrit.crowse.pl$au=OP>

The Kenyon Review
<http://www.kenyonreview.org/>

Kinetic Poetry
<http://mrl.nyu.edu/~perlin/poetry2/>

Literary Reference Online
<http://www.factsonfile.com>

Literature Online (LION)
<http://www.il.proquest.com/products/pd-product-Lion.shtml>

Literature Resource Center
<http://www.gale.com/LitRC/>

LitLinks
<http://www.bedfordstmartins.com/litlinks/>

Long Shot
<http://www.longshot.org/>

Lost Poets of the Great War
<http://www.emory.edu/ENGLISH/LostPoets/>

Low Probability of Racoons
<http://www.hphoward.demon.co.uk/poetry/>

Mr. William Shakespeare and the Internet
<http://shakespeare.palomar.edu/>

Mudlark: An Electronic Journal of Poetry & Poetics
<http://www.unf.edu/mudlark>

NMEDIAC: The Journal of New Media and Culture
<http://www.ibiblio.org/nmediac/>

The Online Books Page
<http://digital.library.upenn.edu/books/>

PoemFinder
<http://www.poemfinder.com/login.asp>

Poems That Go
<http://www.poemsthatgo.com/>

Poetry
<http://www.poetrymagazine.org/>

Poetry and Prose of the Harlem Renaissance
<http://www.nku.edu/~diesmanj/poetryindex.html>

Poetry.com: The International Library of Poetry
<http://poetry.com>

Poets & Writers
<http://www.pw.org/>

Poets' Corner
<http://www.theotherpages.org/poems/>

Poets.org: The Academy of American Poets
<http://www.poets.org/index.cfm>

Project Gutenberg
<http://www.gutenberg.net/>

Representative Poetry Online: Version 3.0
<http://eir.library.utoronto.ca/rpo/display/index.cfm>

Riding the Meridian
<http://www.heelstone.com/meridian/>

Sonnet Central
<http://www.sonnets.org/>

Southern Poetry Review
<http://www.spr.armstrong.edu/>

APPENDIX (continued)

UbuWeb, Visual, Concrete, Sound
<http://www.ubu.com/>

VISPO LANGU(IM)AGE
<http:vispo.com/misc/links.htm>

Voice of the Shuttle Technology of Writing
<http://vos.ucsb.edu/browse.asp?id=2733>

Walt Whitman Collection
<http://etext.lib.virginia.edu/whitman/>

William Blake Archive
<http://www.blakearchive.org/>

Word Circuits: New Media Poetry
<http://www.wordcircuits.com/>

World Poetry Database: World Poetry
<http://www.lingshidao.com/waiwen/index.htm>

From Celluloid to Digital:
Electronic Resources for Film Studies

Rebecca S. Albitz

SUMMARY. The Internet offers a large number of free Web sites for those researching films and film-related subjects, but their veracity can be suspect. Happily, there are also reliable sites, both free and supported by a number of commercial firms, representing key film studies research and reference products. This article highlights some of the most useful free and commercial electronic resources currently available to film researchers. *[Article copies available for a fee from The Haworth Document Delivery Service: 1-800-HAWORTH. E-mail address: <docdelivery@haworthpress.com> Website: <http://www.HaworthPress.com> © 2005 by The Haworth Press, Inc. All rights reserved.]*

KEYWORDS. Film studies, television studies, electronic resources, Internet resources, electronic databases, indexing and abstracting services

INTRODUCTION

Electronic resources for the study of the sciences and social sciences have proliferated during the past ten years, but those for the arts and hu-

Rebecca S. Albitz is Electronic Resources and Copyright Librarian, The Pennsylvania State University, 126S Paterno Library, University Park, PA 16802 (E-mail: rsa4@psu.edu).

[Haworth co-indexing entry note]: "From Celluloid to Digital: Electronic Resources for Film Studies." Albitz, Rebecca S. Co-published simultaneously in *Journal of Library Administration* (The Haworth Information Press, an imprint of The Haworth Press, Inc.) Vol. 43, No. 3/4, 2005, pp. 55-63; and: *Evolving Internet Reference Resources* (ed: William Miller, and Rita M. Pellen) The Haworth Information Press, an imprint of The Haworth Press, Inc., 2006, pp. 55-63. Single or multiple copies of this article are available for a fee from The Haworth Document Delivery Service [1-800-HAWORTH, 9:00 a.m. - 5:00 p.m. (EST). E-mail address: docdelivery@haworthpress.com].

manities have lagged behind. Ironically, the humanities subject based on a specific technological development, film studies, has lagged even further behind than its Arts and Humanities counterparts in the development of electronic reference works and indexing and abstracting services. Conversely, film fans embraced the Internet quickly. Every film, actor, actress, and director seems to have at least one Web site devoted to his or her work, creating an immense amount of film-related sites that must be culled through to find those with truly useful information. This article will examine scholarly commercial products, based on published print resources, focused on a scholarly audience, and will explore free resources that have developed a reputation for reliability and stability.

The first determination film scholars make before selecting appropriate research resources is the focus of their research. Film, as one of the more popular mass mediums in this country, has become a tool in almost every discipline in the humanities and social sciences. And, within film studies as a discipline, a proliferation of theoretical approaches makes seemingly irrelevant resources critical. For example, if a research project is exploring the psychological effects of film or television viewing, as many studies of violent behavior in children have done, *PsychInfo* or other psychology-focused products would be relevant. If the interest is in exploring the film itself and how it was received at the time of release, the researcher would gather contemporary reviews and articles from magazines or newspapers which would reflect the reception of a film, the stars, and director. In this case a general literature index such as *Reader's Guide to Periodical Literature* provides access to critical primary resources. The educational effectiveness of film use in the classroom would be best researched in *ERIC* or another education-focused resource. Because the resources useful to research in these divergent areas are too numerous to explore in this paper, I will focus on film as a discipline unto itself, and as a text that is studied, not unlike a literary work.

COMMERCIAL PRODUCTS

Indexing and Abstracting Services

For those initiating a research project, locating the standard indexing and abstracting service(s) in their specialty is usually the first step. Film studies has two print indices that have been published since the early 1970s–when academic institutions began to offer film studies courses and programs. The Film and Television Documentation Center at the State University of New York in Albany has been compiling *Film Literature Index* since 1973. Considered the broadest and most comprehensive index for film and television studies, *Film Literature Index* includes records for about 150 film studies and television-specific journals from 30 countries. In addition, indexers review over 200 non-film periodicals for film and television-related articles. Indiana University-Bloomington's Digital Library Program, along with SUNY Albany, were awarded a National Endowment for the Humanities grant to convert this title into an on-line, fully searchable database containing over 700,000 citations. *FLI Online* can be found at <http://webapp1. dlib.indiana.edu/fli/index.jsp>.[1] I have included *FLI Online* with the other commercially-produced electronic products, although the results of this grant-funded project, the digitization of the volumes covering 1976 through 2001, will be available free of charge on the Internet. *FLI Online* offers boolean keyword searching and subject searching, as well as browsing by name, production title, and corporate name. Various filters, such as article language and type (peer reviewed) can be applied to a search. Unfortunately, no plans are in place to continue the project beyond 2001.

The other primary film studies index is known, in print form, as the *International Index to Film Periodicals*. The International Federation of Film Archives (FIAF) has been compiling this index since 1972, focusing primarily on film periodicals, although articles related to television are included. The on-line product, *International Film Archive*, contains articles from those film journals indexed since 1972, and television articles beginning in 1979. Only available on the SilverPlatter platform, *International Film Archive* allows keyword searching, as well as searching by film title, director's name, corporate entity, or other film-specific designations. In separate modules, this product includes a number of other FIAF publications, all of which are cross-searchable. One of these publications is the *International Directory of Film and Television Documentation Collections*, which provides information about FIAF institutional members and their holdings. Another publication, *Treasure from the Film Archives*, includes FIAF institutional members' records for their silent film holdings. Finally, many FIAF members create their own publications, information about which is available through the *Bibliography of FIAF Members*.

Other indexing and abstracting services offer access to film and television journal content, among other disciplines they cover. *The International Index to Performing Arts* includes citations to articles from over

210 international journals on film, dance, theater, performance art, puppetry, and storytelling. Available through Chadwyck-Healy, this indexing service covers performing arts literature from 1864 through the present. Other indices supporting film research include *Wilson's Art Index, Wilson's Humanities Index* as well as the *Modern Language Association (MLA) Bibliography*. While film and television are not the major foci of these titles, they are worth consulting when compiling a comprehensive bibliography. Wilson databases and the MLA Bibliography are available from a variety of third-party information providers.

Filmographies

Bibliographies are standard tools in the study of literature. Knowing what publications are available on a topic gives researchers a snapshot of the universe of information available to them. For those researchers approaching film as a text or as a reflection of the society in which it was produced, a filmography is as essential as the bibliography. Two electronic resources compile information concerning films produced in the United States and Great Britain, with selected titles from other European countries. The first of these is a blend of an indexing and abstracting product and a filmography. The British Film Institute (BFI) has created *Film Index International (FII)* based on its print publication *Summary of Information on Film and Television (SIFT)*, a compilation of information on world cinema gathered over the past 70 years.

FII is comprised of two data files. The first is a filmography, including credits, production information, and plot summaries, as well as selected television program information. Biographical information about film and television personalities comprises the second. These two files interact through hyperlinks, and each entry contains a bibliography of relevant citations. Unfortunately, subject searching is not available; articles can be located only by the film or personality to which they refer. *FII* covers not only British film and television, but also productions from 170 countries, including the U.S. Although not a comprehensive filmography, nor as complete an index as *Film Literature Index, FII* plays a valuable role in locating literature about international cinema. This product is licensed through Chadwyck-Healy.

For the United States, the American Film Institute (AFI) has produced a print catalog of feature films, covering 1893 through 1950 and 1961-1970. In its electronic form, this catalog contains searchable production information and plot summaries, along with AFI-developed subject and genre headings. The credits and subject headings are hyperlinked, allowing the searcher to create filmographies based on topic, performer, director, and other production staff. The AFI defines the scope of this catalog as feature length films produced in the United States or financed by an American production company. Obviously the ten-year gap between 1951 and 1960, which is currently being compiled, and the termination of the project in 1970 prevent the user from obtaining a complete filmography. For those who understand these limitations, however, the AFI catalog is an invaluable history of feature film production in the United States. The AFI Catalog is also available through Chadwyck-Healy. Both the BFI and AFI catalogs can be licensed as a package, which allows users to cross-search these filmographies.

Film Scripts

Film can be studied as a text from a variety of perspectives. One can conduct a close analysis of the shot structure of a film to discern how camera angles, shot composition, and camera movement create meaning for the viewer. Analyzing use of film editing, music, and other production techniques may also suggest a variety of meanings. Using the script itself, both as a literary text and the genesis of a visual product is a widely-used method of film analysis. *American Filmscripts Online*, an Alexander Street Press product, is an electronic collection of selected scripts spanning the history of American film. These scripts are various authorized versions, including the author's personal copies production scripts from film studios and published editions. Faber and Faber and Vintage Press are among the publishers represented, while Warner Brothers, Fox, and Sony are studios that contributed content. Notable screenwriters such as Paul Schrader and Oliver Stone have contributed copies of their own works. Each script is heavily indexed at the scene and word level, allows users to search themes, words used in context within a scene and character traits such as nationality, religion, and age. Records for each film and person include both bibliographic and biographical information. When completed, *American Filmscripts Online* will contain 1,000 screenplays.

Video Reviews/Distributors

Finally, for researchers who are interested not just in feature films, but also in documentaries and educational titles, *Video Librarian Plus* includes over 15,000 full-text video reviews. The Web site for the print journal *Video Librarian*, this product includes a searchable database of over 1,000 video distributors. Because smaller distribution companies or filmmakers themselves may choose to retain distribution rights to their works, many sources for documentary and educational film and video purchase can be difficult to find. For this reason a distributor's database is invaluable for building a strong video collection.

FREE INTERNET RESOURCES

General Film Sites

While all the previously-mentioned commercial electronic products were developed from print resources, the following free products were created for and on the Internet, and have developed a reputation as reliable information resources. The most popular of these is the *Internet Movie Database* (*IMDb*) <http://www.imdb.com>.[2] Touted as the Earth's biggest movie database, with over 376,000 titles and 1,400,000 records for actors, actresses, producers, directors, writers, and other cast and crew members, *IMDb*'s goal is to include as many films and television programs with complete credits and plot summaries as possible. Site users themselves contribute credits, plot information, and reviews as well as corrections to other contributions. The *IMDb* has launched a commercial site called *IMDb pro*, focusing on the information needs of those working in the entertainment industry <https://secure.imdb.com/signup/v4/?d=IMDbTab>.[3] The commercial site includes box office figures for United States daily and weekly grosses, international box office receipts, and video rental figures. Entertainment news from *Entertainment Weekly* is available, as well as "in production" charts for over 1,500 film and television projects. For the person who is interested in locating credit or plot information, however, the free site provides ample information, and the accuracy of this information is widely accepted.

While the *IMDb* appeals to film scholars and fans alike because of the breadth of information available, another Web site is geared specifically toward the film studies student or faculty member. The Society for Cinema and Media Studies (SCMS)–formerly, Society for Cinema Studies–is the leading international scholarly film, television, and media organization. SCMS' Web site contains information concerning the organization, upcoming conferences, publications, and awards <http://www.cmstudies.org>.[4] A members-only section offers a membership directory, officer and committee information, job postings, and graduate student information. While membership in the SCMS is not free, the public section of its Web site has useful information for those considering membership.

A thorough Web site combining the scholarly with the popular, the free with the commercial, is *Cinema Sites* <http://www.cinema-sites. com>.[5] A well-organized meta-site, *Cinema Sites'* Webmaster has selected and annotated references to hundreds of media-related Web pages. These categories include electronic journals, film scripts, film reviews, animation, television, and fan sites. Taking on the task of linking to and checking links to sites with a focus on more popular information is a challenge, and broken links are common in these categories. *Cinema Sites'* Webmaster has done a good job of maintaining access to interesting Web sites and has included contact information so that users of this site can notify him of access issues.

Box Office Figures

One of the bigger challenges for film students, pre-Web, was locating both historical and current box office receipts. This information provides a glimpse into the immediate and extended popularity of a film. The Web has a number of box office sites covering films in current release, historic films, and video/DVD sales and rentals. *WorldwideBoxoffice.source* links to a number of different sites focusing on current releases figures, both domestic and international <http://www.worldwideboxoffice.com/ source.html>.[6] It is from these sites that the figures for *WorldwideBoxoffice* are gleaned. *WorldwideBoxoffice* offers receipt figures for over 3,300 film titles, released from approximately 1900 to date <http://www.worldwideboxoffice.com>.[7] Box office entries for each film contain links to the IMDb record for the film for further cast, credit, and plot information. Another site, *Box Office Guru*, provides up-to-date box office information, along with a daily grosses archives back to 1997 <http://www.boxofficeguru.com>.[8] Release schedules for upcoming films and opening weekend figures are also available. A running total of receipts from all-time box office record holders are included.

Television

Many film studies programs have embraced television and other moving media as part of their scholarly realm. The Society for Cinema Studies' change in name to Society for Cinema and Media Studies illustrates this trend. So, any article identifying electronic resources in film studies would be incomplete without mentioning television study resources as well. Almost all of the indexing and abstracting services previously mentioned identify articles concerning television as well as film. The *Internet Movie Database* includes film and television programs, as well as credits for cast and crew members. A metasite devoted to film and television is available from and maintained by Time Lapse.com, a stock footage company. *TVlink* is a clearinghouse for all things film and television on the Web <http://www.timelapse.com/tvlink>.[9] Links to sites for actors, producers and directors, animators, and special effects creators, as well as television stations, film distribution companies, and video distribution companies are listed. Resources related to the content, production, and technology of film and television can be found on this site as well. The Webmaster has provided contact information, encouraging users to report broken or redirected links, adding to the stability of this site.

CONCLUSION

Because film studies focuses on a text that was created initially for entertainment, a plethora of popular materials are available on the Internet. These popular sites raise a number of issues for information seekers, depending on the focus of their research. Therefore anyone interested in the field of film studies should be aware of commercial products as well as those freely available on the Internet. The commercial resources not only allow one to corroborate the information found on the Internet, but also provide different kinds of information, such as subject-searchable citations to journal articles. The recent release of *Film Literature Index Online*, with its free access to scholarly citations on film and television, will change the research behaviors of some, and will be a huge boon to those without access to other commercial products. However, very few researchers have the luxury of free access to a definitive indexing service. For the latest research in film and television, subscriptions to commercial services will continue to be necessary.

NOTES

1. Film and Television Documentation Center & IU Digital Library, *FLI Online*, 4 November 2004, <http://webappt.dlib.indiana.edu/fli/index.jsp> (2 December 2004).

2. Amazon.com, *Internet Movie Database*, <http://www.imdb.com> (2 December 2004).

3. Amazon.com, *IMDb pro.com*, <https://secure.imdb.com/signup/v4/?d=IMDbTab> (2 December 2004).

4. Society for Cinema & Media Studies, <http://www.cmstudies.org> (2 December 2004).
5. David R. Augsburger, *Cinema Sites*, <http://www.cinema-sites.com> (2 December 2004).
6. Chuck Kahn, *WorldwideBoxoffice.source*, <http://www.worldwideboxoffice.com.source.html> (2 December 2004).
7. Chuck Kahn, *WorldwideBoxoffice*, <http://www.worldwideboxoffice.com> (2 December 2004).
8. Gitesh Pandya, *Box Office Guru*, 29 November 2004, <http://www.boxofficeguru.com> (2 December 2004).
9. Timelapse.com, *TVlink*, <http://www.timelapse.com/tvlink> (2 December 2004).

WORKS CITED

Amazon.com. *IMDb pro.com*. <https://secure.imdb.com/signup/v4/?d=IMDbTab> (2 December 2004).

Amazon.com. *Internet Movie Database*. <http://www.imdb.com> (2 December 2004).

Augsburger, David R. *Cinema Sites*. <http://www.cinema-sites.com> (2 December 2004).

Film and Television Documentation Center & IU Digital Library. *FLI Online*. 4 November 2004. <http://webappt.dlib.indiana.edu/fli/index.jsp> (2 December 2004).

Kahn, Chuck. *WorldwideBoxoffice*. <http://www.worldwideboxoffice.com> (2 December 2004).

Kahn, Chuck. *WorldwideBoxoffice.source*. <http://www.worldwideboxoffice.com/source.html> (2 December 2004).

Pandya, Gitesh. *Box Office Guru*. 29 November 2004. <http://www.boxofficeguru.com> (2 December 2004).

Society for Cinema & Media Studies. <http://www.cmstudies.org> (2 December 2004).

Timelapse.com. *TVlink*. <http://www.timelapse.com/tvlink> (2 December 2004).

Popular Web-Based Reference Sources for United States History

Paul A. Frisch

SUMMARY. Obstacles to the efficient, effective discovery of Web-based reference sources for United States history include the vastness of the Web, researchers' unfamiliarity with sophisticated searching techniques, and the tendency of search engines to list results by "relevancy" based on a site's popularity. Reference librarians can facilitate research by offering a list of categorized Web sites which includes meta sites, directories, overviews, timelines and chronologies, data, primary sources (maps, newspapers, documents, pictures, video and audio), U.S. government history, biographies, and writing citation guides. *[Article copies available for a fee from The Haworth Document Delivery Service: 1-800-HAWORTH. E-mail address: <docdelivery@haworthpress.com> Website: <http://www.HaworthPress.com> © 2005 by The Haworth Press, Inc. All rights reserved.]*

KEYWORDS. United States history, American history, reference sources, digital sources, electronic sources, Web sources

---

Paul A. Frisch is Associate Provost, Library, Instructional and Technology Services, Our Lady of the Lake University, 411 S.W. 24th Street, San Antonio, TX 78207 (E-mail: frisp@lake.ollusa.edu).

[Haworth co-indexing entry note]: "Popular Web-Based Reference Sources for United States History." Frisch, Paul A. Co-published simultaneously in *Journal of Library Administration* (The Haworth Information Press, an imprint of The Haworth Press, Inc.) Vol. 43, No. 3/4, 2005, pp. 65-74; and: *Evolving Internet Reference Resources* (ed: William Miller, and Rita M. Pellen) The Haworth Information Press, an imprint of The Haworth Press, Inc., 2006, pp. 65-74. Single or multiple copies of this article are available for a fee from The Haworth Document Delivery Service [1-800-HAWORTH, 9:00 a.m. - 5:00 p.m. (EST). E-mail address: docdelivery@haworthpress.com].

doi:10.1300/J111v43n03_06

A search of the Internet for information about United States history leads to a rich assortment of primary and secondary resources. However, the chances of a quick, successful outcome are thwarted by the vastness of the subject and the uneven quality of retrieved sites in terms of scope, organization, currency of information and links, and bias. Since the Web became popular in the mid-1990s, two published articles have attempted to make quality United States history sources more accessible over the Web. Published in 1996, the first article includes both Gopher and Web sites.[1] The second article describes the growing universe of Web sites.[2] This article will build upon these earlier articles in two ways. First, it will describe the most current sites, a major challenge given the frequency with which new sites appear, and older sites either disappear or are no longer updated. Second, this article will focus mainly on reference sources for the general public, and high school and college students who need assistance selecting and researching a topic, writing the paper, citing the sources, and finding facts.

META SITES, DIRECTORIES, AND OVERVIEWS

These sources will help the researcher who needs an historical overview, an encyclopedia article, or an organized site from which to select a topic.

A Biography of America
<http://www.learner.org/biographyofamerica>

WGBH Boston, funded by Annenberg/CPB, produced this telecourse, video series, and Web site which is aimed at college-level history students. The 26 topics are those frequently found in U.S. history books. Each topic has a transcript of the video in which historians discuss the major issues, an interactive map or time line, a key events chart, and bibliographic citations to print and Web-based sources.

Sage History: An American Experience
<http://www.sagehistory.net>

David Sage, a history instructor at Northern Virginia Community College, developed this site as an introduction to anyone interested in United States history. Each of the 14 time periods and topics has an overview, important dates, documents, and print and Web sources. Also found at this site are links to historic sites, images, an extensive reading list, some biographical sketches, and suggested projects.

Digital History
<http://www.digitalhistory.uh.edu>

This collaboration between the University of Houston, Chicago Historical Society, The Gilder Lehrman Institute of American History, Houston's Museum of Fine Arts, U.S. Department of the Interior's National Park Service, and The Project for the Active Teaching of American History encourages the use of new technologies to enhance teaching and research. It includes an online textbook with 44 chapters, primary sources, biographies, encyclopedia, chronologies, images, maps, writing guides, and historiography.

Encyclopedia Britannica Online
<http://www.eb.com>

This subscription database includes information from Britannica Student Encyclopedia and the Britannica Internet Guide. In addition to its search engine, the most useful features for finding information on United States history are an A-Z alphabetical browse and a subject browse organized into an outline. Each article has internal links to other articles, and citations in MLA, APA, and Britannica style.

AllRefer.com
<http://reference.allrefer.com/encyclopedia/History/United_States_and_Canada.html>

This site has major headings for North American indigenous peoples, Supreme Court, biographies, and general U.S. history articles. Each major heading contains an alphabetical list of articles which are drawn from the Columbia Electronic Encyclopedia (2003).

History Resource Center–U.S.
<http://www.galegroup.com/HistoryRC/P02F.htm>

Thomson Gale has created a subscription database that integrates the content of full-text periodicals, multimedia reference articles, and facsimiles of historical documents. This database can be accessed through person, time period, subject, chronology, full text, and a combination of full text and subject. Search results can include overviews, annotated chronologies, encyclopedic articles, essays, biographies, original documents, full-text journal articles, bibliographies, and annotated Web links.

American History Online
<www.factsonfile.com>

This subscription database from Facts on File brings together nine collections, including biographies of American inventors, entrepreneurs, business visionaries, political leaders, social leaders and activists, First Ladies, presidents, vice presidents, and Supreme Court Justices; *Encyclopedia of American History*; and *Encyclopedia of Battles in North America*. Browsing may be accomplished in six categories–biographies, encyclopedic subject entries, primary sources, timeline, image gallery, and maps and charts. Cross-references appear in the entries. There are illustrations and bibliographies in many entries. There is a subject list of related Web sites.

United States History Index
<http://vlib.iue.it/history/USA>

Created by Dr. Lynn H. Nelson, professor of history emeritus at Kansas University, and now managed by George Laughead of the Kansas Heritage Group, this is the most comprehensive site for links to U.S. history sites. This well organized site has the following six major categories. Bibliography includes gateways and link pages, documents, bibliographies, archives, libraries and book sellers. Materials include databases, electronic texts, Federal resources, journals, historic sites, and U.S. history books. Research aids covers maps, timelines, and references. There are categories for associations and societies, and historians' calendar. There are 20 listings under historical topics, including uncommon ones like Beat Generation, generational studies, and maritime history. There are 13 chronological periods.

TIMELINES AND CHRONOLOGIES

American Cultural History–19th Century
<http://kclibrary.nhmccd.edu/19thcentury.html>

Peggy Whitley and other reference librarians at Kingwood College have created an entertaining, informative decade-by-decade tour of the nineteenth century. Each decade explores the following ten areas: art and architecture; business and the economy; books and literature; migration and immigration; education; news and events; music and theater; pastimes; science and technology; and social movements. Each area offers a brief overview with a picture and links within the text, and a short list of books, videos, and Web sites.

American Cultural History–The Twentieth Century
<http://kclibrary.nhmccd.edu/decades.html>

Peggy Whitley et al. have constructed a decade-by-decade examination of twentieth-century America. Each decade explores the following six areas: art and architecture; books and literature; fads and fashion; historic events and technology; music; and theater, film, and radio. Each area offers a brief overview with a picture and links within the text, Library of Congress browsing call letters, a short list of books, and a few Web sites.

U.S. History Timeline and This Day in History
<http://www.infoplease.com/ipa/A0902416.html>

These are part of the infoplease.com Web site operated by Pearson, a British-based publication and media conglomerate. The timeline offers brief descriptions. Many entries have links to The Columbia Electronic Encyclopedia. "This Day in History" provides brief entries with some having links.

DATA

Historical Census Data Browser
<http://fisher.lib.virginia.edu/collections/stats/histcensus>

Harvard University's Instructional Computing Group has used data from the Inter-University Consortium for Political and Social Research to enable browsing of selected historical census data from 1790 to 1970. Data from 1790 to 1830 focus solely on population characteristics, while selected economic, manufacturing, and agricultural data are available for later censuses. The data are from the county and state level, and once data are retrieved they can be further refined, sorted, and displayed.

How Much Is That Worth Today?
<http://eh.net/ehresources/howmuch/sourcenote.php>

John J. McCusker, a distinguished professor of American history and economics at Trinity University, has created a calculator for comparing the purchasing power of money in the U.S. economy from 1665 to the present. The numbers since 1913 are based on the Consumer Price Index compiled by the United States' Bureau of Labor Statistics. Monetary values prior to 1913 are based on the calculations of economists and economic historians. McCusker notes that finding comparable worth over time is an imprecise process.

PRIMARY SOURCES

Sometimes the request for reference assistance requires an important document, a vital speech, a historic photograph or video clip, or access to old newspaper articles.

AMDOCS–Documents for the Study of American History
<http://www.ukans.edu/carrie/docs/amdocs_index.html>

Maintained by the University of Kansas, this is one of the most comprehensive, organized collection of links to digital documents. Most documents are from the eighteenth and nineteenth centuries with relatively few from the twentieth century. The documents are organized by time period. The find command will also allow a single keyword to be searched.

ProQuest Historical Newspapers
<http://www.chadwyck.com>

Chadwyck-Healey has produced a full-text, keyword searchable database to major American newspapers. Subscribers have access to the *New York Times* (1851-2001), *Wall Street Journal* (1889-1987), the *Washington Post* (1877-1988), and *Christian Science Monitor* (1908-1991). ProQuest is also currently digitizing the *Chicago Tribune* and *Los Angeles Times*. Newspaper articles are retrieved in PDF files.

Perry-Castaneda Library Map Collection–Historical Maps of the United States
<http://www.lib.utexas.edu/maps/histus.html>

The University of Texas map library uses the following categories: early inhabitants, exploration and settlement, U.S. territorial growth, later historical periods, and other historical map sites.

Historical Picture Collections
<http://history.sandiego.edu/gen/documents/clipsources.html>

Steven Schoenherr, an historian at the University of San Diego, has organized links to pictures in such categories as presidents, states, cities and regions, aviation, military, movies and radio, railroads, science and technology, ships, and space images.

Video Clips and Audio Speeches
<http://www.historychannel.com/broadband>

The History Channel has organized video clips under the following categories: featured clips, this day in history, historical icons, military and war, arts and society, science and technology, and television. Audio speeches are categorized by politics and government, war and diplomacy, science and technology, and arts, entertainment and culture.

U.S. GOVERNMENT

The White House
<http://www.whitehouse.gov>

This site provides brief biographies of the Presidents and First Ladies which are searchable by name or date. There are facts about the White House, including art, furnishings, and life in the White House, and an online tour. Events and traditions, such as the Easter egg roll, baseball, and State of the Union, are available. Air Force One, Marine One, and Camp David are covered.

The United States House of Representatives
<http://www.house.gov>

In addition to information on current operations, there is a page of Educational Links which includes the legislative process, Congressional documents and debates (1774-1875), House historical information, key U.S. documents (Declaration of Independence, Constitution, Bill of Rights and amendments), and full text of proposed amendments that were not ratified.

The United States Senate
<http://www.senate.gov.>

This site offers a treasure trove of historical information under the headings "Art and History" and "Reference." Information is available on past senators, institutional development, chronology, party division, historical essays, key U.S. documents (Declaration of Independence, Constitution and Bill of Rights), bibliographies, and glossary.

The Supreme Court Historical Society
<http://www.supremecourthistory.org>

The Society was incorporated as a private, non-profit organization in 1974. It supports educational programs, supports research, and collects artifacts related to the Court's history. "Researching the Court" is the most relevant section for historical information, including voting records, biographies and bibliographies of the Justices, Court procedures and opinions, and the architecture and history of the Supreme Court building.

BIOGRAPHIES

Biography.com
<http://www.biography.com>

This site is related to the Biography Channel, which is part of the A&E Television Networks. There are over 25,000 biographies of present and past figures. The database can be searched by name, keyword (e.g., occupation, place, and event), or an alphabetical index. The entries vary in length with links to Web sites and persons who were related to the biographee's life.

AllRefer.com
<http://reference.allrefer.com>

A keyword search of this free commercial site will produce a list of links for biographical information. The most complete entries are from "encyclopedia," which links to the *Columbia Electronic Encyclopedia.* *InfoPlease.com* also links to the *Columbia Electronic Encyclopedia* and provides highlighted links within the article and a brief bibliography, but *AllRefer.com* has these features plus a list of related topics.

Biographical Directory of American History
<http://www.digitalhistory.uh.edu/biographies/biographies.cfm>

Part of the *Digital History* project previously mentioned, an alphabetical list of primarily deceased, prominent Americans links to entries in Houghton Mifflin's *The Reader's Companion to American History.* Each signed biography has a brief bibliography and links to *see also* references.

American National Biography Online
<http://www.anb.org>

Oxford University Press's subscription database is an ongoing project with over 17,000 biographies with bibliographies and some with illustrations. New biographies are being entered, and there are updates to existing bibliographies and biographies. There are links to other biographies in the database and to external Web sites. *ANB Online* is searchable by full text, subject name, gender, occupation or realm of renown, birth date, birthplace, death date, and contributor name.

RESEARCH, WRITING, AND CITATION GUIDES

These sites will aid students who need assistance in the processes of researching and writing papers and critical book reviews, and citing electronic resources.

A Student's Guide to History
<http://www.bedfordstmartins.com/history/benjamin/content.htm>

This is a brief online version of *A Student's Guide to History, 8th edition (Bedford/St. Martin's, 2000)* by Jules Benjamin, a historian at Ithaca College. This site offers guidance in selecting and researching a topic, and writing for different types of history assignments, such as essays, research papers, book reviews, and comparative book reviews. Within the text there are links to glossary terms and *see* references.

Writing Guides
<http://www.digitalhistory.uh.edu/writing_guides/writing_guides.cfm>

Part of the Digital History project previously mentioned, the Writing Guides page is divided into five sections: How to Write in a History Class; Steps in Writing a Research Paper; Taking an Essay Exam; Writing a Critical Book Review; and Guide for the Grammatically Perplexed.

Citing Electronic Information in History Papers
<http://cas.memphis.edu/~mcrouse/elcite.html>

Maurice Crouse, a historian at the University of Memphis, has maintained this site since 1995. He provides examples for individual works, parts of works, periodicals and journals, newspapers and magazines, abstracts and reviews of individual works, periodicals and journals, electronic mail, electronic conferences, interest groups, newsgroups and lists, searches in online library catalogs and databases, and government publications and legal documents.

CONCLUSION

The popular Web-based sources covered in this article should suffice for researchers below the level of graduate student who need an overview, a fact, or an introduction to the art of historical research and writing. After selecting a topic, the neophyte researcher is ready for more specialized sources. The above discussed *United States History Index* <http://vlib.iue.it/history/USA> should prove adequate in leading the researcher to Web sites which cover specific topics.

NOTES

1. Stanley D. Nash, Miles Yoshimura, and William Vincenti, "American History Resources on the Internet," *College & Research Libraries News* 57 (1996): 82-84, 96.
2. Paul A. Frisch, U.S. History: Primary and Secondary Sources, *College & Research Libraries News* 62 (2001): 991-94.

Evolving Internet Reference in Anthropology: What Our Patrons Want and How We Can Help Them Find It

Wade R. Kotter

SUMMARY. Reference work in anthropology has evolved in a variety of directions with the growth of the Internet and World Wide Web. This discussion of that evolution stresses the ways in which existing Internet resources can be used to answer eight of the most common categories of reference questions in this extraordinarily broad and diverse discipline. These categories were identified through an informal survey of anthropology reference librarians and subject specialists. *[Article copies available for a fee from The Haworth Document Delivery Service: 1-800-HAWORTH. E-mail address: <docdelivery@haworthpress.com> Website: <http://www.HaworthPress.com> © 2005 by The Haworth Press, Inc. All rights reserved.]*

KEYWORDS. Anthropology, cultural anthropology, archaeology, physical anthropology, linguistics

---

Wade R. Kotter is Social Sciences Librarian, Stewart Library, Weber State University, Ogden, UT 84408-2901 (E-mail: wkotter@weber.edu).

[Haworth co-indexing entry note]: "Evolving Internet Reference in Anthropology: What Our Patrons Want and How We Can Help Them Find It." Kotter, Wade R. Co-published simultaneously in *Journal of Library Administration* (The Haworth Information Press, an imprint of The Haworth Press, Inc.) Vol. 43, No. 3/4, 2005, pp. 75-83; and: *Evolving Internet Reference Resources* (ed: William Miller, and Rita M. Pellen) The Haworth Information Press, an imprint of The Haworth Press, Inc., 2006, pp. 75-83. Single or multiple copies of this article are available for a fee from The Haworth Document Delivery Service [1-800-HAWORTH, 9:00 a.m. - 5:00 p.m. (EST). E-mail address: docdelivery@haworthpress.com].

Available online at http://www.haworthpress.com/web/JLA
doi:10.1300/J111v43n03_07

INTRODUCTION

Any librarian who has fielded reference questions in anthropology knows that such questions can present a significant challenge. Anthropology, which can be defined as the scientific study of humankind at all times and in all places, is perhaps the most diverse of all the social sciences. It includes several sub-disciplines, including cultural anthropology, archaeology, anthropological linguistics, and physical anthropology, each with its own research questions, methodologies, and literatures. Reference questions in anthropology can relate to the present or the distant past, to one's immediate locality or to a location far away. They can also relate to generalities about human culture or intimate details of human biology. What ties all these sub-disciplines together is the goal of documenting and explaining human variability, both cultural and biological. Because of this breadth and diversity, any attempt to develop an annotated list of World Wide Web sites for use in anthropological reference runs the risk of losing touch with the information needs of our patrons.

In an attempt to avoid this dilemma, work on this article began with an informal survey of experienced anthropology librarians who subscribe to ANSS-L, the e-mail discussion list of the Anthropology and Sociology Section (ANSS) of the Association of College and Research Libraries. A message was posted twice to the list requesting that individuals send the author a list of the five most important categories of anthropological reference questions based on their experience. A total of 25 individuals responded to these messages. Based on these responses, the author identified eight general categories of anthropology reference questions that reflect the needs of our patrons and serve as the foundation for the remainder of this article.

FINDING INFORMATION
ON A SPECIFIC CULTURAL GROUP

All of the survey respondents mentioned finding detailed information on a specific cultural group as one of the most important categories of reference questions in anthropology. While a search by group name using a general search engine such as Google might yield some useful results, recent years have seen the emergence of three World Wide Web resources that are much more focused and reliable. They also provide excellent models for future developments.

eHRAF Collection of Ethnography: Web
<http://www.yale.edu/hraf/collections.htm>

This subscription-based database is an electronic version of the Human Relations Area Files, an indexed microfiche collection of full-text sources documenting over 300 human societies from around the world. The electronic version allows searching of the collection by group name, location, subject and so forth. It is by far the most comprehensive source of detailed ethnographic information available on the Web. Unfortunately, as a subscription-based product it is only available to those libraries that can afford it.

AnthroSource
<http://www.anthrosource.net>

Developed by the American Anthropological Association (AAA) in partnership with the University of California Press with support from the Andrew W. Mellon Foundation, AnthroSource has the potential to revolutionize reference service in anthropology. The initial version, which became available in January 2005, provides access to a complete full-text archive of 39 AAA publications from the first issue up to 2003. It also provides access to the full text of 11 core AAA journals from 2003 to the current issue, including *American Anthropologist*. Complete access to AnthroSource is available to AAA members and to institutional subscribers. However, anyone with Internet access can search the database, providing bibliographic access to a wealth of primary literature in anthropology. The default simple search looks for terms in all fields, including abstract, article title, keyword, author, and publication year. Searching for the name of a specific cultural group can yield citations to a wealth of primary literature. For example, in late January 2005, a search for articles on the Nuer, a native people of Sudan, yielded 555 articles. Even without access to the full text, AnthroSource is an essential reference resource for anthropology.

Ethnologue
<http://www.ethnologue.com/web.asp>

This freely accessible Web site provides access to information on over 6,000 living languages spoken in countries throughout the world. Produced by SIL (formerly known as the Summer Institute of Linguistics), this extremely useful site provides authoritative information about these languages as well as regularly updated bibliographies. One can search by general keyword and browse by language name, language family, and country.

FINDING BIOGRAPHICAL INFORMATION

Another commonly mentioned category of reference questions in anthropology involves finding biographical information about a specific anthropologist. Although using a general search engine can sometimes yield useful results, the material from such sources is often sketchy and poorly documented. General biographical information on a few very well-known anthropologists can also be found in the standard subscription-based biographical sources and freely accessible Web sites such as biography.com, but only recently has an Internet resource specific to anthropology appeared.

Anthropological Biography Web
<http://www.mnsu.edu/emuseum/information/biography>

This increasingly useful Web site is maintained by anthropology students at Minnesota State University, Mankato. It includes brief biographical sketches on over 700 individuals of relevance to anthropology, both living and deceased. This student project has evolved into a very useful resource for biographical information on anthropologists, although the quality of the sketches varies. In addition to detailed biographical sketches, the best entries include bibliographies of print sources, links to Web sites, and sometimes images as well.

FINDING BOOK REVIEWS

Another oft-mentioned category of reference questions in anthropology involves the search for reviews of a specific book. Although reviews of such books can sometimes be located in the standard book review indexes and some article databases, the fact that many specialized books in anthropology are reviewed only once or twice means that the reviews may never make it into these general indexes. Fortunately, there are two Web sites that help us resolve this dilemma.

AnthroSource
<http://www.anthrosource.net>

In addition to regular articles from AAA journals, AnthroSource (see above) provides access to thousands of book reviews from the same publications. Since anyone with Internet access can search AnthroSource, it is an essential resource for identifying book reviews in anthropology. Unfortunately, AnthroSource does not allow searchers to restrict their search only to book reviews.

Anthropology Reviews Database
<http://wings.buffalo.edu/ARD/>

Developed and maintained at the Department of Anthropology, University at Buffalo, State University of New York, the Anthropology Reviews Database (ARD) provides citations to book reviews published in several core anthropology journals, both print and electronic, as well as the full text of nearly 300 reviews specifically written for the database. The quality of these full-text reviews is quite high. While this site has great potential, its ultimate success will depend on the continuing commitment of its volunteer editorial board.

FINDING IMAGES

Common reference questions in anthropology mentioned by the respondents also include a search for images. In academic libraries, for example, an increasing number of students are looking for images to illustrate their research. As with previous categories, one can sometimes find appropriate images using the image search capabilities of general search engines, but at times this can be a tedious and difficult process. In recent years, however, museums have begun to make their collections, including images, available on the Web. One example is of special relevance to anthropology.

Anthropology Collection Database, California Academy of Sciences
<http://www.calacademy.org/research/anthropology/collections/
collintro.htm>

The Department of Anthropology, California Academy of Sciences, has recently made its collection data available online, including high-quality images of over 10,000 objects. This remarkable site allows the user to search for objects using a variety of criteria, including category, material, culture, and maker's name. It would also be very valuable for anthropologists doing comparative analyses of material culture.

FINDING INFORMATION ON RECENT DISCOVERIES

The informal survey also suggests that users are very interested in locating information on recent discoveries, especially in archaeology and human evolution. Often individuals hear about such discoveries on the news and come to the library looking for additional information. Searching for such information using standard sources can be time-consuming and often results in frustration. However, Web sites that provide subject-specific news links are appearing in increasing numbers on the Web, including two very interesting sites of relevance to anthropology.

Archaeological News
<http://www.archaeological.org/webinfo.php?page=10168>

Produced by the staff of *Archaeology Magazine*, a publication of the Archaeological Institute of America, this site provides reliable, up-to-date archaeological news links and commentary. If a recent discovery has captivated the public interest, chances are it will be mentioned on this site. New stories are added each weekday, with earlier stories archived back several years. For example, in late January 2005, a search for stories on archaeology in Israel yielded stories dating back to October 2002.

Council for British Archaeology's British & Irish Archaeology Newsfeed
<http://www.britarch.ac.uk/newsfeed/index.html>

This innovative newsfeed, which is updated every five minutes, provides links to online news items on archaeology garnered from various British online sources. Links remain on the newsfeed page for two days. While focused on British archaeology, it provides a model of what ought to be done for various regions of the world.

FINDING INFORMATION ON SPECIFIC
ARCHAEOLOGICAL SITES AND ANCIENT CULTURES

Although not mentioned as often as the previous categories, several respondents reported that requests for information on specific archaeological sites and ancient cultures are also quite common. Using general search engines and archaeology meta-sites, one can often find useful but usually limited information. However, in recent years a few Web resources have appeared that have great potential.

eHRAF Collection of Archaeology: Web
<http://www.yale.edu/hraf/collections.htm>

This counterpart to the eHRAF Collection of Ethnography provides access to a fully indexed collection of full-text primary documents on archaeological traditions from various parts of the world. Users can search by several criteria, including site name, archaeological culture, and general keyword. Although the number of archaeological traditions represented is relatively small when compared to its ethnographic counterpart, new traditions are being added on a regular basis. Regardless, it remains a very useful source for specific archaeological information for those libraries that can afford it.

National Archaeological Database
<http://www.cr.nps.gov/aad/TOOLS/nadb.htm>

This freely accessible Web database, a joint project of the National Park Service and the Center for Advanced Spatial Technologies, provides access to a wealth of information on public archaeological research in the United States. It includes citations for over 300,000 archaeological reports of limited circulation, records for thousands of federal archaeology permits, and a mapping application. The archaeological reports are searchable by several criteria, including state, county, author, title, publication date, and work type. In late January 2005, a search for reports on archaeological research in Weber county Utah yielded 74 citations, each of which includes an indication of where the report is housed. The National Archaeological Databases is truly a unique resource and documents the potential of the Web for making literature of limited distribution more widely accessible to scholars and the public at large.

FINDING CAREER INFORMATION

Another category of reference questions identified by several respondents involves requests for assistance in finding career information in anthropology and its sub-disciplines. The primary sources for such information are the major scholarly associations in the field, although the amount and quality of this information vary from association to association.

American Anthropological Association
<http://www.aaanet.org/careers.htm>

As the largest scholarly association of anthropologists in the world, one would expect that the American Anthropological Association Web site would be one of the best sources for career information in the field. Unfortunately, the quantity and quality of information it provides leaves a great deal to be desired, although it does provide a valuable list of links to other sources of career information. Individuals can also order a video entitled *Anthropologists at Work: Careers in Anthropology* at a cost of $35.00 for non-AAA members, but this will be of little use to those seeking reference assistance. The AAA should consider providing a free video stream of this program on its Web site.

Society for American Archaeology
<http://www.saa.org/careers/index.html>

The careers section of the Society for American Archaeology Web site is an excellent resource for individuals considering a career in archaeology. It provides links to a variety of resources, including a well-written FAQ on archaeology as a career. The material on this site should be required reading for anyone considering a career in archaeology and would serve well as a model for other professional associations in anthropology.

American Association of Physical Anthropologists
<http://www.physanth.org/careers/>

This is a useful but brief page that discusses both academic and non-academic careers in physical anthropology. It also includes a few useful links to sources of additional information and provides some valuable advice on the job-search process.

IDENTIFYING FIELDWORK OPPORTUNITIES

The final category of reference questions mentioned by several respondents involves identifying fieldwork opportunities, especially in archaeology. Most meta-sites in anthropology and archaeology include links to fieldwork opportunities, but one specialized site stands out as especially valuable.

AFOB Online
<http://www.archaeological.org/webinfo.php?page'10015>

This is the online version of the *Archaeological Fieldwork Opportunities Bulletin* which has been published annually for many years by the American Institute of Archaeology. It is updated on a regular basis and is searchable by a variety of criteria. Information provided on the main Web page indicates that it is searched by hundreds of users on a weekly basis. Anyone assisting users in finding fieldwork opportunities in anthropology should be aware of this unique resource.

CONCLUSION

There is no doubt that reference librarians have access to a growing number of useful and innovative Internet resources in anthropology to assist them in responding to their users' information needs. But there is also room for significant improvement. In this author's opinion, the greatest room for growth is the development of resources that specifically target the information needs of our users, be they laypersons, students, or scholars. As Internet reference resources in anthropology continue to evolve, reference librarians should be anxiously engaged in helping the developers of these resources understand these information needs.

Exploring LGBTQ Online Resources

Ellen Greenblatt

SUMMARY. This article evaluates several online resources in the field of lesbian, gay, bisexual, and transgender studies, looking at both proprietary resources such as EBSCO's *GLBT Life*® database as well as freely-available resources such as *GLBTQ: An Encyclopedia of Gay, Lesbian, Bisexual, Transgender & Queer Culture.* A variety of resources will be examined, including e-books, such as the *Encyclopedia of Lesbian, Gay, Bisexual and Transgendered History in America*; Web sites, such as *Library Q: The Library Worker's Guide to Lesbian, Gay, Bisexual, and Transgender Resources*; and networking resources, such as *Trans-Academics.org* and *Qstudy-L.* *[Article copies available for a fee from The Haworth Document Delivery Service: 1-800-HAWORTH. E-mail address: <docdelivery@haworthpress.com> Website: <http://www.HaworthPress.com> © 2005 by The Haworth Press, Inc. All rights reserved.]*

KEYWORDS. LGBTQ, lesbian, gay, bisexual, transgender, questioning

---

Ellen Greenblatt is Associate Dean for Access, Collections, and Technical Services, Auraria Library, University of Colorado at Denver and Health Sciences Center Downtown Denver Campus, 1100 Lawrence Street, Denver, CO 80204 (E-mail: Ellen. Greenblatt@cudenver.edu).

[Haworth co-indexing entry note]: "Exploring LGBTQ Online Resources." Greenblatt, Ellen. Co-published simultaneously in *Journal of Library Administration* (The Haworth Information Press, an imprint of The Haworth Press, Inc.) Vol. 43, No. 3/4, 2005, pp. 85-101; and: *Evolving Internet Reference Resources* (ed: William Miller, and Rita M. Pellen) The Haworth Information Press, an imprint of The Haworth Press, Inc., 2006, pp. 85-101. Single or multiple copies of this article are available for a fee from The Haworth Document Delivery Service [1-800-HAWORTH, 9:00 a.m. - 5:00 p.m. (EST). E-mail address: docdelivery@ haworthpress.com].

doi:10.1300/J111v43n03_08

INTRODUCTION AND BACKGROUND INFORMATION

Before plunging into identifying and evaluating LGBTQ online resources, it is important to address several key issues relating specifically to this subject area. Paramount among these is the definition of the
label "LGBTQ."

LGBTQ: The Acronym

The first four letters of this acronym–"LGBT"–stand for lesbians,
gay men, bisexuals, and transgender persons.[1] The fifth letter can be in-
terpreted variously as standing for "questioning individuals" (those in
the process of coming out, i.e., exploring their sexual orientation or gender identity) as well as standing for "queer," a word often used collectively to represent these different communities. In this article, LGBTQ
will be applied in the broadest sense, incorporating lesbians, gay men,
bisexuals, transgender, and questioning people.[2]

Why Lump All These Groups Together?

While lesbians, gay men, bisexuals, and transgender people are
bound together by common values, concerns, and histories, it is their
oppression, more than any other factor, which defines this bond.
Heterosexism affects not only gay men and lesbians, but also bisexuals
who are involved in same-sex affectional and sexual relationships. Sexism and genderism–and the legal and social repressions that result from
these prejudices–profoundly affect lesbians, bisexuals, and gay men as
well as transgender persons. And since one's gender identity does not
necessarily determine one's sexual orientation, some transgender people are doubly persecuted, as they may consider themselves lesbian,
gay, or bisexual as well as transgender.

Too often members of these separate communities (and thereby their
needs and desires) are rendered invisible or subsumed under the needs of
others. It is therefore important to use an acronym that represents each
community in any discussion related to this population group as a whole.

Researching LGBTQ Topics

While this "laundry list" acronym, which delineates the various communities, is the politically correct appellation currently in vogue, over

time various other labels have been applied.[3] The term "homosexual" has long been thought too clinical by gays and lesbians themselves, although it continues to appear in publications by non gay and lesbian writers. Some terms such as "lesbigay" and the more inclusive "lesbigaytr" disappeared almost as quickly as they arose.

Other terms may not be universally accepted or widely used due to their controversial nature. For example, many view the word "queer" as a derogatory slur in much the same way that the African-American community perceives the term "nigger." And while some LGBTQ people may now embrace the word, others still find the term offensive.

Another example is the recently established Library of Congress subject heading, "Sexual minorities," which although intended as a synonym for "LGBTQ," does not truly address the gender-based concerns of transgender and gender-variant people.

Debate rages throughout the transgender community regarding appropriate terminology. Much of this debate focuses on the usage of the terms "transgendered" and "transgender." Many members of the community use "transgender" as an adjective–e.g., transgender persons–feeling that "transgendered" has the same types of negative connotations associated with it as the term "colored" has for people of color and the term "disabled" has for people with disabilities. Others see no problem in using "transgendered" as an adjective, and, in fact, prefer to be called "transgendered persons." Some use the term "transgender" as a noun–e.g., "transgenders" rather than "transgender individuals." And still others avoid this situation altogether by using the terms "trans*" or "trans."

Also, the meanings of words may change over time. For example, in contemporary usage the term "queer" has evolved to include any individuals–heterosexual as well as gay, lesbian, bisexual, and transgender–who do not feel that their sexuality conforms to societal norms.

And while many resources may use the "laundry list" acronym, they may not always list the letters in the same order. Some resources may transpose letters (e.g., "GLBTQ") or omit or add one or more letters (e.g., "LGBT" or "LGBTIQA"), which means that ensuring comprehensive search results entails numerous keyword searches based upon various letter combinations.

As one can see, this constant change in terminology, inclusiveness, and order can make research in this area quite a challenge![4]

Criteria Used in Selecting Resources

The resources considered for this article were evaluated in terms of scope, accuracy, objectivity, authority, stability, and currency and were selected based on their relevance and/or interest to academic researchers and librarians. The resources highlighted here were created by experts in the field, primarily librarians and scholars. Several resources originate from institutions or are collaborations between institutions.

Considering the controversial subject matter, objectivity of the site was an especially important criterion. Raging debates over same-sex marriage and related rights have created a politically charged climate surrounding LGBTQ issues. These days anyone with a modem and an ISP can publish on the Web. Sometimes wonderful resources come out of people's obsessions. Other times people use their pages as "virtual soapboxes." The sites below were assessed for bias and selected on the basis of their affirmation of LGBTQ values and identities.

Stability and longevity were also important considerations, as was the currency of the various sites. However, these last criteria proved the most difficult. Internet sites that have been around for some time can abruptly change, disappear, or be abandoned by their creators. Because many sites are the effort of one or more volunteers, few of them will be maintained indefinitely and with the thoroughness librarians or researchers expect from conventionally published resources. Furthermore, with the increasing commercialization of the Internet, resources that were once freely accessible are increasingly becoming proprietary. This article will examine both types of resources.

PROPRIETARY RESOURCES

GLBT Life® Full Text
<http://www.epnet.com/academic/glbt.asp>

Since its debut in 2003, *GLBT Life* has emerged as the leading database in LGBTQ studies. While the original product was basically an indexing and abstracting service, its publisher, EBSCO, launched a full-text version in 2005. Just prior to that, in late 2004, EBSCO announced a partnership with National Information Services Corporation

(NISC), publishers of *GLBT Life*'s closest competitor, the *Sexual Diversity Studies* database, in which an additional 50,000 records indexed and abstracted from over 3,500 periodicals would be added to *GLBT Life*. Duplicate records were "composited," i.e., NISC and EBSCO combined records, thus retaining unique information from both sources, rather than eliminating duplicates. This partnership increased the number of records in *GLBT Life* to well over 200,000. Another partnership, this one with Salem Press, features chronologies spanning 20th century LGBTQ history. *GLBT Life* also indexes *GLBTQ: An Encyclopedia of Gay, Lesbian, Bisexual, Transgender & Queer Culture. (See p. 91 under Freely Available Resources for more information about this resource.)* EBSCO has also been working closely with LGBTQ archives and organizations, most notably the One National Gay and Lesbian Archives, the Lesbian Herstory Archives, and the Homosexual Information Center, to digitize and index their resources, and thus further expand and enhance the database.

GLBT Life offers researchers several different ways to access and present their data. Researchers can perform both basic and advanced searches of the database; browse the database index; or use the thesaurus that EBSCO specifically developed for *GLBT Life*. There is also a hierarchical journal authority file listing the publications indexed. Researchers can consult this file to get detailed information about each publication as well as a list of all issues available. Another helpful feature is "cited references" through which researchers can identify where particular authors or resources have been cited.

While *GLBT Life* contains much more full-text material than it did when it first appeared, a portion of the database will always consist of abstracting and indexing records. Access to this information can be optimized through use of some of the other resources cited below: in particular, *CatalogQ*, a union list of serial holdings in several LGBTQ organizations, as well as through the online catalogs of various LGBTQ libraries and archives (links to which can be found at *Library Q*).

GenderWatch
<http://proquest.com/products/pt-product-genderwatch.shtml>

While not specifically an LGBTQ database, *GenderWatch* contains quite a bit of relevant material, some of which dates back to the 1970s. This full-text database contains articles from academic journals, alternative press publications, national and regional magazines and newspapers, and conference proceedings in addition to non-serial publications such as books, booklets and pamphlets, and reports. Useful features in *GenderWatch* include the ability to sort results in order of relevance and the capability to search by type of article (e.g., book review, obituary, etc.).

Haworth Frontiers on LGBT Studies
<http://www.haworthpress.com/lgbt/HaworthLGBTjournals.pdf>

The newest proprietary LGBTQ electronic resource collection was introduced in 2005 by The Haworth Press, Inc. This resource includes full text of all the LGBTQ journals and other publications ever published by Haworth. Both current and back issues of journals will be included–over 350 journal issues of the twelve LGBTQ journals published by Haworth. *At press time, Haworth Frontiers on LGBT Studies was not yet available for preview.*

Encyclopedia of Lesbian, Gay, Bisexual and Transgendered History in America
<http://www.galegroup.com/servlet/ItemDetailServlet?region= 9&imprint=000&titleCode=S157E&type=4&id=191586>

An example of a reference work that is published both in print and electronic form, the *Encyclopedia of Lesbian, Gay, Bisexual and Transgendered History in America* consists of over 500 articles of various lengths. It also includes an overview essay on LGBT history in the United States, a chronology of significant events, and a directory of LGBT archives. A comprehensive index rounds out the volume.

The electronic version is available through the *Gale Virtual Reference Library*. While the benefits of having such a reference resource available 24/7 are clear, searching this particular e-book can prove rather cumbersome. Researchers will need to be aware that unless they specifically limit their search to this resource alone, their queries will search all the other titles from the *Gale Virtual Reference Library* to which their library has access. Also, researchers may be frustrated in their attempts to access the supplemental materials such as the chronology and the overview essay. Otherwise, searching is fairly conventional, offering the usual types of searches (i.e., title, keyword, full text, and sources) with the exception of the ability to search image captions.

FREELY AVAILABLE RESOURCES

General LGBTQ Resources

GLBTQ: An Encyclopedia of Gay, Lesbian, Bisexual, Transgender & Queer Culture
<http://www.glbtq.com/>

   Premiering in 2002, *GLBTQ* states its mission as "to serve as most comprehensive, accessible, and authoritative encyclopedia of gay, lesbian, bisexual, transgender, and queer (glbtq) culture."[5] Edited by Claude J. Summers and Ted-Larry Pebworth, both of the University of Michigan-Dearborn, this illustrated encyclopedia contains more than 1,200 articles by 300 contributors spread among three broad subject areas–Arts, Literature, and Social Science. Articles are accompanied by bibliographies and links to related topics. This resource can be searched by keyword or alphabetically by subtopic under the three main topics. There is also a "Special Features" section that includes interviews and archives biweekly "Spotlight" articles. These items can be displayed by date, subject, or popularity. A discussion forum rounds out this resource. A biweekly electronic newsletter is also available to those who wish to subscribe. This product is also indexed by *GLBT Life*. *(See p. 88 under Proprietary Resources.)*

QueerTheory.com
<http://www.queertheory.com/>

   This massive Web site which purports to provide users with "the best online resources integrated with the best visual and textual resources in Queer Culture, Queer Theory, Queer Studies, Gender Studies and related fields"[6] is included here for the sheer bulk of information available. From its very controversial origins in 2000 as a course project on homosexuality produced at a Catholic university, it has grown considerably over the intervening years. The creator of *QueerTheory.com* is Danne Polk, a former instructor at Villanova University and Webmaster of several other sites including the *Philosophy Research Base*.
   Since much of the information contained on this site is generated or solicited from other sources, researchers should verify any information they come across elsewhere. For example, the site's bibliographies seem to be generated from Amazon's Web site. (The site has affiliate re-

lationships with such entrepreneurs as Amazon, TLA Video, Powell's, and Travelocity.com.) Also, most of the topic areas solicit user input and it's unclear whether this information is evaluated before being incorporated into the site. However, the site is well indexed by several different types of indexes (although once again, users have input into the creation of these indexes), including name, author, scholar, subject, book topics, and organizations. It is keyword searchable, and also contains a browsable list of major topics on the home page.

This is a good place to start for hard-to-find topics. However, once again, it is recommended that any information found here be verified elsewhere.

Qstudy-L, The Queer Studies List: Archives
<http://listserv.acsu.buffalo.edu/archives/qstudy-l.html>

Often overlooked by researchers, the archives of electronic discussion lists are treasure troves of information, particularly if they have a well-designed Web interface to aid in information retrieval. *Qstudy-L: The Queer Studies List* is the premier electronic discussion list in the field, with archived messages dating back to July 1994. By examining list traffic, researchers can gather important insights into the growth of the field over the past decade.

Qstudy-L runs on LISTSERV® software, which has a well-developed Web-based search interface. The search page clearly explains the various types of searches possible. Not only can information be retrieved by keyword and phrase searching, but also these can be limited by the subject, author, or date of the e-mail message. Results can be sorted in a variety of ways.

Library Q: The Library Worker's Guide to Lesbian, Gay, Bisexual, and Transgender Resources
<http://library.auraria.edu/libq/>

This site, which celebrates its 10th anniversary this year, was designed specifically to help library workers better serve their LGBTQ patrons. Modeled after its bricks and mortar counterpart–the friendly neighborhood library–this Web site contains information of interest to public and technical services library workers in all types of libraries. Navigating through the various "library departments," one will discover all types of resources developed by the Library Q staff, as well as annotated links to a multitude of resources created by other library workers, bibliophiles, and experts. For example, visit the reference area to find directories, subject guides, pathfinders, checklists . . . even a vertical file. Check out the subject bibliographies in the "Stacks." Or, consult the technical services area for information on subject headings and classification schemes.

International Gay & Lesbian Review (IGLR)
<http://w5.usc.edu:9673/review/iglr/>

Underwritten by the Institute for the Study of Human Resources and the University of Southern California, *The International Gay & Lesbian Review (IGLR)* is edited by Walter L. Williams, director of the ONE Institute Center for Advanced Studies and professor of anthropology at the University of Southern California. This site contains reviews or abstracts to over 1,000 LGBTQ-related books, including some Ph.D. dissertations and master's theses. Since this is a volunteer-run endeavor, the coverage of titles is sporadic rather than comprehensive. Reviews are dependent upon the donations of publishers and the contributions of volunteer reviewers. Some of the reviews were originally published in the *White Crane* journal and on the Web site *GayToday.com*, which the *ILGR* lists as partner book review sites. Although there are some editorial guidelines, reviews come in a wide variety of styles and approaches. Also, a large proportion of the titles at this site contain only abstracts, often based on information supplied by the publisher or taken from the cover or book jacket.

Reviews can be retrieved through a basic keyword search (apparently a full-text search) or alphabetically by title or author of the work being reviewed. The usability of this resource would be greatly improved by instituting advanced searching capabilities.

With these caveats in mind, the *IGLR* is still a useful resource as it fills an important need for LGBTQ researchers. Historically, LGBTQ books were not always reviewed in mainstream review sources and those LGBTQ publications that did review these books were not always held by libraries. It is only recently that researchers have had significantly consistent access to reviews of LGBTQ-related titles, although there are still many LGBTQ titles that are never reviewed. *IGLR* helps bridge the gap in this regard.

CatalogQ
<http://www.catalogq.net/wwindex.html>

CatalogQ is a searchable union serials list for the LGBTQ periodical holdings of the following institutions located in California: the GLBT Historical Society in San Francisco, the ONE Institute and Archives in Los Angeles, the San Francisco Public Library, the June Mazer Lesbian Archives in Los Angeles, the Lavender Library, Archives and Cultural Exchange, Inc. in Sacramento, and the Transgender Periodicals Collection from California State University Northridge. Funded by a Library Services and Technology Act grant, the database, formerly housed at the GLBT Historical Society in San Francisco and now housed at the ONE Institute and Archives in Los Angeles, includes "newspapers, newsletters, magazines, 'zines, journals, and other material published on a periodic basis."

The database is searchable by title; author/publisher/organization; subject; geographical place; and repository. The Web interface is awkward and difficult to search. Searches can be refined through the use of a "word wheel" which returns a browsable index based on the search terms entered. Users can then select the appropriate entry from this index, paste it into the field they are searching, and submit their search. Once they receive their results, they can click on "details" to see owning repositories and their holdings. Combining the data from several autonomous repositories can be problematic. For example, when I tried searching for the *Lesbian Tide*, I found the title listed at least three different ways. However, shortcomings aside, this is indeed a valuable resource for identifying where certain periodical titles are held, especially now that LGBTQ resources are being more widely indexed through databases such as *GLBT Life.*

Other useful lists of periodicals can be found at: *Our Own Voices: A Directory of Lesbian and Gay Periodicals, 1890s-2000s* <http://www. clga.ca/Material/PeriodicalsLGBT/inven/oov/oovint.htm> compiled by the Canadian Lesbian and Gay Archives and *Northwest GLBT Journals and Other Serial Publications* <http://faculty.washington.edu/alvin/ nwjcat.htm> compiled by Alvin Fritz at the University of Washington Libraries. The online catalogs of LGBTQ archives and libraries are also useful resources to consult. *Library Q* contains a listing of catalogs and booklists <http://library.auraria.edu/libq/opacs.html>.

*The Lesbian, Gay, Bisexual and Transgender Religious Archives
Network (LGBTRAN)*
<http://www.lgbtran.org/index.htm>

A project of the Chicago Theological Seminary, The Lesbian, Gay,
Bisexual and Transgender Religious Archives Network (LGBTRAN)
bills itself as "a resource center and information clearinghouse for the
history of LGBT religious movements."[7] The aim of this relatively new
organization is to help LGBTQ religious groups learn how to organize
and preserve their archival resources and to direct and connect researchers with LGBT religious collections.

The Web site contains three major resource sections. There is a "Collections Catalog" listing relevant LGBT religious collections with links
to finding aids and/or repositories whenever possible. This list can be
displayed in a variety of ways: by title, organization, person, faith/tradi-
tion, geographical place, and subject heading (loosely based on the Library of Congress scheme). Another section features an exhibit of
historically significant documents from a variety of religious traditions.
And a final section, called the "Pioneers Gallery," provides brief biographical sketches and photos of leaders in LGBT religious movements. The site also includes a suggested list of repositories for those
considering donating their personal papers as well as a library housing
publications generated by members of the organization.

Lesbian Resources

Lesbian History Project: A Lesbian History Research Site
<http://www-lib.usc.edu/~retter/main.html>

Yolanda Retter, director of the UCLA Chicano Studies Research
Center Library and Archive and curator of the Lesbian Legacy Collection at the One National Gay and Lesbian Archives, created this site to
promote lesbian visibility on the Internet, especially in regards to lesbians of color. The site is intended to enhance access to online resources
relating to lesbian history and to provide support and space to gather,
document, publicize, and preserve work on lesbian history. A major
goal of the site is to aid researchers in locating primary source materials
and to encourage networking between community-based and institu-
tionally affiliated scholars in the field. Although it appears that not all of
the sections are updated on a regular basis, this grass-roots, no frills site

still has quite a bit to offer including an expansive collection of check-lists including "Notable Lesbians of All Colors."

NCLR: National Center for Lesbian Rights
<http://www.nclrights.org/>

The National Center for Lesbian Rights (NCLR) is a national legal resource center committed to advancing lesbian rights through advocacy, legal action, and education. This site contains several excellent downloadable publications primarily directed at issues relating to lesbians, such as parenting and other family concerns, relationship recognition, same-sex marriage, employment, and age-related concerns.

Gay Men's Resources

The World History of Male Love
<http://www.androphile.org/>

Dedicated to celebrating the tradition of same-sex love between men, this striking Web site explores the phenomenon through various lenses including world mythology and folklore, art, history, and literature. Truly international in scope and intent (the main page has been translated into six languages), the site includes information about male love around the globe and throughout history. The "Library" contains literary examples of male love from antiquity through modern times, as evidenced in myths, folktales, essays, poetry, biography, and fiction. The "Museum" contains artistic renderings of male love, featured in different cultural "halls," e.g., the "Greek Hall," "Chinese Hall," etc.

The "Guided Tour" is a cleverly designed feature, combining literature and art related to a particular theme, e.g., "Heroic Homosexuality: Male love in the time of the Greeks." The aptly-named "Symposium" provides a forum for discussion. Created by the mysteriously anonymous "Androphile Gay History Project," the site contains both a site map and a search feature.

Gay Pulp Fiction Database
<http://128.148.7.229:591/gaypulp/>

Consisting of over 4,600 volumes of gay men's pulp fiction, this growing collection housed at Brown University also contains some lesbian pulp titles. While the titles are non-circulating, the accompanying searchable database is a wonderfully rich resource for those researching this genre. The searchable fields include author, pseudonym, title, publisher, date, source, and notes. Browsable fields include author, title, publisher, and date. Note: Lesbian books can be identified by inputting "lesbian" in the notes field.

Bisexual Resources

Bisexual Resource Center
<http://www.biresource.org/>

The Bisexual Resource Center (BRC) site offers an enormous collection of bisexual resources, including several downloadable educational pamphlets plus directories, bibliographies, etc. The best bisexual resource available by far, this site contains an extensive assortment of information and links. A volunteer effort, this Web site does suffer from its share of broken and obsolete links.

Bisexuality-Aware Professionals Directory
<http://www.bizone.org/bap/>

This nationwide directory helps bisexuals find professionals–including therapists, health professionals, educators, coaches, pastoral and religious workers, attorneys, body workers, computer, business, and financial professionals, travel agents, and others–who are sensitive to the unique needs and sensibilities of bisexual people. The site lists eight criteria that pertain to bisexuality-awareness, including recognizing bisexuality as a "valid lifestyle"; understanding how bisexual issues differ from gay and lesbian issues; and attending or organizing workshops on the topic of bisexuality. To be listed in the directory, professionals must meet at least three of those eight criteria. Once the professionals explain to the directory coordinator about how they meet the requisite criteria, they are eligible for a free listing in the directory. The site is relatively new and most categories only contain a handful of listings, but as the word spreads, the directory should grow significantly.

Transgender Resources

Gender.org: Gender Education and Advocacy
<http://www.gender.org/>

Produced by Gender Education and Advocacy (GEA), a national organization which "seek[s] to educate and advocate . . . for all human beings who suffer from gender-based oppression in all of its many forms,"[8] this information-rich site offers several significant resources, including "Trans-Portal," a database of trans*-related Web resources, downloadable educational guides on a variety of topics including "Gender Variance: A Primer" and "Ethical Guidelines for Gender Education," and the National Transgender Library & Archive (including lists of its holdings current as of 1998).

Trans-Academics.org
<http://www.trans-academics.org/>

Trans-Academics.org is the accompanying Web site to the electronic discussion list of the same name. The list and site offer a positive environment for people of all gender identities to discuss issues of importance to the trans* community, especially as they relate to research in the field. The site contains several wonderful resources including instructional materials, a bibliography of required reading, and a glossary of "LGBTQI Terminology."[2] Founder and creator, Eli R. Green, works at New York's Hetrick-Martin Institute and serves on the board of the National Transgender Advocacy Coalition and as chair of its Research Committee.

Transhistory.org: Transsexual, Transgender, and Intersex History
<http://www.transhistory.org/>

Transhistory.org, a site cobbled together by a group of "hobbyist historians and transactivists," focuses on the history and experiences of transsexual, transgender, and intersex persons in the 20th century. Although apparently not updated since 2001, the site is for the most part self-contained and therefore there are few broken links. However, it appears to have been abandoned before it was completed (witness the many unlinked headings under each topical category). Nonetheless, the site still contains several useful resources concerning trans* history, including a "TransHistory Timeline" and biographies of key individuals along with histories of significant organizations.

CONCLUSION

This is only a small, yet varied, sampling of the many LGBTQ resources available online. Many more can be found by visiting *Library Q*

<http://library.auraria.edu./libq>. The Internet has played a significant role in the LGBTQ community. For many community members, isolated either geographically in rural areas or socially by the stigma attached by society to variant sexual orientation or gender expression, it has become a virtual lifeline–a place where, anonymously and in relative privacy, they can find the information they so desperately seek. For other community members, it has become an essential networking and community organizing tool.

Early on the LGBTQ presence on the Web was the work of enthusiastic volunteers working on their own or in small groups to create much needed resources. As time has passed, many of these volunteer-based sites have simply been abandoned due to a variety of reasons, including burnout, cost, lack of institutional support, and an ability to keep up with technical advances, among other reasons. However, there are still many functioning Web sites that owe their existence to these dedicated volunteers.

With the information needs of the LGBTQ community becoming more commercially viable, the for-profit sector is not only creating and packaging collections of online resources, but sometimes also buying out or taking over resources that were once freely available on the Web–such as The Haworth Press's recent acquisition of the *International Journal of Transgenderism*, an electronic journal once freely available on the Web.

While online information resources of interest and pertaining to the LGBTQ community are proliferating, the nature of these resources is certainly shifting. It will be interesting to see what types of changes the future brings.

ENDNOTES

1. For definitions of these and other terms used throughout this article, please see the glossary at the end.

2. Due to space constraints, other groups occasionally included in the LGBTQ mix–e.g., intersex people and allies–will not be specifically included in this article, although several of general and trans* sites do contain resources on intersexuality.

3. A prime example of the changing nature of terminology is the group that is now called the American Library Association Gay, Lesbian, Bisexual and Transgendered Round Table which began as the Task Force on Gay Liberation and then changed to the Gay Task Force and then to the Gay and Lesbian Task Force and then to the Gay, Lesbian, and Bisexual Task Force before adopting its current name.

4. Although this article will use the acronym "LGBTQ" in general to refer to lesbians, gay men, bisexuals, transgender and questioning people, whenever a resource is

discussed in this article, the acronym or terminology featured in that particular resource will be used. This can be rather confusing and is certainly indicative of the lack of a common or agreed-upon terminology.

5. *GLBTQ: Frequently Asked Questions,* 2004, <http://www.glbtq.com/about/faqs.htm> (15 December 2004).

6. *QueerTheory.com,* 2004, <http://queertheory.com/> (15 December 2004).

7. *The Lesbian, Gay, Bisexual and Transgender Religious Archives Network,* 2004 <http://www.lgbtran.org/index.htm> (15 December 2004).

8. Gender Education and Advocacy, Inc., *Gender.Org,* 2003, <http://www.gender.org/> (15 December 2004).

APPENDIX

LGBTQ Glossary[1]

Allies are straight (i.e., non-LGBTQ) people who combat heterosexism, biphobia, homophobia, and transphobia.

Biphobia is prejudice toward bisexuals.

Bisexuals are people who are romantically and sexually attracted to people of the same and opposite sex. They may or may not be non-monogamous or even sexually active.

Gay men are men who are romantically and sexually attracted to other men.

Gender expression is how people communicate their gender identity. People who conform to societal gender norms are said to have congruent gender expression and gender identity.

Gender identity is how people self-identify in regard to their gender. For example, they may self-identify as male, female, transgender, or other gender variant.

Gender is a cultural construct as opposed to sex, which is biologically defined. Used to classify attitudes, behaviors and other forms of expression, gender is applied in different ways by different cultures. In dominant Western society, the concept of gender is rigidly defined and limited to a male/female dichotomy. In other cultures, including many Native American cultures, gender is more fluid and broadly applied.

Gender variant people are those who are unable to or choose not to conform to societal gender norms.

Genderism manifests itself as the exclusion of people who do not conform to societal gender norms. It can also be defined as prejudice or bias against gender variant people.

Heterosexism is the belief in the inherent superiority of heterosexuality and its right to cultural dominance.[2]

Homophobia is prejudice against lesbian and gay people. It is sometimes also applied more broadly to LGBTQ people.

Intersex people are people whose external genitalia, sex chromosomes, or internal reproductive organs are not distinctively male or female.

Lesbians are women who are romantically and sexually attracted to other women.

LGBTQ is the collective abbreviation used for lesbians, gay men, bisexuals, transgender and questioning people in this article.

Questioning individuals are those who are engaged in self-discovery and exploration of their sexual orientation and/or gender identity.

Sexual orientation is the inclination or capacity to develop intimate emotional and sexual relationships with people of the same sex (lesbian or gay), the opposite sex (heterosexual), or either sex (bisexual).

Transgender persons are persons who literally "transgress" societal definitions of gender. An umbrella term applied to people whose gender behavior, expression, or identity does not conform to the sex they were assigned at birth, transgender is applied to a broad range of gender variant people, such as cross-dressers, transsexuals, and drag queens, among others. Sometimes abbreviated as "trans*" or "trans."

Transphobia is prejudice toward transgender people.

---

1. These definitions are based in part upon the following resources: Gender Education and Advocacy, Inc., *Gender Variance: A Primer*, 2001, <http://gender.org/resources/dge/gea01004.pdf> (15 December 2004), and Safe Schools Coalition, *Glossary*, n.d., <http://www.safeschoolscoalition.org/glossary.pdf> (15 December 2004).
2. Audre Lorde, "There Is No Hierarchy of Oppressions," *Interracial Books for Children Bulletin* 14 (1983), 9.

Women and Gender Studies
Internet Reference Resources:
A Critical Overview

Cindy Ingold

SUMMARY. The field of women and gender studies has matured over the last decade with many colleges and universities now offering undergraduate majors, and several others offering master's and doctoral degrees. Coinciding with the growth of the discipline and the growth of published materials, there has been a concurrent evolution of electronic resources in women and gender studies, both proprietary and freely available on the Web. This article provides a general overview with annotations of selected online resources in women and gender studies. *[Article copies available for a fee from The Haworth Document Delivery Service: 1-800-HAWORTH. E-mail address: <docdelivery@haworthpress.com> Website: <http://www.HaworthPress.com> © 2005 by The Haworth Press, Inc. All rights reserved.]*

KEYWORDS. Women's studies, gender studies, online resources, Internet, World Wide Web

---

Cindy Ingold is Women and Gender Resources Librarian, University of Illinois, Urbana-Champaign, 415 Main Library, 1408 West Gregory Drive, Urbana, IL 61801 (E-mail: cingold@uiuc.edu).

[Haworth co-indexing entry note]: "Women and Gender Studies Internet Reference Resources: A Critical Overview." Ingold, Cindy. Co-published simultaneously in *Journal of Library Administration* (The Haworth Information Press, an imprint of The Haworth Press, Inc.) Vol. 43, No. 3/4, 2005, pp. 103-117; and: *Evolving Internet Reference Resources* (ed: William Miller, and Rita M. Pellen) The Haworth Information Press, an imprint of The Haworth Press, Inc., 2006, pp. 103-117. Single or multiple copies of this article are available for a fee from The Haworth Document Delivery Service [1-800-HAWORTH, 9:00 a.m. - 5:00 p.m. (EST). E-mail address: docdelivery@haworthpress.com].

Available online at http://www.haworthpress.com/web/JLA
doi:10.1300/J111v43n03_09

INTRODUCTION

As a discipline within institutions of higher education in the United States, women's studies has become more firmly established in the last ten to fifteen years. The Web site *Women's Studies Programs, Departments, & Research Centers* (see description below) maintained by Joan Korenman has links to over 700 sites for programs, departments, and centers from around the world. Over 600 of these sites are within the United States. The field of women's studies has grown from its evolution in the women's movement of the late 1960s and early 1970s when only a handful of classes were taught on college campuses to today where many universities now offer undergraduate majors in women's studies and more and more are beginning to create graduate programs. Consequently, the amount of scholarship and publishing on women and gender studies has grown substantially. Along with this has been the tremendous growth of Internet related resources for women and gender studies. Currently, the Web offers a vast amount of information for women and gender studies; indeed we are now at a point where there are so many resources available on the Internet that finding the quality resources can be daunting.

CRITERIA

This paper provides an overview of some of the best Web sites for women and gender studies, concentrating on those sites which have an academic or scholarly focus. To determine which women and gender studies sites to include, the author relied on several important criteria. First and foremost, I focused on sites created by academic librarians or scholars in the field of women's studies. Women's studies scholars and librarians are the ones who know the discipline the best, the ones who work with the literature every day, the ones who teach classes. Many sites have been created by the very people who saw a need which was not being addressed by other online resources. Second, I concentrated on sites which have for the most part been around for several years. Many of the Web sites featured here began in the early to mid-1990s and are still considered the best. Third, I made an effort to include Web sites which empower and educate women and girls. The Internet can be a powerful tool for transformational change, and many of the resources cited in this article have as one of their goals to educate and empower women.

Finally, I concentrated on sites that covered a wide range of subjects, because I could not include all of the excellent women's studies Web sites in this brief article. I also concentrated on sites whose focus was broadly conceived, because these tend to lead users to other significant sites. For a current listing of women's studies Web sites in individual disciplines, readers are referred to the general/meta sites listed below, especially the *Women's Studies Librarian's Office, University of Wisconsin System* Web site, and the *WSSLinks: Women and Gender* Web site. The recently published annotated bibliography *Women's Studies: A Recommended Bibliography* edited by Linda A. Krikos and Cindy Ingold (Libraries Unlimited, 2004, 3rd ed.) provides annotations to Web sites in 19 subjects as well as annotating the core print English language literature.

PROPRIETARY RESOURCES

In the 1990s, women's studies faculty and librarians had very few online databases to choose from. The databases that were available often provided very little full text, indexed only selected titles, and often did not index periodicals from cover to cover. With the growth of the discipline and the advocacy of women's studies librarians, there now are a large number of online indexing and abstracting sources, full-text databases, and digitized collections for women's studies. For a comparison of the features of many of these resources, readers should check out the Web page maintained by the Collection Development Committee of the Women's Studies Section of the Association of College and Research Libraries within the American Library Association <http://www.libr.org/wss/projects/electronic.html>. The Instruction Committee of the WSS also has created database instruction guides for several proprietary online databases. They are available at <http://www.libr.org/wss/projects/guides.html>.

Indexing and Abstracting Sources

Women's Studies International (1972 to date)

This product, available from National Information Services Corporation (NISC), is the single best online indexing source for women's studies literature. The content of the database derives from six separate files: *Women Studies Abstracts*, which has contributed over 72,000 records;

the *Women's Studies Database* created at the University of Toronto Library; four files from the Women's Studies Librarian's Office, University of Wisconsin System; a MEDLINE subset on women; *Women of Color and Southern Women: A Bibliography of Social Science Research* produced at the University of Memphis between 1975-1995; and *Women's Health and Development: An Annotated Bibliography* of holdings from the World Health Organization. NISC adds additional titles including Internet documents, articles from professional journals, conference papers, books, book chapters, selected popular literature, government reports, working papers, and Web sites. Because of its depth and breadth of coverage for literature on women and gender studies, Women's Studies International is one online database to which all libraries should subscribe. Unfortunately, the software provided by NISC is not the most intuitive.

Full-Text Databases

Contemporary Women's Issues (1992 to date)

Contemporary Women's Issues or CWI is available from the following vendors: OCLC FirstSearch, the Gale Group, and LexisNexis. This resource includes the full text of several women's studies periodicals although the dates of coverage for the full text can vary. The real strength of the database is the inclusion of newsletters, research reports from Non-Governmental Organizations (NGOs) and other associations, as well as other types of reports and materials which many libraries would not subscribe to or collect. The earliest records in CWI date back to the early 1990s. The database is multidisciplinary, covering topics such as health and reproductive issues, domestic violence, legal and educational issues, employment, gender equality, politics and human rights, and women's studies as a discipline. It does not cover women in the arts and humanities except for including book reviews. This is an excellent resource that provides access to much of the gray literature.

GenderWatch

GenderWatch, available from ProQuest Information and Learning, is another full-text database which covers 175 women's studies publications including newsletters, periodicals, books, proceedings, conference reports, and governmental and NGO reports. A very select number of titles go back to the 1970s, but the majority of titles coverage is from the 1980s and 1990s. The database is also multidisciplinary, covering many of the same topics as CWI; however, GenderWatch does cover the arts and humanities better than CWI.

Digitized Collections

The Gerritsen Collection–Women's History Online, 1543-1945.

The Gerritsen Collection from ProQuest Information and Learning is the digitized version of the materials collected by C. V. and Aletta Jacobs Gerritsen in the late 1800s. The collection spans more than four centuries and fifteen languages, and has over 4,700 publications. The online version includes two million pages of images as they appeared in the original printed works. Two segments comprise the collection: periodicals make up 25 percent of the collection, and monographs make up 75 percent.

Alexander Street Press offers several impressive digitized collections, most notably North American Women's Letters and Diaries.

FREELY AVAILABLE WEB SITES

The Web sites listed below generally meet all of the criteria discussed in the beginning of this article. Many other valuable women and gender studies Web sites exist but space considerations limited listing to only a small number. The Web sites listed below are excellent sites to know and use for reference purposes. Additionally, most of these sites will lead users to other useful Internet resources.

General/Meta Sites

FeMiNa
<http://www.femina.com/>

FeMiNa created by Cybergrrl, Inc. provides a searchable directory of "female friendly sites and information on the World Wide Web." The front page provides a Yahoo-like directory including the following topics: Arts and Humanities, Business and Finance, Computers and Science, Education, Entertainment, Family and Motherhood, Girls, Health and Wellness, Media and Publications, Regional, Recreation and Leisure, and Society and Culture. FeMiNa also features a site of the month, and a link to the latest women's news which tends to be health-related or consumer information. There are several opportunities to provide feedback and to get involved including online surveys and quick polls. Because of its Yahoo-like structure, this site would appeal to the general public.

Gender, Race, and Ethnicity in Media
<http://www.uiowa.edu/~commstud/resources/GenderMedia/femmedia.html>

This site was created by Karla Tonella, a librarian at the University of Iowa. The site is organized by the following categories: advertising, African American, Asian American, assorted gender and media links, cyberspace, feminist media, indexes and directories, Latin American, LesBiGay, Native American and other indigenous peoples, print media, television and film, and other media and mixed media. Under each category, users are directed to either full-text articles and reports, or other Web sites.

Women's Studies Database, University of Maryland
<http://www.mith2.umd.edu/WomensStudies>

This is the premiere database for the discipline of women's studies. Begun in 1992, the site serves "those people interested in the women's studies profession and in general women's issues." It provides a wealth of information for women and gender studies faculty and graduate students including conference listings, calls for papers, employment listings, and syllabi from women's studies courses. It also provides reviews of current films, often from a feminist perspective, which have been culled from radio broadcasts and other resources. A reading room provides access to papers on a variety of topics; a section titled "Program Support" provides access to sites about pedagogy, curriculum policies, theory information, and establishing a major; and a link called "Gender Issues" provides access to other Web sites. This Web site provides valuable information for faculty, scholars, and students in the field.

Women's Studies Librarian's Office, University of Wisconsin System
<http://www.library.wisc.edu/libraries/WomensStudies/>

The Women's Studies Librarian's Office at Wisconsin was established in 1977, and has been a guiding source for many women's studies librarians and faculty. The site gives information about the publications of the office, *Feminist Collections: A Quarterly of Women's Studies Resources*, *Feminist Periodicals*, and *New Books on Women and Feminism*, including a full-text link to several articles from *Feminist Collections*.

Links by subject provide access to a wealth of other Web sites. Librarians can find a link to feminist and women's publishers and to a database of core books in women's studies. The core books database, created by the Women's Studies Section of the Association of College and Research Libraries within the American Library Association, provides citations to books in print for over forty subjects. Users can also find links to homepages of feminist magazines and journals, and access to *WAVE: Women's Videos Database*, as well as a list of video distributors. For librarians at college and research libraries with responsibilities in women and gender studies, this site is an essential resource.

WSSLinks: Women and Gender Studies Web Sites
<http://libr.org/wss/WSSLinks/index.html>

WSSLinks is maintained by the Women's Studies Section of the Association of College and Research Libraries. The authors, all academic librarians, state that the purpose "is to provide access to a wide range of resources in support of Women's Studies." The page is subdivided into the following subjects: general sites, archives, art, business, culture (mostly literature), education, film, health, history, international, lesbian sites, music, philosophy, politics, science and technology, and theology. Each of these pages offers a consistent design making it very easy for users to navigate within the pages. Individual subject pages are organized depending on the best approach for that subject, so, for example, the page on Women and Business includes Associations/Organizations/Centers, Biographies of Prominent Business Women, Directories of Women Owned Businesses, Electronic Discussion Forums, Newsletters and Journals, Resources for Business Start Ups, and Statistical Sources while the page on Theology includes General Sites, followed by links arranged by specific religions. Librarians with expertise in these subject areas maintain these pages assuring high quality and currency. The only weakness of WSSLinks is that its coverage of subjects is limited.

Feminist Theory and Women's Studies as a Discipline

Feminist Theory Website
<http://www.cddc.vt.edu/feminism/enin.html>

The Feminist Theory Website, available in English, French, and Spanish lists two major goals: to encourage a wide range of research into feminist theory, and to encourage dialog between women (and men) from different countries around the world. The Web site provides information about various fields within feminist theory including everything from body studies to sexuality; from critical theory to postmodernism; from liberal feminism to radical feminism. Each link within the thirty-one different categories of feminism provides a bibliography of articles and books on that topic, a list of critical thinkers within that field, and a link to Web sites if they exist. The home page also provides links to different national/ethnic feminisms which are organized by country or region, and to information on individual feminists. The latter section is arranged alphabetically and provides brief biographical information on each feminist thinker, a summary of the person's major themes, and a bibliography of sources, if available, by the person. The Web site contains over 5,400 bibliographical entries. Created by Dr. Kristin Switala and hosted by the Center for Digital Discourse and Culture at Virginia Tech University, the Feminist Theory Website premiered on the Internet in November 1997, and provides an excellent introduction and overview to feminist theory.

NWSA: National Women's Studies Association
<http://www.nwsa.org>

NWSA, founded in 1977, is "committed to support and promote feminist teaching, research, and professional and community service at the pre-K through post-secondary levels." The organization is the main professional association for women's studies faculty, scholars, and professionals. The organization Web site provides links for women's studies program directors to network, information for students, lists of conferences and calls for papers, a job bank, and current news.

Women's Studies Programs, Departments, & Research Centers
<http://research.umbc.edu/~korenman/wmst/programs.html>

Joan Korenman of the University of Maryland created this resource of more than 700 women's studies programs, departments, and research centers around the world that have Web sites. Korenman arranges the programs alphabetically, listing programs in the United States first followed by those outside the United States. The programs and departments offering graduate degrees or concentrations are noted in a brief annotation. Korenman also offers a link to institutions offering online degrees. Other useful sites cataloging women's studies programs are Gerri Gibbi's page <http://creativefolk.com/directories.html>

and the Artemis Guide to Women's Studies in the U.S. <http://www. artemisguide.com/> which lists 371 programs in the United States arranged alphabetically by state. Smith College also provides a page to graduate programs in the United States <http://www.smith.edu/wst/ gradlinks.html> although it has not been updated in over one year.

Activist, Political, Law

American Association of University Women
<http://www.aauw.org/>

The American Association of University Women or AAUW, founded in 1881, is one of the oldest advocacy organizations for women in the United States. AAUW is composed of three corporations. The Association advocates education and equity for women and girls; the Educational Foundation provides scholarships for graduate women around the globe; and the Legal Advocacy Fund works to fight sex discrimination in higher education. The Web site provides current information on AAUW's research and activities including listing conferences.

Feminist Majority
<http://www.feminist.org>

The mission of the Feminist Majority Foundation is to "develop bold, new strategies and programs to advance women's equality, non-violence, economic development, and most importantly, empowerment of women and girls in all sectors of society." The Feminist Majority Foundation Online offers the best single source for feminist activism on the Internet. Buttons from the front page provide a wide array of links to information, current news, and opportunities to get involved and take action. Examples of the categories one can link to include a "Feminist Internet Gateway" which provides a well organized resource to other Web sites; a link for "Student Activism"; information on health issues including breast cancer; and a link to feminist careers. The "Feminist Internet Gateway" provides a current list of links to women and gender organizations in many fields.

NOW: The National Organization for Women
<http://www.now.org>

The National Organization for Women (NOW) claims it is the largest organization for feminist activists in the United States with 500,000 members from all 50 states and the District of Columbia. Founded in 1966, NOW strives to bring about equality for all women by working to "eliminate discrimination and harassment in the workplace, schools, the justice system, and all other sectors of society; secure abortion, birth control and reproductive rights for all women; end all forms of violence against women; eradicate racism, sexism and homophobia; and promote equality and justice in our society." The NOW site allows users to get involved and take action, and to check out current issues ranging from abortion rights to economic equity from Title IX to women in the military. Each of the current issues links provides background information on the topic, current advocacy being done, and NOW's stand on the issue. Users can also find out about local chapters.

Women's Human Rights Resources
<http://www.law-lib.utoronto.ca/diana/mainpage.htm>

The purpose of Women's Human Rights Resources, maintained by the Bora Laskin Law Library, University of Toronto, "is to help researchers, students, teachers, and human rights advocates locate authoritative and diverse information on women's international human rights via the Internet." The site is organized under three broad categories which reflect the goals of the Web site's creators: "Share Knowledge," "Support Advocacy," and "Promote Scholarship." The first category includes a Women's Human Rights Resources Database, which lists hundreds of articles, documents, and links related to international women's rights and legal issues. The second category lists human rights advocacy guides which bring together key documents from the international and regional human rights systems and UN bodies. The third section includes detailed research guides providing overviews on various topics, and a link to graduate fellowships in reproductive health law and women's rights.

Science, Technology, and Medicine

Center for Information Technology
<http://www.umbc.edu/cwit/index.html>

The Center for Information Technology was established in 1998 by Joan Korenman with the following goals: "to encourage more women and girls to prepare for careers and become leaders in information technology; to communicate information related to the richness and breadth of women's lives, concerns, and possibilities using technology; to foster research concerning gender and information technology." The home page offers a current listing of books, curricular resources, girl-related resources, a speakers' bureau, and a link to related Web sites. Of special note is the link for Web sites relating to women's issues in science and technology. As with all of Korenman's sites, information is current and relevant.

Center for Reproductive Rights
<http://www.crlp.org/>

Formerly known as the Center for Reproductive Law and Policy, the Center for Reproductive Rights is "a non-profit legal advocacy organization dedicated to promoting and defending women's reproductive rights worldwide." This site offers information on the following topics: legal advocacy, human rights, equality, adolescents, safe pregnancy, contraception, and abortion. By clicking on each subject, users can access the latest information on the topic, with cross-references to additional publications, cases, legislative policy, statutes, and press releases. The site is available in Spanish and French, and includes an index.

International Women's Health Coalition
<http://www.iwhc.org/>

The International Women's Health Coalition (IWHC) works on health policies and programs that promote the rights and health of women and girls. Founded in 1984, IWHC works "to build political will and influence the policies of governments, donors, and international agencies to secure girls' and women's sexual and reproductive health and rights." First, IWHC provides professional assistance and financial support to local organizations in Africa, Asia, and Latin America. Second, IWHC keeps abreast of current information to inform debates in the United States and abroad. Lastly, the organization advocates at intergovernmental conferences, and other international agencies. The Web site provides current information on policy issues, links to events such as conferences, and information on the four issues the organization focuses on: youth health; HIV/AIDS; safe abortion; and the right of women to control their own sexuality. Another useful site is Women's Health from the World Health Organization <http://www.who.int/topics/womens_health/en/> which provides fact sheets on women's health issues and links to other sites.

Global Issues

International Center for Research on Women
<http://www.icrw.org>

The International Center for Research on Women was founded in 1976 to fill the "gaps in understanding the complex realities of women's lives and their role in development." ICRW works in partnership with other organizations on research and advocacy issues affecting women with special concern in the following areas: adolescence, HIV/AIDS, nutrition and food security, poverty reduction, reproductive health, violence against women, and women's rights. Under each of these project areas, users will find research reports and a list of current activities being done in the specific area.

International Women's Rights Action Watch
<http://iwraw.igc.org/about.htm>

The International Women's Rights Action Watch (IWRAW) was created in 1985 at the World Conference on Women in Nairobi, Kenya "to promote recognition of women's human rights under the Convention on the Elimination of All Forms of Discrimination Against Women (the CEDAW Convention), a basic international human rights treaty." IWRAW functions as the primary international Non-Governmental Organization to facilitate human rights for women and families. The Web site provides links to publications, information on the Fourth World Conference on Women held in Beijing in 1995, the status of CEDAW and current actions, and links to other Web sites. Because of the importance of CEDAW for advancing women's rights worldwide, this is an important source of current information on women's rights issues worldwide.

Women Watch
<http://www.un.org/womenwatch>

Women Watch is the central gateway to information and resources on women's equity through the United Nations system. A directory of UN resources includes categories on gender mainstreaming, international instruments and treaties, thematic issues, information on women by various world regions, and information on gender training. An especially useful feature of Women Watch is the section "Statistics and Indicators" which includes reports and databases on statistics relating to women and children. Notable reports include the *World's Women 2000: Trends and Statistics* highlighting data in a wide number of fields including families, health, education and work; *State of the World's Children*; *Human Development Reports*; and a host of other reports from UN agencies and other intergovernmental agencies.

Under the category United Nations entities, users will be directed to other UN agencies and organizations working on women's issues. Notable among these other agencies is UNIFEM <http://www.unifem.org/>, the women's fund at the United Nations, which provides financial and technical assistance to programs "that promote women's human rights, political participation and economic security." The Division for the Advancement of Women <http://www.un.org/womenwatch/daw/index.html> established in 1946 "advocates the improvement of the status of women of the world and the achievement of their equality with men." Finally, INSTRAW, the International Research and Training Institute for the Advancement of Women, <http://www.un-instraw.org/en/index.html> carries out research and training activities dedicated to the advancement of women.

Women of Color

Black American Feminism
<http://www.library.ucsb.edu/subjects/blackfeminism/>

Black American Feminism, compiled by Sherri L. Barnes, Associate Librarian at the University of California, Santa Barbara, is a bibliography citing sources in subject areas within the humanities, social sciences, and health, medicine and science. The time period is the nineteenth century to the present, "with the majority of references representing the very influential contemporary black feminist thought that emerged in the 1970s and continues today." The bibliography is arranged into four broad disciplines: Arts and Humanities; Social Sciences; Education; Health, Medicine and Science, and includes six sections by format: (Auto) Biographies, Memoirs, and Personal Narratives; Interviews; Speeches; Multidisciplinary Anthologies; Periodicals: Special Issues; and Web Sites. Each of the four disciplines is further subdivided into more specific categories. Each category is prefaced with a quotation by a famous African American woman and then sources are listed alphabetically by author's last name. Barnes includes citations from professional, scholarly, popular, mainstream and alternative magazines, journals, newspapers, and books.

Women of Color Web
<http://www.hsph.harvard.edu/grhf/WoC/index.html>

The mission of the Women of Color Web site is to provide "access to writings by and about women of color in the U.S." Created by the Global Reproductive Health Forum at the Harvard School of Public Health, the authors provide access to writings on feminisms, sexualities, and reproductive health and rights related to women of color. Each of the three sections takes users to full-text articles or papers by leading feminist writers including bell hooks, Patricia Hill Collins, and Barbara Smith. The site also provides teaching tools including syllabi, a list of organizations, and a link to discussion lists.

Statistical

Gender Stats: Databases of Gender Statistics
<http://devdata.worldbank.org/genderstats/home.asp>

Gender Stats is an electronic database of gender statistics made available through the World Bank. The data are presented in various modules including summary information by country; thematic data; gender monitoring data; or data by region of the world. The thematic data include poverty indicators, education, health, basic population, and labor force indicators. The database is continuously updated; data sources include national statistics, UN sources, and World Bank surveys.

WIDNET
<http://www.focusintl.com/widnet.htm>

WIDNET, the women in development network, includes statistics organized by the following world regions: Africa, Asia, Oceania, the Americas, and Europe. Each region includes statistics on population, family, households, health, education and training, labour, and power, which are statistics on the numbers of women in government. Statistics are from the United Nations publication, *The World's Women 1995–Trends and Statistics.*

CONCLUSION

Clearly, the field of women and gender studies has become more mainstream in the last ten years. As disciplines grow, the literature of the discipline also evolves. In the case of women's studies, there has been a steady growth of online databases including indexing and abstracting services, full-text databases, and digitized collections. Additionally, World Wide Web sites have been created, many of which serve as important reference resources for librarians, scholars, and students. This article provided an overview of some of the best Web resources for women and gender studies.

Internet Reference Sources
for Asian Studies

Lisa Klopfer

SUMMARY. This essay discusses Internet reference works for Asian Studies. Internet reference works are difficult to delimit, since the new formats and functions of the Internet have created new genres. Subject guides and directories do not qualify as reference sources, but the characterization of other forms of information on the Internet is still vague. The standards for evaluating Internet sources are also still in flux. Nonetheless, using a rule of thumb definition, a select number of Internet resources for Asian Studies are reviewed. *[Article copies available for a fee from The Haworth Document Delivery Service: 1-800-HAWORTH. E-mail address: <docdelivery@haworthpress.com> Website: <http://www.HaworthPress.com> © 2005 by The Haworth Press, Inc. All rights reserved.]*

KEYWORDS. Internet, reference, genres, Asian Studies

INTRODUCTION

It is now widely accepted that scholars and students alike look to the Internet for research resources. As many librarians have noted, usually

---

Lisa Klopfer is Assistant Professor and Librarian, Eastern Michigan University, 100 Halle Library, Eastern Michigan University, Ypsilanti, MI 48197 (E-mail: lisa.klopfer@emich.edu).

[Haworth co-indexing entry note]: "Internet Reference Sources for Asian Studies." Klopfer, Lisa. Co-published simultaneously in *Journal of Library Administration* (The Haworth Information Press, an imprint of The Haworth Press, Inc.) Vol. 43, No. 3/4, 2005, pp. 119-128; and: *Evolving Internet Reference Resources* (ed: William Miller, and Rita M. Pellen) The Haworth Information Press, an imprint of The Haworth Press, Inc., 2006, pp. 119-128. Single or multiple copies of this article are available for a fee from The Haworth Document Delivery Service [1-800-HAWORTH, 9:00 a.m. - 5:00 p.m. (EST). E-mail address: docdelivery@haworthpress.com].

doi:10.1300/J111v43n03_10

with a touch of regret if not outrage, students frequently look to the Internet first, and, if the information found is satisfactory, they may not look any further.[1] For Asian Studies, this development will not lead to the death of scholarship as some academics have foretold. In fact, the Internet has actually broadened and enlivened this field. This is because, first, the Internet offers information to a much wider range of users than ever before had access to specialized library collections; and second, because that information itself includes materials that were never available at all until they were digitized. Thus, scholars can now easily search distant collections such as *Mapping Asia* <http://www.asiamap.ac.uk/index.php> or the *Asian Reading Room* of the Library of Congress <http://www.loc.gov/rr/asian/>, or learn about on-going research in Asia at sites such as the *South Asian Studies Programme*, National University of Singapore <http://www.fas.nus.edu.sg/sas/research.html>, all of which used to require difficult communications and long time delays. Students have access to an extraordinary range of cultural materials and interactive teaching tools such as the Perry-Castañeda Library (University of Texas at Austin) *Asian Maps* collection <http://www.lib.utexas.edu/maps/asia.html>; the interactive atlases in *The Silk Road Project* <http://www.silkroadproject.org/>; photo and document exhibitions such as *Paper Gods* <http://www.columbia.edu/cu/lweb/eresources/eimages/eastasian/papergods/> or Stefan Landsberger's *Chinese Propaganda Poster Pages* <http://www.iisg.nl/%7Elandsberger/>; and popular culture resources such as *Popular Culture of Japan: An Annotated Directory of Internet Resources* <http://newton.uor.edu/Departments&Programs/AsianStudiesDept/japan-pop.html>.

This richness, however, has left librarians scrambling to catch up. It is now difficult to keep track of all the Internet resources even in a restricted topic area, let alone all of Asian Studies. Luckily, Asian Studies has been well served· on the Internet by the hard work and broad vision of T. Matthew Ciolek, Head of the Internet Publications Bureau, Research School of Pacific and Asian Studies, Australian National University. He publishes, among other things, *The Asian Studies WWW Monitor* <http://coombs.anu.edu.au/asia-www-monitor.html>, *The AnthroGlobe Bibliographies* <http://coombs.anu.edu.au/Biblio/biblio_index.html>, and the *Asian Studies WWW Virtual Library* <http://coombs.anu.edu.au/WWWVL-AsianStudies.html>. These resources, combined with the relatively new *Portal to Asian Internet Sources* (PAIR) initiative <http://webcat.library.wisc.edu:3200/PAIR/>, are so rich that it is almost redundant to list any other sites.

The goal of this paper, however, is to discuss specifically *reference* works on the Internet, which brings up another set of questions. As the Internet continues to expand from gopher sites to portals to blogs and beyond, the functional definition of "reference" becomes blurry. We shall start by discussing this question before moving on to analyze specific Internet reference works of interest to librarians, teachers and students in Asian Studies.

WHAT IS A REFERENCE WORK ON THE INTERNET?

Reference sources are typically defined as works that are designed to be consulted rather than read from cover to cover. This immediately begs the question, what Internet source is NOT designed to be consulted rather than read from start to finish? And yet many Internet formats do not fit the typical format of reference works. Reference works are further defined as containing entries or files that are presented in an organized manner (usually alphabetical) and are indexed and cross-referenced.[2] Given the flexibility of hypertext and of keyword searching on the Internet, this definition needs examination if not expansion if it is to be practical.

A typical reference book defines a realm of coverage, defines the universe of materials it is pointing to, and offers a structure in which searching and browsing for topics within that defined range can be accomplished (usually through alphabetical lists and indexes). As noted, on the Internet, a new set of genres complicates these functions. Online dictionaries and encyclopedias follow the paper models most closely. Through searching or browsing, the user accesses a finite set of information that is organized into uniform chunks (definitions, short essays). The power of hyperlinks and of keyword searching, however, has opened up a huge new range of possibilities for online reference.

The most obvious of these are the Web pages that organize and annotate links to other Web pages. Subject guides created by librarians are now ubiquitous, but their content is extremely variable. Comparison of five such guides chosen from a Google search found a remarkable lack of overlap in resources, including the recommended Web links.[3]

More expansive than subject guides, Internet directories and virtual libraries provide more access to Internet resources, usually without reference to non-digital sources. These pages might more properly be compared to a catalog than a reference work. Indeed, some of the best of these resources code their entries using Dewey (as BUBL does)[4] or Dublin Core standards with Library of Congress Subject Headings (as

PAIR does).[5] These indexes to Web sites differ from library catalogs, however, because the sources they point to are not under the control of the indexers. While a library selects its sources and then indexes every one of them, subject guides and other Internet indexes select and index only a tiny portion of the possible sites. Unlike library materials, the indexed Internet sources may change or disappear (even the citations to Web pages in this article, for example, cannot promise to point to the same source that was viewed by the author at the time of citation).

Internet directories also suffer from a lack of reliable structure. Each one is organized differently; there are no authority records for author or title, let alone subject headings (excepting BUBL and PAIR); and there is no provision for Boolean searching. Lastly, while library indexes point to relatively comparable kinds of materials (books, multimedia, series, journals), subject guides and portals provide links to materials that vary extremely in their size and specificity, so that, for example, the same list of links may point to a huge commercial portal, a map database, or a single report on a personal Web page.

Then there are specific genres such as online atlases, which usually have few index features and, because of their visual content, are difficult or impossible to search internally. Listserv archives and blogs can also be sources of information, but they are even more disorganized (for example, *Sushicam* <http://www.sushicam.com/> entries are sorted chronologically and can only be searched by keyword).[6]

What counts as reference sources on the Internet remains a question ripe for debate among librarians, one that might enrich our discussions of paper reference works as well. For the purposes of this paper, subject guides and directories shall be ruled out. As noted, they are not really comparable to a paper reference work, and they are easy to find and quite fluid in content, which makes them impractical subjects for review such as this. Instead, the focus shall be on less ubiquitous and more specific sources that are perhaps more difficult to locate on the Web but can offer accurate, useful information.

EVALUATING INTERNET REFERENCE SOURCES

Even if a set of genres is delimited as online reference, there is still the question of how to evaluate Internet reference sources. As James H. Sweetland has pointed out, standard criteria for evaluating Web pages have not been settled.[7] Sweetland notes that *Choice* reviewers, perhaps limited by space and the demands of their readers, emphasize usability over authority, accuracy, and reliability.[8] Sweetland also comments on the futility of published reviews of bibliographies of Web sites, because of their ephemeral nature. This author has produced one guide to Web resources relating to Asia[9] as have others,[10] but such publications are rapidly made obsolete in a way no book review ever is. In only a few years after their creation, many of the listed sites have changed their content so radically that the reviews no longer apply, not to mention those that have simply ceased to exist at the cited URL.

Sweetland lists a number of standards used for Web site evaluation, but none of them seem practical. Indeed, it seems clear that standards for evaluation will continue to be in flux just as much of the formats and functions of the Internet itself continue to change.

In this essay, reviews will emphasize authority and accuracy of content, and will evaluate the work in light of similar published and Internet sources. Usability is only a criterion if there are specific barriers to consider.

INTERNET REFERENCE SOURCES FOR ASIAN STUDIES

Encyclopedias

Encyclopedias are iconic of reference works. Most Internet encyclopedias function similarly to paper ones, with the added advantages of keyword searching and hypertext cross references. *Encarta* <http://encarta.msn.com> is a Microsoft product (the fact is difficult to ignore because of the logos, links, and advertisements for other Microsoft products, including a "premium" version of the encyclopedia requiring payment). The limited number of signed and unsigned articles (a larger number of articles were only available for paying customers) do not cite authoritative sources. Some include a list of further reading. The article on Indonesia, however, found significant lapses and biases. The article reflects the American bias against the Sukarno regime, and does not even mention the non-aligned movement or the Bandung conference. Strangely, the article differs from the same entry in the UK version of *Encarta* (<http://uk.encarta.msn.com/>), which is unsigned. Some content areas for Asian Studies were simply unavailable in the free version of *Encarta*, including sample searches for "Dalits," "Austronesian Languages" and "Prostitution in Thailand."

The online *Columbia Encyclopedia* <http://uk.encarta.msn.com/> does somewhat better on all topics tested, while still misrepresenting the history of Suharto's rise to power.[11] The content of the articles in both sources is appropriate for students up to high school or beginning college.

Wikipedia <http://en.wikipedia.org/wiki/Main_Page> is a new form of encyclopedia, one that could not exist except on the Internet. It describes itself as "a free-content encyclopedia that anyone can edit."[12] No ads confuse or mislead users on this site, and the structure takes full advantage of hypertext. While *Encarta* only offers a single directory browse or keyword searching, *Wikipedia* offers multiple category schemes, including academic disciplines, Dewey, and even Roget's Thesaurus classification.[13] Articles are unsigned, but registered users may append comments and even edit the entries. The entry for "Dalit" is (as yet) little more than a definition but it includes a (very short) list of further readings and external links, and a useful comment pointing out the limits of the entry.[14] The entry on Austronesian languages included links to the two most useful external sources: *Ethnologue* <http://www.ethnologue.com>, *Austronesian Language Database* <http://language.psy.auckland.ac.nz/>, and a third dead link to what appears to have been a personal home page (demonstrating the weakness of this genre). Because of *Wikipedia*'s unorthodox method of compilation, one is reminded to question its content. But in fact, users should be just as suspicious of the content of more standard reference works, even ones that claim to be authoritative such as *Encarta*. The citations and discussions in *Wikipedia* both emphasize and partially vitiate the fact that all such works have inherent biases.

Map and Image Collections

The Internet is rapidly becoming an excellent source of maps and satellite images, taking advantage of Geographic Information Systems (GIS) as well as zooming and hyperlinking in images. The *National Geographic Map Machine* <http://plasma.nationalgeographic.com/mapmachine> is excellent, and should be a major study and teaching tool at all educational levels. Specific to Asia, the *Perry-Castañeda Library Map Collection* from the University of Texas, Austin <http://www.lib.utexas.edu/maps/asia.html> offers scanned images of publicly accessible maps, including historical ones. The online collection for Asia, however, is not deep, relying almost entirely on U.S. government sources. Serious scholars will have to continue to visit physical libraries for most colonial era maps and subject-specific maps.

For photographs of architecture, a growing non-profit site is the *Asian Historical Architecture* page <http://www.orientalarchitecture. com/>. This site accepts images contributed by users and offers citations to published works on Asian art and architecture. The images are useful for reports and lectures, but are rarely of enough quality to be published (although the authors of the page suggest arrangements can be made).[15]

Reference Sources for Teachers

Teachers often do not want in-depth sources, but instead prefer materials that are organized in ways appropriate for classroom use. Columbia University's *Asia for Educators* <http://afe.easia.columbia.edu/> only seems to cover East Asia, although the "in construction" areas suggest more is to come. The excerpts of primary sources are properly cited, but quite limited. A teacher would still have to use a physical library (or, as the site urges, online bookstores) to seek out more background. The *Asian Educational Media Service* <http://www.aems.uiuc. edu/HTML/sitemap.html> is, as the name implies, simply an index of teaching media available through purchase (it includes a few free Internet videos). The *Global History Sourcebook* <http://www.fordham. edu/halsall/global/globalsbook.html> is, in contrast, extremely rich in content. Primary sources are arranged chronologically within geographic areas (such as "Persia" or "Hellenistic World"). The sources are often linked to external pages, which leads to the usual problem of out-of-date URLs. The advantage of a "global" approach is that Asian history is more contextualized; but there are also separate pages for "Indian history" (which, oddly, includes pre-history and areas not part of modern India), "East Asian history" (China, Japan and Korea), and "Islamic history." The sibling *Modern History Sourcebook* <http://www. fordham.edu/halsall/mod/modsbook.html> has a section on "Asia since 1900." Another source for documents in the modern history of Asia is the *UCLA Center for East Asian Studies* document page <http://www. isop.ucla.edu/eas/documents/doc-index.htm>. It includes Cambodia, Indonesia, Laos, Nepal, and Vietnam in addition to the usual East Asian countries.

CONCLUSION: ASIAN STUDIES STILL NEEDS LIBRARIES

Asian studies itself is a messy subject area, covering multiple continents and academic disciplines. It would seem, therefore, to be a good test of the Internet, where the virtual bringing together of disparate materials is easier than in physical collections. T. Matthew Ciolek has demonstrated that the Asian Studies presence on the Web is strong and growing. Nonetheless, the number of good reference sources is low. The greatest opportunity for Internet reference in Asian Studies would seem to lie in collaborative projects such as the *Wikipedia* and the *Asian Historical Architecture* page, where world-wide participation could build up a virtual collection that would otherwise never exist at all. In the future, we will certainly see more efforts to standardize font sets for various scripts, and more sophisticated translation software. As GIS functionality improves, we may see datasets available in that format. In the meantime, however, good reference works for Asian Studies still remain primarily in paper.

NOTES

1. W. Lee Hisle, "Top Issues Facing Academic Libraries: A Report of the Focus on the Future Task Force," *College & Research Libraries News* (November 2002) and Scott Carlson, "Students and Faculty Turn to Online Library Materials Before Printed Ones, Study Finds," *The Chronicle of Higher Education* (3 October 2003) <http://chronicle.com/free/2002/10/2002100301t.htm> (accessed 31 December 2004).

2. Heartsill Young, ed., *The ALA glossary of library and information science* (Chicago: American Library Association, 1983) and Marcia Bates "What Is a Reference Book?" in *For information specialists: Interpretations of reference and bibliographic work,* Howard D. White and Marcia J. Bates (Norwood, NJ: Patrick Wilson, 1992).

3. The guides visited were from University of Otago Library (New Zealand) <http://www.library.otago.ac.nz/subject_guides/asian.html>, University of Georgia Libraries <http://www.libs.uga.edu/researchcentral/subjectguides/asian.html>, Seattle University <http://www.seattleu.edu/lemlib/ResearchPath/SubGuides/Asian_Studies.htm>, Berea College <http://www.berea.edu/library/sublist/SubAST.html>, and Denison University <http://www.denison.edu/library/researchsubject/asian.html>, all accessed 31 December 2004.

4. *BUBL Link* <http://bubl.ac.uk/> (accessed 31 December 2004).

5. *PAIR: Portal to Asian Internet Sources* <http://webcat.library.wisc.edu:3200/PAIR/> (accessed 31 December 2004).

6. For other blogs, see *Best Blogs in Asia* <http://www.misohoni.com/bba/> (accessed 31 December 2004).

7. James H. Sweetland, "Reviewing the World Wide Web–Theory versus Reality," *Library Trends,* 48 no. 4 (2000): 748-768.

8. Ibid., 766-767.

9. Lisa Klopfer, "Southeast Asian Studies Online Resources," *College & Research Libraries News.* 64 no. 2 (2003): 96-99.

10. Sheau-yueh J. Chao and Ching Chang, "Internet Resources on Asian Studies: A Guide to the Best Sites of 2003," *Collection Building,* 22 no. 4 (2003): 186-207. Avail-

able through Emerald <http://www.emeraldinsight.com/0160-4953.htm> and Jana Sackman Eaton, "Using Computer Assistance in Teaching About Asia," *Journal of Educational Media & Library Sciences*, 39 no. 4 (2002): 374-381.

11. *The Columbia Encyclopedia*, 6th ed. New York: Columbia University Press, (2001-04). <www.bartleby.com/65/>.

12. Main page, *Wikipedia* <http://en.wikipedia.org/wiki/Main_Page> (accessed 31 December 2004).

13. Category schemes, *Wikipedia* <http://en.wikipedia.org/wiki/Wikipedia%3ACategory_ schemes> (accessed 31 December 2004).

14. Talk: Dalit (outcaste), *Wikipedia* <http://en.wikipedia.org/wiki/Talk%3ADalit_% 28outcaste%29> (accessed 31 December 2004).

15 "FAQ: Can I publish these photos in a book?" *Asian Historical Architecture* <http://www.orientalarchitecture.com/> (accessed 31 December 2004).

WORKS CITED

Asian Historical Architecture. <http://www.orientalarchitecture.com/> (accessed 31 December 2004).

Bates, Marcia. "What Is a Reference Book?" in *For Information Specialists: Interpretations of Reference and Bibliographic Work*. Howard D. White and Marcia J. Bates. Norwood, NJ: Patrick Wilson (1992).

Best Blogs in Asia. <http://www.misohoni.com/bba/> (accessed 31 December 2004).

BUBL Link. <http://bubl.ac.uk/> (accessed 31 December 2004).

Carlson, Scott. "Students and Faculty Turn to Online Library Materials Before Printed Ones, Study Finds." *The Chronicle of Higher Education* (3 October. 2003).

Chao, Sheau-yueh J. and Ching Chang. "Internet Resources on Asian studies: A Guide to the Best Sites of 2003." *Collection Building* 22 no. 4 (2003): 186-207. Available through Emerald <http://www.emeraldinsight.com/0160-4953.htm>.

Ciolek, Matthew T., ed. *The Asian Studies WWW Monitor* <http://coombs.anu.edu.au/ asia-www-monitor.html> (accessed 31 December 2004).

Ciolek, Matthew T., ed. *The AnthroGlobe Bibliographies* <http://coombs.anu.edu.au/ Biblio/biblio_index.html> (accessed 31 December 2004).

Ciolek, Matthew T., ed. *Asian Studies WWW Virtual Library* <http://coombs.anu. edu.au/WWWVL-AsianStudies.html> (accessed 31 December 2004).

The Columbia Encyclopedia, 6th ed. New York: Columbia University Press (2001-04). Available at <www.bartleby.com/65/>.

Columbia University. C. V. Starr East Asian Library. *Paper Gods* <http://www.columbia. edu/cu/lweb/eresources/eimages/eastasian/papergods/>.

Eaton, Jana Sackman. "Using Computer Assistance in Teaching About Asia." *Journal of Educational Media & Library Sciences* 39 no. 4 (2002): 374-381.

Eng, Robert Y. *Popular Culture of Japan: An Annotated Directory of Internet Resources* <http://newton.uor.edu/Departments&Programs/AsianStudiesDept/japan-pop. html> (accessed 31 December 2004).

Hisle, W. Lee. "Top Issues Facing Academic Libraries: A Report of the Focus on the Future Task Force." *College & Research Libraries News* 63 no.10 (2002): 714-715.

Klopfer, Lisa. "Southeast Asian Studies Online Resources." *College & Research Libraries News* 64 no. 2 (2003): 96-99.

Landsberger, Stefan. *Chinese Propaganda Poster Pages* <http://www.iisg.nl/%7Elandsberger/> (accessed 31 December 2004).

Library of Congress. *Asian Reading Room.* <http://www.loc.gov/rr/asian/>.

Mapping Asia. <http://www.asiamap.ac.uk/index.php>.

National University of Singapore. *South Asian Studies Programme.* <http://www.fas.nus.edu.sg/sas/research.html>.

PAIR: Portal to Asian Internet Sources. <http://webcat.library.wisc.edu:3200/PAIR/> (accessed 31 December 2004).

The Silk Road Project <http://www.silkroadproject.org/>.

Sushicam. <http://www.sushicam.com/> (accessed 31 December 2004).

Sweetland, James H. "Reviewing the World Wide Web–Theory versus Reality." *Library Trends* 48 no. 4 (2000): 748-768.

University of Texas at Austin. Perry-Castañeda Library. *Asian Maps* <http://www.lib.utexas.edu/maps/asia.html>.

Wikipedia. <http://en.wikipedia.org/wiki/Main_Page> (accessed 31 December 2004).

Young, Heartsill ed. *The ALA Glossary of Library and Information Science.* Chicago: American Library Association (1983).

The Internet in Latin America:
Development and Reference Sources

Molly Molloy

SUMMARY. This article chronicles the development of the Internet in Latin America and the evolution of reference and research information of use to scholars in the interdisciplinary field of Latin American Studies. It describes selected reference resources including public domain/open access and subscription databases, electronic journal aggregators, and Web sites that provide full text of historical materials, abstracts, and citations to journal articles, books, dissertations and other academic resources, government information, statistics, and news. *[Article copies available for a fee from The Haworth Document Delivery Service: 1-800-HAWORTH. E-mail address: <docdelivery@haworthpress.com> Website: <http://www.HaworthPress.com> © 2005 by The Haworth Press, Inc. All rights reserved.]*

KEYWORDS. Latin America, Internet, development, history, reference sources, research

THE DEVELOPMENT OF THE INTERNET
IN LATIN AMERICA

Information does not exist in isolation from the individual, organization, or other entity that creates it. Researchers need to know about the

Molly Molloy is affiliated with the New Mexico State University Library, Box 30006, MSC 3475, Las Cruces, NM 88003 (E-mail: mmolloy@nmsu.edu).

[Haworth co-indexing entry note]: "The Internet in Latin America: Development and Reference Sources." Molloy, Molly. Co-published simultaneously in *Journal of Library Administration* (The Haworth Information Press, an imprint of The Haworth Press, Inc.) Vol. 43, No. 3/4, 2005, pp. 129-147; and: *Evolving Internet Reference Resources* (ed: William Miller, and Rita M. Pellen) The Haworth Information Press, an imprint of The Haworth Press, Inc., 2006, pp. 129-147. Single or multiple copies of this article are available for a fee from The Haworth Document Delivery Service [1-800-HAWORTH, 9:00 a.m. - 5:00 p.m. (EST). E-mail address: docdelivery@haworthpress.com].

dynamics of information production and dissemination in their disciplines and in the countries or regions that they study. In the interdisciplinary field of Latin American Studies, librarians must be aware of how academic publishing functions in the region, the characteristics of the book trade, and how to obtain materials or provide access to information produced outside of the commercial realm by governments, education, and the non-governmental organization (NGO) sector. Librarians must understand how the mass media operate in different countries and how to obtain newspapers so that an archive will exist for future historians. Latin Americanist librarians have been engaged in these activities for many years and their efforts have created excellent research collections that have fostered the growth of new knowledge.

My career as an academic librarian began at the same time that the Internet became accessible to more than just the techies and geeks in higher education. From my perspective as a specialist in Latin American area studies, it seemed that researchers should take advantage of this new tool for information dissemination that promised to break through some of the barriers of time, distance, and economics that made access to information from Latin America difficult. As the Internet became an important tool for scholarly communication and research and entered the information universe in Latin America in the 1990s, academic librarians recognized the need to use the Net to increase access to traditional sources of information (online newspapers, academic journals, newsletters, etc.) and to take advantage of the production and dissemination of new sources of information.

Long before traditional published sources appeared on the Internet, scholars, activists, journalists, and others were creating and disseminating unique information from and about the region to the rest of the world, often information produced by groups and individuals excluded from the commercial or traditional academic information world, such as activist groups, guerrilla organizations, and other minority or marginalized sectors of the population (Cleaver 1998, Molloy 1998). The primary value of the Internet has always been as a medium of communication and a vehicle for the formation of community. The Internet is a "network of networks" of people keeping each other aware of events and sharing information to solve problems, to publicize situations requiring action, and to facilitate the creation of new knowledge. The Internet can create communities of affinity without geographic limitations.

In a previous paper, I explored in some detail, the development of the Internet in Latin America within the framework of several interrelated themes: the use of Internet communication for development and democracy; the influence of entertainment and commerce; and the economics of the gap in access to information technologies in Latin America (Molloy 2000). While universities, international organizations, governments, and private businesses played an important role in institutionalizing Internet communications in Latin America, it should be noted that NGOs took on much of the earliest technical, educational, and outreach work in the late 1980s and early 1990s to bring Latin America online. Social change activists, often members of local groups dealing with human rights, environment, peace, labor, or other issues recognized the potential of new technologies to enable them to connect with people in other parts of the world who were working on similar issues or who had an interest in receiving information about their activities (Lane 1990, Keck and Sikkink 1998).

In the pre-Internet era, beginning as early as 1985-86, the Association for Progressive Communications (APC) provided access to electronic mail for many groups involved in progressive social movements in Latin American countries–the earliest NGO networks in the region were in Nicaragua and Brazil (Frederick 1993, Association for Progressive Communications 2004, Pasch 1997). It can be argued that the conjunction of Internet communication and the growth of civil society in Latin America created a synthesis such that: "Throughout Latin America and the Third World . . . such groups (grassroots NGOs) have risen to prominence in the last ten to fifteen years–thanks in no small measure . . . to their ability to creatively use new information and communication technologies–exerting their influence all the way from the struggle to redefine (and democratize) daily life to the realm of international relations" (Norsworthy 1997, p. 268).

Optimism about the social benefits of Internet connectivity in Latin America prevailed throughout the 1990s; however, the more recent boom fueled by online entertainment and commercial applications and the growth of private Internet service providers that followed took away much of the vanguard status that progressive organizations had acquired (Gomez 1998). The commercial boom enabled many more people in Latin America to obtain access to the Internet, but as Gomez points out (2000), the Latin American Internet became a "hall of mirrors" reflecting, and in some ways exacerbating, huge inequalities already present in these societies.

The *1999 Human Development Report* of the United Nations Development Program (UNDP 1999) focused on the contradictions of globalization: a world in which the benefits of growth and prosperity had become more and more unevenly distributed. Thirty years ago, the income ratio of the richest to the poorest countries was 30-to-1; by 1999 it had grown to 74-to-1. The report details the "double-edged sword" potential of the Internet to break down barriers and facilitate social change and/or to reinforce the inequalities of access to the Internet in rich and poor countries. "Those with income, education and–literally–connections have cheap and instantaneous access to information. The rest are left with uncertain, slow, and costly access. When people in these two worlds live and compete side by side, the advantage of being connected will overpower the marginal and impoverished, cutting off their voices and concerns from the global conversation" (UNDP 1999, 6).

There is no lack of literature on the general problem of the "digital divide" in Latin America (Panos Institute 1998, Hamelink 1998, Haymond 1998, Carty 2000, Everett 1998). Everett examined the position of aid agencies in funding information technology as a tool for promoting economic development and political reform, but found that: "The Internet is far from being the free and open exchange that the advertisers and other enthusiasts claim. In terms of both content and accessibility it reflects the same inequalities of race, class, gender and the global order which exist in the 'real world'" (Everett 1998, 392).

By 2003, most Latin American governments had articulated policies aimed at promoting Internet access and connectivity and thus working toward the alleviation of inequalities (Summits of the Americas 2004). A recent study (Hawkins and Hawkins 2003) looked at the connections between government policies and Internet access in Latin America. Their data show that the level of Internet use is strongly associated with the overall wealth of the countries and the corresponding development of the telecommunications infrastructure (659). The only government policy shown to have a significant impact on the level of Internet access was the implementation of changes in telecommunications tariff structures (660).

The Internet, like so many technologies before it, is not being introduced onto a *tabula rasa*; rather, it is inserted into an existing set of highly unequal social and economic relations. In the case of Latin America, it is not even a static situation of inequality–the period of the 1990s, when the Internet was introduced in the region, was one of growing inequalities in distribution of wealth and resources. However, there is the potential, thanks to private investment, government policies, and the continuing efforts of progressive communities, to create the space for activism, education, research, and other socially beneficial activities. Critical and well-informed users and producers of information may, in the long run, be much more important than hardware, infrastructure, and commercial investment.

In 2004, Tim Berners-Lee, credited as the inventor of the World Wide Web, received a $1.2 million Millennium Technology Prize in Helsinki, Finland. In his acceptance speech, Berners-Lee said that if he had patented his ideas and demanded royalty fees, he would never have succeeded in creating and implementing the communication protocols and markup language that have become essential to what became the open and inter-operable World Wide Web, accessible through any computer platform anywhere in the world. His statement emphasized the Internet's "spirit of openness and sharing" as an essential catalyst to creativity and invention (Shannon 2004).

The recent trend toward the "harvesting" of metadata from archives of open access scholarly information sources and making these archives accessible to Web searchers through deep indexing is one way that the Internet may be moving toward fulfilling the dreams of its founders and the "access is power" optimists of the 1990s: that useful and reliable information would become freely available to all–not just to those in wealthy countries or to the privileged few in poorer world regions like Latin America. Librarians and other information scientists are finding evidence to show that open access sources do have a greater impact on the research community than articles published in journals that are only accessible by paying high subscription fees (Antelman 2004).

Eugene Garfield, the citation database pioneer and founder of the Institute for Scientific Information (ISI) has speculated that open access may improve readership and citation impact (quoted in Antelman, 372-373). ISI's Journal Citation Reports (JCR) are used extensively in academia to determine the relative research impact of a select list of journals across disciplines. ISI currently monitors the presence of open access journals in its citation databases to determine if open access increases research impact. The most recently published study, released in October 2004 and based on the 2003 Journal Citation Reports, concludes that while "more of the currently available open access journals rank in the lower half of their subject category" there are some open access titles in the top ranks (McVeigh 2004).

It is important to note that the JCR methodology focuses on a measurement of the research impact of *journals*, not individual articles (Antelman 373). ISI's October study points out the complexity in evolving open access distribution models, including the fact that many publishers permit self-archiving of individual articles by authors, that these archives are increasingly available through Web searching, and thus the availability of articles outside the "package" of the published journal may also affect research impact. The ISI reports note the important role of regional journals in open access publishing, specifically the Scientific Electronic Library Online (SciELO), which encompasses a growing list of Latin American titles (Thomson ISI 2004).

ANNOTATED GUIDE TO REFERENCE SOURCES FOR LATIN AMERICAN STUDIES

The resources listed here provide access to scholarly literature, news and news archives, periodicals, statistics, and government information focused specifically on Latin America. I have included a few general sources that may be especially relevant to Latin American Studies. Some sources mentioned are very specific and are provided as examples of the kind of unique and useful information that is available via the Internet; however, this list is not intended to be comprehensive. Directory sites such as the Latin America Network Information Center (LANIC) provide the best access to the constantly changing array of sites in the region. These online resources will provide a variety of information including complete bibliographic citations and abstracts and/or full text. In some cases, the database will provide external links to the full text of articles or documents. Access to full text depends on whether the end user is willing to pay for documents or whether the source material is provided through a paid subscription maintained by the library or other institution providing the database access. For all resources listed, I indicate whether access is OPEN or via SUBSCRIPTION.

Americas Program
<http://www.americaspolicy.org/>
OPEN

The Americas Program Web site provides policy briefs and analysis from the Interhemispheric Resource Center (IRC) <http://www.irc-online. org> on topics such as economic integration and sustainable development, U.S. policy, and Latin American political, social and economic affairs, etc. The site includes data and reports on current U.S.-Mexico border issues <http://www.americaspolicy.org/index/usmex/index.php> and an archive of published policy papers and newsletters back to 1995

<http://www.americaspolicy.org/clearinghouse.html>. The IRC is a not-for-profit research and advocacy organization located in New Mexico.

Biblioteca Virtual de Ciencias Sociales de América Latina y el Caribe, Consejo Latinoamericano de Ciencias Sociales (CLACSO)
<http://www.clacso.org/wwwclacso/espanol/html/biblioteca/fbiblioteca.html>
OPEN

This site from CLACSO provides free access to more than 4,000 full-text books, periodical articles, reports, and conference papers by social sciences researchers in Latin America and the Caribbean.

CIAONET: Columbia International Affairs Online
<http://www.ciaonet.org>
SUBSCRIPTION

Columbia International Affairs Online (CIAO) is a comprehensive source for theory and research in international affairs. CIAO provides full text of working papers, reports, and articles from many international relations research centers and think tanks and full text of books published by Columbia University Press. Latin American countries and issues are well-represented in CIAO content. For access and subscription information, see: <http://www.ciaonet.org/frame/subscribefrm.html>.

CLASE/PERIODICA
<http://www.oclc.org/support/documentation/firstsearch/databases/dbdetails/details/ClasePeriodica.htm>
SUBSCRIPTION

OCLC Firstsearch provides access to these two periodical databases produced by the Universidad Nacional Autónoma de México (UNAM). CLASE indexes documents published in Latin American journals specializing in the social sciences and humanities; PERIODICA covers the sciences and technology. Together the databases provide more than 300,000 bibliographic citations to articles, essays, book reviews, conference proceedings, and technical reports published in more than 2,600 journals from 24 different Latin American countries. This database does not provide links to full-text articles. Access to database producers is available from the Dirección General de Bibliotecas at UNAM: <http://dgb.unam.mx>.

Federal Reserve Bank of Dallas
<http://www.dallasfed.org/index.html>
OPEN

The Federal Reserve Bank of Dallas is an excellent source for economic information on the U.S.-Mexico border region and Latin America. It provides full-text access to economic data, reports and analysis. The Center for Latin American Economics, CLAE <http://www.dallasfed.org/latin/index.html> is a research institute attached to the Federal Reserve Bank of Dallas. CLAE focuses its research efforts on issues of particular concern in Latin America and provides full-text access to working papers, research reports, statistics, and other documents via this Web site.

Handbook of Latin American Studies–HLAS
<http://lcweb2.loc.gov/hlas/>
OPEN

The Handbook of Latin American Studies is produced by the Hispanic Division of the Library of Congress and is provided free of charge to Web users worldwide. HLAS provides abstracts and complete bibliographic information for published materials and online resources from and about Latin America on a wide range of topics in the humanities and social sciences, selected and annotated by specialists in the field. HLAS has been published since 1936 and the print volumes constitute a comprehensive and growing bibliography of the scholarly literature in Latin American Studies. The online database contains more than 80,000 citations and grows at the rate of about 10,000 citations annually. HLAS includes citations to books, journal articles, theses and dissertations, online resources, and materials in other formats such as CD-ROMs. For more information on the history and content of this resource, see: <http://lcweb2.loc.gov/hlas/salalm.html>.

Hemeroteca Digital de Chihuahua
<http://www.inpro.com.mx/english/index2.html>
SUBSCRIPTION

The Hemeroteca Digital de Chihuahua, provided by Información Procesada (INPRO), contains full-text articles from Mexican newspapers and magazines from and about the state of Chihuahua and the U.S.-Mexico border region. Most of the information in the database is in Spanish, although it does contain articles from some regional U.S. publications that cover the border region. In addition to local papers from Ciudad Júarez and Chihuahua, the database contains articles that pertain to Chihuahua and the northern border region from many other Mexican publications. Time coverage: 1976 to the present. This database is very specific, but it is an excellent example of a regional information provider developing unique archival content of use to serious researchers. For more information about access to this database, e-mail: informes@inpro.com.mx.

Hispanic American Periodicals Index (HAPI)
<http://hapi.gseis.ucla.edu>
SUBSCRIPTION

HAPI provides access to the contents of more than 500 social sciences and humanities journals from and about Latin America with coverage from 1970-present. HAPI is a source for authoritative, worldwide information about Central and South America, Mexico, the Caribbean basin, the U.S.-Mexico border region, and Hispanics in the United States. Subject coverage ranges from current political, economic, social, and business issues to Latin American arts and letters. HAPI Online contains complete bibliographic citations to articles, book reviews, documents, original literary works, and other materials. HAPI provides coverage of many regional journals that are not included in other online databases. Produced by the UCLA Latin American Center, HAPI includes more than 210,000 citations, and grows at the rate of about 8,000 records a year. Beginning in 2003, HAPI provides links to articles that are available full text through several commercial sources and through journal Web pages. For more information see: <http://hapi.gseis.ucla. edu/hapi/html/free/about.shtml>.

Independent Media Center–Indymedia
<http://www.indymedia.org>
OPEN

The Independent Media Center is an excellent example of social activists taking advantage of the Internet to disseminate alternative news from many different world areas. Indymedia describes itself as "a collective of independent media organizations and hundreds of journalists offering grassroots, non-corporate coverage." Latin American news is posted to Indymedia from Argentina, Bolivia, Brazil, Chile, Colombia,

Ecuador, Mexico, Peru, and Uruguay. It is an excellent source for current news coverage from an alternative perspective.

InfoLatina: ISI Emerging Markets
<http://www.securities.com/corp/infolatina.html>
SUBSCRIPTION

InfoLatina provides current and archival access to the full text of a large array of Mexican publications, including newspapers, magazines, government documents, legislation, and jurisprudence. For some publications, the archive goes back to the early 1980s. The commercial service, Internet Securities, acquired the InfoLatina database in 2000 and merged the content with other global and Latin American news and business sources provided through the Web site. Trial subscriptions are available. For more information on subscriptions and access, see: <http://www.securities.com/corp/infolatina.html?ms=0&section=contact>.

INFO-LATINOAMERICA: Latin American Information System
<http://www.nisc.com>
SUBSCRIPTION

Produced by the National Information Services Corporation (NISC), INFO-LATINOAMERICA covers regional business, economics, politics, and social issues. This database began as Info-South from the University of Miami's North-South Center and coverage goes back to 1988; content is updated weekly. INFO-LATINOAMERICA includes abstracts of Latin American newspaper and some journal articles; most content from 1996-forward is full text or includes links to full text on the Web. Coverage tends toward English-language news and business sources from more than 1,500 international newspapers, journals, news magazines, newsletters, media broadcasts, conference proceedings, and other print publications. English translations of foreign media broadcasts are provided by the World News Connection (see p. 145). See: <http://www.nisc.com/factsheets/qila.htm> for more information.

INFORME–Revistas en Español
<http://www.galegroup.com/servlet/ItemDetailServlet?region= 9&imprint=000&titleCode=INFO1&type=4&id=172023>
SUBSCRIPTION

INFORME is provided by the Thomson Gale Group. The database provides full-text access to more than 140 Spanish and bilingual academic and popular periodicals. Archival coverage is not consistent, but full text for some titles is included back to the mid-1990s. Subject coverage includes news, politics, arts and letters, social sciences, as well as popular entertainment, sports, and fashion magazines. INFORME is one of the first products from a mainstream, commercial information provider to include significant Spanish-language and Latin American content to non-specialized academic and public libraries. The INFORME title list is available: <http://www.galegroup.com/tlist/sb5022.html> and a fact sheet: <http://www.gale.com/pdf/facts/inform.pdf>.

J-STOR
<http://www.jstor.org/>
SUBSCRIPTION

J-STOR is a membership organization providing a full-text archive of the complete runs of several hundred major academic journals in the sciences, social sciences, and humanities. Some journal archives cover more than 100 years of research. Latin American Studies titles in the current J-STOR collections include: *Hispanic American Historical Review*, *Journal of Interamerican Studies and World Affairs*, *Journal of Latin American Studies*, *Latin American Perspectives*, and *Latin American Research Review*. Inclusion of archival Latin American content in J-STOR should continue to grow and will make it possible for many smaller college and university libraries to provide access to specialized journals that are not part of their print holdings.

Latin American Network Information Center (LANIC)
<http://lanic.utexas.edu>
OPEN

LANIC is headquartered at the University of Texas at Austin and is the premier Internet directory for Latin American information. LANIC provides links to thousands of information resources from and about Latin America. Many LANIC projects continue to provide full-text access to archival materials of use to researchers. The following are examples of LANIC resources and projects.

Electronic Text Collections
<http://lanic.utexas.edu/project/etext/>

Full texts of Presidential messages from Mexico and Argentina dating back to the mid-19th Century; translations into English of more than

37 years of Castro's public speeches, interviews, and press conferences; archives of several Latin American journals and conference proceedings, etc.

Latin American Open Archives Portal (LAOAP)
<http://lanic.utexas.edu/project/laoap/>

LAOAP (under development) uses the Open Archives Initiative Protocol for Metadata Harvesting (OAI-PMH) to develop a database to provide access to social sciences "grey literature" (working documents, pre-prints, research reports, statistical documents) produced by Latin American research institutes, NGOs, and some government agencies. It is anticipated that the repositories indexed by the LAOAP will be integrated into other open access archives to facilitate access via open Web search engines.

Association of Research Libraries Latin American Research Resources Project (ARL-LARRP)
<http://lanic.utexas.edu/project/arl/>

In addition to the LAOAP and the Presidential Messages databases, LANIC and ARL have collaborated to create a database of the Tables of Contents (LAPTOC) of more than 800 humanities and social sciences journals published in Latin America. The journals covered in LAPTOC are specifically chosen because they are not likely to be included in other databases (such as HAPI). Indexing is provided by Latin American specialists at participating ARL libraries; members facilitate interlibrary loan of articles to other participating libraries.

A selection of other LANIC pages:

LANIC Newsroom: <http://lanic.utexas.edu/info/newsroom/>

Media and Communication: <http://lanic.utexas.edu/subject/media/>

Journalism: <http://lanic.utexas.edu/la/region/journalism/>

Magazines: <http://lanic.utexas.edu/la/region/epub/>

Newspapers: <http://lanic.utexas.edu/la/region/news/>

Academic journals: <http://lanic.utexas.edu/la/region/journals/>

Photography: <http://lanic.utexas.edu/la/region/photography/>

Government: <http://lanic.utexas.edu/subject/government/>

Human Rights: <http://lanic.utexas.edu/la/region/hrights/>

U.S.-Mexico Border: <http://lanic.utexas.edu/la/mexico/usmex/>

Maps: <http://lanic.utexas.edu/la/region/map/>

Statistics: <http://lanic.utexas.edu/la/region/statistics/>

Libraries & Reference: <http://lanic.utexas.edu/subject/libraries/>

Latin America Data Base (LADB)
<http://ladb.unm.edu/>
SUBSCRIPTION

The LADB has been published by the Latin American and Iberian Institute at the University of New Mexico since 1986 and at that time it was one of the first online databases for Latin American research, disseminating weekly bulletins of news and economic and political analysis via e-mail and providing access to an online archive via a telnet connection. LADB currently produces three weekly electronic news bulletins about Mexico (SourceMex), Central America and the Caribbean including Cuba (NotiCen), and South America (NotiSur). These are available on the Web and/or by e-mail with a subscription. LADB's searchable archive of over 24,000 articles since 1986 is updated weekly. This is a unique, content-rich archive and current awareness source for economic and political information on Latin America. See <http://ladb.unm.edu/info/prices/> for prices and trial account information. E-mail: <info@ladb.unm.edu>.

LatinFocus
<http://www.latin-focus.com/>
OPEN

LatinFocus, "the leading source for Latin American economies," contains data from government sources, economic forecasts, market analysis covering economic performance, political risk assessments, and financial market developments. LatinFocus includes full-text documents providing economic indicators (GDP, unemployment, CPI, stock market, exports, imports, etc.) from 1995 onward for Argentina, Brazil, Chile, Colombia, Mexico, Venezuela, and Latin America as a whole. The database also includes recent news articles and commentaries, fact sheets, charts, economic briefings, and related links for individual countries. LatinFocus sells publications and some specialized services via subscriptions, but the free resources on the Web site are an excellent research tool.

LexisNexis Academic Universe
<http://www.lexis-nexis.com/universe>
SUBSCRIPTION

This general database for news and legal research is available through many U.S. academic libraries. It includes full-text access to thousands of news sources, including several dozen Spanish-language titles. The best segments for Latin American news are "North/South American News" and "Spanish Language News." Searches can be restricted to these sets of publications. LexisNexis provides access to several specialized publications such as the *Latin American Weekly Report*, *Latin American Newsletters*, *Latin American Regional Reports*, *Latin American Economy and Business*, *Latinnews Daily*, as well as information on the region from thousands of daily newspapers and other periodical sources.

National Security Archive
<http://www2.gwu.edu/~nsarchiv/>
OPEN

The National Security Archive is an independent non-governmental research institute and library located at George Washington University in Washington, DC. The National Security Archive collects and publishes declassified documents acquired through the Freedom of Information Act (FOIA). Complete collections are available for purchase in published and microfiche formats and online via subscription, but the Web site provides selections of full-text primary research collections online in a section entitled: Electronic Briefing Books, <http://www2.gwu.edu/~nsarchiv/NSAEBB/index.html>. Latin American topics available online include: Argentina's Dirty War, CIA in Latin America, Contras, Cocaine and Covert Operations, the Tlatelolco Massacre, Human Rights and the Dirty War in Mexico, Kennedy and Castro, Chile Intervention, Oliver North File, War in Colombia, U.S. Policy in Guatemala, and many other topics.

OAIster
<http://www.oaister.org>
OPEN

OAIster is an open access archive project of the University of Michigan Digital Library and provides a searchable database of more than 4.7 million (as of December 2004) articles, documents, graphics, photographs, sound recordings, videos, and other digital objects made freely available on the Internet by more than 390 institutions and organizations including many university special collections and archives. OAIster encompasses as broad a collection of resources as possible in many formats and with no restrictions on subject parameters. It is also possible to restrict searches to specific collections included in the database. OAIster is accessible to the entire Internet community. While OAIster does not focus specifically on Latin America, sample keyword searches reveal significant Latin American content. Examples: Latin America* restricted to image format = 108 items; Mexico images = 8,969; Mexico and all document types = 15,332; Nicaragua and all document types = 305 items.

Political Database of the Americas
<http://www.georgetown.edu/pdba/>
OPEN

The Political Database of the Americas is produced at Georgetown University and provides political documents and data for all countries in the hemisphere, including texts of constitutions and laws, electoral systems and historical election data, political party platforms and histories, judicial information, and more.

Red de Revistas Científicas de America Latina y El Caribe (RedALyC)
<http://www.redalyc.com/>
OPEN

The Red de Revistas Científicas de America Latina y El Caribe, España y Portugal provides full-text access to more than 130 journals in social sciences and humanities published in many Latin American countries, Spain and Portugal. RedALyC is conceived as an open access portal for academic information produced in the region. Using the slogan, "La ciencia que no se ve, no existe/Science that is not seen does not exist," RedALyC has taken a giant step forward in providing access to academic research produced in Latin America. It is anticipated that the visibility of the full text of these journals will increase the citation rates and global research impact of Latin American scholarship.

Sistema de Información sobre Comercio Exterior/Foreign Trade Information system (SICE)
<http://www.sice.oas.org/>
OPEN

SICE is the Foreign Trade Information System of the Organization of American States. The Web page contains full text of official documents and other information relating to trade agreements and treaties, intellectual property rights organizations, investment treaties, a glossary, and related links to other Web sites, arranged by topic and by country concerning trade in the Western hemisphere. Most of the documents available via SICE are provided in English and Spanish and portions of the site are available in English, Spanish, French, and Portuguese.

SciELO
<http://www.scielo.org/>
OPEN

The Scientific Electronic Library Online, SciELO, is a vanguard open access digital library of full-text articles from science and social science journals from Latin America and Spain. The original SciELO project was developed by a consortium of Brazilian research institutes, and has developed as a model for cooperative electronic publishing of scientific journals on the Internet. SciELO was designed to meet the scientific communication needs of developing countries, particularly Latin America and the Caribbean. Current projects exist in Brazil, Chile, Cuba, Spain, Mexico, Colombia, Peru, Costa Rica, and Venezuela. SciELO content is especially strong in the fields of public health, agriculture, biomedicine, and allied health sciences. SciELO titles feature prominently in the ISI research impact studies of open access journals and are accessible via Google Scholar <http://scholar.google.com>.

SCIRUS
<http://www.scirus.com>
OPEN

SCIRUS is a comprehensive science-specific Internet search engine that provides access to scientific, scholarly, technical, and medical data on the Web. Like Google Scholar, SCIRUS provides links to open access scientific information, as well as links to articles that may be available via purchase or subscription. I have included it in this list because keyword searches yielded many relevant articles and sites with Latin American content, including links to open access archives such as SciELO.

World News Connection
<http://wnc.fedworld.gov>
<http://wnc.dialog.com/>
SUBSCRIPTION

World News Connection (WNC) provides access to a wide array of news articles, conference proceedings, television and radio broadcasts, periodical articles, and other publications. Translations of foreign language broadcast and print sources are provided by the National Technical Information Service (NTIS) and produced by analysts at the Foreign Broadcast Information Service (FBIS), a sub-agency of the CIA. WNC provides English translations of news broadcasts worldwide, with extensive coverage from more than 25 Latin American and Caribbean countries. News stories and translations are generally available online within 24-72 hours of broadcast. Online archival coverage goes back to 1995. Although the database content is created and maintained by NTIS, online subscription access to the WNC is provided through DIALOG, <http://wnc.dialog.com/>. For more information on subscribing, contact: <customer@dialog.com>.

CONCLUSIONS

I began writing about the development of the Internet in Latin America in 1994 and have posted various chronologies and resource lists online (Molloy 1999). Until very recently, the Internet as a reference source for Latin American Studies was a way to access gigabytes of information on the latest events (daily newspapers, current issues of popular magazines, travel and tourism information, political and human rights alerts, basic government information) but provided only limited access to deep news archives or scholarly resources. As can be seen from the selective list of reference resources above, this broad but shallow information pool is changing and growing with the most interesting and substantive advances coming from scientific journal publishers, research centers, and NGOs in the region.

The current challenge for librarians and scholars is to find meaningful ways to participate in the evolution of the Internet from a communication tool into a functioning virtual library. While the Internet does not provide the kind of controlled subject access and the bibliographic or inventory control that exists in a research library, new digital projects using the Open Archives Initiative Protocol for Metadata Harvesting (OAI-PMH) are creating online access to large repositories of quality research information. Regional electronic publishing initiatives such as the Scientific Electronic Library Online (SciELO) and the Red de Revistas Científicas de América Latina y El Caribe (RedALyC) now provide free, open access to the full contents of hundreds of academic journals published in Latin America, the Caribbean, and Spain. Advanced Internet search engines such as Google make it possible to find quality information on the open Web. New relationships between Google and global academic publishers, including those from Latin America (launched as Google Scholar in late November 2004), are creating the beginnings of a real virtual library for academic research in Latin American Studies.

BIBLIOGRAPHY

Antelman, Kristin. 2004. Do open-access articles have a greater research impact? *College & Research Libraries* 65, 5: 372-382.

Association for Progressive Communications. 2004. The Association for Progressive Communications: Internet and ICTs for Social Justice and Development. <http://www.apc.org/english/index.shtml>.

Carty, Winthrop. 2000. Public education's information gap. *NACLA Report on the Americas* 33, 4 (January/February): 36-38.

Cleaver, Harry M., Jr. 1998. The Zapatista effect: The Internet and the rise of an alternative political fabric. *Journal of International Affairs* 51 (Spring): 621-640.

Everett, Margaret. 1998. Latin America On-Line: The Internet, development, and democratization. *Human Organization* 57, 4 (Winter): 385-393.

Frederick, Howard. 1993. Computer networks and the emergence of global civil society. In *Global Networks: Computers and International Communication*, ed. Linda M. Harasim, 283-295. Cambridge, MA: MIT Press.

Gomez, Ricardo. 1998. The nostalgia of virtual community: A study of computer-mediated communications use in Colombian non-governmental organizations. *Information Technology and People* 11, 3: 217-234.

Gomez, Ricardo. 2000. The hall of mirrors: The Internet in Latin America. *Current History* 99, 634 (February): 72-77.

Hamelink, Cees. 1998. The People's Communication Charter. *Development in Practice* 8, 1 (February): 68-74.

Hawkins, Eliza Tanner and Kirk A. Hawkins. 2003. Bridging Latin America's digital divide: Government policies and Internet access. *Journalism and Mass Communication Quarterly* 80 (3): 646-665.

Haymond, Ruel. 1998. Internet accessibility in Latin America. *Educational Technology Research and Development* 46 (3): 116-117.

Keck, Margaret and Kathryn Sikkink. 1998. *Activists beyond borders: Advocacy networks in international politics*. Ithaca: Cornell University Press.

Lane, Graham. 1990. *Communications for progress: A guide to international e-mail*. Nijmegen, Netherlands: Antenna/Interdoc; London: Catholic Institute for International Relations (CIIR); Brussels, Belgium: Environment & Development Resource Centre (EDRC).

McVeigh, Marie. 2004. *Open access journals in the ISI citation databases: Analysis of impact factors and citation patterns*. Thomson Scientific, October 2004. <http://www.thomsonisi.com/media/presentrep/essayspdf/openaccesscitations2.pdf>.

Molloy, Molly. 1998. Internetworking as a tool for advocacy and research: The case of Chiapas News, 1994-1996. In *SALALM in the Age of Multimedia: Technological Challenge and Social Change: Seminar on the Acquisition of Latin American Library Materials (SALALM)*, ed. Peter A. Stern, 12-23. Austin: SALALM Secretariat. A version of this paper is available online: <http://lib.nmsu.edu/staff/mmolloy/chiapasnews.htm>.

Molloy, Molly. 1999. LA GUIA: Internet resources for Latin America. <http://lib.nmsu.edu/subject/bord/laguia/>.

Molloy, Molly. 2000. Background on the development of the Internet in Latin America. <http://lib.nmsu.edu/subject/bord/laguia/netdev.html>.

Norsworthy, Kent. 1997. Computer communications, civil society, and UT-LANIC. In *Societies Under Constraint: Economic and Social Pressures in Latin America: Seminar on the Acquisition of Latin American Library Materials XL*, ed. Robert A. McNeil, 266-287. Austin: SALALM Secretariat.

Pasch, Grete and Carmen Valdés R. 1997. The dawn of the Internet era in Guatemala. International Federation of Information Processing. <http://www.nortropic.com/la/ifip.htm>.

Shannon, Victoria. 2004. Pioneer who kept the Web free honored with a technology prize. *New York Times*, June 14, 2004. (Accessed December 1, 2004 via LexisNexis Academic Universe.)

Summits of the Americas Information Network. 2004. *Connectivity in the Americas*. <http://www.summit-americas.org/Quebec-Connectivity/connectivity-eng.htm>.

Thomson ISI. 2004. *The impact of open access journals: A citation study from Thomson ISI*. (April 2004). <http://www.isinet.com/media/presentrep/acropdf/impact-oa-journals.pdf>.

United Nations Development Program. 1999. *1999 Human Development Report: Globalization with a Human Face*. New York: Oxford University Press. Online: <http://hdr.undp.org/reports/global/1999/en/>.

World Bank. 1998. *World Development Report 1998/99: Knowledge for Development*. Washington, DC: World Bank. Also available online: <http://www.worldbank.org/wdr/wdr98/>.

Creating a Web Resource:
African American Kentuckian Profiles

Reinette F. Jones

SUMMARY. For far too many years we have been unable to fulfill requests for a current biographical reference on African American Kentuckians. In response, two librarians, Reinette Jones and Rob Aken, created Notable Kentucky African Americans <http://www.uky.edu/Subject/aakyall.html>, a continuously updated online reference source that is tailored to the profiles of African Americans in and from Kentucky. *[Article copies available for a fee from The Haworth Document Delivery Service: 1-800-HAWORTH. E-mail address: <docdelivery@haworthpress.com> Website: <http://www.HaworthPress.com> © 2005 by The Haworth Press, Inc. All rights reserved.]*

KEYWORDS. Kentucky, African Americans, reference, Web resource

DEVELOPMENT OF THE WEB PAGE

For many years, students, faculty, and community members would request biographical information on African American Kentuckians at

---

Reinette F. Jones is Librarian I, University of Kentucky, IDRC/Storage Library, Third Floor King Annex, Lexington, KY 40506 (E-mail: rjones@uky.edu).

[Haworth co-indexing entry note]: "Creating a Web Resource: African American Kentuckian Profiles." Jones, Reinette F. Co-published simultaneously in *Journal of Library Administration* (The Haworth Information Press, an imprint of The Haworth Press, Inc.) Vol. 43, No. 3/4, 2005, pp. 149-159; and: *Evolving Internet Reference Resources* (ed: William Miller, and Rita M. Pellen) The Haworth Information Press, an imprint of The Haworth Press, Inc., 2006, pp. 149-159. Single or multiple copies of this article are available for a fee from The Haworth Document Delivery Service [1-800-HAWORTH, 9:00 a.m. - 5:00 p.m. (EST). E-mail address: docdelivery@haworthpress.com].

doi:10.1300/J111v43n03_12

the University of Kentucky reference desks with only limited success. In response, in 2003, librarians Reinette Jones and Rob Aken created Notable Kentucky African Americans <http://www.uky.edu/Subject/aakyall.html>. It is a continuously updated online reference source tailored to the profiles of African Americans in and from Kentucky. The Web page has become a very enlightening library endeavor that has been so well received by patrons that the information has grown considerably with hundreds more entries than were ever anticipated. The project has developed from the initiative of two librarians into a patron-driven online source, with the majority of the new information coming from those who use and view the Web page.

The original planning called for one to two hundred brief biographical profiles and a few new entries were to be added each quarter. But that plan was soon scrapped and the page has developed at its own pace. Librarian Reinette Jones researches and verifies new entries and writes the profiles. Librarian Rob Aken edits the profiles and adds them to the Web page.

It is a no-frills page, a .txt (ASCII) file with html mark-up. Listed are persons of African descent who were born in Kentucky or have resided in the state and have contributed to the well-being of others. The time frame is from the earliest history up to the present. Entries may be viewed as a complete list or by categories/subjects listed in the drop-down box at the top of the page. There is always the search option using the browser find command. The individual profiles are in alphabetical order by last name in the following format: name (in bold), birth date-death date, Kentucky hometown or county, a brief profile, and the title of at least one source for additional information. It is preferable to list a source that is available in a Kentucky library, but that is not always possible.

The initial purpose of the Web page was to satisfy the few reference requests that never escalated in number, but continued to be asked each semester, year after year. The page was made available late September 2003 via the University of Kentucky library's Internet resources pages. Soon afterwards, the page could also be found using Yahoo, Google, and other search engines. A bibliographic record of the page is now also available in FirstSearch and in the University of Kentucky Libraries online catalog InfoKat. The increased exposure has brought more visitors to the site, which has led to frequent e-mails with contributions, corrections, and requests for more information. The e-mail messages come from around the nation and there are a few from other countries. Persons forwarding the messages are individuals listed on the Web page, their relatives, librarians, authors, researchers, students, educators, genealogists, and other curious souls.

There has been a steady flow of incoming information and the page has grown from the initial 100 or so entries to more than 500 entries after six months, to the present 900 entries. The perpetual waiting list has no less than 100 names to be researched and verified and more information is received each month.

In our first attempts to stick to a quarterly update schedule, it was erroneously concluded that the incoming information would begin to decrease before too long. But little did we know that the influx of information would hold constant for an indefinite time period. As seasoned librarians, we thought that we knew the library collections fairly well. We had honed our searching skills over the years and we had a pretty good grasp of the subject matter and the parameters for presenting it on the Web. Yet, as the page continued to quickly grow, it was necessary for us to also widen our views about who was notable and we had to relinquish some of the control of the page content in order for the information to be most useful to patrons.

The unexpected outcome of receiving quality data that made it possible to add up to 100 names to the Web page each month was the telling sign that there is a lesser-known history hidden in the libraries that fortifies what is being taught in classrooms. As astute as we thought we were, there is actually a group of researchers who know how to find the needed sources much better than the librarians and it is only a few–those few who show up at the reference desks–who look toward librarians for answers or help. The concept of patron assistance has been reversed for this project; instead of the librarians guiding patrons to library information, it is the patrons who are guiding the librarians to the library information in order to assist other patrons.

The information is very enlightening and the entire project has been fun. The patrons appreciate the effort. This was most evident when 27 names were selected from the Web page to be used in the publication of daily vignettes in *The Lexington Herald-Leader* during Black History Month 2004. Newspaper readers called and e-mailed the University of Kentucky Libraries and the newspaper to say thank you. Requests were received for the Web address and assistance was sought for finding the Web page as a title in the online catalog. Patrons came to the library to request the individual titles found on the Web page. There were requests for paper copies of the Web page from persons in Kentucky communities who did not have computers in their homes. They were directed to their nearest public library.

Printed copies of the Web page would not be provided because it would be a costly enterprise in terms of time and it would take more than 100 sheets of paper per request, plus packaging and postage. Notable Kentucky African Americans is strictly an online resource. The time dedicated to the page is used for researching, verifying, and updating the information and the Web page. On average, five research hours per week will yield fifteen new entries, and it takes about an hour to edit and add the new entries to both the complete file and the separate categories on the Web. The hour also includes the addition of new categories, when necessary.

The decision was made early on to use the terms provided by the contributors in naming the categories/subjects, because their terms best define who and what we were being asked to add to the page. LC subject headings could have been used for each grouping, but terms such as "My Old Kentucky Home" better define the history of race relations than would the subject heading of "Kentucky songs and music." The group headings also have the expandability to include other pertinent information, for example the story of the African American descendents of My Old Kentucky Home family.

There are presently 77 categories and the most recent ones added are automobile dealerships, wrestling, biologists, and corrections facilities. They represent what has been the outer spectrum of employment opportunities and professions. The three largest categories are educators, business, and politics; these are some of the jobs that have historically been more available to African Americans in Kentucky. One of the categories that has grown the most recently is librarians, library collections, and libraries. It was known that Henderson, KY, had the first public library and Louisville, KY, had the first library-training program, both exclusively for African Americans. But, it was learned from contributors that there were actually earlier African American librarians, in particular, Isaac E. Black, a law librarian in Covington, KY, from 1869-1874.[1]

The page is filled with this type of rewarding information. Marcus Henderson at the Central Kentucky Technical College said it best: "Ms. Jones, great site; substantive material that needs to be propagated to every school in the state. This site highlights the importance of knowledge of self and its ability to promote positive identity development for those who are unsure about our tremendous contributions to the fabric of this nation."[2]

Adding to Mr. Henderson's words, the case of African American librarians is a prime example of national contributions. Within the boundaries of Kentucky, there existed the earliest and ongoing history of African American public libraries and the training of African American librarians. This asset has had a major influence on generations of patrons who learned how to locate information about African Americans within library holdings. However, that influence received a severe blow when the number of African American librarians within the state decreased by more than 70% beginning in 1980.[3] In contrast, the number of published titles began increasing while the number of individuals who had assisted in accessing the information began decreasing and their expertise was not replaced, not even with electronic catalogs and databases. This is part of the reason why the present scenario has come about with this project, patrons guiding the librarians to the sources in order to assist other patrons.

It is because of the patrons' willingness to assist us that the project has gotten off the ground so quickly. The greatest amount of the librarians' time is spent researching incomplete information and bad links. One-third of the entries have links to other Web pages for additional information, but as is common, the links change or the destination page is removed. If another valid link can not be found, then a source in some other format will be listed. For most of the profiles, a paper source is listed for additional information. Less than half the contributed names and leads can be found in electronic databases such as Biography and Genealogy Master Index or the online version of the state newspapers, *The Lexington Herald-Leader* and *The Louisville Courier-Journal.*

Surprisingly, 90% of the contributed information has been valid including titles and authors. The remaining 10% of the contributions are not necessarily invalid, but a sufficient amount of information was not submitted or it can not be verified. The page has a high degree of accuracy, and thanks to the contributors, their efforts have saved an enormous amount of research time in locating additional names and information. None of this had been anticipated in the initial planning stage. At the end of the first year, so many changes had taken place that we had to take a break and regroup.

The Web page was evaluated to make sure that it was still on track with the University of Kentucky Libraries' mission statement and goals. And it was. The mission statement is as follows: "As the major research library in the Commonwealth, we provide comprehensive access to information essential to teaching, research, and service at the University of Kentucky, through our human resources and maximum use of technology. As library staff meets these needs for the University community, we extend information services to the Commonwealth and make unique holdings available to the world."[4]

Next, the collection development policies were reviewed. Included in all subject selectors' acquisitions duties is the responsibility for selecting titles related to African Americans, and this includes the Special Collections Department which selects titles relating to Kentucky. Also, for several years there has been A Guide to Internet Resources that includes general African American sites and Kentucky sites. The Notable Kentucky African Americans Web page is a perfect fit between the two areas as a serial title, a Web-based reference resource, and as a catalog. The selectors' past acquisition choices were a determining factor as to the amount of information found within the University of Kentucky library collections. Overall, they have done fairly well; at least 70% of the titles listed on the Web page can be found in the University of Kentucky Libraries.

The last part of the evaluation was redefining the Web page and its purpose. The original purpose had to be changed because the page was no longer a reference tool primarily for University of Kentucky patrons. A much larger group was using the page and contributing to the page. Why this had not been an obvious possibility during the planning stage was a nagging question that needed to be answered, because it would help to better define the future purpose and existence of the Web page.

Based entirely on the number of e-mail messages received, patrons in search of biographical reference sources on African American Kentuckians are in dispersed locations within Kentucky and around the country. Therefore, when help is sought from librarians, it appears that there are few requests from any one location. The Notable Kentucky African Americans Web page has become a place to deposit the knowledge. It also provides an opportunity for librarians to join the conversation on a more regular basis, and in doing so, librarians have been introduced to the particulars of a patron group that has not been so visible to the library.

Who knew that there was so much information? The answer to that question is that no one knew and if we had known, then restrictions probably would have been put in place to control the size of the Web page and the pace of its growth. Letting the page grow freely has allowed for the inclusion of different people, some of whom are not African American, and the inclusion of lesser known historical events and accomplishments, and the persons that made them happen. All of this has helped in redefining the Web page as a continually updated reference serial that exists at the pleasure of the University of Kentucky Libraries and is available to all who care to use it. The focus is still primarily African American Kentuckians and all contributions are welcomed.

The Web page may or may not continue to grow at the same rate it did the first year. But, one of the important things learned is that there are persons who have created their own bibliographies and guides from information that is deeply embedded within library collections, within special collections and historical and genealogical societies, within personal collections, and on the Web. And because of these bibliographies and guides, accurate contributions could be expediently forwarded to the University of Kentucky to be added to the Web page.

Why share the information freely? The sharing of knowledge benefits everyone involved; every one contribution that is added makes for a much larger pool from which to draw new information. Also, it is a matter of pride in dispelling the misconception that there is not much written about African American Kentuckians. Much of the information is extant but embedded within collections, which means that a patron has to find a likely source and search the content between the covers for the desired information. It is a laborious task due to the way the information has forever been packaged and published, and it is especially true with reference sources, which will be further discussed in the next section.

A BRIEF OVERVIEW OF ALTERNATIVES

One of the greatest benefits of the Web page is its value as an online reference guide to the literature found within titles. Front-end reference sources that focus on African American Kentuckians are rare and though it is a very relevant topic, it is an area that has not been revolutionized by library technologies or the Web. Other than the Notable Kentucky African Americans Web page, there are only three dated references dedicated to the subject. The titles are in paper, one of which is also on microfiche. The titles are not interrelated.

The first, *Biographical Sketches of Prominent Negro Men and Women of Kentucky*, was published in 1897 and has fifty names. The second, *The Fascinating Story of Black Kentuckians: Their Heritage and Traditions*, was published in 1982. The index was published five years later and it is owned by fewer than ten libraries in the state. The third title, *Profiles of Contemporary Black Achievers of Kentucky*, was published in 1983 and provides a list of profiles within 44 pages. All three titles are the result of original research and interviews, and there is little duplication of names and information between the three sources. Redundancy is more prevalent in the reference publications with a national scope, particularly those that are published as a serial.

This is not to say that other reference titles are not useful, whether they are in paper or online, but it takes a lot of searching in a lot of titles to find biographical information on African American Kentuckians, especially when there is not a geographic index. To put that statement in perspective, the names of African American Kentuckians can be found in general and subject specific reference titles, but there will be few or no names in any given volume. The same is true for the titles dedicated solely to Kentucky or African Americans. The exception is the early 1900s volumes of *Who's Who of the Colored Race* and *Who's Who in Colored America*.

There seems to have been a much stronger relationship in the past between those who were considered notable in Kentucky and the publishers of the African American reference titles. This was probably true due to the publication of an earlier work by Kentuckian, William J. Simmons, author of the reference title *Men of Mark* in 1887. The title was a forerunner to the African American *Who's Who* publications and was an added incentive to the inclusion of Kentuckians in future publications.

However, in spite of the strong beginning, the fact of the matter is that not much original research has been done for a reference work on African American Kentuckians beyond the three previously mentioned titles, and it should not be assumed that the Web has made a major difference. Only a third of the individual profiles are referenced to the Web from the Notable Kentucky African Americans Web page. There is not a wealth of new scholarly information being published in this medium in reference to African American Kentuckians. Also, much of what is available falls into three dominant themes: slavery, the Civil War, and the Kentucky Derby. While these are perfectly legitimate historical events, there are many other noted events, accomplishments, and associated people that can be researched in a library and other historical holdings.

Getting hits on the Web is most beneficial when a name or background information is known beforehand. For example, knowing the name of John Chenault and his background as an author, freelance writer, poet, playwright, and musician made it a lot easier to find the John Chenault Web page <http://www.liben.com/JCBio.html>, than it would have been simply knowing that he was employed at the University of Louisville Libraries. In this particular case, Mr. Chenault's Web page provided background information that would never be found in a library collection.

Searching the online catalogs of Kentucky libraries individually or as a group through the Kentucky Virtual Library Gateway <http://www.kyvl.org/> will result in a few potential biographical titles. There are not many African American Kentuckians about whom single volume biographical works have been written. The writing and publishing of such titles has occurred on a small scale and this is most evident when searching the worldwide union catalog WorldCat <http://www.oclc.org/worldcat/>. A keyword or subject search using the terms "African Americans," "Kentucky," and "biograph*" (truncated) will result in at most 116 titles in various media, mostly books. The publication dates range from 1850 to the present, and 65% of the dates are 1980 and later. Twenty-three of the earliest works are available in full-text online through the University of North Carolina at Chapel Hill project, Documenting the American South <http://docsouth.unc.edu/>.

The absolute best virtual collection is the Kentuckiana Digital Library <http://kdl.kyvl.org/>, which has included access to images of materials relating to African American Kentuckians that can be found in special collections, archives, and oral history collections from around the state. For a look inside recent book titles, Amazon's Search Inside the Book <http://www.amazon.com/exec/obidos/tg/browse/-/10197021/002-8061776-0852816> is an option. When using this source–yes it is a source–there will be quite a few hits that are off the mark within the large listing of titles. But, the joy of finding relevant information between the pages and online can offset some of the annoyance of having to search through hundreds of titles. Searching online by keyword is much more accurate and efficient than randomly flipping through the pages of hundreds of titles hoping to catch a glimpse of the desired information.

In the search for articles, many databases provided by the libraries will result in some hits. Those that will yield the most relevant results are subscription databases such as JSTOR, LexisNexis, and the newspaper databases, *The Lexington Herald-Leader* and *The Louisville Courier-Journal*.

More of the relevant articles will be found in local serial publications and older journals that are not indexed in an electronic database or available full-text online. Examples of such titles are the *Berea College Magazine*, *The Louisville Defender*, *Register of the Kentucky Historical Society*, *The Brown American*, *The African Watchman*, and *Opportunity*. It is within these types of publications that patrons will find the names of such persons as Raoul Cunningham and Rev. William A.

Jones, Sr., two of Kentucky's Civil Rights leaders, and Joshua and Matilda Dunbar, the parents of poet Paul L. Dunbar.

Until there is a better mechanism for locating biographical information on African American Kentuckians, there will be the challenge of creating a comprehensive guide to the literature that is accessible to the largest clientele. The Web page, Notable Kentucky African Americans is only the beginning of an answer. In a perfect world it would be possible to look inside all collections in Kentucky and to search all available databases, similar to Amazon's Search Inside the Book, using one interface to search it all. Someday, maybe it will happen.

CONCLUSION

For now, Notable Kentucky African Americans is one more option. Over the next year the Web page will once again be allowed to develop, but with some additional enhancements. A source index will be added, which will contain all of the titles that appear on the Web page. It will be noted if a title can be found in the University of Kentucky Libraries, other Kentucky Libraries, or elsewhere. Also, there are plans to subdivide the three largest categories: business, education, and politics. These categories will probably become even larger as the second phase of the research takes place–locating and verifying more information within journals and other serial publications. Up to this point, the Web page has not been a time burden and it is hoped that the time it takes to locate more citations in serial publications will be as minimal as that for the books.

As a final note, there have been discussions within the University of Kentucky Library System about turning the Web page into a Web database. For now, it is nothing more than a discussion. Final decisions will be made next year following the reorganization of the library personnel and the library Web pages.

NOTES

1. Harris, T. H. H. Creating windows of opportunity: Isaac E. Black and the African American Experience in Kentucky. Register of the Kentucky Historical Society 2000 98(2): 155-177.
2. Marcus Henderson, "African Americans in Kentucky Web Page," 13 December 2004, personal e-mail, (20 December 2004).

3. This is according to the numbers for African American librarians in Kentucky found in the EEO Files of the U.S. Census for 1980, 1990, and 2000.

4. *Initiative, Mission & Vision Statement*. 3 December 2004. University of Kentucky Libraries. 28 November 2004 <http://www.uky.edu/Libraries/lcvision.html>.

WORKS CITED

A Guide to Internet Resources. Ed. Rob Aken. 29 September 2004. University of Kentucky Libraries. 28 November 2004 <http://www.uky.edu/Subject/>.

Census '90 Detailed Occupation by Race, Hispanic Origin and Sex. U.S. Census Bureau. 21 December 2004 <http://censtats.census.gov/eeo/eeo.shtml/>.

Census 2000 EEO Data Tool. U.S. Census Bureau. 21 December 2004 <http://www.census.gov/eeo2000/>.

Department of Commerce Bureau of the Census. 19th Census of the United States. (1980 Census Population, VI Characteristics of the Population, Chapter D, Detailed Population Characteristics, Part 19, Kentucky) (p. 19-248). Washington, DC: Government Printing Office.

Documenting the American South. Ed. UNC University Library. 9 November 2004. University of North Carolina at Chapel Hill. 28 November 2004 <http://docsouth.unc.edu/index.html>.

InfoKat. 11 August 2003. University of Kentucky Libraries. 28 November 2004 <http://infokat.uky.edu/cgi-bin/Pwebrecon.cgi?DB=local&PAGE=First>.

Initiative, Mission & Vision Statement. 3 March 2004. University of Kentucky Libraries. 28 November 2004 <http://www.uky.edu/Libraries/lcvision.html>.

Kentuckiana Digital Library. Kentucky Virtual Library. 28 November 2004 <http://kdl.kyvl.org/>.

Notable Kentucky African Americans. Ed. Reinette F. Jones and Rob Aken. 16 November 2004 University of Kentucky Libraries. 28 November 2004 <http://www.uky.edu/Subject/aakyall.html>.

Search Inside the Book. Amazon.com, Inc. 28 November 2004 <http://www.amazon.com/exec/obidos/tg/browse/-/10197021/104-4449208-7895147>.

WorldCat. OCLC. 28 November 2004 <http://www.oclc.org/worldcat/>.

Frontiers of Effort:
Librarians
and Professional Development Blogs

Melissa Laning
Catherine Lavallée-Welch
Margo Smith

SUMMARY. This article defines blogs and distinguishes them from other Web sites. A brief history of the blog format is included along with an exploration of the growth and acceptance of blogs as a professional information reference source for librarians. The authors review the literature on blogs and recommend a set of criteria for determining the value of blogs as a professional development tool. They also review examples of Weblogs meeting the screening criteria. *[Article copies available for a fee from The Haworth Document Delivery Service: 1-800-HAWORTH. E-mail address: <docdelivery@haworthpress.com> Website: <http://www.HaworthPress.com> © 2005 by The Haworth Press, Inc. All rights reserved.]*

KEYWORDS. Blogs, Internet sources, librarianship, reference sources, Weblogs

Melissa Laning is Assessment & Resource Planning Librarian, Ekstrom Library (E-mail: melissa.laning@louisville.edu); Catherine Lavallée-Welch is Electronic Resources Librarian, Kersey Library (E-mail: catherine.lavallee-welch@louisville.edu); and Margo Smith is Collection Access & Management Librarian, Ekstrom Library (E-mail: margo.smith@louisville.edu), all at the University of Louisville, Louisville, KY 40292.

[Haworth co-indexing entry note]: "Frontiers of Effort: Librarians and Professional Development Blogs." Laning, Melissa, Catherine Lavallée-Welch, and Margo Smith. Co-published simultaneously in *Journal of Library Administration* (The Haworth Information Press, an imprint of The Haworth Press, Inc.) Vol. 43, No. 3/4, 2005, pp. 161-179; and: *Evolving Internet Reference Resources* (ed: William Miller, and Rita M. Pellen) The Haworth Information Press, an imprint of The Haworth Press, Inc., 2006, pp. 161-179. Single or multiple copies of this article are available for a fee from The Haworth Document Delivery Service [1-800-HAWORTH, 9:00 a.m. - 5:00 p.m. (EST). E-mail address: docdelivery@haworthpress.com].

Available online at http://www.haworthpress.com/web/JLA
© 2005 by The Haworth Press, Inc. All rights reserved.
doi:10.1300/J111v43n03_13

INTRODUCTION

Professional development is a continuous process in which one is engaged in life-long learning in order to update his or her skills, knowledge, and competencies in a chosen career. The library world may be one of the most rapidly changing work environments due to advances in technology and the proliferation of sources of information. Managing an LIS career requires time and effort and there are no set rules that apply to all. Over the World Wide Web, there are different kinds of Web sites that can help a librarian in his or her professional development. This article focuses on a specific type of Web site, the blog.

This article introduces the concepts of Weblogs and blogging, and describes their use and functionalities. It also discusses the value of blogs as a professional development tool for librarians and other information professionals. Criteria for evaluating LIS-related blogs as professional development tools are then proposed. Finally, a list of blogs corresponding to those criteria is given.

WHAT IS A BLOG?

The term blog comes from "Web Log" and now refers to a specific type of Web site composed of content organized in the form of dated entries, in reverse chronological order. Laurel A. Clyde described blogs as taking " the form of a diary, a news service (or summaries of and links to current news items on a topic), a collection of links to other Web sites, a series of book reviews, reports of activity on a project, a journal or diary, a photographic record of an event or activity."[1]

Blogs are an example of what is called "social software" which is software built around the support for conversational interaction between individuals or groups, social feedback, and social networks. Other examples of social software are e-mail, chat, instant messaging, wikis, networking Web sites such as Friendster, multi-user dungeons, and collaborative filters like Amazon readers' recommendations.[2]

Blogs first started in the late 1990s and were mostly lists of links organized by dated entries. Jorn Barger coined the term "Weblog" at the end of 1997. The number of blogs grew gradually until July 1999 when *Pitas*, the first free blogging tool was launched. Hundreds of blogs were then created, spurred on by the launch, one month later, of other do-it-yourself services such as Blogger and Groksoup.[3] Supported by the new technology, the phenomenon quickly grew because of its appeal and its ease of use. There are now millions of blogs on the Web and several authoring tools.

If blogs were more personal ventures at the beginning, professional and corporate blogs are now quickly developing as a major subset of the Blogverse. Blogs by libraries and librarians are no exception. Some of the oldest LIS blogs include oss4lib <http://oss4lib.org/>, librarian.net <http://oss4lib.org/>, <http://oss4lib.org/>, and AcqWeb <http://www.acqweb.org/>, all created in 1999.

One difference that distinguishes a blog from other Web sites is the technology used to build it. Weblogging software permits the most casual of computer users to publish quickly and easily on the Web, without having to know HTML. Interfaces are intuitive, using icons like those in word processor software. Publication is timely and the content can be edited quickly and as frequently as needed.

The second difference is the content. Typically, the contents of a blog are more dynamic than those of a more run-of-the-mill Web site. The primary purpose of the blog is to communicate up-to-the minute information, in short increments as opposed to a Web site in which only a part of the content might be dynamic. For example, a news page for an organization's Web site may be the only portion of the site that routinely changes. Of course, a Web site can be comprised of more traditional pages and include a blog for dynamic content.

A third difference is the purpose of the sites. As with other social software, one of the objectives is to create communication between the blogger and his/her reader. There are several functionalities that appear in blogging software that permit interaction between the participants: commenting, citing, referring, and even co-authoring.

Most of the blogging software products available share common functionalities. The extent of their use is obviously the choice of the blog editor.

- *Ads:* Some free services will include commercial advertisements in the blog if it is hosted on their servers. Bloggers may also choose to place ads to generate revenue.
- *Archives:* This feature permits readers to retrieve previous posts based on date of entry. The archive can appear in daily, weekly, or monthly increments depending on the tool.
- *Audio posting:* Some services have the capability to host streaming audio entries, e.g., Audblog by Blogger.
- *Blogroll:* This feature is a list of the other blogs the editor/publisher reads.

- *Categories:* This feature allows categorization of posts by subject. Headings are created and assigned by the blogger so that readers can retrieve all entries for a particular subject area of interest.
- *Commenting:* Most services permit readers to post their own comments on an entry. The comments are then available for others to read and comment on further. Commenting can be turned off.
- *Draft:* This is the ability to save a post as a draft, before publication.
- *Feed:* This feature allows the content of a blog to be automatically pulled into an aggregator each time it is updated. An aggregator is a software application that permits reading the content of several blogs in one location. The two main types are RSS and Atom.
- *Image posting:* Most services make it possible to include images in posts. Some blogs are entirely dedicated to pictures.
- *Permanent link:* This feature creates a separate URL for each post, making it easier to link to a specific post.
- *Pre- and post-date entries:* This feature provides a direct link to the entries posted directly before and after a searched permanent link.
- *Recent posts:* Some services automatically list the titles of a pre-determined number of recent posts.
- *Search engine:* This makes it possible to add a search engine to a blog.
- *Template:* Most services will offer blog templates with pre-coded layouts to less HTML-savvy bloggers.
- *Time, date, and author stamps:* This allows each post to include the date and time of publication, and the name of its author. The date and time can be edited and the name can be chosen.
- *Title:* This feature offers the possibility of giving each post a unique title.
- *Trackback:* This feature creates a link between two blogs that permit one to see where a particular post has been cited.[4]

There are currently over four hundred blogs dealing with library and information issues published by librarians or by libraries as an organization. They cover different types of libraries and different special interests. There are blogs, for example, for science librarians, youth services librarians, cataloguing librarians, or blogs that cover the use of technology in libraries, legal issues in libraries, and open access publishing. Others monitor the media and other sources for local, national, and international news in the field.

Blogs can alleviate information overload by helping the reader filter the important news in any domain. The information has been pre-evaluated, summarized, annotated, commented upon, and delivered to them on a timely basis. Similar to an alerting service or a selective dissemination of information service, blogs can pinpoint information of interest. The reader can use blogs as a professional development tool to stay abreast in the LIS field, and follow new resources, technological advances, research, vendor activity, new materials, conferences, and job postings.

LITERATURE REVIEW

Because blogs are a relatively new format, the literature on blogs, especially in a professional context, is somewhat limited. Until the past year, it is likely that many people have never even heard the word or concept mentioned in their regular reading; however 2004 has seen a large increase in exposure for blogs.

For example, a search of the EBSCO Academic database using "Weblogs" as a search term identifies no hits before 1999, three in 1999/2000, nine in 2000/2001, forty in 2001/2002, one hundred sixty-six in 2002/03, and two hundred sixty-two in 2003/2004. Finding any items published prior to 1999 requires searching through multiple indexes.

The focus of most relevant articles from 1997-2000 is on the art and experience of blog practice, and can best be described as self-absorbed. As early adopters discovered this new tool for expression, they promoted the practice and their own work by spreading the word through newsletters and other less traditional outlets. Of course they also used their own blogs and Web pages to expound on the topic. *We've Got Blog: How Weblogs Are Changing Our Culture* is a compilation of these early writings and provides insight into the excitement experienced by some of the first bloggers as they discovered a new, easy, and very immediate way to share information on a topic of personal and often intense interest.[5]

Another current in the literature is the "how-to" article or book. One book that has been well reviewed is *Blogging: Genius Strategies for Instant Web Content* by Biz Stone, but at this point numerous others are available.[6] A third focus of the popular literature is the blog history, covering the growth of the blogger community, or blogosphere, as well as the evolution of blog styles. This past year has seen a vast increase in the number of blog history articles, most likely due to the increased attention blogs received during the 2004 Democratic and Republican Conventions. One of the first blog historians is Rebecca Blood who wrote "Weblogs: A History and Perspective" in 2000.[7] In 2004, *Time* published 15 articles about blogs including one with a blog timeline.[8] A noticeable difference in the selections from previous news items from the 2004 *Time* selections is that they are about, and not by, bloggers, and there is a somewhat more analytical approach than previously noted.

Starting in 2001/02, blogs also start to appear in more academic literature sources, particularly in education journals. The general thrust of many of the more recent articles is on the use of blogs as a new pedagogical tool, and they provide case studies of blog usage.[9] Another body of literature discusses the blog as a tool of scholarly communication.[10]

The library-related literature on blogs follows basically the same timeline and evolution as the general literature. Beginning in 2001/02, there are a small number of articles that introduce the concept of blogs, provide instruction about how to create them, and introduce case studies of library usage.[11] One early entry is "You Must Read This: Library Weblogs" by Walt Crawford. He covers blog basics, categorizes types of blogs, and discusses the potential value of blogs. An important aspect of Crawford's article is that he considers the latter issue from the perspective of the readers, not the writers of blogs. This is one of the first indications that blogs might be considered a tool for professional development.[12]

A more recent overview is the essay "Throw Another Blog on the Wire: Libraries and the Weblogging Phenomena" by Harder and Reichardt.[13] They offer a formal definition of a blog and even more evidence that blogs can be a good professional development reference source for librarians. The authors also point out that blogs can be used to communicate information updates to both internal and external audiences. A very recent article in the library literature describes the blog usage by a group of law librarians within the same firm to keep each other informed about such matters as password changes, new resources, and information about vendor visits.[14]

BLOG ANALYSIS

As more and more librarian-focused blogs emerge, their role and value in professional communication become a legitimate question. The

Libdex <http://www.libdex.com> Web site, one of several online indexes of library-related Web sites, links to approximately 150 library Weblogs created by U.S. librarians and nearly 70 more created by librarians in other countries. The authors reviewed all the U.S. Weblogs listed on Libdex as well as the selections from Canada, England, France, and Germany. Despite the tremendous variety of topics covered and stylistic differences, the majority fell into three categories or types: personal musings or diaries, bulletin boards of activities, and topical.

In addition to developing this overall schema, the authors screened the entries based on whether or not they fit the definition of a reference tool and conveyed information intended for the professional development of the reader. Lastly, the authors developed a set of criteria for evaluating the quality of the blogs that met all the other filters for inclusion in this review.

Examples of blogs in the personal musings category include: Collecting My Thoughts <http://collectingmythoughts.blogspot.com>; DrWeb's Domain <http://drweb.typepad.com>; indierocklibrarian <http://www.indierocklibrarian.com>; and, Bloug <http://louisrosenfeld.com/home/>. This type of blog may contain entries of interest to other librarians, but generally their value has more to do with entertainment than professional development. Furthermore, it is also doubtful that they would meet any established definition of a reference tool since the content is quite idiosyncratic and unpredictable.

Examples of blogs in the bulletin board category include: Chi Lib Rocks! <http://radio.weblogs.com/0111803/>; ILL News <http://www.sls.lib.il.us/ill/blog>; and, h20boro lib blog <http://www.waterborolibrary.org/blog.htm>. The purpose of this type of blog is more clearly information sharing than the personal musings type; however in most cases the intended audience were users of a particular library or service. Chi Lib Rocks! is an example of this blog type used for professional development information-sharing, by listing all types of LIS-related learning opportunities within a specific geographic area. This format seems amenable to professional development usage, but has not been fully exploited for that purpose.

Topical blogs were the category most likely to be considered as a professional development reference tool. Of course, not all topical blogs created by librarians are focused on improving the practice of librarianship; however most of the sources reviewed in this article are from that category.

In the Blogverse, a good blog is one that is frequently "bloggrolled" or linked by other blogs. BlogStreet <http://www.blogstreet.com/biq100.html> ranks blogs according to the number of times a blog is blogrolled. It also assigns a Blog Influence Quotient (BIQ) for those blogs linked by high-ranked blogs.

The authors chose a more qualitative set of criteria for including items in this review. They are:

- Title or tag lines immediately convey the blog's topic or focus
- Posts are updated regularly and most recent is no more than one month old
- Posts are brief and contain links to further resources
- Posts are consistent with blog's focus
- Posts are archived both chronologically and by subject
- Site contains a search box
- Site uses good graphic design principles
- Blog's lifespan exceeds one year

CONCLUSION

Rapid advances in technology have both alleviated and exacerbated the demands on librarians in their efforts to provide resources and access to resources for their user communities. In this environment, most librarians would agree that professional development is a necessary component in maintaining quality, on-going library services. In their article, "Integrating Informal Professional Development in the Work of Reference," Karla J. Block and Julia A. Kelly offer several informal methods of professional development to supplement more formal methods. Two of the informal methods suggested are, "e-sessions," in-house presentations on a particular database or special topic and "AskRef," a locally created database of unusual, common or difficult reference questions.[15]

Blogs can be an ideal addition to a list of informal methods of professional development. They can provide a forum for discussion about a particular topic or serve as a reference work that is consistently updated by an expert in the field, much like an alerting service. Furthermore, blog technology is easy to use so that creating a blog can itself be considered a form of professional development.

BLOG LIST

The blogs listed below are ones that the authors selected for their usefulness as professional development tools. They are, for the most part, topical blogs.

beSpacific: Accurate, Focused Law and Technology News *<http://www.bespacific.com/>*

The posts, which are updated almost daily, cover law and technology news, particularly where they intersect. There is an emphasis on issues such as copyright, privacy, and censorship that have a significant impact on information policy and librarianship practice.

Each segment of the post briefly describes a news item and provides links to relevant documents. The entries are separated with several visual cues so that the reader can easily scan the day's news for topics of interest. One of the features that distinguish this blog from others is that each entry is labeled with one or more topic headings that become the basis for archiving by topic. This technique gives the reader an understanding of where to look in the archives for similar articles.

beSpacific has been public since early 2003 and has an archival record back to August 2002. Its creator is Sabrina I. Pacifici, a law librarian with extensive experience in legal publishing. She developed *LLRX.com*, which is still published, in 1996; it was one of the first "Webzines" focused on legal issues.

Confessions of a Science Librarian *<http://www.jdupuis.blogspot.com/>*

John Dupuis, author of the Confessions, is a science librarian at York University in Toronto, Canada. His blog supplies information tidbits of interest to science and engineering librarians. He also offers information on more general LIS subjects and electronic resources. Occasionally, Dupuis includes entries on science fiction literature and computer chess, two of his personal interests.

The blog has been published since the end of 2002. Entries are regular, concise, and relevant. The various articles from the sci-tech or other LIS literature that Dupuis selects are particularly interesting and thought-provoking. He also regularly explores the lighter, funnier side of science. The blog contains a search box, a feed, and chronological archives, but no topical archives.

EngLib: for the sci-tech librarian
<http://www.englib.info/>

The posts cover news and other information specifically of professional interest to sci-tech librarians, such as conference and product news. Occasionally, a more personal post will appear such as the recent announcement of a colleague's bypass surgery. Links to relevant documents, Web sites, or people are embedded within each entry.

Posts appear at least a few times each week, and often daily, and the archives date from February 2002. The posts for each day are clearly divided and each brief entry has a separate headline. Archival posts can be retrieved from either a category or date index.

Catherine Lavallée-Welch is the creator of *EngLib* and she is a sci-tech librarian at the University of Louisville.

The Handheld Librarian
<http://www.handheldlib.blogspot.com/>

This site is for librarians using and working with handheld technologies. It provides information about books, articles, conferences, workshops, and other opportunities for learning more about handhelds. In addition, this site also features posts from others who have questions about handheld technology applications, creating a more informal and interactive space.

Posts are made on an irregular basis but are frequent enough to still be current. The archives, which go back to early 2002, are only available from a chronological index. A feature that is being beta tested on this site is called BlogChat, which allows the reader to interact with the bloggers in real time.

Tom Dennis, Mary Peterson, Lori Bell, Terri Ross Embry, Tom Peters, Peg Burnette, and Barbara Fullerton, who created/maintain this blog, are from various institutions.

The In Season Christian Librarian
<http://www.inseasonchristianlibrarian.blogspot.com/>

A site designed for a very specific audience–librarians in Christian academic libraries. The posts provide brief commentary and links to information resources, television programs, and events primarily about the theology and practice of Christianity. Some of the references are to items about religion in general, other religions, or occasionally to other resources unrelated to religion, e.g., National Book Award winners Web site. Overall, however, the focus and intended audience is very clear.

Entries are updated daily during the week and sometimes on weekends. The archives are only arranged chronologically, although there is a list by title of recent, previous posts.

There is no information provided except through reading the posts about the individual writing them.

The Kept-Up Academic Librarian
<http://keptup.typepad.com/academic/>

The Kept-Up Academic Librarian is a relatively new blog, begun in February 2004; its purpose is to help academic librarians to stay abreast of news and development in the higher education field. Its editor, Steven J. Bell, is the director at the Gutman Library at the Philadelphia University.

This blog is updated several times a week with posts covering student life, academic affairs, and technological and financial issues among others.

The usual blog characteristics are all present for an effective browsing (topic and chronological archives, a list of recent posts and permanent links) but the page doesn't have a search engine. The design is efficient and easy to read with visible links. There is a companion "Keeping Up" Web site with a series of links to help information professionals with self-guided professional development <http://staff.philau.edu/bells/keepup/>.

librarian.net
<http://librarian.net/>

librarian.net is a classic LIS blog and one of the most widely read and cited. Being on the Internet since 1993, and blogging since December 1999, Jessamyn West has since enjoyed a reputation as an opinion maker in the library world and as a "radical librarian." She gives her opinion on a wide range of library issues and monitors the media for LIS references. Ms. West reports on her travels to events and meetings. In addition, she is a frequent presenter at conferences.

The blog went through a few incarnations through the years. While the present layout is pleasant and understated, it is difficult to differentiate between the entries. Finding the permanent link for each entry is also a bit tricky. The blog has an FAQ, a booklist the editor has been reading, and recommended links. Entries are posted almost every day.

Library Stuff
<http://www.librarystuff.net/>

The byline indicates that this is the "library Weblog dedicated to resources for keeping current and professional development." Steven M. Cohen, a law librarian based in New York State, has been publishing the popular blog *Library Stuff* since August 2000. Cohen provides entries that consist of brief comments and embedded links, which reflect the library and technology worlds. He was named one of the *Library Journal*'s Movers and Shakers in 2004.

The blog content would be more accessible if there were topical categories for the entries. A search box would also be a helpful addition. There are no additional links in the sidemenu but rather a listing of the editor's presentations and publications.

The SciTech Library Question
<http://stlq.info/>

The STLQ blog, as it is more commonly known, is directed, "but not restricted," as its byline says, to engineering and science librarians. The two editors, Geoff Harder and Randy Reichardt, are academic librarians from the University of Calgary, Alberta. There are also other occasional contributors.

Besides science and engineering resources and news, other topics are covered such as technology issues and more wide-ranging matters like open access publishing. The authors often reproduce, with permission, discussions happening on various listservs. The posts are sometimes lengthy. The right-hand menu offers interesting lists of Web sites, blogs, and feeds of interest to sci-tech librarians.

LISNews
<www.lisnews.com>

LISNews is an excellent example of a collaborative blog. Each day, blog collaborators post a variety of subjects that are LIS-related, either local, national, or international in focus. Started by Blake Carver in November 1999, the blog consists of volunteer contributors who provide the content and anyone may suggest a story.

There are several tools with which to navigate through the voluminous content: categories, sections, archive, most recent posts listings, top stories listings, a search engine, and feeds. Additional options are available for registered users. By creating an account, readers can set up their own blog, filter and monitor discussions, receive the headlines by e-mail, and become an author.

Each entry is clearly indicated and there is an icon that illustrates each category to which the entry belongs. While an icon can be a useful tool for recognition of the category, the LISNews icons are somewhat distracting. The number of hits each entry has received is tabulated below the entry. Comments are numerous and often spirited.

Open Access News
<http://www.earlham.edu/~peters/fos/fosblog.html>

The entry for the blog on *Libdex* briefly notes the purpose of the blog and lists its creator, Peter Suber. The blog's intention is further defined on the front page, top of the right sidebar: "The main purpose of the blog is to gather and disseminate news about the open-access movement, and to harness the energy and knowledge of a wide group of contributors in doing so." There is another link to an expanded version of the blog's charge as well as an article by Peter Suber on the definition of Open Access. Links to the author's philosophy, vita, and other related interests further define the blog's focus.

The entries are archived weekly starting with 5/26/02. There is a site search box powered by *Atomz*. Readability is excellent with brief daily entries that are link-rich with related corporate affiliations, articles, and open access journal citations.

Open Stacks–Promoting Literacy for All
<http://openstacks.net/os/>

The site is well designed, with clear fonts. The single sidebar is outlined in black with the same dark khaki-colored background as the main part of the page. At the bottom of each daily entry is the time the entry was posted, a link for commentary, number of trackbacks, and the category under which the entry is filed. However on 10/16/04, Mr. Greg

Schwartz, the author of the blog, noted that comments were no longer a feature of his blog due to the "spam nuisance factor."

Each entry is assigned a category that allows the entry to be collocated. The categories are listed on the sidebar of the front page, e.g., accessibility, news, and professional development. Each category has varying numbers of entries. The categories are helpful for searching, but including a search engine would enhance accessibility.

The tone is informal and personal; for instance Mr. Schwartz thanks the person who gave him the idea to move his content columns to the left. Mr. Schwartz shares accessibility and usability tips with users, such as a link to "Designing a more usable World" sponsored by the Trace Center at the University of Wisconsin which promotes "Universal Design" principles.

There is an interesting blogroll entitled "My Feeds" that is categorized by LIS, news, "Web geekiness," and miscellany. LIS has more than 100 entries, news has 6 entries, and Web geekiness has about 30 entries. The sidebar also includes a list of the author's favorite sites about blog technology.

oss4lib–Open Source Systems for Libraries
<http://www.oss4lib.org/>

The responsibility for and authority of the blog are readily visible on the front page with several topic links at right top corner that include "About" which states the mission of the blog: "Our mission is to cultivate the collaborative power of open source software engineering to build better and free systems for use in libraries"; the blog's provenance and start date are respectively, Yale Medical Library, 1999.

The topic label "Projects" lists 95 open source programs related to library technology, like *Citation Manager*, an online citation database for end user and *Pears*, for text storage and retrieval.

The bi-monthly entries are arranged by names of open system projects and date of posting; latest entry is from 2004/11/15. There are always at least 2 entries per month. The content is definitely directed toward the librarian-technologist with advanced computer programming skills.

The content archives are arranged by date via *SourceForge.net*, which lists e-mail headings as the subject. The result is somewhat uneven and ranges from "John Doe is out of the office" to threads of discussions like "Re: Reviews of *BibX*."

Peter Scott's Library Blog
<http://blog.xrefer.com/>

Peter Scott, an academic librarian at the University of Saskatchewan Library, is the well-known editor of this blog sponsored by electronic publisher *xrefer*.

The great attraction to this blog is the quantity and quality of the entries. Numerous entries are made every day on this blog and cover the whole range of LIS issues and news from around the world. There are no categories for the entries but there are fourteen links of interest to librarians on the left sidebar area of the front page: recent books, associations, conferences, journals, academic library blogs, school library blogs, etc.

A convenient Google Search box for the site is located at the top of the first page that also provides a button for a total Web search or one limited to Mr. Scott's blog. The site's layout is streamlined with one background color, one font, three font sizes, and no outline borders.

The scope of the blog covers a variety of library issues from Canada, the U.S., and the UK with occasional international entries, e.g., a link to presentations from the 9th European conference of medical libraries. There are regular title updates about e-resource providers, e.g., Emerald e-journal provider, and a list of titles available from the EBSCO Journal Service, EJS (1/31/04).

There are regular announcements of online versions of library, technology and topical journals, e.g., *Library Quarterly* (University of Chicago Press) and *Journal of Endocrinology* available via HighWire Press. A fun feature is the Friday brainteaser from *xrefer* on a variety of topics such as rock n' roll history, names of obscure hobbies, etc.

The ResourceShelf: Resources and News for Information Professionals
<http://resourceshelf.freepint.com/>

Mr. Gary Price is the author of the blog and in the "bio" post the blog is described as follows: "This daily electronic newsletter is where he posts news and other resources of interest to the online researcher." Given the wide scope of coverage and ease of use, this is a modest description.

The blog's first entry is dated 3/1/01. Entries are archived by month and there are an average of 15-20 posts per month. Even without a list of categories posted, many daily entries are consistently subdivided by categories, e.g., "Resources, Reports, Tools, Lists, Full-Text documents," "Resource of the Week," "Professional Reading Shelf." Entries for the category "Professional Reading Shelf" cover broad professional interests and are often subdivided, e.g., "Professional Reading Shelf: Librarianship," and "Professional Reading Shelf: Cataloging." Another example of subdivisions use is "Information Quality–Web" and "Information Quality–Health Information."

There is wide-ranging representation of resources related to library type, current affairs, and general technology issues, as well as government and private resources. The variety seems endless and yet the recurring categories provide a sorting function that is not rigid. This is the only site reviewed which provides a search box for the entire site as well as a search box for the month currently viewed. The site's currency, depth, and consistency are ideal for continuing professional development.

Retrofitted Librarian: News and Information for San Francisco Bay Area Library Workers
<http://retrofittedlibrarian.blogspot.com/>

Ms. Susan Rosenblatt started the blog in November 2002 to address general and technical issues related to librarianship. In May 2003, she re-focused the blog to California-related library issues. The blog is well-designed, easy to read, and archived every month since November 2002. Links to presentations are provided when available, and summaries of presentations are provided in "bulleted" format when no direct links are present. A visit to the entry for November 2003 indicates that approximately 75% of the entries are linked descriptions of conferences/workshops. Three of the four links checked were still available. "Retrofitted Librarian" is an excellent model for a location-based, professional interest blog. There are many entries about the USA PATRIOT Act and how libraries throughout California have responded with policies about patron records. Numerous entries are included about California legislation affecting both public and academic libraries.

Scholarly Electronic Publishing Weblog
<http://info.lib.uh.edu/sepb/sepw.htm>

Charles W. Bailey's blog presents a comprehensive and current bibliography about electronic scholarly publication. The bibliographic entries are arranged by title of the source for which links are provided. Two samples from the entry of October 11, 2004 include the articles, "Do Open-Access Articles Have a Greater Research Impact?" from

College & Research Libraries, 65, no. 5 (2004), and the article "News and commentary about the open access movement," *SPARC Open Access Newsletter*, no. 78 (2004), by Peter Suber.

The earliest entry is dated June 7, 2001 and all entries are archived monthly. The predicted day for the next update is just under the day of the preceding update. All entries are cumulated by month/year.

The layout is text-only annotated bibliography style. There are no sidebars. More than half of the entries are briefly annotated.

At the bottom of the monthly page there is a separate "bottombar" which includes a link to the license agreement for using the Weblog, contact information, and the authorship statement.

The Shifted Librarian
<http://www.theshiftedlibrarian.com/>

Ms. Jenny Levine provides her definition of the shifted librarian as "someone who is working to make libraries more portable." She believes that "NetGen" patrons expect information to come to them, rather than the patron going to the information.

The site focuses primarily on access technology issues for public libraries with some entries related to academic library access issues. There is a search box for the entire site. For instance there is an entry in which she discusses RSS feeds, their use in the K-12 classroom, and linking with the public library. There are other entries that report on and link to articles of interest such as the *Christian Science Monitor* article about the Braille version of Harry Potter in 13 volumes.

The tone is conversational and the entries stay focused. The first entry appeared on January 13, 2002 with monthly entries thereafter. The site is archived by month. First entry of November 2003 was an explanation that there would be a hiatus. The first page sidebar includes a blogroll of approximately 150 entries that are not arranged in alphabetical or subject order, but which are fun for browsing.

User Education Resources for Librarians
<http://libeducation.blogspot.com/>

Teresa Hartman, librarian at the University of Nebraska Medical Center, authors the blog. A clear statement of the blog's purpose is on the top sidebar on the front page. It states, "Topics and issues that will be posted here: user education, distance education support, e-learning support, librarianship, information access." The content focus is medical librarianship with links to recent articles related to medical library issues, e.g., "eMedicine," and "10 best medical sites" in publications such as the *Boston Globe, Business Week,* and *Wired.*

There are regular entries for "call for papers" from the Medical Library Association, and the Special Library Association divisions. The brevity of each entry makes the blog an ideal current awareness resource.

The blog began in November 2003 and is consistently updated. The monthly archives are posted on the front-page sidebar. The use of one font with ample white space lends itself to easy reading. There was a hiatus of roughly three months that is succinctly explained. Fortunately, Ms. Hartmann had resumed the blog with her characteristically robust and varied entries.

NOTES

1. Laurel A. Clyde, "Library Weblogs." *Library Management* 25.4/5 (2004): 183-189.

2. Stowe Boyd, "Are You Ready for Social Software?" *Darwin Magazine* (May 2003) (Accessed on 11/22/2004).

3. Rebecca Blood, "Weblogs: A History and Perspective. 7 September 2000" *rebecca's pocket.* <http://www.rebeccablood.net/essays/weblog_history.html> (Accessed on 11/22/2004).

4. C. Lavallée-Welch, "Jumping on the Blogwagon for Libraries." Brick and Click Libraries Symposium, October 22 2004, Maryville, MO: pp. 68-76.

5. John Rodzilla, ed. *We've Got Blog: How Weblogs Are Changing Our Culture.* Cambridge, MA: Perseus Publishing, 2002.

6. Biz Stone, *Blogging: Genius Strategies for Instant Web Content.* Indianapolis: New Riders Publishers, 2002.

7. Blood.

8. Lev Grossman, "Meet Joe Blog." *Time* 163:25 (June 21, 2004): 65-69.

9. For examples of the literature in this area see: Jo Ann Oravec, "Bookmarking the World: Weblog Applications in Education." *Journal of Adolescent & Adult Literacy* 45:7 (April 2002): 616-621; Greg Weiler, "Using Weblogs in the Classroom." *English Journal* 92:5 (May 2003): 73-75; Oravec, "Blending by Blogging: Weblogs in Blended Learning Initiatives," *Journal of Educational Media* 28:2-3 (October 2003); and Christian Wagner, "Put Another (B)log on the Wire: Publishing Learning Logs as Weblogs," *Journal of Information Systems Education* 14:2 (July 2003): 131.

10. For examples see: David Glenn, "Scholars Who Blog: The Soapbox of the Digital Age Draws a Crowd of Academics." *The Chronicle of Higher Education* 49:39 (June 6, 2003): A14; and Robert J. Ambrogi, "Seek and Ye Shall Find–With the Right Search Engine." *Legal Times* (July 12, 2004): 18.

11. For examples see: Steven M. Cohen, "RSS for Non-Technie Librarians." *LLRX.com* (June 3, 2002). http://www.llrx.com/features/rssforlibrarians.html (Accessed on 8/2/2004); Doug Goans and Teri M. Vogel, "Building a Home for Library News

with a Blog." *Computers in Libraries* 23:10 (November/December 2003): 20-26; Steven A. Stone, "The Library Blog: A New Communication Tool." *Kentucky Libraries* 67:4 (Fall 2003): 14-15; and, Cohen, "Library Weblogs." *Public Libraries* 43:1 (January/February 2004): 26-27.

12. Walt Crawford, "You Must Read This: Library Weblogs." *American Libraries* 32:9 (October 2001): 74-76.

13. Goeffrey Harder & Randy Reichardt, "Throw Another Blog on the Wire: Libraries and the Weblogging Phenomena." *Feliciter* 49:2 (2003): 85-88.

14. Diahann Munoz, "Blogs Hit the Library: How One Law Firm's Librarians Found a Way to Stay Connected." *Legal Times* (July 5, 2004): 29.

15. Karla Block & Julia A. Kelly, "Integrating Informal Professional Development into the Work of Reference." *The Reference Librarian* 72 (2001): 207-217.

Psyched About Psychology Internet Resources

Alice J. Perez

SUMMARY. What resources does the reference librarian use to assist people conducting research in the vast field of psychology? This article surveys resources, both free and proprietary, which can help the reference librarian assist students and faculty. Included in this article are descriptions of proprietary and freely available Web sites (databases, encyclopedias, dictionaries, Web megasites, test information, and yearbooks); Sage: the UCSD Library's gateway to the Web; and psychology research guides. *[Article copies available for a fee from The Haworth Document Delivery Service: 1-800-HAWORTH. E-mail address: <docdelivery@haworthpress.com> Website: <http://www.HaworthPress.com> © 2005 by The Haworth Press, Inc. All rights reserved.]*

KEYWORDS. Psychology, psychological, Internet, Web sites, tests, megasites, yearbooks, research guides, pathfinders

---

Alice J. Perez is Bibliographer/Reference Librarian, Cognitive Science, Psychology and Education, Social Sciences and Humanities Library 0175R, 9500 Gilman Drive, University of California, San Diego, La Jolla, CA 92093 (E-mail: ajperez@ucsd.edu).

[Haworth co-indexing entry note]: "Psyched About Psychology Internet Resources." Perez, Alice J. Co-published simultaneously in *Journal of Library Administration* (The Haworth Information Press, an imprint of The Haworth Press, Inc.) Vol. 43, No. 3/4, 2005, pp. 181-194; and: *Evolving Internet Reference Resources* (ed: William Miller, and Rita M. Pellen) The Haworth Information Press, an imprint of The Haworth Press, Inc., 2006, pp. 181-194. Single or multiple copies of this article are available for a fee from The Haworth Document Delivery Service [1-800-HAWORTH, 9:00 a.m. - 5:00 p.m. (EST). E-mail address: docdelivery@haworthpress.com].

Available online at http://www.haworthpress.com/web/JLA
© 2005 by The Haworth Press, Inc. All rights reserved.
doi:10.1300/J111v43n03_14

INTRODUCTION

The psychology collection at the University of California, San Diego, Social Sciences and Humanities Library focuses on experimental psychology and supports the six broad areas taught by the Department of Psychology: Behavior Analysis; Biopsychology; Cognitive Psychology; Developmental Psychology; Sensation and Perception; and Social Psychology. There are many significant psychology resources which are only available in print; however, many important resources are now available electronically or in both formats. This list is by no means comprehensive, but is rather selective.

A section on tests has also been included because many psychology programs require students to find test information.

Reference librarians typically teach library classes how to search the PsycINFO, PsycARTICLES and PubMed databases to psychology and human development students. This survey will help not only those librarians new to the field of psychology, but also those who need a refresher on psychology resources.

DATABASES

Proprietary

PsycINFO

Although many librarians are familiar with the PsycINFO database, many students are not. In the library classes I teach, I continue to encounter seniors who have not heard of, let alone searched PsycINFO.

PsycINFO is produced by the American Psychological Association and is the primary database for psychological and behavioral sciences literature. Coverage is from 1840 to the present and is international in scope. PsycINFO indexes journal articles, books, book chapters, theses, dissertations, and reports. The database provides citations and abstracts. Many journal articles indexed in PsycINFO are available online. The PsycINFO database can be searched by author, title, keyword, descriptor (subject heading), and through the use of many other field codes. Descriptors (subject headings) can be identified via the online thesaurus or the print version entitled *Thesaurus of Psychological Index Terms*.

PsycARTICLES

The PsycARTICLES database is another product from the American Psychological Association. It is a full-text database which only indexes journal articles, at the present time, from 53 different journals. Everything contained in PsycARTICLES is contained in PsycINFO; think of it as a subset of PsycINFO. Coverage is from 1985 to the present from journals published by the American Psychological Association, the APA Educational Publishing Foundation, Canadian Psychological Association, and Hogrefe & Huber. PsycARTICLES can be searched by author, title, and keyword, but not by descriptor. People may search the PsycINFO database by descriptors because everything contained in the PsycARTICLES database is indexed in the PsycINFO database.

PsycARTICLES also provides the ability to view the current or past issues of its journals. This feature is very popular with faculty, who more and more frequently do their reading and research from their offices.

Two popular features in PsycINFO and PsycARTICLES are "Alert" and "Create a Bibliography." The Alert feature is very popular with faculty and graduate students. An Alert allows you to submit a search which the database automatically searches for each time the database is updated. Both PsycINFO and PsycARTICLES are updated on a weekly basis. An e-mail is sent to you containing the new content or if new content was not added to the database, you are nonetheless notified.

The other feature "QuikBib" (Create a Bibliography) is popular with undergraduates. This feature became available in June 2004 and is also available in PsycARTICLES. It allows people to mark particular records from their search results to create a bibliography. The marked records are saved; a document format is selected from four options: HTML, Text, RTF, or MS Word; and a bibliographic style is chosen from six different styles: APA, AMA, Chicago, MLA, Turabian, and Uniform (Uniform Requirements for Manuscripts Submitted to Biomedical Journals). Lastly the user clicks on the Create button, and voila, the bibliography is available to print or download.

Free

PubMed

This database is provided by the National Library of Medicine. It provides citations and abstracts from the biomedical journal literature.

Coverage is from 1953 to the present and is international in scope, although most records are from English language journals. The beauty of searching PubMed is that one can enter search terms and the database automatically searches for the terms in up to four different lists. It begins by looking in the MeSH (Medical Subject Headings) and if not found in MeSH, the database continues to look for the terms in the Journal Translation Table, followed by the Author Index. If a term is not found in any of its lists, it will search all fields of a record. PubMed calls this feature "Automatic Term Mapping."

DATABASES FORTHCOMING

Proprietary

The following products, all in the area of psychology, are definitely worth investigating.

ProQuest Psychology Journals

A full-text database from ProQuest Products. It contains over 400 top psychology and related publications for the student and the mental health professional. The database includes hundreds of journals published in the United States and several published in Canada, and the United Kingdom.

PsycBOOKS

A full-text database of books and chapters, including out of print books, published by the American Psychological Association and other publishers. As of November 2004, the database includes 585 books and 9,923 chapters. Many of the books were published by the American Psychological Association during 1950-2003. The database also includes the exclusive online release of 1,500 entries from the APA/Oxford University Press, *Encyclopedia of Psychology*. This new database will be updated on a monthly basis.

PsycCRITIQUES

A full-text database containing reviews of current psychology books. This database replaces the print journal *Contemporary Psychology:*

APA Review of Books which ceased as a print publication in December 2004. The initial database will include approximately 4,000 reviews from 1995-2003. Each weekly online release will then include approximately 15 reviews of psychological books from the current copyright year.

PsycEXTRA

A gray literature database from the American Psychological Association. It indexes material written for the professional, but not included in peer-reviewed journals. Materials indexed will include newsletters, newspapers, technical and annual reports, government reports, pamphlets, etc.; hence there is no overlap with PsycINFO. The initial size of the database will contain approximately 60,000 records and will be updated on a weekly basis.

Psychology and Behavioral Sciences Collection

A comprehensive, full-text database from EBSCO Information Services, covering topics in emotional and behavioral characteristics, psychology and psychiatry, mental processes, anthropology, and observational and experimental methods. The database contains over 500 journals.

Sage Full-Text Collections: Psychology

A full-text database of thirty journals published by Sage and participating societies. Many of the journals were included in the 2003 ISI Journal Citation Reports. At the present time the database includes 15,800 articles.

ENCYCLOPEDIAS

Proprietary

International Encyclopedia of the Social & Behavioral Sciences
<http://www.elsevier.com/wps/find/bookdescription.cws_home/601495/description#description>

A major reference work covering the social and behavioral sciences, this resource is published both in print and online. The editors-in-chief are Neil J. Smelser and Paul B. Baltes, and there are 52 section editors. The work was published by Elsevier in 2002. This encyclopedia is a principal reference tool for the psychology researcher. It covers 39 sections and includes 4,000 articles. It is useful for the patron in need of background information on a broad topic or by the advanced researcher looking for in-depth information on a specific topic. Online access is available via ScienceDirect.

Free

Encyclopedia of Psychology
<http://www.psychology.org/>

This encyclopedia is made available by William Palya, Department of Psychology, Jacksonville State University. The database is arranged hierarchically and the first page contains a list of eight categories: Career, People and History, Environment Behavior Relationships, Publications, Organizations, Resources, Paradigms and Theories, and Underlying Reductionistic Machinery. Librarians will find the Resources category the most useful. The Resources Web page contains additional categories such as Ethical Issues, MegaSites, Statistics, etc., with links to Web sites dealing with these broad topics. One can also look at new sites added to the database, the popular sites, or a random site. Using the Search option, one can search a word or conduct a Boolean search for a list of Web sites dealing with a specific topic.

DICTIONARIES

Proprietary

A Dictionary of Psychology
<http://www.oxfordreference.com/views/BOOK_SEARCH.html?book=
t87&subject=s20>

This dictionary was written by Andrew M. Colman, and it was published by Oxford University Press, 2001. It is available in print, and online as part of the Oxford Reference Online database. It contains over 10,000 entries and in addition to psychology, covers related disciplines such as nursing, sociology, social work, and education.

WEB MEGASITES

Free

AmoebaWeb
<http://www.vanguard.edu/faculty/ddegelman/amoebaweb/>

Maintained by Dr. Douglas Degelman, Professor of Psychology at Vanguard University of Southern California. The site includes two groupings of 36 categories in total. The first group of nine categories includes: APA Style & Writing, Career Preparation, Full-Text Journals, General References, Graduate Study, Online Tests, Parenting, Research Participation, and Research Scales. The second larger grouping contains 27 categories organized by psychological topic in alphabetical order from Applied Psychology to Therapy. You may also conduct a search via its search box located on the main page. The site also includes a "What's New?" link to the most recent additions to its Web site, and another link to its featured Web site of the month.

Psych Central: Dr. Grohol's Mental Health Page
<http://psychcentral.com/>

Created by John Grohol, author of *The Insider's Guide to Mental Health Resources Online* (Guilford, 2003). This Web site includes the following categories: Internet Resource Directory (professionally-reviewed support groups, articles, Web sites and more, organized by topic), Disorder Symptoms & Treatments (specific symptom checklists and detailed treatment information), Community Support Forums (you may join the community of people grappling with mental health and relationship issues), Quizzes & Tests (get personalized anonymous scores and instant quiz answers for free), World of Psychology Blog (psychology commentary and interesting news and research from around the Web, blogged regularly), Medication Library (prescription drug reference guide), and Psychology Articles & News (interesting articles written by professionals on a wide range of topics). This site was first launched in 1995.

Psych Web
<http://www.psywww.com/>

Created by Russell Dewey, Georgia Southern University. This Web site contains links to careers in psychology, full-text books available online, psychology departments on the Web, and more. According to its Web site it has been on the Internet for a decade now. You may search by the categories located on the left-hand side bar or via a Google search on the main Web page. The various categories on the left-hand side bar are: APA Style Resources, Books, Brochures, Careers in Psychology, Commerce, Departments, Find Anything, Mind Tools, Psychology of Religion, Scholarly Resources, Self-Help Resources, Self-Quiz for Introductory, Sport Psychology, States of Consciousness, and Tip Sheets.

PsychCrawler
<http://www.psychcrawler.com/>

This Web site is a product/search engine from the American Psychological Association. At the present time it indexes nine different Web sites: American Psychological Association; APA Public Information; National Institute of Mental Health; National Institute on Drug Abuse; The Substance Abuse and Mental Health Services Administration; U.S. Department of Health and Human Services, Center for Mental Health Services; National Clearinghouse for Alcohol and Drug Information; Sidran Foundation (Sidran Institute is a non-profit organization devoted to helping people who have experienced traumatic life events); and National Center for Post-Traumatic Stress Disorder. The site also includes search tips.

PsychScholar
<http://psych.hanover.edu/Krantz/>

Developed by John Krantz, Hanover College. The Web site consists of Web resources for psychological scholars and budding psychological scholars. The psychological scholar side of the Web page contains links to Research and Scholarship, Teaching, Connecting with Colleagues, and a General category. The budding scholar side of the page contains links to Research, Studying and Classes, The Next Step (explore different areas of psychology, links to psychology career resources, and links to psychology departments) as well as a General category.

Social Science Information Gateway–Psychology Gateway
<http://sosig.esrc.bris.ac.uk/psychology/>

The Web site provides high quality Internet sites on many subjects, psychology being one of them. The Social Science Information Gateway (SOSIG) is part of the UK Resource Discovery Network. The Psychology Gateway consists of 18 sub-sections from General Psychology to Sport Psychology or you may conduct a search via its search box. There is also a link to its "Top 50 Psychology sites," the top 50 sites most visited in the SOSIG Psychology section for a specified time period.

TESTS

Free

ETS Test Collection
<http://www.ets.org/testcoll/index.html>

The Test Collection Database contains descriptions of over 20,000 tests held at the Educational Testing Service library. Tests in Microfiche (TIM) is a subset of this collection and consists of over 1,000 actual tests. These tests are available for purchase from the Educational Testing Service. If the "availability" field indicates "Tests in Microfiche" or "PDF" one can obtain the test from ETS. All other tests must be obtained through the publisher, author, or other source listed in the "availability" field of the test description. The information is this field, however, is current as of the time ETS received it; one may need to locate up-to-date contact information.

FAQ/Finding Information About Psychological Tests
<http://www.apa.org/science/faq-findtests.html>

This Web site is from the American Psychological Association. It includes information on how to find both published and unpublished tests. It also provides summaries of four important test resources, *Tests in Print, Mental Measurements Yearbook, Tests,* and *Test Critiques.*

Full Instruments Available in: ETS Tests in Microfiche Collection
<http://libraries.uta.edu/helen/test&meas/Table%20of%20contents/
ETSTestsInFiche2004.htm>

Compiled by Helen Hough, Central Science Librarian, Central Library, University of Texas at Arlington. This Web site is a complete online listing of the test titles contained in the ETS Tests in Microfiche Collection (Educational Testing Service). Tests can then be acquired from ETS.

Mental Measurements Yearbook Indexes
<http://www.unl.edu/buros/index00.html>

An online version of the *Mental Measurements Yearbook* (MMY) from the Buros Institute of Mental Measurements. Indexing begins with the 9th edition, 1985 to the present. You can search the complete index alphabetically by test title, individual editions by test title, or by subject via the 19 categories in the classified subject index. Test reviews can be found in the print version of the *Mental Measurements Yearbook* or some can be found via the companion Web site *Test Reviews Online*.

Test Reviews Online (Mental Measurements Yearbook)
<http://buros.unl.edu/buros/jsp/search.jsp>

This companion Web site, also from the Buros Institute of Mental Measurements, provides information on over 4,000 commercially available tests and reviews of over 2,000 of these tests. You can search alphabetically by test title, by category (divided into 18 categories) or via a keyword search. Reviews can be found in the print version of *Mental Measurements Yearbook* or purchased online via this Web site. Coverage is from the 9th edition, 1985 to the present edition of the *Mental Measurements Yearbook*.

Proprietary

Health and Psychosocial Instruments (HaPI)
<http://www.ovid.com/site/catalog/DataBase/866.jsp?top=2&mid=3&bottom=7&subsection=10>

A product from Behavioral Measurement Database Services. This database provides information on measurement instruments such as questionnaires, checklists, rating scales, etc., in the health sciences, psychosocial sciences, organizational behavior, and library and information science. Coverage is from 1985 to the present.

YEARBOOKS

Annual Review of Psychology
<http://www.annualreviews.org/catalog/2004/ps55.asp>

This product is published by Annual Reviews. The series covers 30 different fields from the biomedical, physical, and social sciences, and is published on an annual basis. The *Annual Review of Psychology* is available in both print and online. This distinguished reference source provides critical reviews of psychology literature written by leaders in the field. According to the 2004 print volume, the online version will provide digital add-ons to the print.

SAGE

<http://libraries.ucsd.edu/sage/sage.html>

Sage is the UCSD Library's gateway to the Web and was launched in 2000. It is a database of electronic resources licensed for UCSD students, faculty, and staff, designated [UCSD Only] as well as some freely available sites on the Internet. These resources have been selected by our library subject specialists as being valuable for research by students, faculty, and staff. Sage includes Web sites, electronic journals, electronic books and reports, and databases of all types.

Sage is arranged both by subject and type. At the present time there are 107 subjects ranging from Aerospace Engineering to Urban Studies and Planning, and 57 types ranging from Article Databases to Web Megasites. Each subject's main page includes a list of Featured Sites; these are sites deemed most essential by the subject specialist. A site can also be designated a Key Site. A Key Site designation will list the site at the top of the page under each type (in alphabetical order if more than one type is designated a Key Site). See Sage–Psychology URL listed below for examples.

Sage–Psychology
<http://libraries.ucsd.edu/sage/subjects/psychology.html>

The Psychology section of Sage is maintained by me as the Psychology Librarian for UCSD. The first page lists the Featured Sites which includes those sites that I deemed most useful for students, faculty, and staff at UCSD. At the present time there are 36 types listed for Psychology from Article Databases to Web Megasites. During October 2004 the Sage Psychology Web page was accessed a total of 247 times from 89 different visitors (many are repeat customers!).

ONLINE GUIDES FOR PSYCHOLOGY

A Google search for psychology guides will retrieve hundreds of online guides located at various libraries around the globe. Listed below are several psychology online guides from a variety of academic libraries. Note the different approaches to the guides yet all contain the necessary information for the psychology researcher at their respective campuses.

Boston College, Boston College Libraries. *Research Guide: Psychology*. [Updated 22 November 2004; cited 29 November 2004.] <http://www.bc.edu/libraries/research/guides/s-psychology/>

University Library, California State University, Long Beach. *Psychology*. [Updated 12 October 2004; cited 29 November 2004.] <http://www.csulb.edu/library/subj/psychology.html>

The Libraries of the Claremont Colleges, Claremont University Consortium. *Psychology Research Guide*. [Updated 27 September 2004; cited 29 November 2004.] <http://libraries.claremont.edu/research/rguides/psych/>

Olin & Uris Libraries, Reference Department, Cornell University Library. *Psychology: A Research Guide*. [Updated 19 April 2004; cited 29 November 2004.] <http://www.library.cornell.edu/olinuris/ref/psychologyref.html>

Emory University General Libraries. *Psychology Research Guide*. [Updated 26 July 2004; cited 29 November 2004.] <http://web.library.emory.edu/subjects/socsci/psychol/psyc/>

Mount Holyoke College, Mount Holyoke College Library. *Psychology*. [Updated 1 November 2004; cited 29 November 2004.] <http://www.mtholyoke.edu/lits/library/guides/psych.shtml>

Northwest Missouri State University, Owens Library. *Psychology Research Guide*. [Updated July 1999, links verified June 2004; cited 29 November 2004.] <http://www.nwmissouri.edu/library/courses/psychology/>

Oklahoma State University Library. *Psychology Research Guide*. [Updated 3 May 2004; cited 29 November 2004.] <http://www.library.okstate.edu/hss/chaney/psychology/psyc.html>

San Diego State University, Library and Information Access. *Subject Guide for Psychology.* [Updated 2 November 2004; cited 29 November 2004.]
<http://infodome.sdsu.edu/research/guides/psych/psychres.shtml>

University of Massachusetts Amherst, University of Massachusetts Amherst Libraries. *Psychology Research Guide.* [Updated 2004; cited 29 November 2004.]
<http://www.library.umass.edu/subject/psychology/>

University of California, San Diego, Social Sciences and Humanities Library. *Psychology Resources: A Select List.* [Updated 30 November 2004; cited 30 November 2004.]
<http://sshl.ucsd.edu/collections/psycguide.html>

BIBLIOGRAPHY

American Psychological Association. *E-Products.* [2004; cited 24 November 2004]. <http://www.apa.org/eproducts/>.

American Psychological Association. *FAQ/Finding Information About Psychological Tests.* [updated 2004; cited 30 November 2004]. <http://www.apa.org/science/faq-findtests.html>.

American Psychological Association. *PsychCrawler: Web sites currently in the index.* [updated n/a; cited 30 November 2004]. <http://www.psychcrawler.com/plweb/pcsites.html>.

Annual Reviews. *Annual Reviews Welcome.* [updated 2004; cited 30 November 2004]. <http://www.annualreviews.org/index.asp>.

Buros Institute of Mental Measurements. *Frequently Asked Questions: What Is Test Reviews Online?* [updated n/a; cited 30 November 2004]. <http://www.unl.edu/buros/faq.html>.

Buros Institute of Mental Measurements. *Mental Measurements Yearbook Indexes.* [updated n/a; cited 30 November 2004]. <http://www.unl.edu/buros/index00.html>.

Degelman, Douglas, Vanguard University of Southern California. *AmoebaWeb: Psychology on the Web!* [updated 21 November 2004; cited 30 November 2004]. <http://www.vanguard.edu/faculty/ddegelman/amoebaweb/>.

Dewey, Russell, Georgia Southern University. *Psych Web.* [updated 2004; cited 30 November 2004]. <http://www.psywww.com/>.

EBSCO Information Services, Bibliographic and Full Text Databases. *Psychology and Behavioral Sciences Collection.* [updated n/a; cited 29 November 2004]. <http://www.epnet.com/academic/p&bsc.asp>.

ETS Test Collection. *Frequently Asked Questions.* [updated 03 October 2003; cited 24 November 2004]. <http://www.ets.org/testcoll/faq.html>.

ETS Test Collection. *How to Order a Test.* [updated 03 October 2003; cited 4 January 2005]. <http://www.ets.org/testcoll/order.html>.

Elsevier.com. *Products–International Encyclopedia of the Social & Behavioral Sciences.* [updated 2004; cited 24 November 2004]. <http://www.elsevier.com/wps/find/bookdescription.cws_home/601495/description#description>.

Grohol, John. *About Psych Central.* [updated 24 November 2004; cited 24 November 2004]. <http://psychcentral.com/about/>.

Hough, Helen, University of Texas at Arlington. *Full Instruments Available in: ETS Tests in Microfiche Collection.* [updated 22 December 2004; cited 4 January 2005]. <http://libraries.uta.edu/helen/test&meas/Table%20of%20contents/ETSTestsInFiche2004.htm>.

Krantz, John, Hanover College. *PsychScholar: A collection of web resources for psychological scholars and budding psychological scholars.* [updated 29 September 2003; cited 30 November 2004]. <http://psych.hanover.edu/Krantz/>.

National Library of Medicine. *PubMed Tutorial–Using PubMed–How It Works–Automatic Term Mapping.* [updated July 2004; cited 24 November 2004]. <http://www.nlm.nih.gov/bsd/pubmed_tutorial/m2006.html>.

Ovid. *Products and Services–Health and Psychosocial Instruments (HaPI).* [updated 2004; cited 24 November 2004]. <http://www.ovid.com/site/catalog/DataBase/866.jsp?top=2&mid=3&bottom=7&subsection=10>.

Oxford Reference Online. *A Dictionary of Psychology.* [updated 2004; cited 24 November 2004]. <http://www.oxfordreference.com/views/BOOK_SEARCH.html?book=t87&subject=s20>.

Palya, William, Jacksonville State University. *Encyclopedia of Psychology.* [updated 24 November 2004; cited 24 November 2004]. <http://www.psychology.org/>.

ProQuest Information and Learning Company, ProQuest Products. *ProQuest Psychology Journals.* [updated 2004; cited 29 November 2004]. <http://www.proquest.com/products/pd-product-PsycJournals.shtml>.

Sage Full-Text Collections. Psychology. [updated 2003; cited 29 November 2004]. <http://www.sagefulltext.com/home.aspx?id=1>.

Sidran Institute. *About the Sidran Institute.* [copyright 1995-2003; cited 3 January 2005]. <http://www.sidran.org/about.html>.

Social Science Information Gateway. *Psychology Gateway.* [updated 2004; cited 30 November 2004]. <http://sosig.esrc.bris.ac.uk/psychology/>.

UCSD Libraries. *Sage.* [updated 18 September 2003; cited 10 January 2005]. <http://libraries.ucsd.edu/about-sage.html>.

Internet Resources for Education Reference

Linda Marie Golian-Lui

SUMMARY. This article focuses on the current status of the Internet for reference tools in the field of education as of 2005. Several categories of resources are highlighted: commercial databases, government and educational association Web sources, and specialty Web pages. The chapter concludes with a Webliography of the Internet sites highlighted in the article. *[Article copies available for a fee from The Haworth Document Delivery Service: 1-800-HAWORTH. E-mail address: <docdelivery@haworthpress.com> Website: <http://www.HaworthPress.com> © 2005 by The Haworth Press, Inc. All rights reserved.]*

KEYWORDS. Education, Internet resources in education, Internet research in education, online research in education, online resources in education

INTRODUCTION

Education leaders, practitioners, and students have a voracious need for reference information. Many reference needs in education center on

---

Linda Marie Golian-Lui is University Librarian/Director, Edwin H. Mookini Library and Graphic Services, University of Hawaii at Hilo, 200 West Kawili Street, Hilo, HI 96720 (E-mail: golianlu@hawaii.edu).

[Haworth co-indexing entry note]: "Internet Resources for Education Reference." Golian-Lui, Linda Marie. Co-published simultaneously in *Journal of Library Administration* (The Haworth Information Press, an imprint of The Haworth Press, Inc.) Vol. 43, No. 3/4, 2005, pp. 195-208; and: *Evolving Internet Reference Resources* (ed: William Miller, and Rita M. Pellen) The Haworth Information Press, an imprint of The Haworth Press, Inc., 2006, pp. 195-208. Single or multiple copies of this article are available for a fee from The Haworth Document Delivery Service [1-800-HAWORTH, 9:00 a.m. - 5:00 p.m. (EST). E-mail address: docdelivery@haworthpress.com].

doi:10.1300/J111v43n03_15

195

direct support for classroom teachers and the growing complexity of laws, curriculum mandates, testing, and the inclusion of special need students into the traditional classroom. At any given time, there is a need for instant access to resources that address policies, grants, technology integration, student evaluation, school finance, professional development, fundraising, counseling, community relations, crisis handling, disaster intervention, and classroom management.

Research shows that support for Internet reference resources is increasing among library users. According to the *2004 Library Journal/Trendwatch Graphic Arts Academic Reference Survey*, academic library patrons have chosen a preferred format for reference, and it is electronic.[1] The primary reasons for the support of this format among academic reference users involve the Internet's convenience to information and the numerous additional features supported with the technology. This growing format preference is playing a significant role in the proliferation of Internet reference resources in all subject areas, including education.

This article summarizes some of the significant changes in the field of educational Internet reference resources in the last few years, calls attention to a few selection tools for reviewing the continuously growing number of education Internet reference resources, and highlights a few specific resources.

ERIC'S EXTREME MAKEOVER IN 2004

One of the most significant changes in the area of Internet reference resources for Education occurred with the implementation of changes in the Education Resources Information Center (ERIC).[2] ERIC was one of the very first online bibliographic database providers, established in 1966 as a subject-themed clearing-house for education. ERIC's mission was to gather, index, and input bibliographic information to make journal articles and gray literature available in education. ERIC has been, and continues to be, a favorite and reliable educational reference resource. With well over a million records, ERIC is the largest database of electronic reference information and resources in the field of education.

ERIC's 2004 extreme makeover is a direct result of the Education Sciences Reform Act of 2002 (PL 107-2790). According to the staff at ERIC, one of their prime motivations for this change is to make it easier to include more full-text documents or journals. The Education Sciences

Reform Act of 2002 is expanding ERIC's content coverage and avenues for information dissemination.

ERIC's changes in 2004 reflect increased integration of patron suggestions and major changes to the role of clearinghouses in education information dissemination.

While the inclusion of additional full-text documents and journals is highly welcomed, there are some current concerns and confusion among ERIC users about increased costs for similar services. Like any high quality reference tool, the ERIC makeover will need several years of fine-tuning and continued efforts. Luckily, ERIC's makeover is a collaborative process that includes user feedback, advisory boards, and focus groups. There is the potential for many exciting developments and enhancements ahead for ERIC and the reference information it provides. URL: <http://www.eric.ed.gov>.

ADDITIONAL TRENDS AND CHANGES

In 2005 many librarians, researchers, and publishers are actively addressing the issues of open access to journals, research findings, and reference data. The concept of open access is definitely on the rise, with proposals that information and research resulting from public funds should be made freely available. Increased access to educational reference data and resources that received public funding is a notable situation that should be monitored. This will have a tremendous impact on Internet reference resources in education.

Educational resources on the Internet continue to be developed in patterns established by other subject fields such as business and math. Therefore, it is very likely that the trend of new Internet reference tools in the field of education should explode. Many resources currently available only in a print format will become available in an Internet format in the near future. Vast amounts of reference data currently only available in print format will migrate into the Internet, and an overall increase in the availability of high quality e-books is also expected.

Finally, the future for specialized and independent educational Internet clearinghouses is not bright. The significant changes in ERIC over the past three years indicate that information once provided in print (and more recently electronically) through clearinghouses will continue the aggressive transition into reference monographs (both print and electronic), data sets, and databases as a combination of both free and fee-based resources.

SELECTION TOOLS

Regardless of format, librarians must continue to rely upon selection tools for the effective purchase of library materials, including Internet education reference resources. Most monographic vendors now provide their library clients with information concerning new electronic databases, e-books, and Internet reference resources as part of their approval plan services. Two tools for providing quality reviews for educational Internet reference resources are *Choice Reviews Online* and the annual "Reference" special supplemental issue *of Library Journal.* Both of these tools provide reviews of Internet reference resources written by subject specialist librarians. URL: <http://www.choiceonsite.org/>.

Although printed monographs on educational Internet sites tend to become quickly outdated, one printed resource providing good insight into the growing world of Internet resources for education is *Essential Websites for Educational Leaders in the 21st Century*[3] by James Lerman. Released in 2004, this reviewing tool is organized into twenty-five major areas of interest such as assessment, lesson plans, administration, and curriculum resources. Each chapter includes an annotated bibliography of six to twenty Internet sites supporting the specific area. The book is complemented by an identically organized compact disc for easy access to all Internet sites mentioned in the book.

RECOMMENDED INTERNET RESOURCES

Some of the more noteworthy Internet resources for the education community are listed below. These recommended resources are organized into the following three categories: commercial databases, government and education-sponsored Internet Web sites, and special interest education Internet Web sites and reference resources. Many variables, such as number of users, remote access, consortium pricing, and database packages affect the final institutional price for all the commercial databases and some of the special interest education Internet Web sites listed. Institutions interested in purchasing access to these Internet reference resources should contact the publisher directly for details.

Commercial Databases

In the area of education full-text aggregated databases, four major vendors have risen to the top of the information-providing pyramid:

ProQuest, EBSCO, Thompson/Gale, and H. W. Wilson. A complete review of the major educational resources provided by these commercial vendors is beyond the scope of this article. In summary, all four vendors provide reliable and excellent subject coverage of Internet education resources.

ProQuest Online Information Service provides access to thousands of current periodicals and newspapers directly supporting education reference. Many sources are updated daily and contain full-text articles dating back to 1986. Some information services provide deep backfiles of archival material as part of their expanding digitization project of 5.5 billion pages from their microfilm collection.

ProQuest lists 43 Internet products in direct support for education reference, including e-books, newspapers, ERIC access, aggregated journal products, dissertations, and specialized collections. The company provides a mix of article searching, information access, and information delivery. The searching interface is effective for both the novice and professional researcher.

ProQuest Education Journals provides information on hundreds of educational topics, covering almost 400 leading education journals. The database covers not only the literature on primary, secondary, and higher education but also special education, home schooling, adult education, and hundreds of related topics.

ProQuest Professional Education & Education Complete provides access to more than 300 full-text magazines that address all aspects of K-12 education. This service is expanded in its *ProQuest Education Complete* with an additional coverage of 200 full-text journals and indexing/abstracting for another 280 more.

Canadian Business and Current Affairs provides a focus on Canadian education information. Over 400 journals are in the collection, with selective coverage back to the 1970s. Academic, administrative, professional, and topical journals are all included, as well as newsletters and education association highlights.

ProQuest Career and Technical Education is designed for both students and instructors. This product provides excellent coverage for vocational information for community colleges, two-year institutions, public libraries, and high schools offering technical courses such as healthcare, building trades, auto mechanics, sales and retail, accounting, photography, graphic design, nursing, and technology. The database covers over 400 publications. This is an excellent reference resource for vocational information including mechanical schematics,

parts listing, ingredient listings, and comparison of medical appara-
tuses. URL: <http://www.il.proquest.com/proquest/>.

Like ProQuest, EBSCO Publishing offers a broad range of full-text
and bibliographic databases designed to meet the reference needs of all
library types worldwide. EBSCO has designed its search interfaces to
interact seamlessly with other electronic resources, effectively creating
a one-stop reference and research environment.

An especially helpful feature is how EBSCO Publishing divides its
Internet products into six specific categories: Academic Libraries, Biomedical Libraries, Government Libraries, School (K-12), Corporate Libraries, and Public Libraries. EBSCO's support for education reference
includes e-books, newspapers, ERIC access, aggregated journal products, and specialized collections. The company provides a mix of article
searching, information access, and information delivery. The searching
interface is effective for both the novice and professional researcher.

One specialized database created by EBSCO is the *Teacher Reference
Center*. This reference resource provides indexing and abstracts for
over 280 of the most popular teacher and administrator trade journals.

In late 2004, EBSCO partnered with the Buros Institute to provide
Internet access to the *Mental Measurements Yearbook*, one of the most
heavily used printed education reference resources since 1938. This
Internet reference resource is one of the most significant Internet reference additions in recent history. The resource provides evaluative
information, written by testing and measurement experts. Each entry
includes a well-written description of the instrument, links to professional reviews, links to research studies using the instrument, reference
information, and contact information. The Internet version is currently
limited to instruments available in the English language, commercially
available for purchase, and new, revised or widely used since the last
printed series update. URL: <http://www.ebsco.com/home/>.

H. W. Wilson's *Education Full Text* is marketed as a full-text proprietary database. This Internet resource is based upon the popular paper
resource, *Education Abstracts*, which provides author, title, subject, and
abstract coverage of more than 650 core educational periodicals and
full-text coverage of 270 journals. Although the dates of coverage are
typically 1994 to date, H. W. Wilson continues to expand the dates of
full-text coverage. This commercial product can be purchased directly
from H. W. Wilson or from an aggregator service such as ProQuest or
EBSCO. Primarily used as a research tool, *Education Full Text* also
provides statistical and factual data information in the education field

through the coverage of educational trade journals, yearbooks, and some monographs.

Education Index Retrospective is a new product that complements the *Education Full Text* product highlighted above by providing abstracts and indexing between 1929 and 1983. Author, title, subject, and abstract coverage of more than 650 core education periodicals is provided. URL: <http://www.hwwilson.com/>.

Thomson Gale serves education reference needs through a wide variety of print and Internet resources. The company is best known for its long history in the reference publishing field and has a reputation for breadth and convenience of its education data, including homework help, health questions, and business profiles.

Testing & Education Reference Center was released in 2004, and provides career and entrance testing information for people preparing for higher education and civil service careers. One of the greatest strengths of this Internet reference resource is the broad coverage of samples of specialized college entrance, graduate school, military, trade school, and civil servant exams. The database also provides basic reference information on colleges, universities, and other adult education opportunities. Information on specific state tests like CAHSEE (California State Exit-Level Exam) is also provided. URL: <http://www.gale.com/Testing&Education/>.

Corbis Images for Education is a unique Internet reference resource dedicated to educational images. There are 400,000 digital images available from its popular art, historical, nature, science, and space collections are available for use in a variety of learning-related applications, including class projects and assignments, presentations, lesson plans, Web coursework, and much more. The license that comes with this product is a broad-rights educational use license, which allows library patrons, faculty, staff, and students to access the entire collection for any educational purpose. The images are accessible via a secure Web site that allows authorized users to easily search and download images from an on-premise terminal or via remote IP-based authentication. The images and the education license are perfect to support image reference requests typical of public library, K-12, and higher education learning. URL: <http://education.corbis.com/artandhistory.aspx>.

Other Commercial Internet Resources

In 2004, another welcomed addition of high quality electronic education journal access became available from SAGE publishing. *Educa-*

tion: A SAGE Full-Text Collection includes the full-text coverage of 19 journals published by SAGE and its participating societies. Coverage goes back 36 years, and encompasses over 7,000 articles. It covers such subjects as assessment, multilingual education, curriculum, early childhood education, educational administration, and educational policy. URL: <http://www.csa.com/csa/factsheets/sageduc.shtml>.

Peterson's Education Portal is the Internet version of the well-known series of printed Peterson reference resources used for college searches and the application process. The site includes online practice tests for many popular entrance exams including the GRE, GMAT, and SAT. The site provides users with helpful information necessary for making informed decisions about future education and career directions. The resource includes a financial aid database, providing access to nearly $5 billion worth of scholarships, and grant information. URL: <http://www.petersons.com>.

Facts on File Curriculum Resource Center is an Internet reference collection of printable teacher handouts designed to supplement and support middle school, high school, and junior college curricula. The product provides reference and supplemental information across broad core subject areas including U.S. history, world history, science, math, health, physical education, and geography. Much of the information is provided in visual maps and data representations such as time lines and diagrams. URL: <http://www.fofweb.com/SellSheets/05035x.pdf>.

Kraus Curriculum Development Library is a searchable Internet reference database that provides curriculum information and examples to over 5,500 documents on a wide variety of subjects covered in Pre K–12th Grade and Adult Basic Education. The resource provides direct links to curricula examples from State departments of education, federal government agencies, colleges/universities, regional educational consortia, and non-profit educational organizations. Curricula are selected on the basis of currency, quality, content, and geographic distribution. The database allows searching for lesson plans, learning activities, instructional strategies, educational frameworks, teaching techniques, learning objectives, grading, and links to educational legislation. URL: <http://www.kcdlonline.com/>.

Government Web Sites

United States Department of Education strives to ensure equal access to education and promotes educational excellence throughout the nation. Its Internet site provides reference information concerning U.S. national priorities for improving education. The site provides links to funding opportunities, educational statistics, news summaries, free and fee based federal publications and products, and directory contact information for workers and the various departments and divisions organized under the U.S. Department of Education. URL: <http://www.ed.gov/>.

National Library of Education is the federal government's main reference and resource center for education information. It is charged with being the nation's collector and creator of education research information. This Internet site is filled with a wide variety of reference resources including statistics, historical timelines, legislative updates, subject bibliographies, and links to many educational associations. URL: <http://www.ed.gov/NLE>.

National Center for Education Statistics is part of the U.S. Department of Education that is considered a primary reference resource for education statistics. It is considered the primary federal entity for the collection and analyzation of data related to education in the United States and also provides similar information for many other nations. The NCES has a congressional mandate to collect, collate, analyze, and report complete statistics on the condition of American education. In the past few years, NCES has greatly improved the organization of its Internet information. NCES provides access to nearly 2,000 publications and data products and provides information on more than 40 NCES programs and surveys. The most significant reference assistance provided by NCES involves statistical information, with recent improvements on how to build your own tables using data from NCES surveys. Special links to quick educational statistics, tables, and figures are available at this site. URL: <http://nces.ed.gov/>.

National Center for Early Development and Learning is a research project supported by the U.S. Department of Education's Institute for Educational Sciences (IES). Administratively based at the FPG Child Development Institute, NCEDL is a collaborative project with the University of Virginia and UCLA. Premiering in 2004, the NCEDL Internet site was designed with the primary goal of assisting the translation of research into practice and with broadly communicating findings. The site has five main sections: News, Research, People, Products, and Sites that are searchable with a very easy to use internal search engine. URL: <http://www.fpg.unc.edu/~ncedl/>.

Special Resources

Encyclopedia of Education is an essential reference tool released in 2002 by Macmillian Reference in both print and Internet versions. The Internet option offers 24/7 remote access, circulation of reference content, and cross searching of over 850 articles that contain bibliographies, with many articles including links to Internet sites. Editor James W. Guthrie, assisted by nearly 1,000 contributors from various schools, basically adheres to the same goals and format exhibited in the previous edition. He and his colleagues offer the views, in lengthy, comprehensive essays, of the institutions, people, processes, roles, and philosophies inherent in teaching practices. This fully-revised second edition offers a complete view of the institutions, people, processes, roles, and philosophies found in educational practice in the United States and throughout the world. Features include 121 biographies of influential educators; profiles of historic colleges and universities; profiles of organizations active in the field; and an appendix of full-text primary source documents including education-related legislation, international treaties, and testing methods. URL: <http://www.gale. com/servlet/ItemDetailServlet?region=9&imprint=541&titleCode=M98& type=4&id=173295>.

Developing Educational Standards is an Internet reference site that supports the arduous task each state faces in developing, implementing, researching, evaluating, and reporting educational standards. This site indexes and makes direct links to a wide assortment of educational standards sources through out the nation in one convenient place. URL: <http://edstandards.org/Standards.html>.

Web Feet is a comprehensive subject guide to quality free resources available on the Internet. The product provides a collection of pre-selected, annotated, and cataloged Internet sites that are reviewed by librarians, subject experts, educators, and editors. The resource includes six collections: K-8 Collection; K-12 Collection; Core Collection (for grades 6-12 and adult); Health Collection; Public Library Collection; and Academic Library Collection. The Internet resource supports the ability to search by grade level and specific curriculum disciplines. URL: <http://www.webfeetguides.com/>.

The Research Libraries Group, a nonprofit membership corporation of universities, national libraries, archives, and other memory institutions, has produced the *RedLightGreen* Internet site from the quality collections among the members. *RedLightGreen* debuted in 2003 as a special Internet searching tool designed specifically for undergraduates using the Web to find reliable and quality information. The product provides information from more than 130 million books for education and research. More importantly, the searching interface links students back to their campus libraries for the books they select. It is a unique search engine that looks like Google, Yahoo, and other familiar Web search engines. URL: <http://www.redlightgreen.com/>.

Gateway to Educational Materials is a consortium effort providing educators with quick and easy access to thousands of educational reference resources found on various federal, state, university, non-profit, and commercial Internet sites. The site changes frequently and provides spotlights of current events that teachers can use in the classroom. URL: <http://www.thegateway.org/>.

Educator's Reference Desk is marketed as a resource that uses over a quarter century of experience of providing high-quality resources and services to the education community. The Internet site organizes more than 2,000 lesson plans and other online classroom information fact sheets. URL: <http://eduref.org>.

The *Education Commission of the States* was established in 1967 to help state leaders shape educational policy and to inform policymakers interested in particular education topics. The site organizes policies by topic and by state. The site provides a daily roundup of the nation's top education news and a weekly bulletin highlighting state policy trends, new reports, upcoming meetings and events, and new Web site links. URL: <http://www.ecs.org/>.

Special Education Resources on the Internet is a collection of Internet-accessible information of interest to anyone involved in special education, including parents. The site contains numerous reference resources that help educators and parents better understand the behavioral, medical, legal, and social issues involved with special education. URL: <http://seriweb.com.>.

Educational Testing Service (ETS) is one of the largest private educational measurement organizations. Its *Test Collection* includes an extensive library of over 20,000 tests and other measurement devices dating from the early 1900s to the present. The site provides sample questions from current tests, including some foreign tests from Canada, Great Britain, and Australia. URL: <http://www.ets.org/testcoll/index.html>.

Digital Resources for Evaluators is another reference Internet site providing information on testing and other measurement instruments. Although not as robust as the ETS product, the site does link the user to helpful contact information concerning other associations, professional consultants, companies that conduct testing and evaluations, and online versions of selected evaluation tools. An especially helpful reference tool is the digitized copy of standards and checklists. URL: <http://www.ets.org/testcoll/index.html>.

EvaluTech is a product of the Southern Regional Education Board's Educational technology cooperative. The Internet site provides access to more than 10,000 reviews of software and other educational resources. The site also evaluates both free and fee based Internet resources in many K-20 fields, especially in language arts, mathematics, social studies, and sciences. URL: <http://www.evalutech.sreb.org/>.

CONCLUSIONS

Today's education professionals are challenged by the need to constantly update their knowledge, skills, and expertise. The popularity of the Internet and the enhancements offered by electronic reference tools are making this reference information format a preference among all types of library users. The development of additional quality Internet reference resources in the field of education will surely explode in the next few years.

To successfully find reference information, today's education practitioners need a fundamental knowledge of the discipline, the discipline's vocabulary, and a basic understanding of how to combine words and phrases that will retrieve the reference information they seek in an electronic format. This can be frustrating for those new to the field of education and to those new to the use of Internet reference resources.

Like traditional print resources for educational reference, Internet resources run a wide range from those with exceptional value to those with questionable reliability. Like print resources, users of Internet reference resources need to carefully scrutinize each reference source for validity, reliability, point of view, currency, credentials, and other criteria.

Quality Internet reference resources are not always free or cheap. The challenge of balancing library funds with patron needs is the fundamental principle of all library collection development activities. Finding quality education Internet reference information on the Internet is easier today than just a few years ago. However, librarians still have much to do and much to learn about the art and practice of using and promoting these reference resources with our users.

NOTES

1. Andrew Richard Albanese, "The Reference evolution." *Supplement to the Library Journal,* (November 15, 2004): 10.
2. Carol Tenopir, "Online databases: ERIC's extreme makeover." *Library Journal,* (September 1, 2004): 36.
3. James Lerman, *Essential Websites for Educational Leaders in the 21st Century* (Lanham, Maryland: Scarecrow, 2004).

WEBLIOGRAPHY

Choice Reviews Online [Online]. Retrieved February 7, 2005. URL: <http://www.choiceonsite.org/>.

Corbis Images for Education [Online]. Retrieved February 7, 2005. URL: <http://education.corbis.com/artandhistory.aspx>.

Developing Educational Standards [Online]. Retrieved February 7, 2005. URL: <http://edstandards.org/Standards.html>.

Digital Resources for Evaluators [Online]. Retrieved February 7, 2005. URL: <http://www.ets.org/testcoll/index.html>.

ERIC [Online]. Retrieved February 7, 2005. URL: <http://www.eric.ed.gov>.

EBSCO [Online]. Retrieved February 7, 2005. URL:<http://www.ebsco.com/home/>.

Education: A SAGE Full-Text Collection [Online]. Retrieved February 7, 2005. URL: <http://www.csa.com/csa/factsheets/sageduc.shtml>.

Education Commission of the States [Online]. Retrieved February 7, 2005. URL: <http://www.ecs.org/>.

Educational Testing Service Test Collection [Online]. Retrieved February 7, 2005. URL: <http://www.ets.org/testcoll/index.html>.

Educator's Reference Desk [Online]. Retrieved February 7, 2005. URL: <http://eduref.org>.

Encyclopedia of Education, 2nd Edition [Online]. Retrieved February 7, 2005. URL: <http://www.gale.com/servlet/ItemDetailServlet?region=9&imprint=541&titleCode=M98&type=4&id=173295>.

EvaluTech [Online]. Retrieved February 7, 2005. URL: <http://www.evalutech.sreb.org/>.

Facts on File Curriculum Center Collection [Online]. Retrieved February 7, 2005. URL: <http://www.fofweb.com/SellSheets/05035x.pdf>.

Gateway to Educational Materials [Online]. Retrieved February 7, 2005. URL: <http://www.thegateway.org/>.

H. W. Wilson's Education Full Text [Online]. Retrieved February 7, 2005. URL: <http://www.hwwilson.com/>.

Kraus Curriculum Development Library [Online]. Retrieved February 7, 2005. URL: <http://www.kcdlonline.com/>.

National Center for Early Development and Learning [Online]. Retrieved February 7, 2005. URL: <http://www.fpg.unc.edu/~ncedl/>.

National Center for Education Statistics [Online]. Retrieved February 7, 2005. URL: <http://nces.ed.gov/>.

National Library of Education [Online]. Retrieved February 7, 2005. URL: <http:// www.ed.gov/NLE>.

Peterson's Education Portal [Online]. Retrieved February 7, 2005. URL: <http://www. petersons.com>.

ProQuest [Online]. Retrieved February 7, 2005. URL: <http://www.il.proquest.com/ proquest/>.

RedLightGreen [Online]. Retrieved February 7, 2005. URL: <http://www.redlightgreen. com/>.

Thomson Gale [Online]. Retrieved February 7, 2005. URL: <http://www.gale.com>.

Thomson Gale Testing and Education Reference Center [Online]. Retrieved February 7, 2005. URL: <http://www.gale.com/Testing&Education/>.

Special Education Resources on the Internet [Online]. Retrieved February 7, 2005. URL: <http://seriweb.com.>.

United States Department of Education [Online]. Retrieved February 7, 2005. URL: <http://www.ed.gov/>.

Web Feet [Online]. Retrieved February 7, 2005. URL: <http://www.webfeetguides. com>.

Avoiding Accidental Tourism: Reference Resources for Travel Research

Ellen M. Krupar
Nicole J. Auer

SUMMARY. Tourism's size and importance are underrated. *National Geographic* speculates that tourism is the largest industry in the world, generating one trillion dollars a year, and just for the United States, travel receipts for 2002 were $67,451,000. For all of that activity, most patrons and librarians are only aware of booking Web sites such as Travelocity. This paper will discuss industry-specific sites that offer information for researchers and for travelers interested in going off the beaten path. *[Article copies available for a fee from The Haworth Document Delivery Service: 1-800-HAWORTH. E-mail address: <docdelivery@haworthpress.com> Website: <http://www.HaworthPress.com> © 2005 by The Haworth Press, Inc. All rights reserved.]*

KEYWORDS. Tourism, hospitality, travel, Internet, Web sites

Ellen M. Krupar (E-mail: kellen@vt.edu) and Nicole J. Auer (E-mail: auern@vt.edu) are both affiliated with the University Libraries, Virginia Tech, PO Box 90001, Blacksburg, VA 24061-9001.

[Haworth co-indexing entry note]: "Avoiding Accidental Tourism: Reference Resources for Travel Research." Krupar, Ellen M., and Nicole J. Auer. Co-published simultaneously in *Journal of Library Administration* (The Haworth Information Press, an imprint of The Haworth Press, Inc.) Vol. 43, No. 3/4, 2005, pp. 209-225; and: *Evolving Internet Reference Resources* (ed: William Miller, and Rita M. Pellen) The Haworth Information Press, an imprint of The Haworth Press, Inc., 2006, pp. 209-225. Single or multiple copies of this article are available for a fee from The Haworth Document Delivery Service [1-800-HAWORTH, 9:00 a.m. - 5:00 p.m. (EST). E-mail address: docdelivery@haworthpress.com].

Available online at http://www.haworthpress.com/web/JLA
doi:10.1300/J111v43n03_16

BIBLIOGRAPHIES

Tourism Research Links
<http://www.waksberg.com/>

Gives links to research in tourism topics with a focus exclusively on the academic side. Subjects covered include event management and sustainable development. Links are also given for government and professional organizations in tourism. Compiled by Rene Waksberg.

Virtual Laboratory for Leisure, Tourism & Sport
<http://playlab.uconn.edu/frl.htm>

Gives alphabetic lists of references by topic which include: Economic Impact of Sport and Tourism, Ecotourism, Sport Tourism, Information Technology in Tourism and Hospitality, Tourism in the Middle East, Tourism Forecasting/Time Series Analysis, etc. Created and updated by Andrew Yiannakis, director of the Virtual Laboratory for Leisure, Tourism and Sport, University of Connecticut. Most lists were somewhat out-of-date with updates from 1995-2003.

DATA SOURCES

Bureau of Transportation Statistics
<http://www.bts.gov>

Provides statistical information on travel within the United States, including information on traffic patterns and reasons for travel. There are also data on border crossings from Mexico and Canada. Data are also available by type of transportation including monthly data on traffic levels, flight delays, mishandled baggage, oversales, and consumer complaints for the airline industry. Some of the data are dated to 2001, based on the latest National Household Travel Survey.

Economic Census of the United States
<http://www.census.gov/econ/census02/>

Performed every five years, the Economic Census gathers financial and employment data on the industries of the United States. The data are offered at the national, state, county, and MSA level. The industry series gives data at the industry level. The next travel data will be released in 2005.

Office of Travel & Tourism Industries (International Trade Administration, Department of Commerce)
<http://tinet.ita.doc.gov/>

Provides information on tourism development, tourism policy, and data on inbound and outbound travel to and from the U.S. When it is snowing, you can see how many U.S. citizens are traveling to the Caribbean this year! Many areas are still under development.

DATABASES

Hospitality and Tourism Index

This new database being offered by EBSCO is composed of the defunct *Articles in Hospitality and Tourism, Lodging, Restaurant & Tourism Index* and the *Cornell Hospitality Database*. It is the best entry-way to academic articles directly related to tourism. By subscription only.

Mintel Research Reports
<http://www.mintel.com>

Offers research reports on many different industries drawn from secondary information by providers such as Simmons, IRR, and ACNeilson as well as proprietary primary research. The focus is on segments (i.e., coffee) rather than on broad industry categories (i.e., food industry) and offers some brand-level information. Geographic regions covered are the United States, United Kingdom, and the European Union. Two areas of direct interest include Travel and Leisure. Sample reports include Airline Loyalty Programs and Casino Gambling in the United States. Reports are superseded once they are updated, but a backfile of reports may be offered to academic libraries in the near future. One potential snag for academic libraries is that the license agreement prohibits walk-in usage.

National Recreation Database (Canadian)
<http://www.lin.ca/>

Free database offered by Canada's Lifestyle Information Network of government sources on leisure, including tourism. Searchable by keyword, demographic, and topic. Most publications are available through full-text links.

National Tourism Databases
<http://www.msue.msu.edu/msue/imp/modtd/mastertd.html>

Free database created by Michigan State University Extension Tourism Area of Expertise. Offers topic and keyword searching of extension publications such as bulletins, reports, videos, and training programs dealing directly with topics in tourism such as the economic impact of tourism on individual states. Some material is available in the database or contact information is provided for the publication.

INDUSTRY INFORMATION

Industry information is available for tourism in most of the business industry sources, sometimes under such subjects as leisure or travel. There are many associations that also provide information on tourism as a whole or in a segment of the industry. Unfortunately, some of them only offer that information for members of the association. Listed here are the associations and Web sites that offer substantive information for the non-member. Beyond industry overviews, several news and Web portals give access to current updates on the industry.

Airlines

Air Transport Association
<http://www.airlines.org>

As the only trade organization for the principal U.S. airlines, the ATA offers its members the latest industry news, information about government affairs, economics, ATA publications, and operations and safety information. ATA members also have access to a "Members Only" section unavailable for review for this annotation.

International Air Transport Association
<http://www.iata.org>

A trade association that consists of 270 airlines focused on international travel, both passenger and cargo. While most information offered requires subscription or purchase, some information is available for free, including a State of the Industry report, some statistics, and press releases on the industry.

Ecotourism/Geotourism/Sustainable Tourism

The Heisenberg Uncertainty Principle says that you can not observe something without changing what you are trying to observe. This is true in tourism, where even the act of observing or visiting can destroy the object of the travel. A *News in Science* article discusses the Lascaux caves, which had been closed for forty years because of fungus that grew due to alterations in the cave's entrance. Even after the closing, the cave paintings continued to be threatened by fungus probably brought in by workmen fixing the air-conditioning system aimed at keeping fungus out of the caves (*News*). Other sites are similarly menaced by tourism. Mark Fineman lists several areas threatened by tourists, ranging from cave-ins in England, damage to Notre Dame Cathedral, and wear on Mexican pyramids, to trash strewn over Mount Everest (Fineman, E16). Ecotourism is an effort to build an alternative to destructive tourism, either by restricting the numbers of tourists, forbidding tourism in sensitive areas, or charging compensatory rates for tourism to environmentally sensitive areas.

Conservation International
<http://www.ecotour.org/>

Conservation International focuses on sites that have threats to their biodiversity. While not a direct booking site, CI provides information about ecotourism destinations in the threatened areas, including a general description, available activities, location and access, facilities, and contacts for arranging a trip.

International Centre for Ecotourism Research
<http://www.gu.edu.au/centre/icer/>

Hosted by Griffith University in Australia, the center focuses on the environmental impact of tourism and the rise of ecotourism. Available full text are the green guides for tourist activities, including off-road tours, whitewater rafting, whale watching, scuba diving, and small boat tours. Also available are lists of publications and research created at the Centre.

National Geographic Sustainable Tourism Resource Center
<http://www.nationalgeographic.com/travel/sustainable/index.html>

Offers a handbook on evaluating the level of sustainability for companies and destinations, links to TravelWatch articles on sustainable tourism, ratings of destinations on sustainability, and directories of links for sustainable tourism at the tourism professionals, travelers, and resident level.

The International Ecotourism Society (TIES)
<http://www.ecotourism.org>

Provides information about the ecotourism industry including research articles, statistics, and a newsletter on the topic.

United Nations International Year of Ecotourism
<http://www.uneptie.org/pc/tourism/ecotourism/iye.htm>

The United Nations designated 2002 as the International Year of Ecotourism. Events were held in that year, and several publications are available at the Web site including general guides to ecotourism, standards of practice, and results of the summits.

Hoteliers

American Hotel and Lodging Association
<http://www.ahma.com>

AH&LA is a dual membership association that supports members at the federal and state level by providing them with information on governmental affairs, industry news, conventions, and career services. AH&LA products and services include its own *Lodging Magazine*, research reports, and fee-based local market data from Smith Travel Research. Educational opportunities are offered though AH&LA's Educational Institute. However, some information may be somewhat outdated, since most of the press releases were from 2003. On the other hand, this site does offer a Lodging Industry Report using the latest information available from the U.S. Department of Commerce. Property, Allied, or International memberships are available, as are memberships for faculty and students.

American Resort Development Association
<http://www.arda.org>

This Washington, D.C.-based trade association represents the vacation ownership and resort development industries and offers free consumer information, fee-based research reports, legislative information, and services for members.

Bed & Breakfast and Unique Inn Brokers
<http://www.bbteam.com>

Gives inns for sale and articles to help aspiring bed and breakfast owners. Articles cover topics including Anatomy of an Inn Sale, Financing Startup B&Bs with an SBA Loan, and Inn Financing Without Tears.

Yellow Brick Road
<http://www.yellowbrickroadnl.com>

Gives resources for the aspiring innkeepers including: advice for looking for an inn to purchase, financing the purchase, training opportunities, and state-by-state links to local associations and realtors for Bed & Breakfast inns.

News Sources

Ehotelier
<http://www.ehotelier.com/>

Gives access to Internet information useful to employees in the hotel industry, including breaking news drawn from newswires, a free hotelier newsletter, a directory of links to hotel chains, a directory of hotel schools, and an industry discussion forum.

Hotel Interactive
<http://www.hotelinteractive.com/>

Gives access to news briefs and research information focused on hotel and lodging news, hotel development, hotel management, and trade links. Offers further lodging research after a free registration in a Hospitality Insider section.

Hospitality Net
<http://www.hospitalitynet.org/index.html>

Gives access to searchable industry and financial news in the hotel industry. Also gives information about market research reports within the hotel industry, some of which give good data in the summaries and some of which are available in full text.

Overview Sources

CrossSphere: The Global Association for Packaged Travel
<http://www.crosssphere.com/>

An association for tour operators, CrossSphere provides information on market segment assessments, trends in packaged travel, and brief reports on current topics.

Travel Industry Association of America (TIA)
<http://www.tia.org>

An association that covers all of the travel industry, TIA offers many statistics on the travel industry, including demand, pricing, markets, Internet usage for travel, industry performance, and more. Much is only available for a fee or by membership in the organization; however, some material is available for free. TIA also provides current information, including analysis of legislation and its impact on the travel industry.

World Travel and Tourism Council
<http://www.wttc.org>

A trade association solely made up of the business leaders from the private sector of tourism, the World Travel and Tourism Council focuses on promoting the large economic effect of travel and tourism. Free publications include ones that focus on economic impact of tourism, rankings of counties on their offering of a competitive environment for tourism, and guides for sustainable tourism.

World Tourism Organization
<http://www.world-tourism.org>

A specialized agency of the United Nations, the World Tourism Organization (WTO) consists of 144 countries, 7 territories, and 300 members from the private sector. Focused on the development of sustainable tourism, the WTO provides statistics, research, news releases, and programs on tourism around the world.

Restaurant Sources

National Restaurant Association
<http://www.restaurant.org>

Includes a membership of 60,000 companies. The National Restaurant Association, in conjunction with the National Restaurant Association Educational Foundation, provides its members with the latest information on governmental issues, industry forecasts and reviews, growing a business, health and nutrition, career and educational opportunities, conferences and events, and much more. Industry reports are available for sale from its online store and members can contact the association's Information Service and Library by phone or e-mail. The public can access its Dining Guide to find links to national dining guides and to their local restaurant associations, tourism boards, and newspaper dining sections.

Web Portals

Hospitality Index
<http://www.hospitality-index.com/Default.htm>

Manufacturing, service, and supplier index for the hospitality industry. Companies are listed by their major products or services in such categories as: Foodservice Equipment and Supplies, Cleaning and Maintenance, Guest Amenities, etc. Searchable by product keyword and company name.

Hospitality-Industry.com
<http://www.hospitality-industry.com/>

Offers links to hospitality Web sites sorted by broad subject category. The sites are searchable by keyword and the site offers forum area, latest hospitality news, and a free newsletter.

Hotel Resource
<http://www.hotelresource.com/>

Web portal that offers subject listing of links for finding hotel industry suppliers and resources such as real estate, global hospitality portals, research, directories, etc.

Leisuretourism.com
<http://www.leisuretourism.com>

This portal offers access to news in the tourism and leisure areas and articles pulled from CAB Abstracts originally published as the *Leisure, Recreation and Tourism Abstracts*. Coverage begins in 1974 and requires a subscription.

Booking

Rather than evaluate all major booking sites, which are almost identical, this section will concentrate on more unusual booking and travel information sites, either for particular audiences or for specific types of travel.

List of the major booking sites: Travelocity, Orbitz, Cheaptickets. com, Priceline.com, Hotwire.com, Expedia.com., Yahoo! Travel, eBookers.com, American Airlines, Delta Airlines, Southwest Airlines, U.S. Airways, Continental, JetBlue.

Bed and Breakfast Guest Houses and Inns of America Network
<http://www.bedandbreakfast.com>

Gives links to 27,000 bed and breakfast inns worldwide, including hot deals for some of them. The inns are searchable geographically and a reservation request can be e-mailed directly from the listing. The site also provides area reports on either a city or a theme, such as the Northern Shenandoah Valley in Virginia. The site also organizes the B&B Awards which are based on votes by people visiting the Web site. Tips for staying at a B&B are also provided, including: tipping, choosing an inn, and finding pet-friendly inns. If after staying at one, you are inspired to run a B&B, there are also a FAQ on "Is Innkeeping for me?" and links to inns for sale.

Earthwatch
<http://www.earthwatch.org>

Offers the opportunity to volunteer in scientific research and education. Choose from more than 130 expeditions in 47 countries. You can search for expeditions by time period, location, or field of study. Members of an expedition pay for a share of the costs and must pay for travel to the project site. Expeditions in archaeology, biodiversity, conservation research, cultural diversity, endangered ecosystems, global change, oceans, and world health are available.

Earthfoot Poster Board
<http://www.earthfoot.org/>

Earthfoot is a Web portal that provides listing for ecotourism tours, focused on the smaller operators. Listings are sorted by location and by preferred activity. Individual listing for the tours include general description of the tour, general fee information, and booking information.

Elderhostel
<http://www.elderhostel.org/>

Oh, to be 55 or older. If you are, you can join the 170,000 Elderhostel participants in around 10,000 programs in 90 countries. The focus is on lifelong learning with themed trips in North America, education trips on ships and barges, volunteering with service programs, arts and culture, outdoors, and intergeneration with grandchildren. There are no membership fees and tuition is all-inclusive except for travel to the site within the U.S. and Canada.

Hostelling International–American Youth Hostels
<http://www.hiayh.org>

Although membership to this organization is only free for those 18-years old or younger, others can still join and benefit from this network of youth hostels around the United States. Help with planning a trip overseas is also available through links to travel tips and resources, as well as through links to Web sites for youth hostel organizations around the world.

Sustainable Travel
<http://www.responsibletravel.com>

The site links to thousands of holidays focused on sustainable travel listed by: location, activity, and accommodations.

United States Tour Operators Association
<http://www.ustoa.com>

Member of this association must operate in the U.S., have 18 referrals from industry and financial sources, have a certain volume of tours, have operated at least three years under the same management, carry a million dollars of professional liability insurance, adhere to the association's ethical standards, and bond their tours with a million dollars of insurance against bankruptcy. Once a tour operator becomes a member, the company can display the logo of the association assuring travelers of the tour standards. The Web site offers a directory of members searchable by company name, destination, activity, and tour preference.

Health While Traveling

National Center for Infectious Diseases: Travelers' Health
<http://www.cdc.gov/travel/>

Offers health information including information about location, disease, vaccinations, insect protection, outbreaks, and general guidelines on how to avoid becoming ill while traveling.

Travel Health Online
<https://www.tripprep.com/scripts/main/default.asp>

Gives information on health considerations in individual countries, prevention, identification and treatment of specific diseases, and a directory of medical providers worldwide. Requires free registration.

Travel Planning

American Automobile Association
<http://www.aaa.com>

This site contains all sorts of information and tips for car buyers, car owners, and those traveling. One can check out the news page for updated news briefs, book or plan a vacation on AAA's Travel page, or find out more about AAA's many savings, financial, and insurance services. Members can have TripTiks created for them online.

European Travel Commission
<http://www.visiteurope.com>

The ETC is a non-profit marketing organization comprised of national tourism offices of 33 European nations whose purpose is to promote travel to Europe and their individual countries. Some useful links about Europe include weather, tips for preparing for travel to this region, a list of major events, maps and images of Europe, their pressroom items, and a link for hot deals. Links for each of the 33 member countries take the reader to an overview, fast facts, and contact information for that country. One more click takes you directly to that country's tourism Web site.

National Geographic Travel
<http://www.nationalgeographic.com/travel/>

Offers destination guides to specific sites in the United States and Canada which include Things to Do and See, When to Go, Getting There, How to Visit, and Activities. Destination sites are sorted geographically by region or by listings by state or alphabetic. Also features a trip-finder by keyword, region, country and activity.

National Park Service
<http://www.nps.gov>

Despite its name, the National Park Service actually is in charge of many locations beyond the National Parks. Such sites include battlefields, monuments, rivers, preserves, cemeteries, and historic sites. The sites are searchable alphabetically, geographically, by theme (wars, mountains, fossil/dinosaurs, etc.) or by activity (biking, camping, boating, hiking, fishing, etc.). Each location has information on: accessibility, activities, facts, for kids, management docs, plan your visit, history and culture, fees, facilities, nearby attractions, weather and climate, education programs, nature and science, and special events. Planning your visit information includes operating hours and seasons, getting there, and getting around. Be aware that even though the slogan of the National Park Service is "Experience Your America," some of the more popular sites require permits before you can camp there. If actual travel is too much, some of the more popular National Park Service sites have Web cams.

Recreation Vehicle America
<http://www.rvamerica.com>

As "The home of the RV industry on the Internet," this Web site provides a wide array of information for consumers as well as for retailers. Directories, industry news, and chat rooms and bulletin boards are just a few of the types of resources offered.

Tourism Offices Worldwide Directory
<http://www.towd.com>

Directory of all official tourism Web sites including government offices, convention centers, visitor bureaus, and others that provide travel information to the public. Booking and travel agents are not included.

U.S. Department of State Travel
<http://travel.state.gov/>

Includes Background Notes and Travel Warnings about countries where Americans should not travel and guides to traveling as an American overseas which go beyond the usual advice of pretending to be a Canadian. Some tips for traveling overseas handouts are region based and some are topic based, such as Health Issues and Safety Issues. Also contains information for international travelers visiting the United States.

World Chamber of Commerce Directory
<http://www.chamberofcommerce.com>

Most chambers have a visitor's guide on their sites; this directory provides a union site to find the one that covers the area of interest. Searching is by city name and a list of top travel spots is provided.

Yahoo! Travel
<http://travel.yahoo.com/>

Combines travel guides with bookings for transportation, accommodations, vacation packages and deals. Has links to the international versions of this United States travel site.

BIBLIOGRAPHY

Fineman, Mark. (1990, August 5). Nations act to save treasures from trampling of tourists. *Austin American Statesman*, E16. Retrieved December 25, 2004, from Factiva.

International marketing data and statistics. (2004). London: Euromonitor.

National Geographic sustainable tourism resource center (n.d.). Retrieved November 15, 2004, from <http://www.nationalgeographic.com/travel/sustainable/index.html>.

News in science: Environmental and nature (2003, April 1). Retrieved November 22, 2004, from <http://www.abc.net.au/science/news/enviro/EnviroRepublish_821227.htm>.

APPENDIX

List of All Web Sites Used in This Article

Air Transport Association–<http://www.airlines.org>

American Automobile Association–<http://www.aaa.com>

American Hotel and Lodging Association–<http://www.ahma.com>

American Resort Development Association–<http://www.arda.org>

Bed & Breakfast and Unique Inn Brokers–<http://www.bbteam.com>

Bed and Breakfast Guest Houses and Inns of America Network–
<http://www.bedandbreakfast.com>

Bureau of Transportation Statistics–<http://www.bts.gov>

Conservation International–<http://www.ecotour.org/>

CrossSphere: The Global Association for Packaged Travel–
<http://www.crosssphere.com/>

Earthfoot Poster Board–<http://www.earthfoot.org/>

Earthwatch–<http://www.earthwatch.org>

Economic Census of the United States–
<http://www.census.gov/econ/census02/>

Ehotelier–<http://www.ehotelier.com>

Elderhostel–<http://www.elderhostel.org/>

European Travel Commission–<http://www.visiteurope.com>

Hospitality Index–<http://www.hospitality-index.com/Default.htm>

Hospitality-Industry.com–<http://www.hospitality-industry.com/>

Hospitality Net–<http://www.hospitalitynet.org/index.html>

Hostelling International–American Youth Hostels–<http://www.hiayh.org>

APPENDIX (continued)

Hotel Interactive–<http://www.hotelinteractive.com/>

Hotel Resource–<http://www.hotelresource.com/>

International Air Transport Association–<http://www.iata.org>

International Centre for Ecotourism Research–
<http://www.gu.edu.au/centre/icer/>

Leisuretourism.com–<http://www.leisuretourism.com>

Mintel Research Reports–<http://www.mintel.com>

National Center for Infectious Diseases: Travelers' Health–
<http://www.cdc.gov/travel/>

National Geographic Sustainable Tourism Resource Center–
<http://www.nationalgeographic.com/travel/sustainable/index.html>

National Geographic Travel–<http://www.nationalgeographic.com/travel/>

National Park Service–<http://www.nps.gov>

National Recreation Database (Canadian)–<http://www.lin.ca/>

National Restaurant Association–<http://www.restaurant.org>

National Tourism Databases–
<http://www.msue.msu.edu/msue/imp/modtd/mastertd.html>

Office of Travel & Tourism Industries (International Trade Administration, Department of Commerce)– <http://tinet.ita.doc.gov/>

Recreation Vehicle America–<http://www.rvamerica.com>

Sustainable Travel–<http://www.responsibletravel.com>

The International Ecotourism Society (TIES)–<http://www.ecotourism.org>

Tourism Offices Worldwide Directory–<http://www.towd.com>

Tourism Research Links–<http://www.waksberg.com/>

Travel Health Online–<https://www.tripprep.com/scripts/main/default.asp>

Travel Industry Association of America (TIA)–<http://www.tia.org>

United Nations International Year of Ecotourism–
<http://www.uneptie.org/pc/tourism/ecotourism/iye.htm>

United States Tour Operators Association–<http://www.ustoa.com>

U.S. Department of State Travel–<http://travel.state.gov>

Virtual Laboratory for Leisure, Tourism & Sport–
<http://playlab.uconn.edu/frl.htm>

World Chamber of Commerce Directory–
<http://www.chamberofcommerce.com>

World Tourism Organization–<http://www.world-tourism.org>

World Travel and Tourism Council–<http://www.wttc.org>

Yahoo! Travel–<http://travel.yahoo.com/>

Yellow Brick Road–<http://www.yellowbrickroadnl.com>

Finding Your Future:
College and Career Information
on the Internet

Kara J. Gust

Holly A. Flynn

SUMMARY. This article reviews a sampling of free and proprietary college and career resources, available via the Internet. Sites reviewed provide comprehensive information on a variety of colleges and careers and address a number of related college/career guidance issues and special topics. Selected test preparation sites are also reviewed. Sites and resources included are suitable for any college and careers collection and useful to subject selectors and reference librarians. *[Article copies available for a fee from The Haworth Document Delivery Service: 1-800-HAWORTH. E-mail address: <docdelivery@haworthpress.com> Website: <http://www.HaworthPress.com> © 2005 by The Haworth Press, Inc. All rights reserved.]*

KEYWORDS. College guides, career guides, test preparation, Internet resources

Kara J. Gust is Assistant Instruction Librarian, Michigan State University Library, 100 Library, Michigan State University, East Lansing, MI 48824 (E-mail: gustk@msu.edu).

Holly A. Flynn is Mathematics Librarian, Vernon G. Grove Research Library, Michigan State University, D101 Wells Hall, East Lansing, MI 48824 (E-mail: flynnhol@msu.edu).

[Haworth co-indexing entry note]: "Finding Your Future: College and Career Information on the Internet." Gust, Kara J., and Holly A. Flynn. Co-published simultaneously in *Journal of Library Administration* (The Haworth Information Press, an imprint of The Haworth Press, Inc.) Vol. 43, No. 3/4, 2005, pp. 227-245; and: *Evolving Internet Reference Resources* (ed: William Miller, and Rita M. Pellen) The Haworth Information Press, an imprint of The Haworth Press, Inc., 2006, pp. 227-245. Single or multiple copies of this article are available for a fee from The Haworth Document Delivery Service [1-800-HAWORTH, 9:00 a.m. - 5:00 p.m. (EST). E-mail address: docdelivery@haworthpress.com].

Available online at http://www.haworthpress.com/web/JLA
© 2005 by The Haworth Press, Inc. All rights reserved.
doi:10.1300/J111v43n03_17

INTRODUCTION

Whether it be discovering the ideal college major and campus setting, uncovering new online educational opportunities, or seeking information on that "first real job" or a completely new career, both prospective college students and working professionals can find high-quality college and career guidance through the WWW. Many well-established publishers now offer online versions of their college resources that used to exist only in print, microform, and/or CD-ROM such as CollegeSource catalogs, Peterson's guides, and College Board guides. Similarly, career guides that were once only published in print are now available electronically from WetFeet and Vault. Various print directories and guides have been transformed into customizable, one-stop search portals, providing instant access to college degree and program information, career guidance, test preparation materials, advice on resumé writing, and online articles providing additional information. More importantly, in these online resources, publishers have recognized the need for the inclusion of guides to distance education, career education courses, and online degree programs.

Previous literature provides a solid foundation of essential print resources in the area of college guides. Riedinger provides the framework for a strong collection of college guides: general guides and directories, ancillary works such as test preparation materials, specialized guides for particular fields of study, and international study guides. Both he and Grundt also review essential print and software resources produced by Peterson's, The Career Guidance Foundation, The College Board, and ETS, covering undergraduate and graduate schools, degrees/majors, financial aid and scholarships, admissions details, and study abroad programs. Other authors, such as Holden and Buschman, review college guides that focus on opportunities in higher education for non-traditional students, women, minorities, Christian and Jewish students, and for students with special needs.

A strong foundation of literature about career guides also exists. White reviews career exploration resources for libraries: cover letter, resumé, and interviewing guides; company and industry information sources; and salary data. Olver offers suggestions on setting up a career center in a library, including which materials are needed and how they should be organized for optimum browsability. Finally, Lee adds that college students expect a high level of interactivity when searching for career information, an issue addressed by the career Web sites reviewed in this paper.

Many of the resources reviewed in these articles still remain the best for finding college and career information; however, many now also have electronic counterparts that provide excellent college and career search opportunities for the electronic environment. There are also many new high-quality online resources that are great additions to any college/career guide collection. This article reviews a selection of both freely available and/or subscription-based college and career resources on the Web. Resources reviewed are organized into four categories: "College and Career All-in-One Resources" that provide one-stop access to college, career, test preparation materials, and more; followed by "College Resources" only; "Career Resources" only; and "Test Preparation Resources" only. College guide sites reviewed include comprehensive college information: degrees and programs offered, key facts and statistics, and financial aid and tuition information. Sites included cover both U.S. and international colleges and universities and information for non-traditional, minority, and international students. Career resources include sites with information on available positions in the U.S. and abroad, company and industry information, cover letter, resumé, and interviewing guides, salary data, and professional certification. Sites reviewed are just a small sampling of the many college/career information sites now available on the Web.

COLLEGE AND CAREER ALL-IN-ONE RESOURCES

CollegeBoard.com
<http://www.collegeboard.com>

At CollegeBoard.com, The College Board provides an excellent and comprehensive Web site for searching for information on over 3,600 colleges and universities, numerous College Board tests, and over 450 careers. Navigation is very easy through separate, audience-directed links for students, parents, and educators.

The "College QuickFinder" offers quick access to a college by doing a name or keyword search. Searches and colleges recently viewed can be saved to a personalized listing by registering for a free collegeboard. com account. The "College MatchMaker" provides many additional searching features. Schools can be searched by:

- Type: two-year vs. four-year, public vs. private, religious affiliations, co-ed or same-sex, historically black colleges and universities, and Hispanic-serving institutions (as designated by the Federal government).

- Location: regions, states, or distance from a specific zip code.
- Campus Life: rural/urban setting, school size, on-campus or co-ed housing availability, ethnicity of student population, percentages of international students and out-of-state students, and services/accommodations for persons with disabilities.
- Specific Activities and Sports: fraternities and sororities, choral groups, bands, student newspapers, and Division I sports for both men and women.
- Academic Majors (search by keyword or browse by category).
- Technology: availability of Internet access in dorms or requirement of personal computers.
- Admission Criteria: specific test (ACT, SAT) or interview requirements, percentage of applicants accepted, and high school GPA of first-year students. Students may also compare their test scores to those at selected institutions. College searches can also be limited to those schools where the application deadline has not yet passed.
- Cost and Financial Aid: specific in-state and out-of-state tuition ranges, and need-based versus non need-based financial aid awarded.

Additional helpful features include the comparison of schools side-by-side, tips and news related to college searching and applications, information on college visits, and basic guides and FAQs related to planning for, applying to, and paying for college.

Another extensive section of the site provides details on various College Board tests: SAT & Subject Tests, PSAT/NMSQT, AP, and CLEP. Significant information for each test is provided such as test center locations, dates, fees, preparation tips, and many free practice questions and tests.

CollegeBoard.com also offers excellent resources and tools in locating information on hundreds of careers. The "Career Browser" allows users to browse careers by category and title, and access career profiles that include details such as the nature of the job, working conditions, training, earnings, job outlook, and more. A detailed "Majors & Careers" section provides resources on choosing a college major and why it matters, planning for jobs and internships, lists of jobs that require a college education, the "ten hottest careers," and "ten industries with the fastest employment growth."

Most resources at CollegeBoard.com are freely available, but it does offer users the option of saving lists of careers and majors and building resumes online through "My Road," a customizable, subscription-based portal. Overall, CollegeBoard.com is an easy-to-use, complete, and highly useful college/career search resource.

The Princeton Review
<http://www. princetonreview.com/>

The Princeton Review, already a leader in college and career publications, makes a great addition to the Web with its highly practical and extremely well-designed one-stop search portal, complete with a wealth of college, career, and test preparation resources.

The Princeton Review's "College" portion of its Web site offers the unique and personalized "Counselor-O-Matic," an advanced search engine that matches prospective college students' previous academic and extracurricular characteristics to their future academic and college preferences. By signing up for a free account, users can save their histories and preferences and modify their answers and profiles. Users create profiles based on answering a series of questions based on several academic, social, and personal qualities such as high school attended, course load, GPA, class rank, highest standardized test scores, involvement in extracurricular or volunteer activities, sports or music involvement, ethnic background, and gender. Users may also enter their preferences for college, including specific majors or fields of study; religious affiliation; location; size; student body characteristics; cost of tuition; financial aid available; and availability of music, sports, or fraternities/sororities. Profiles of each school include all of the above as well as admissions information, links to online applications (if available), information about visiting each campus, and the school's rankings according to a number of academic and student life factors. Especially useful is the "What students say" section of each profile which includes direct quotes and opinions from students attending that particular school. The "College" site is complete with SAT/ACT preparation resources as well, including free online practice questions and tests, test-taking tips and advice, and fee-based online courses and tutoring.

The Princeton Review also has an extensive online collection of resources on graduate schools, including specific business, law, and medical schools. Information is provided on many specific entrance exams required such as the GRE, GMAT, LSAT, and MCAT. For each test, there are links to free online practice tests, test-taking strategies, and fee-based online courses and tutoring. Additional graduate education links include career-oriented programs offered by various schools, advice on choosing a graduate school, distance education articles, and financial resources available.

The Princeton Review's one-stop search portal is also complete with career information. Its "Career Research & Planning" section includes a "Career Quiz" that matches personal interests to potential careers, advice on choosing a career, interview tips, and possible internships available. Careers and internships can be searched by keyword or browsed alphabetically. Easy-to-read profiles of each career feature segments on: "A Day in the Life," "Quality of Life," "Past and Future," "Facts and Figures," "Majors," "Graduate Programs," and "Internships."

Hobson's CollegeView®
<http://www.collegeview.com/>

Hobson's CollegeView® is an extensive, freely available, one-stop search service for college, career, and test preparation information. Hobson's "College Search" offers access to profiles of more than 3,800 colleges and universities throughout the U.S. and Canada. Schools and universities can be searched by a variety of criteria including name, public vs. private, areas of study, ethnicity, school type (including vocational and community college), athletics, student body size, religious affiliation, location, city size, and more. The search feature is very easy to navigate and multiple criteria selections can be searched at once, including more than one major or area of study. School profiles include links to key facts, an information request form, printable application, and campus tour (if available). The key facts about each school include majors and degrees offered, student body statistics, student life services available, athletics, admission details for domestic and foreign students (including tests required), tuition and fees, financial aid, and scholarship details. Key facts for each school can also be saved or printed in PDF format and searches can be saved by creating a free account. The most unique feature of CollegeView® is its multimedia virtual campus tours for selected schools.

The additional benefits of CollegeView® include numerous guides and links on searching for specific areas of study and types of schools, studying abroad, college life, types of financial aid, and scholarships available. Specific links for Hispanic and Canadian students are also provided. CollegeView® also provides links to test preparation materials for the PSAT, SAT, ACT, and TOEFL, including selected practice questions.

Hobson's CollegeView® search portal is further enhanced with its extensive "Career Center," offering a tremendous amount of information on career planning and searching, as well as tips on interviewing and resumé writing. Careers can be searched by keyword, browsed alphabetically, or browsed by category. The advanced career search allows users to search occupations by personal characteristics and job duties, related areas of study, training and education required, physical demands, and compensation. Job profiles provide wide-ranging details on working conditions, employers, salary, job outlook, education and experience, and job-specific sample resumés.

COLLEGE RESOURCES

CollegeSource® Online
<http://www.collegesource.org>

Since its inception as the Career Guidance Foundation in 1971, CollegeSource, Inc. has continued its dedication to making finding college guides and college information easier with today's technology. Its premiere subscription-based resource, CollegeSource® Online, continues to be the leading resource in identifying colleges and accessing their catalogs. CollegeSource® Online contains current college catalogs (and some from previous years as well) from both public and private two-year, four-year, and graduate schools, for a total of about 28,000 catalogs from more than 4,200 institutions. Of those institutions, approximately 550 are international colleges and universities. It provides a profile of every accredited college within the U.S., along with a link to their college home page, financial aid information, admission requirements and fees, and a map of the school's location and other travel information via Expedia.com.

Several advanced search features provide access to college profiles and catalogs based on majors/degrees, tuition, geographic location (country, state, proximity to a certain city), enrollment, and affiliations. There is also an alphabetical listing of all colleges and universities by institution name. The catalog full-text search provides an extremely useful KWIC "hits summary," displaying excerpts from the PDF catalog immediately before and after each hit. College catalogs are provided in their entirety in PDF format (with hyperlinked table of contents and index), and full printing capabilities. An essential resource for any college collection.

Peterson's Education Portal
<http://www.petersons.com>

Peterson's has a long history and well-established reputation for providing educational information to individuals, institutions, and libraries. It is no surprise then that it presents one of the best and most complete college guide sites freely available. Through audience-directed links, Peterson's Education Portal offers numerous links and resources for prospective undergraduates, graduates, and adult learners.

The "College Bound" center of this site allows prospective undergraduates to search for colleges by name or keyword, location (including specific state, country, or urban/rural setting), tuition, enrollment size, student/faculty ratio, average GPA, type of school (two-year, four-year, public, private, all men's, or all women's), sports programs, and religious denomination. Each college profile is complete with school description and contact information, link to college Web site, link to online application (if available), as well as key statistics and details on students, faculty, campus facilities, majors, academic programs, libraries, on-campus computer technology, athletics, and more. The "College Bound" section for undergraduates also features helpful resources on preparing for the SAT and ACT, applying for financial aid, and studying abroad (including a search for study abroad programs).

Another great advantage of Peterson's is its inclusion of resources for graduate, non-traditional, and distance education students. The "Graduate Bound" section offers specific resources for graduate students such as a search feature to locate graduate schools and programs by name or keyword, test preparation links, financial aid/loan resources, and tips for writing personal statements and essays. The "Adult Learners" section targets non-traditional students who may search for distance learning programs by area of study, degrees awarded, name of school, keyword, and on-campus requirements (if any). The search also allows users to search for continuing education courses that do not require a specific degree. Those students wanting to be recruited by schools have the option of creating an online profile of their personal background and preferred courses of study.

Additional site links include general information on financial aid, test preparation, and important articles and FAQs on choosing a college and major, graduate school, and distance learning education.

Peterson's Career College Foundation
<http://www.petersons.com/cca/default.asp>

Part of Peterson's Education Portal and "Career Education" site, the Career College Foundation provides an excellent resource for those looking for private and post-secondary schools, institutes, colleges, and universities that offer career-specific educational programs. Colleges and schools can be searched by programs of study and/or by name, and then further refined by state or city. Profiles of schools, colleges, or institutes provide basic contact information, Web address, brief descriptions of programs, financial aid, and admissions information. This site is a great addition to Peterson's Education Portal and highly useful search for vocational, technical, and career education programs.

USNews.com: Rankings & Guides
<http://www.usnews.com/usnews/rankguide/rghome.htm>

Although this site boasts a variety of the highly popular *U.S. News and World Report* college rankings, it now also offers many additional free and subscription-based online college guidance resources. Some of these include a detailed school directory, containing key statistics on more than 1,800 colleges and universities in the U.S. and Canada; and a college search feature allowing prospective students to search for schools on selected criteria such as name, location/metro area, distance from home, campus setting, cost, size, majors/academic programs offered, student/faculty ratio, religious affiliation, extracurricular activities offered, varsity sports, and more. Both the A-Z directory and college search function offer a snapshot of each school including basic contact information, Web site link, basic tuition, campus setting, student body information, and *U.S. News* ranking. More detailed facts and statistics for each school are available via subscription. This site also provides "College Step-by-Step," a very helpful practical guide offering tips and advice on getting started with a college search, building a great application, finding financial assistance and opportunities, and locating further articles on college searching.

ClassesUSA
<http://www.classesusa.com>

ClassesUSA is an excellent resource for adults seeking distance learning classes and programs. It provides access to continuing education classes, online degree programs, graduate and post-graduate degrees, corporate training, professional certifications, CD/video training, education financing, and test preparation.The site can be browsed by degree, program, or featured universities. Links to specific degrees offer a description of the degree and program as well as a form to request more information. An easy-to-use, good starting point for those interested in browsing online continuing and distance education programs.

Residential Colleges and Collegiate Universities Worldwide *<http://www.collegiateway.org/colleges/>*

For those students interested in attending residential-style colleges, this site provides a solid listing and collection of individual Web sites of Oxford/Cambridge-style residential colleges at universities around the world. A brief history of the residential college model with a summary of the first universities to establish them up to the more recent universities to institute such colleges is included. It also provides a geographical listing of residential college home pages from universities throughout the world, including Australia, Canada, China, Germany, Ghana, Great Britain, India, Malaysia, Mexico, The Netherlands, New Zealand, Singapore, and the United States. This site is part of a larger Web site called "The Collegiate Way: Residential Colleges and Higher Education Reform" <http://www.collegiateway.org>. "The Collegiate Way" has more general information and recommended reading for students, parents, and faculty on residential colleges and their benefits.

CollegeNET *<http://www.collegenet.com>*

CollegeNET is an easy-to-use search engine for finding colleges and universities by various search options. The basic keyword search allows schools to be searched by name or keyword. A custom search is also available allowing users to search by specific criteria: type of institution (2-year, 4-year, vocational, etc.), public versus private, religious affiliation, tuition range, undergraduate enrollment, intercollegiate sports offered, state/region, proximity to a certain zip code or city, and average high school GPA of the freshman class.

U.S. Journal of Academics *<http://www.usjournal.com/>*

The U.S. Journal of Academics is designed specifically for international students searching for programs of study available at U.S. colleges and universities. Schools listed include four-year liberal arts colleges, community colleges, English language centers, and summer schools located throughout the United States. Schools can also be browsed geographically and searched according to academic preferences such as degree level, field of study, amount of tuition affordable, and geographic preference (region of the U.S.). This site is also unique in that it can be viewed in eleven languages. Profiles of colleges include a link to the college Web site, college description, programs offered, and estimates on tuition and living expenses. Other quality information on this site includes travel advice, English-language testing information, student insurance, visa regulations, and more.

RWM Vocational Schools Database
<http://www.rwm.org/rwm/>

Recommended by and linked from the U.S. Department of Education, this database lists schools providing vocational training in all 50 states. Schools can be browsed first by state, then occupation.

Nationwide and International Honors Programs
<http://www.indiana.edu/~iubhonor/nchc/other.php3>

Maintained by the Indiana University Honors College, this site is both helpful and unique in that it provides a listing of college and university honors programs throughout the U.S.

CAREER RESOURCES

CareerJournal.com
<http://www.careerjournal.com>

CareerJournal.com is the career site of the *Wall Street Journal*. The information on this freely available Web site is wide-ranging and not just geared toward business executives. Visitors have the option of creating a free personal account through which they can access the jobs database and submit an entry to the resume database. They can also participate in various message boards, where they can express their views on issues such as overseas outsourcing.

Even without creating a personal account, users can access a vast array of valuable materials through CareerJournal.com. The Web site contains many articles about current events, such as the recent Presidential election's impact on the job market. Patrons can also take various quizzes to gauge their understanding of anger management or job satisfaction, as well as search a calendar of career events according to state. Job-hunting advice is another highlight, with informative articles about resumes, cover letters, interviewing, and networking. Visitors can also search for corporate recruiters in various industries.

An extensive portion of CareerJournal.com is also comprised of salary information, including many articles on salary negotiation. The "salary search" is a terrific feature, allowing one to search the average salary of numerous professions by zip code and retrieve lengthy explanations of salary information for that field by way of full-color bar graphs.

CareerJournal.com is not just for people looking for a new career, however, but also for those interested in researching other career topics. It contains an interesting section called "Managing your Career" with information on planning for retirement, diversity issues, balancing work and family, and more. In addition, it offers advice on scholarships and finding a graduate school. Finally, when patrons scroll to the bottom of the page, they can sign up to get an RSS feed of new material added to CareerJournal.com.

This Web site is part of a family of *Wall Street Journal* Web sites, which include StartUpJournal.com (URL: <http://www.startupjournal.com/>) and RealEstateJournal.com (URL: <http://www.realestatejournal.com/>). StartUpJournal.com is geared toward entrepreneurs, and RealEstateJournal.com contains useful information on relocation services.

CareerOneStop
<http://www.careeronestop.org/>

CareerOneStop is billed as just that: one stop shopping for all of your career information needs. According to the Web site, "in line with the Department of Labor's vision for America's Labor Market Information System, CareerOneStop is a collection of electronic tools, operating as a federal-state partnership, and funded by grants to states." It is actually the portal to three Web sites: Career InfoNet, America's Job Bank, and the Service Locator.

Career InfoNet (URL: <http://www.acinet.org/acinet/default.asp>) is the place to go for background information on various careers. One of its most interesting features is the Video Library, through which users can download, at no charge, 450 videos in Quick Time on various careers and industries. Visitors can also look up a list of the fastest growing occupations by education level, and find out the salary range for various jobs. Further details provide which careers require licensure or certification in each state. For job seekers, there is a step-by-step resumé tutorial. For employers, there is a "Job Description Writer"–a tutorial on how to write better job descriptions. The page can be automatically translated into nine different languages. Various means of contacting Career InfoNet, including a toll-free phone number for assistance, are also provided.

America's Job Bank (URL: <http://www.ajb.org/>) is one of the largest job databases on the Internet. One of its more distinctive features is the freely available "Search Scout," which automatically e-mails registered users new job listings, according to their pre-selected criteria.

The America's Servicelocator (URL: <http://www.servicelocator.org/>) allows users to search for career service centers in their area. These include unemployment offices, centers where people can receive counseling to deal with the loss of a job, and vocational education centers.

WetFeet
<http://www.wetfeet.com>

When college students are preparing to graduate and look for their first job, they are likely to be lacking in experience. Undergraduates cannot possibly know everything about the industry they are preparing to enter. One resource that can help with this information gap is WetFeet.com, which specializes in offering "insider information" on dozens of industries. Libraries with career collections should also consider purchasing some of WetFeet's print publications. The WetFeet Web site is a terrific supplement to their insider guides, offering a great deal of free information. When visitors first enter the site, all of the WetFeet insider guides are organized by industry on the left-hand side of the screen. By creating a personal login, users can also access free monthly newsletters and most of the features on the Web site. Interviews with the CEOs of large corporations, and profiles of these companies are included as well. As with many career Web sites, there is also a database of jobs that employers have posted.

WetFeet has several other unique features, including "ResumeEdge"–a step-by-step resumé tutor, and the MAPP–a self-assessment test that matches personality with career choices. WetFeet also has a discussion board for jobseekers to express their concerns or questions. For those who have been offered a position, WetFeet offers insider advice on salary negotiation and profiles of major cities for those who are relocating.

Most of the features on WetFeet.com are free once the user registers. Its insider guides are available in print and PDF format and can be purchased directly through WetFeet.com. They are also available through NetLibrary (URL: <http://www.netlibrary.com>).

Vault
<http://www.vault.com>

A site very similar to WetFeet is Vault, which also publishes a collection of insider information guides to various careers. Vault also offers a free job board, free newsletters, and free profiles of various major corporations. One interesting feature is the Electronic WaterCooler™, which is a collection of company-specific message boards where employers can answer questions submitted by potential employees. The Vault's career guides are also available through NetLibrary.

Goinglobal.com
<http://www.goinglobal.com>

For anyone considering a career overseas, goinglobal.com is a highly useful resource. Goinglobal. com publishes guides for 23 countries on five continents. Each guide is approximately 120 pages long and offers cultural advice, employment trends, embassy listings, professional organizations, job search resources, and advice on obtaining work permits and visas.

The Going Global Career Guides are proprietary and are available from several sources. The 2004 full-text PDF guides are available in the ABI-Inform file of the ProQuest Research Library (URL: <http://proquest.umi.com>). They are also available through Goinglobal.com and NetLibrary. By subscribing, the guides can be searched by country, keyword, or topic by an unlimited number of simultaneous users.

Goinglobal.com offers several free features, as well. Patrons can find out about study abroad and international internships. There are many great "hot topics" articles written by international career advisors, on issues such as immigrating with children. Finally, a free database of international jobs is also available.

U.S. Department of Labor, Bureau of Labor Statistics
<http://www.bls.gov/>

When looking for employment statistics, there is only one place to go: the Bureau of Labor Statistics. While most of the Web sites discussed so far have been about finding a job, this Web site is from a rather different approach: the government's role in employment. Thousands of statistics are available from this site including:

- The current unemployment rate and ten years worth of historic data
- Major work stoppages
- Number of workplace injuries, illnesses, and fatalities
- Mass layoffs
- Labor turnover
- Foreign labor statistics for industrialized countries
- Collective bargaining agreements

The Web site also includes wages by area and occupation, a list of frequently asked questions, and a career information page for children.

For the jobseeker, the most useful resources on this Web site are the full-text, freely available publications. For instance, the *Occupational Outlook Quarterly* (URL: <http://www.bls.gov/opub/ooq/ooqhome.htm>) is a magazine with articles on various career issues, such as "how to get a job in the federal government." An index and archives are provided. Print subscriptions are also available from this Web site.

Industries at a Glance (URL: <http://www.bls.gov/iag/iaghome.htm>) contains profiles of twelve different industries. Eleven of these industries are in the private sector; the twelfth industry includes all government and publicly-held jobs.

The Career Guide to Industries (URL: <http://www.bls.gov/oco/cg/home.htm>) provides insight into careers in 42 industries. This publication includes information on working conditions, earnings and benefits, advancement opportunities, and needed training. It is a companion to the *Occupational Outlook Handbook* (URL: <http://www.bls.gov/oco/home.htm>), which provides information about numerous career choices. This publication details what workers do on the job and expected job prospects. Finally, each entry points users to outside organizations for more information on each career.

TEST PREPARATION RESOURCES

LearnATest.com
<http://www.learnatest.com>

Whether one is preparing to move on to graduate school or to receive certification in a particular profession, standardized tests play an important role. LearnATest.com can help with both of these needs. Published by Learning Express Library, LearnATest.com offers over 100 different kinds of practice exams. Persons working toward graduate school can practice taking the GRE, GMAT, MCAT, LSAT, and more. Those preparing for career changes can practice taking the certification exams for Nursing, teaching, real estate, law enforcement, and more. Other tests include the ASVAB (the test used by the military) and the U.S. Citizenship Test.

LearnATest.com is a proprietary resource, available for individual libraries or consortia to subscribe to Learning Express Library. LearnATest.com can be used by an unlimited number of persons at a time. Users are asked to create a login so that the program can save their results. Once users complete a practice test, LearnATest.com gives them a score, and even offers some individual analysis of scores. Results can be printed and students can retake the practice tests when they are ready. The tests are timed to simulate a real-life test-taking situation.

One drawback to LearnATest.com is that the practice tests are not considered to be "official tests" by their testing bodies. While LearnATest.com is a terrific way to study for the GRE, for example, students taking that test are also encouraged to visit the Educational Testing Service's Web site to download an official practice test.

Educational Testing Service (ETS)
<http://www.ets.org>

For over 50 years, the Educational Testing Service (ETS) has been a leader in research and test assessment resources. It is the premiere non-profit organization that administers a number of tests important to higher education, including the SAT, CLEP, GRE, GMAT, TOEFL, and many others. Through the freely available Web site, ETS.org, detailed information about each test is provided, with links to sample test questions, test preparation resources, and test registration. A complete test directory allows access to more information and can be browsed by topic or alphabetically by test name. Online access is also available to the ETS Test Collection, an extensive test library of over 20,000 tests and measurement devices from the 1900s to the present. This test library can be searched through an online search feature called TestLink.

Kaplan's Test Prep and Admissions
<http://www.kaptest.com/>

Kaplan, already one of the premiere leaders in test preparation materials, now offers extensive information about standardized admissions and licensing tests for colleges, graduate schools, medical and health sciences programs, and English proficiency. Through Kaplan's Test Prep and Admissions Web site visitors can search for information on a variety of tests such as the ACT, PSAT/SAT, GRE, GMAT, LSAT, MCAT, CPA, and TOEFL. For each test, the site offers links to a brief overview, with test time, format, and topics tested; free practice tests and questions; test registration; and premium subscription services available such as online courses and private tutoring. Additional links allow users to find a number of free test-taking strategy and admissions seminars and workshops available, searchable by zip code or state.

CONCLUSION

With the development of both free and proprietary online college and career guidance resources, finding future education and career opportunities has become faster, more accessible, and much more personal. As print reference materials continue to be transferred to electronic formats, many educational and vocational publishers are producing more and more online versions of their college and career resources. These online versions provide great additional benefits such as customizable searches, personal accounts and portals, and automated search engines that match preferences to majors and careers. By moving these collections to the Web, publishers are also addressing their users' needs as many prospective college students and job seekers may not be in positions to access print-only resources, such as working professionals looking to take distance education courses.

The foundation for a strong print collection of college/career/test preparation resources has long been established through Peterson's, The College Board, Vault, Bureau of Labor Statistics, ETS, and others. Through these publishers and additional providers, this foundation should continue to be built upon for the electronic environment with the inclusion of the incredibly rich online collection of college and career search portals, guides, and Web sites.

WEBLIOGRAPHY

Career Guidance Foundation, *CollegeSource® Online*, 10 November 2004, <http://www.collegesource.org/>, (1 November 2004).

ClassesUSA, Inc. *ClassesUSA*, 2004, <http://www.classesusa.com/>, (16 November 2004).

CollegeBoard.com, Inc. *College Board*, 2004, <http://www.collegeboard.com/>, (3 November 2004).

CollegeNET, Inc. *CollegeNET*, 2004, <http://www.collegenet.com/>, (7 November 2004).

Educational Testing Service, *ETS.org*, 28 June 2004, <http://www.ets.org>, (24 November 2004).

Goinglobal.com, *Homepage*, 2004, <http://www.goinglobal.com>, (18 November 2004).

Hobson's CollegeView®, <http://www.collegeview.com>, (7 September 2005).

Indiana University Honors College, *Nationwide and International Honors Programs*, 31 October 2002, <http://www.indiana.edu/~iubhonor/nchc/other.php3>, (6 November 2004).

Kaplan, Inc. Kaplan's Test Prep and Admissions, 2004, <http://www.kaptest.com/>, (23 November 2004).

Learning Express Library, *LearnATest*, 2004, <http://www.learnatest.com>, (18 November 2004).

NetLibrary, *Homepage*, 2004, <http://www.netlibrary.com>, (18 November 2004).

O'Hara, Robert J., *Residential Colleges and Collegiate Universities Worldwide*, 20 August 2004, <http://www.collegiateway.org/colleges/>, (16 November 2004).

RWM.org, *RWM Vocational School Database*, 29 October 2004, <http://www.rwm.org/rwm/>, (5 November 2004).

The Princeton Review, Inc. *The Princeton Review*, 2004, <http://www.princetonreview.com/>, (16 November 2004).

Thomson Peterson's, *Peterson's Education Portal*, 2004, <http://www.petersons.com/>, (2 November 2004).

Thomson Peterson's, *Peterson's Career College Foundation*, 2004, <http://www.petersons.com/cca.default.asp>, (17 November 2004).

United States Bureau of Labor Statistics, *Career Guide to Industries*, 2004, <http://www.bls.gov/oco/cg/home.htm>, (18 November 2004).

United States Bureau of Labor Statistics, *Homepage*, 2004, <http://stats.bls.gov>, (18 November 2004).

United States Bureau of Labor Statistics, *Industries at a Glance*, 2004, <http://www.bls.gov/iag/iaghome.htm>, (18 November 2004).

United States Bureau of Labor Statistics, *Occupational Outlook Handbook*, 2004, <http://www.bls.gov.oco/home.htm>, (18 November 2004).

United States Bureau of Labor Statistics, *Occupational Outlook Quarterly*, 2004, <http://www.bls.gov/opub/ooq/ooqhome.htm>, (18 November 2004).

United States Department of Labor, *America's Career InfoNet*, 2004, <http://www.acinet.org/acinet>, (18 November 2004).

United States Department of Labor, *America's Job Bank*, 2004, <http://www.ajd.dni.us/>, (18 November 2004).

United States Department of Labor, *America's Servicelocator*, 2004, <http://www. servicelocator.org>, (18 November 2004).

United States Department of Labor, *CareerOneStop*, 2004, <http://www.careeronestop. org>, (18 November 2004).

University Microfilms International, *ProQuest*, 2004, <http://proquest.umi.com>, (18 November 2004).

U.S. News & World Report, L.P., *USNews.com: Rankings & Guides*, 2004, <http:// www.usnews.com/usnews/rankguide/rghome.htm>, (14 November 2004).

usjournal.com, LLC, *U.S. Journal of Academics*, 1 November 2003, <http://www. usjournal.com/>, (15 November 2004).

Vault.com, *Homepage*, 2004, <http://www.vault.com>, (18 November 2004).

Wall Street Journal, *CareerJournal.com*, 2004, <http://www.careerjournal.com>, (18 November 2004).

WetFeet.com, *Homepage*, 2004, <http://www.wetfeet.com>, (18 November 2004).

REFERENCES

Grundt, L. "College Guides That Make the Grade." *Library Journal* 117, no. 10 (1992): 83-87.

Holden, K. A. "Alternative Perspectives on College Guides." *Behavioral & Social Sciences Librarian* 10, no. 2 (1991): 57-77.

Lee, Catherine A. "Characteristics of Generation X and Implications for Reference Services and the Job Search." *The Reference Librarian* 55 (1996): 51-59.

Olver, Lynne. "Qualifications Required for a Library Career Center," *American Libraries* 33, no. 7 (2002): 60-61.

Riedinger, E. A. "Resources for Special Library Collection Development in Educational Advising." *Special Libraries* 86 (1995): 272-278.

White, Gary W. *Help Wanted: Job & Career Information Resources.* Chicago, IL: Reference and User Services Association, American Library Association, 2003.

ESL (English as a Second Language) Web Sites: Resources for Library Administrators, Librarians, and ESL Library Users

John Hickok

SUMMARY. Due to immigration patterns over the past few decades, librarians and library administrators at all levels–public, school, and academic–are increasingly welcoming library users who speak English as a Second Language (ESL). Not surprisingly, growth has also occurred in the ESL teaching profession (referred to as TESOL–Teaching English to Speakers of Other Languages), including the proliferation of many Web sites for both teachers and students. This article discusses these sites, particularly in the context of how they may be of help to libraries. *[Article copies available for a fee from The Haworth Document Delivery Service: 1-800-HAWORTH. E-mail address: <docdelivery@haworthpress.com> Website: <http://www.HaworthPress.com> © 2005 by The Haworth Press, Inc. All rights reserved.]*

KEYWORDS. Internet resources, Web sites, ESL (English as a Second Language), TESOL (Teaching English to Speakers of Other Languages), immigrants, minorities

John Hickok is TESOL Librarian, California State University Fullerton, 800 North State College Boulevard, Fullerton, CA 92834 (E-mail: jhickok@fullerton.edu).

[Haworth co-indexing entry note]: "ESL (English as a Second Language) Web Sites: Resources for Library Administrators, Librarians, and ESL Library Users." Hickok, John. Co-published simultaneously in *Journal of Library Administration* (The Haworth Information Press, an imprint of The Haworth Press, Inc.) Vol. 43, No. 3/4, 2005, pp. 247-262; and: *Evolving Internet Reference Resources* (ed: William Miller, and Rita M. Pellen) The Haworth Information Press, an imprint of The Haworth Press, Inc., 2006, pp. 247-262. Single or multiple copies of this article are available for a fee from The Haworth Document Delivery Service [1-800-HAWORTH, 9:00 a.m. - 5:00 p.m. (EST). E-mail address: docdelivery@haworthpress.com].

INTRODUCTION

The number of people who speak English as a Second Language (ESL) has increased in the U.S. over the past few decades, largely due to immigration patterns. The U.S. Department of Education has noted this, reporting that for 1999s student age groups (5-24 year olds), 13.7 million spoke a language other than English at home–a doubling from two decades earlier.[1] Additionally, the 2000 Census reported that of the U.S. adult population, a full 37 million speak another language at home besides English.[2] This demographic change has implications for librarians and library administrators at all levels–public, school, and academic–as increased numbers of ESL speakers visit libraries. Additionally, the geographic distribution of ESL library visitors has increased as well. The stereotypical big-city immigrant magnets (New York, Los Angeles, Miami, etc.), while still magnets, are not alone; Midwest states are encountering, for example, increased numbers of Spanish-speaking Mexican and Latin American immigrants.

Not surprisingly, growth has also occurred in the ESL teaching profession (referred to as TESOL–Teaching English to Speakers of Other Languages), including the proliferation of many Web sites for both teachers and students. In the mid-1990s, as the Internet was first becoming popular, there were only a handful of Web sites dedicated to ESL. These were not necessarily sites from official organizations, like *TESOL.org*, but rather from individuals–ESL instructors in the U.S. and abroad who were enthusiasts in this "new" medium of communication. Examples include Charles and Lawrence Kelly posting lesson ideas in 1995 (to eventually become *The Internet TESL Journal*) and Dave Sperling posting ESL Q&As for students, also in 1995 (to later become *eslcafe.com*). Sperling and his site, in particular, became somewhat of a catalyst for the explosion of other ESL Web sites. Due to the wild popularity of his site (thousands of hits daily), in 1998 he converted to a ".com" site, and began featuring advertising. Certainly the evident potential for advertising revenues was an influence in the many .com ESL Web sites that soon followed. This is not to say that all .com ESL Web sites have only profits in mind. Although commercial by designation, many offer significant free resources (activities, lesson plan ideas, etc.).

Paralleling .com sites, ESL/TESOL publishers also made their entrance onto the Web. Today, there are dozens of large-corporation ESL/TESOL publishers on the Web–offering detailed catalogs of their materials–as well as hundreds of smaller and regional ESL/TESOL publishers. Brokers of ESL/TESOL publishers are also now online, offering educators and librarians "one stop shopping" for ESL resources.

However, .com sites were not the only sites to grow on the Web; many "non-.com" sites similarly developed. ESL departments and faculty at educational institutions began creating ".edu" sites (example: Purdue University's *Online Writing Lab* at <http://owl.english.purdue. edu/handouts/esl/index.html>, providing grammar and writing help for ESL students), and ESL-related organizations began launching their official sites, such as *TESOL.org*, and *NABE.org*. Today, when considering all domains (.com, .org, .edu, etc.) there are thousands of ESL-related Web sites. And when considering individual ESL contributions on the Web–such as an ESL teacher's activity ideas posted on a personal homepage–then the numbers grow even larger. In fact, ESL-related sites have become so numerous that it becomes a challenge for ESL educators and students to sort through them all to find relevant content. Internet search engines, such as *google.com*, can help find specific key-worded sites, but otherwise, they yield overwhelming lists (a simple keyword search of "ESL" on *google.com* currently produces over 7 million hits!). A more helpful strategy is taking advantage of annotated "Webliographies," or lists, of ESL Web sites (more on this, following).

With this plethora of ESL-related Web sites in mind, the context of libraries again arises. Can these sites be of help to libraries? Most certainly. Professional and organizational ESL/TESOL Web sites can be of interest to library administrators in several ways: sociopolitical news on ESL demographics, standards for ESL instruction, bilingual resources, and so forth. ESL/TESOL publisher sites can be of interest to librarians in the collection development of ESL/TESOL books and materials. And sites designed for ESL teachers and students–offering lessons, activities, quizzes, etc.–can also be of benefit to librarians. Teaching ideas presented there can be used by librarians to improve library instruction and reference assistance to ESL students/learners. Learning resources there can be recommended to these students/learners. A frequent reason ESL students/learners visit libraries is to find materials to assist learning English–whether books or videos or test preparation aids, etc. Small libraries–especially schools or public branches–may not have extensive ESL learning material, so the wealth of learner-oriented activities/quizzes/tutorials/lessons on ESL Web sites can become a valuable supplemental resource in the library. That is, however, only if librarians are aware of them.

This article will discuss many of the valuable, prominent ESL Web sites currently available, arranging them in the following four categories: professional and organizational ESL/TESOL sites, ESL/TESOL Webliographies, ESL/TESOL publisher sites, and finally, resource sites for ESL educators and ESL students/learners.

PROFESSIONAL AND ORGANIZATIONAL ESL/TESOL SITES

Tesol.org
<http://www.tesol.org>

Just as ALA represents the library profession, TESOL–the professional association founded in 1966–stands to represent the ESL teaching profession. Its Web site gives news and information for and about the profession, elements of which are of interest to libraries: standards, position statements (e.g., the bilingual education debate), community outreach initiatives, etc.

[State abbreviation]tesol.org
<http://www.tesol.org/s_tesol/sec_document.asp?CID=420&DID=2248>

Besides the national TESOL association, nearly every U.S. state has a state TESOL association and Web site. These associations focus on the specific needs of that state. For example, California's site, *catesol.org*, addresses California-specific issues–such as instructional changes from a 1998 proposition ending bilingual education. Consulting with these state sites could provide helpful information to libraries in assessing their own state's climate on bilingual/language learning issues. A list of all state TESOL Web sites can be found at: <http://www.tesol.org/s_tesol/sec_document.asp?CID=420&DID=2248>.

Ncela.gwu.edu
<http://www.ncela.gwu.edu>

The National Clearinghouse for English Language Acquisition (NCELA), formerly the National Clearinghouse for Bilingual Education (NCBE), is an entity of the U.S. Department of Education to collect information on ESL learning in the U.S. It contains statistics on spoken languages, information on diversity outreach, FAQs on current legislation, and more.

Cal.org
<http://www.cal.org>

The Center for Applied Linguistics is a private, non-profit organization dedicated to language learning research and improvement since 1959. Its Web site hosts an impressive selection of professional resources: research papers, instructional materials, and valuable directories and centers (sub pages)–for example, the Center for Adult English Language Acquisition, where adult literacy programs are discussed in detail (of value to public libraries offering such programs).

Nabe.org
<http://www.nabe.org>

The National Association of Bilingual Education has a coalition membership of teachers, administrators, parents, and more–all favoring bilingual education. They share some goals, but not all, with TESOL. NABE has, in recent years, become a political advocacy group as legislation against bilingual education has arisen in various states. Its site is helpful for libraries in following the current controversies. NABE's site also provides links to its various state affiliate associations.

Literacynet.org/esl
<http://www.literacynet.org/esl>

This Web site is a subdivision of the National Institute for Literacy (*nifl.gov*), a jointly administered program by the departments of Education, Labor, and Health and Human Services. At this site are complete administration resources for conducting literacy programs, instruction, and outreach to ESL learners. It includes materials, training, links, and more.

Acrl.org/is
<http://www.acrl.org/is>

The Web site of the Instruction Section of the Association of College & Research Libraries features a bibliography of "Instruction for Diverse Populations." This includes a section on ESL/international learners, for which this author was the first contributor. The bibliography is an annotated listing of articles, books, and Web sites specifically addressing the issue of assisting these learners in libraries.

Aaiep.org
<http://www.aaiep.org>

uciep.org
<http://www.uciep.org>

These are Web sites of twin associations of Intensive English Programs (IEPs)–the American Association of Intensive English Programs and the University Consortium of Intensive English Programs. These sites are important for libraries to be aware of, as they list and link to IEPs nationwide. Libraries–whether an academic library sharing the same campus with an IEP, or a public library with a independent IEP nearby–can then plan for IEP student usage of the library accordingly.

ESL/TESOL WEBLIOGRAPHIES

It is beyond the scope of this article to try to list and describe every ESL/TESOL site on the Web; there are simply too many. However, there are sites that *do* try to maintain such lists–Webliographies. Some are more comprehensive than others, but all are helpful. Keeping their links updated, however, is a universal challenge for all of them.

Linguistlist.org
<http://www.linguistlist.org>

Self-proclaimed as "the world's largest online linguistic resource," this site is impressive. Its resources and links are extensive. Under the category of *Teaching & Learning→ESL & EFL*, there are hundreds of links for both students (activity sites, grammar tip sites, etc.) and teachers (lesson plan sites, teaching tips sites, etc.).

Iteslj.org/links
<http://iteslj.org/links/>

The Internet TESL Journal's link page is also impressive. Two side-by-side columns–one for students, one for teachers–list dozens of categories (writing, idioms, handouts, etc.) and within each, up to a hundred or more links. All links go to a variety of ESL/TESOL Web sites–some by educators at .edu sites, others by .com companies.

Cal.org/resources/ncbe/esldirectory
<http://www.cal.org/resources/ncbe/esldirectory>

CAL maintains a good Webliography as well, categorized into several areas for both teachers (lesson ideas, assessment, materials, etc.) and students (activities, grammar help, tutorials, etc.).

Eslcafe.com
<http://www.eslcafe.com>

Although Dave Sperling's popular site is primarily a resource site for students, it does maintain a categorized and annotated link page (Webliography) for both teachers and students. Teachers can find annotated links to sites on training, testing procedures, and more; students will see annotated links to sites for games, activities, pronunciation drills, etc.

Englishclub.com/webguide
<http://www.englishclub.com/webguide>

This is a ".com" site similar to *eslcafe.com*, although based out of England. Its Webliography is annotated, and is well organized into categories: vocabulary, grammar, lesson plans, etc. Links for both teachers and students are featured.

English-online.net
<http://www.english-online.net>

tefltesl.free-online.co.uk
<http://www.tefltesl.free-online.co.uk>

These two British Webliographies offer many annotated links. The first, in particular, even evaluates the linked sites using a subjective ranking grid.

Englishnetlinks.com
<http://www.englishnetlinks.com>

Englishwebguide.com
<http://www.englishwebguide.com>

Esldesk.com/esl-links/index.htm
<http://www.esldesk.com/esl-links/index.htm>

These Webliographies offer few or no annotations (sometimes just links only), but nonetheless provide a good assortment of categories–e.g., activities, games, online dictionaries, etc.

Dir.yahoo.com
<http://dir.yahoo.com>

directory.google.com
<http://directory.google.com>

vivisimo.com
<http://www.vivisimo.com>

The Web directories found in popular Internet search engines also provide annotated Webliographies of ESL sites. Yahoo's directory path is: Social Science → Linguistics and Human Languages → Languages → Specific Languages → English → English as a Second Language. Google's is: Arts → Education → Language Arts → English → English as a Second Language. Vivisimo, least known of the three, actually provides better subcategorizing (folders, in the left frame).

[Individuals' Webliographies]

Several individual ESL educators attempt to maintain Webliographies on personal homepages. While not as comprehensive as others, they can often provide insightful annotations. These include: <http://www.angelfire.com/yt/efl>, <http://www.geocities.com/teflthing>, <http://www.csun.edu/~hcedu013/eslplans.html>, <http://www.clas.ufl.edu/users/rthompso/tman.html>, and <http://guides.library.fullerton.edu/tesol/websites.htm>.

Esloop.org
<http://www.esloop.org>

The "ESL Loop" does not categorize its list of sites. Rather, it is a random collection of linked ESL sites (the same idea as "Web Rings"). The lack of categorization is a significant drawback, but at least all participating sites are annotated.

ESL/TESOL PUBLISHER SITES

There are hundreds, if not thousands, of ESL/TESOL publishers if one considers *all* categories–large corporate publishers, small presses, local and regional publishers, etc. The publisher sites below represent national publishers with longstanding traditions of publishing in the ESL/TESOL arena. These publishers are consistently seen at national and state TESOL conventions, year after year. For a more comprehensive list of ESL/TESOL publishers, the Webliographies discussed earlier, or standard publisher directories (e.g., *American Book Trade Directory*) can be consulted.

Brokers

The following brokers–superstores offering ESL materials from multiple publishers–offer "one stop shopping."

Altaesl.com
<http://www.altaesl.com>

Located in northern California, ALTA ESL is one of the largest and most comprehensive brokers. Its online catalog features multiple categories, levels, formats, etc.

Delta-systems.com
<http://www.delta-systems.com>

Competitive with ALTA, and offering in impressive selection as well, Delta is located in Illinois, with an equally strong online catalog.

Millereducational.com
<http://www.millereducational.com>

Located in southern California, Miller Educational Materials has a particularly strong emphasis on Elementary ESL materials.

Multiculturalbooksandvideos.com
<http://www.multiculturalbooksandvideos.com>

This broker has a strong emphasis on videos, but not just for ESL only–learning other languages too.

Publishers

Longman.com
<http://www.longman.com>

One of the largest ESL publishers, its parent company is Pearson Education. Other publisher labels under the same Pearson corporate umbrella are: Prentice-Hall, Scott-Foresman, Addison-Wesley, Dominie, and Penguin.

Heinle.com
<http://www.heinle.com>

Heinle & Heinle likewise has a long history of ESL publishing. Its parent company is Thompson Learning, which also owns the Newbury-House publisher label.

Oup.com/us/esl
<http://www.oup.com/us/esl>

Oxford University Press publishes many ESL materials, including its well-known picture dictionary (offered in many languages).

Cambridge.org/pubs/catalog
<http://www.cambridge.org/esl-efl>

Cambridge ESL is also a longstanding ESL publisher, and has a strong showing of academic/linguistic/teacher preparation materials.

Tesol.org
<http://www.tesol.org/s_tesol/seccss.asp?CID=6&DID=7>

TESOL, the national association, is itself a publisher. It offers various products, but its main emphasis is items on teacher development.

Mhcontemporary.com
<http://www.mhcontemporary.com>

Contemporary Publishers, of the McGraw-Hill parent company, specializes in adult and basic education ESL.

Press.umich.edu/esl
<http://www.press.umich.edu/esl>

The University of Michigan Press offers many ESL materials.

Ballard-tighe.com
<http://www.ballard-tighe.com>

Ballard & Tighe has a strong emphasis on testing materials.

Steck-vaughn.com
<http://www.steck-vaughn.com>

Steck-Vaughn, of the Harcourt parent company, has a strong emphasis on adult and vocational ESL.

Macmillaneducation.com
<http://www.macmillaneducation.com>

While not specifically designated as ESL, Macmillan publishes dictionaries and general English learning texts.

Newreaderspress.com
<http://www.newreaderspress.com>

New Readers Press, of the ProLiteracy parent company, has a strong emphasis on literacy, reading, and vocational ESL.

Prolinguaassociates.com
<http://www.prolinguaassociates.com>

Pro Lingua Associates has a strong emphasis in elementary and activity books.

Barrons.com
<http://www.barronseduc.com/english-language-arts.html>

Barrons, best known as a consumer-oriented study guide publisher, has a strong emphasis on ESL test preparation materials.

ETS.org
<http://www.ets.org/store.html>

Educational Testing Service, the well-known publisher of educational tests (in particular, the TOEFL, for ESL students), itself publishes test preparation materials.

RESOURCE SITES FOR ESL EDUCATORS AND ESL STUDENTS/LEARNERS

As noted, there are many thousands of ESL Web sites–impossible to list and annotate in this article. Therefore, in the listing and annotations which follow, only a representation of many of the more prominent ESL Web sites (established, consistent track records) is offered. Certainly, any subjective listing like this is open for debate; there are countless other sites that could be listed as well, but are not listed for lack of space. Therefore, to explore a fuller, more comprehensive listing of ESL Web sites, one should consult the Webliographies previously discussed.

An important note to make is that on many sites with free resources, particularly .com sites, there are also many "teasers"–that is, links that, when clicked, provide only a sample or description of some resource, and then state that the full resource is available for sale from an advertiser. This is unfortunate, but a reality–.com sites have to pay for their real estate on the Web, and do so with advertising.

Iteslj.org
<http://www.iteslj.org>

The Internet TESL Journal is a longstanding and comprehensive ESL resource site; it offers many resources–from games to lesson plans to grammar explanations–submitted by ESL educators from around the world.

Eslcafe.com
<http://www.eslcafe.com>

One of the most popular ESL sites on the Internet. Offers helpful teaching ideas for teachers, and a wide variety of aids (quizzes, activities, etc.) for students.

Englishclub.com
<http://www.englishclub.com>

tefl.net
<http://www.tefl.net>

These are twin sites, offering resources similar to *eslcafe.com*, for both students and teachers. *Tefl.net* focuses more on teachers' resources.

Englishforum.com
<http://www.englishforum.com>

Like *Englishclub.com* this is an England-based site with activities/quizzes/links for students, and lesson ideas/book recommendations/links for teachers.

ESLgold.com
<http://www.eslgold.com>

Advertises "hundreds of pages of free English teaching and learning materials for both students and teachers," and has a good category menu.

Marksesl.com
<http://www.marksesl.com>

Advertised as a "mega-portal to everything that's ESL," it does impress; many submenus of resources–from flash cards to grammar tools–are available. It provides a considerable list of links. The site is maintained by an ESL teacher in Korea.

Towerofenglish.com
<http://www.towerofenglish.com>

On the Web since 1998, Tower of English provides resources (lessons, quizzes, idioms, tests, etc.) by categories and linking.

Eslmonkeys.com
<http://www.eslmonkeys.com>

Another multipurpose site for both students (activities, quizzes, etc.) and teachers (lessons, job board, etc.); it is maintained by two ESL teachers/entrepreneurs.

Eslpartyland.com
<http://www.eslpartyland.com>

While not as comprehensive as others, it offers more informal activities, on movies, music, etc. The teacher lesson ideas and links page are good.

Esl.about.com
<http://www.esl.about.com>

This popular Internet information site also provides a helpful section on ESL. It provides articles and materials for teachers, and activities/reference for students.

Tesol.net
<http://www.tesol.net>

linguistic-funland.com
<http://www.linguistic-funland.com>

These two are twin sites, maintained by a linguist/Webmaster, and offer an impressive assortment of links, activities, and information. *Tesol.net* should not be confused with *Tesol.org*, which links to the professional association, TESOL.

Rong-chang.com
<http://www.rong-chang.com>

Maintained by a PhD ESL educator, this site has a wealth of activities, lessons, quizzes, and more–very useful for classroom applications.

Englishpage.com
<http://www.englishpage.com>

This site is another .com multi-resource site, but provides many tutorials and interactive exercises that are custom-written (not just links to elsewhere).

Usingenglish.com
<http://www.usingenglish.com>

Provides a nice menu of resources–grammar reference, online quizzes and activities, teacher handouts, etc. Registering (free) provides access to even more.

Englishlearner.com
<http://www.englishlearner.com>

Maintained by a Hungarian ESL teacher, it focuses on tests and quizzes for students (and tips for implementing, for teachers).

Manythings.org
<http://www.manythings.org>

Maintained by the creators of the Internet TESL Journal, this site is filled with word games, puzzles, quizzes, exercises, slang, proverbs, and much more. While it is designed for students, it is of value to teachers in activity planning.

A4esl.org
<http://a4esl.org>

The Internet TESL Journal creators are behind this site as well; it is replete with submitted quizzes, tests, exercises, and puzzles from ESL educators around the world.

Esl-lab.com
<http://www.esl-lab.com>

Titled "Randall's ESL Cyber Listening Lab," this site provides streaming audio listening segments with comprehension quizzes (most useful for students, but ideal for teachers to use as supplements to lessons).

Englishlistening.com
<http://www.englishlistening.com>

real-english.com
<http://www.real-english.com>

Both of these are streaming audio or video sites, with listening comprehension tests. However, unlike *Randall's* (above), they only offer a limited assortment of segments for free; the rest are by paid subscription only.

English-zone.com
<http://www.english-zone.com>

This site has some free resources, but otherwise, is a subscription site; access to all other quizzes, activities, etc., is by paid subscriptions.

1-language.com
<http://www.1-language.com>

Many fewer resources than other sites, but this site still has several good activities, quizzes, and links of use to both students and teachers.

Johnsesl.com
<http://www.johnsesl.com>

A multi-resource site maintained by an ESL teacher, it is rich with activities, quizzes, vocabulary exercises, and more (some are interactive and require Javascript).

Eleaston.com
<http://www.eleaston.com>

This tutorial and help site for English learners is actually maintained by a software engineer (with a great interest in English), not an ESL teacher or company.

Eslflow.com
<http://www.eslflow.com>

This site authorship is not credited, but does provide a very good assortment of elementary-intermediate activities for ESL teachers to use in the classroom.

Bogglesworld.com
<http://www.bogglesworld.com>

Pumpkinandcompany.com
<http://www.pumpkinandcompany.com>

These two sites (not related) are maintained by ESL teachers from around the world, and contain an assortment of lesson plans, handouts, activities, and more–emphasizing elementary levels.

NOTES

1. U.S. Department of Education, National Center for Education Statistics. *The Condition of Education, 2003.* Indicator 4: Participation in Education–Language Minority Students. (Washington, D.C.: GPO, 2003), 21 <http://nces.ed.gov/programs/coe/2003/section1/indicator04.asp>.

2. U.S. Census 2000, in *Statistical Abstract of the United States 2004.* (Washington, D.C.: GPO, 2004), 46 <http://www.census.gov/prod/2004pubs/04statab/pop.pdf>.

Accessing Legal and Regulatory Information in Internet Resources and Documents

Yvonne J. Chandler

SUMMARY. The quantity of legal and government information accessible through online delivery has increased tremendously. Information technology has revolutionized the way much of this information is disseminated by government and the way that researchers access it. The increase in publication can be attributed to two factors: the government's efforts to create a virtual depository of publications and the capability of Internet technology to provide personalized "feeds" of topic-specific information through Web logs and RSS news aggregators. In this article, finding tools, primary and secondary sources of legal and regulatory government information will be identified and described including search engines and guides. *[Article copies available for a fee from The Haworth Document Delivery Service: 1-800-HAWORTH. E-mail address: <docdelivery@haworthpress.com> Website: <http://www.HaworthPress.com> © 2006 by The Haworth Press, Inc. All rights reserved.]*

KEYWORDS. Legal research–United States, government information, Internet legal resources, blogs–legal, laws and legislation–United States,

Yvonne J. Chandler is Associate Professor, University of North Texas, School of Library and Information Sciences, PO Box 311068, Denton, TX 76205 (E-mail: chandler@lis.admin.unt.edu).

[Haworth co-indexing entry note]: "Accessing Legal and Regulatory Information in Internet Resources and Documents." Chandler, Yvonne J. Co-published simultaneously in *Journal of Library Administration* (The Haworth Information Press, an imprint of The Haworth Press, Inc.) Vol. 44, No. 1/2, 2006, pp. 263-324; and: *Evolving Internet Reference Resources* (ed: William Miller, and Rita M. Pellen) The Haworth Information Press, an imprint of The Haworth Press, Inc., 2006, pp. 263-324. Single or multiple copies of this article are available for a fee from The Haworth Document Delivery Service [1-800-HAWORTH, 9:00 a.m. - 5:00 p.m. (EST). E-mail address: docdelivery@haworthpress.com].

government publications, regulations–United States, United States law–bibliography

INTRODUCTION

The law . . . should surely be accessible at all times and to everyone

Franz Kafka

Since the dawn of the Internet age, the quantity of legal and government information being published and made accessible through online delivery has increased tremendously each year. Legal and government information is available from a number of sources on the Internet. Content providers include the United States government, state governments, law schools, private law firms, and private corporations. This information has expanded from a minimal amount of federal government and court information to a highly visible online presence for each state and federal government branch, legislature, department, and/or agency. New resources are added to the Web every day. This availability to government information does truly make the law more accessible to everyone. With RSS technology, desired information is served directly to researchers customized according to their interests in a "feed" of topic-specific news headlines.

The two most significant databases of legal and regulatory information are the subscriber systems of Lexis and Westlaw. There are many freely accessible Web sites where legal and regulatory information can be found. Although there has been a significant increase in the amount of legal information accessible on the Internet, there are limitations on the scope and coverage of this information on Web sites. There are still no significant retrospective archives of freely accessible legal information resources on the Internet. Current and more recent information is well covered on the Net. The government documents and information published on the Internet do not include editorial enhancements or corrections that you will find using the commercially published documents.

WHAT IS LEGAL AND REGULATORY INFORMATION?

Law is the entire body of principles, precedents, rules, regulations, and procedures intended to assure order and justice in a civilized society. It includes constitutions, legislation, decisions–federal, state, and local, civil and criminal.[1] The primary sources of Anglo-American law are created and produced by the judicial, legislative, and administrative branches of government at the federal, state, or local government levels. Much of legal and regulatory information consists of those recorded rules that society will enforce and the procedures that can implement them. Representing the interests and information needs of all citizens, these courts, administrative offices, and legislative bodies produce legal information to meet the mission of the governmental institution. The primary responsibility for making law belongs to the legislative authority–the Congress, state legislatures, and municipal councils; judges are expected to interpret the law and report in the form of opinions, at most filling in gaps when constitutions or statutes are ambiguous or silent; and the administrative departments or agencies are directed by the legislature to create rules and regulations to implement the goals and policies of the laws. At all governmental levels, the branches of government that are empowered to disseminate this information to citizens produce legal information. Legal information includes federal or state judicial rulings or administrative decisions, legislation that is signed into laws or municipal ordinances, rules and regulations, presidential or gubernatorial documents, agency serials or reports, and local ordinances that must be followed by all citizens and government agencies.

While legal and government information affects all citizens, there is a hesitation or uneasiness by non-legally trained individuals to attempt to use this information. Because of the specialized nature, organizational systems, and language of legal and government information, it is more difficult to use than other sources of information. In addition to these factors, the use of legal and government resources is problematic for a number of other reasons:

1. Legal and government information is constantly growing as cases are continuously being decided and pieces of legislation, rules, or regulations are being passed or revised.
2. The majority of legal and government information is created, released, and published by courts, the legislatures, and departments or agencies. In order to access this information, researchers must know the correct jurisdiction or agency that produced the needed information. That is, in addition to the subject of the information needed, in many cases the researcher must know the creator of the legal and government information.

3. Users must consider sets of resources rather than individual volumes, as is characteristic of traditional information tools. In order to find the specific legal information you are looking for, a user must know the set of volumes where the law is published. The rulings of the courts are published in sets that are added to as new decisions are rendered. The title of the volume will not have any relation to the specific piece of information being researched. In addition, the volumes of these sets are always being revised, new information added, or other information removed as a result of the changes in the law. These books of primary authority contain references to the principles and specific rules of law in a given branch of law, as well as citations to relevant statutes and judicial decisions.
4. Legal and government information is published as either "official" or "unofficial" publications. The government publishes or contracts with a commercial publisher to publish the "official" documents. Its statute or court authority officially sanctions publication. "Unofficial" publications are published by private publishers or companies not legislatively endorsed to publish the government information. The "unofficial" publications duplicate the documents in the "official." These private publishers are faster than the government publishers and provide critical research tools as added value to their versions of the cases.
5. Traditional catalogs, indexes, databases, and other finding aids used in libraries for other subject disciplines are not used to identify legal and government information resources. American law has been systematized and organized by subject matter. But, the terminologies to describe the finding tools for legal information, as well as their titles, are different than any other information resources.
6. Bibliographic citations used to find information resources are different for legal and government publications than for other subject disciplines and are unique for each type of resource.

CURRENT STATE OF LEGAL AND GOVERNMENT INFORMATION ON THE INTERNET

Nowadays, accessing legal information by computer is a much more straightforward undertaking. Resources to identify, access, and retrieve legal and government information are available in print, micro-media, and computer-assisted electronic database formats. Information technology of the 21st century has revolutionized the way much of this information is disseminated by the judiciary, legislature, and administrative agencies and the way that all citizens and information users may access it. Users no longer need specialized resources or have to wait for weeks or even months to access many legal and government information resources. The number of legal and government information resources that are published or made available on the Internet is continuing to grow at a phenomenal rate.

Federal, state, and local government departments and agencies are committing to electronic dissemination of the primary sources of law, which include case decisions, legislation, laws, reports, rules, and regulations, via the Internet to disseminate this information to the public. Secondary sources of the law are also digitally published on the Internet. These resources include directories of legal professionals and experts, encyclopedias, dictionaries, legal forms, treatises, citation manuals, legal newspapers, and law reviews or journals. Law schools, courts, government agencies, and law firms also produce, in-house, a variety of legal information resources, special reports, opinion letters, articles, guidebooks, or legal memoranda available through the Internet. Electronically published reports or studies by law school students, faculty, libraries, attorneys, or other participants in the legal process provide valuable information on the Internet.

The monumental increase in online publication can be attributed to a number of factors. First and foremost are the federal government's efforts during the past 10 years to develop an online, virtual depository of government publications and information. The passage of Public Law 103-40, known as the Government Printing Office Electronic Information Enhancement Act of 1993, was the first step made towards increasing the availability of the wealth of information and products produced by the government and making them freely accessible through electronic technology.[2] This act called for the GPO to develop an electronic directory of federal information, to operate an electronic storage facility for online access to federal information, to disseminate government information products online, to provide a system of online access to major government publications, and to provide online access to depository libraries. GPO Access was created after the passage of this Act and serves as a portal to the works of government in all branches providing free electronic access to a wealth of information products produced by the federal government. The growth of citizen use of the Internet has made this tool an increasingly attractive and effective dissemination mechanism for federal government agencies, courts, and the Congress to offer a more cost-effective and user friendly program for providing citizen access to federal documents.

Via GPO Access, the government meets the responsibilities identified in Title 44 of the United States Code (44 U.S.C. Section 1911) stipulating that public access to official government information products disseminated through the Federal Depository Library Program (FDLP) must be maintained permanently in regional depository libraries and by depository libraries not served by a regional library. Since online products are not physically distributed to depository libraries for retention, GPO has assumed responsibility for the provision of permanent access to government information products residing on GPO Access servers. One major change that GPO Access made to improve this site was the simplifying of the URL address for the site. Originally the URL for GPO Access was <http://www.access.gpo.gov>. Last year the URL was changed to the simpler and more direct <http://www.gpoaccess.gov>. The simplification of the URL made the site much more user friendly and accessible for all citizens.

The federal government is making a major commitment to electronic networking as a primary means of providing access to government information and of obtaining services. Internet technologies, such as the World Wide Web, hold great potential for dissemination of this public information faster, more extensively, and more efficiently. The goal of using these technologies in government has presidential support. In his February 2002 budget submission to Congress, President Bush outlined a management agenda for making government more focused on citizens and results, including expanding electronic government, or E-Government. E-Government uses improved Internet-based technology to make it easy for citizens and businesses to interact with the government, save taxpayer dollars, and streamline citizen-to-government communications. In a 2002 memo, President Bush wrote that "administration's vision for government reform is guided by three principles: government should be citizen-centered, results-oriented, and market-based."[3] The principles are woven into the five government-wide reform goals outlined in the Administration's Management Agenda: strategic management of human capital, budget and performance integration, competitive sourcing, expanded use of the Internet and computer resources to provide government services (Electronic Government or E-Government), and improved financial management. Effective implementation of E-Government is important in making government more responsive and cost-effective. The President signed the E-Government Act of 2002 on December 17, 2002, with an effective date for most provisions of April 17, 2003.

In January 2005, at the ALA Midwinter Conference in Boston, Superintendent of Documents, Judith C. Russell, announced that GPO would produce and distribute only the 50 titles listed on the "Essential Titles for Public Use in Paper Format." The GPO would publish all other publications as online documents. This move will make a profound impact on access to government information in formats most usable to the American public. The *Essential Titles List*, last revised in 2000, does not include important materials including maps, geological information, administrative decisions, and other legal materials, as well as Senate and House reports, documents, and hearings that inform the citizenry of the workings of Congress. Many in the library community have expressed concern about the abrupt and complete elimination and distribution of print, noting that this move represents a major disruption to the FDLP's role of ensuring no-fee, permanent access to government information. Librarians and information users opposing this move point out that GPO has not yet established a reliable system to ensure delivery, version control, authenticity, permanent public access, and preservation of government information products disseminated online. Opponents believe that these changes will deprive citizens of their ability to access important authentic government information in the most usable format that will best meet their information needs. Further, many citizens are economically or technologically disadvantaged and cannot make use of necessary technological infrastructure to access electronic government information. It is important to remember that the goal of the FDLP is to provide government information to the American people in a convenient and useable format, not to make it convenient for the administrative agency responsible for that dissemination. Public Printer Bruce James remarked that GPO must change with the times and that the GPO of the 21st Century must use "the technologies of today and tomorrow not yesterday to keep this vision alive."

The library community has long embraced the move to digital technologies, and libraries are on the front lines of developing systems that provide the public with easy, reliable, and permanent access to authentic government information. In an April 2004 hearing on GPO oversight, representatives from five library associations testified that the FDLP should not completely eliminate print distribution because the difficult challenges of the digital life cycle remain unresolved: the authentication, permanent public access to and preservation of electronic government information. It is important that the government recognize the need to validate the authenticity and integrity of an electronic document, whether it is available through GPO Access or located on agency, congressional, or court Web sites. It is not enough to disseminate and preserve digital documents; users must be assured that the electronic government information that they locate and use is authentic.

The second major change in legal information access is the improved capability of Internet technology to provide personalized information. The most exciting innovation in the legal information world over the past five years is the application of Web log technology to this field. The *Merriam Webster's Dictionary* defines blog as a Web site that contains an online personal journal with reflections, comments, and hyperlinks. They are Web sites that use the form of a chronologically ordered online journal.[4] A Web log author–or "blogger"–can publish and maintain an ongoing, informative dialogue with an unlimited number of readers. Blogs filter information and archive it in an enduring chronological manner.

The first Web logs appeared in the early 1990s and were collections of links categorized or compiled by authors. Early Web logs were more personal insights or opinions by the creator, rather than useful information. Since 1999, blogging has become more popular as a communication device on the Internet. The creation of Web logs–called blogs or as the term has been coined in the legal information arena–"blawgs"–has seen an explosion of interest and activity over the past three years. Blogs have existed in large numbers since 1997, but Ambigi states that today there are estimated to be from 20,000 to more than one-half million blogs. *Merriam Webster's* reported in December 2004 that "blog" topped the list of the top ten words of the year. *The Wall Street Journal* reported that blog readership grew in 2004, driven by the election year. But the study found that only 38% of users know what a blog is because of the seamless presentation of information in this format. An indicator of the popularity of blogs is that the blog "Ernie the Attorney," maintained and created by Ernest E. Svenson, a litigator with a New Orleans firm, had more links to his blog than five of the largest law firms' conventional Web site. URLs: <http://radio.weblogs.com/0104634/> or <http://www.ernietheattorney.net/>.

These Web logs, blawgs, or personal Web pages created by attorneys, judges, law school professors, librarians, and publishers contain a myriad of content from personal opinion, articles, commentary, legal news, and current interest updates to reviews of legal Web sites. On some sites, bloggers almost act as journalists for the legal field. For example, *beSpacific*, maintained by Sabrina I. Pacifici, a DC area law librarian and publisher of Law Library Resource Xchange, spotlights news, resources, and information technology related issues. In 2003, Genie Tyburski wrote that "blawgs tend to discuss hot topics and current news which interests the general public more than the dry legal articles you find in more traditional sites."[5] Taking blog technology to the next generation are "news aggregators." For people wanting to receive continuously current legal research and government information, they can subscribe to receive a news aggregator. A news aggregator tracks the information an individual is interested in and organizes the information on a personal Web news page. The aggregators use RSS technology, which stands for "rich site summary" or "Really Simple Syndication." RSS provides a format for organizing online information sources and the content of news-like sites, including Web logs, news services, and Web sites that make their content available in RSS. The aggregator software and services collect those syndicated feeds and present them to end users in a variety of ways. For example, the U.S. Department of State, Bureau of Public Affairs provides RSS feeds for top stories from the State Department home page–daily press briefings, press releases, and remarks by the Secretary of State. With RSS technology, desired information is served directly to researchers customized according to their interests in feeds of topic-specific news headlines.

GUIDES OR INTERNET MEGA SITES FOR ACCESS TO LEGAL AND GOVERNMENT INFORMATION

To begin researching legal and regulatory information, there are starting points often called "portals" or "indexes" or "guides" that serve as gateways to the Internet's resources. Guides, specialized indexes, or directories for government and regulatory information on the Internet include Web sites or pages created by law schools and universities, law firms, government departments or agencies, commercial publishers, law school libraries, law firm libraries or marketing departments, courts, and commercial companies. There are catalogs and guides designed to assist researchers, students, or every day consumers in knowing where to find the legal information that they are attempting to locate. These guides are an important tool used to find legal information because of the specialized language and arrangement of court decisions, laws, and regulations. Because legal information is growing on a daily basis–as the federal and state courts, legislatures, and administrative offices are continuously making new laws or regulations–this information is not static. These compendia provide an important link to these resources on the Internet. Guides are available in both book format and online to assist a researcher in identifying the most authoritative and useful resource to go to on the Internet to locate certain types of information. In addition, the volatility of the Internet must also be taken into account as it is constantly changing as new sites are being added, created, or removed.

Guides to Government Information

Arguably the best source on the Web for federal government documents and information, GPO Access, the official site of the U.S. Government Printing Office, recently redesigned its numerous pages and changed the address location. URL: <http://www.gpoaccess.gov>. The U.S. Government Printing Office (GPO) prints, binds, and distributes publications of Congress, executive branch departments and agencies, and the judicial branch. GPO Access is a far-reaching repository of documents from the three branches of government. It includes the U.S. Code, the Congressional Record, the Code of Federal Regulations, the Federal Register, and much more. GPO based the redesign on a series of surveys, usability studies, focus groups, and feedback received through user support. Maintained by the U.S. Government Printing Office (GPO), titles accessible on GPO Access include the *Congressional Record, U.S. Government Manual, U.S. Reports, Code of Federal Regulations*, and *U.S. Code*. GPO Access provides individual directories for each government branch: Judicial–URL: <http://www.gpoaccess.gov/judicial.html>, Legislative Branch Resources–URL: <http://www.gpoaccess.gov/legislative.html>, and Executive Branch Resources–URL: <http://www.gpoaccess.gov/executive.html>.

One of the most historic and well-organized information resources on GPO Access is the Core Documents of U.S. Democracy, an electronic collection providing direct online access to a core group of current and historical federal government documents and information sources through GPO Access. URL: <http://www.gpoaccess.gov/coredocs.html>. This collection was created to provide American citizens with direct and permanent online access this collection of government documents valued as vital to a democratic society. The site includes links to collections of current congressional, presidential, judicial, demographic, regulatory, and economic documents as well as historical materials. Current government documents linked to this page include the *Weekly Compilation of Presidential Documents, Census*

Catalog and Guide, Statistical Abstract, and the *U.S. Government Manual.* Historical documents on this page, termed "Cornerstone Documents," include the *Articles of Confederation, Bill of Rights* and *U.S. Constitution, Declaration of Independence, Gettysburg Address,* and the *Federalist Papers.* There is also a directory of links to current and historical Presidential documents including the *Abraham Lincoln Papers* at the Library of Congress to the *Weekly Compilation of Presidential Documents.* Another guide to historical documents now available in online formats via the Internet is A Century of Lawmaking for a New Nation: U.S. Congressional Documents and Debates, 1774-1873. URL: <http://memory.loc.gov/ammem/amlaw/index.html>. This very special collection includes primary source documents, records, and acts of Congress from the Continental Congress and Constitutional Convention through the 43rd Congress.

Taking the goals of electronic dissemination of government information to the next step is a national pilot project, Government Information Online. URL: <http://govtinfo.org/>. The goal of this project is to create a model for an online cooperative virtual information and reference desk specializing in questions concerning government information and providing live, online help and assistance for researchers. This project is a cooperative effort of more than 30 official depository libraries throughout the United States. The Guide to Law Online is an annotated guide to state, federal, and international document collections created and maintained by the U.S. Law Library of Congress Public Services Division. URL: <http://www.loc.gov/law/guide/>. This compendium includes sites offering the full texts of laws, regulations, and court decisions, along with commentary from lawyers writing primarily for other lawyers. Materials written for law persons are also included as well as other government sites. There are three geographical guides to United States and international resources. GUIDE: United States–URL: <http://www.loc.gov/law/guide/us.html>, GUIDE: Nations of the World–URL: <http://www.loc.gov/law/guide/nations.html>, and GUIDE: International–URL: <http://www.loc.gov/law/guide/multi.html>. It includes links to legal information sites available for every country. The index links to individual directory pages for each nation. Linked from the International Guide is the Global Legal Information Network (GLIN), a database of laws, regulations, judicial decisions, and other complementary legal sources contributed by governmental agencies and international organizations. URL: <http://www.glin.gov/>. GLIN members contribute the official full texts of published documents to the database in their original language. The Multinational Collections Database lists items which reprint the laws and regulations of international jurisdictions on a particular legal topic. URL: <http://www.loc.gov/mulp/>. The Law Library Web site also includes an excellent directory to legal information, Bookmarks–Legal Resources on the Internet, which was created by library staff. URL: <http://www.loc.gov/rr/law/lawresources.html>.

Guides Maintained by the Big Two in the Legal World: Westlaw and Lexis

Two large providers of legal, news, and business data also produce guides to legal information. FindLaw from Thomson West is a gateway to all legal research Web sites. URL: <http://www.findlaw.com>. Started in 1994 as a list of Internet resources prepared for a librarians' workshop, FindLaw has evolved into one of the most popular starting points for finding legal information. FindLaw has one of the highest traffic counts of any legal Web site. It is a multifaceted portal providing a comprehensive directory of legal resources with links to primary legal sources, government resources, Web sites, publications, software, law reviews, mailing lists, discussion groups, and related FindLaw pages. It is like a "Yahoo!" for law, organizing links in a categorized directory. Its core is the free, comprehensive FindLaw Guide, an index of links to resources in more than 30 practice areas, case law, codes, legal associations, and law reviews. FindLaw has portals designed for different audiences. FindLaw for the Public is designed to help non-lawyers find solutions to legal problems with access to lawyer directories and other topical legal information. URL: <http://public.findlaw.com/>. This site includes a variety of state-specific legal content and expanded general legal content. FindLaw for Legal Professionals is designed to provide easy access to practice-specific information including legal news, case law, and analytical articles on specific topics. URL: <http://lp.findlaw.com/>. There are also FindLaw pages for Business and for Corporate Counsel sites designed to meet the unique information needs of those audiences. URLs: <http://smallbusiness.findlaw.com/> and <http://corporate.findlaw.com/>.

The FindLaw LawCrawler is a Web-wide search engine with a focus on legal sites. A second search engine at FindLaw searches the full text of online law reviews. FindLaw provides some full-text content, not the least of which is the largest freely accessible database of United States Supreme Court opinions, federal appellate court reports, and state court decisions. Thomson West Group purchased FindLaw in January 2001, adding the West Legal Directory and other original content.[6] When

Thomson West Group purchased FindLaw, it expanded the legal news resources and career centers, added CLE and incorporated the West Legal Directory. Four years after this purchase by the largest commercial legal publisher, FindLaw is more diverse and professional looking in its presentation, but it is still free to use by all.

Thomson West's major online publishing rival, LexisNexis also maintains an extensive online resource for legal information. The Web site lexisONE from LexisNexis is a free Web community aimed at solo attorneys and small firms, but it is also very useful for researchers and ordinary citizens to use to access government information and legal resources. URL: <http://www.lexisone.com/>. This site was launched in July 2000 featuring Supreme Court cases since 1790 and selected federal and state cases for the past five years, 6,000 legal forms, 60,000 court forms, articles written for legal practitioners, a newsletter– lexisONE Alert, and the *Martindale-Hubbell Lawyer Locator* including the Experts and Services Directory. This searchable directory includes more than 50,000 experts, consultants, investigators, litigation support, process servers, and other essential legal resources. The lexisONE Legal Web Site Directory is an extensive collection of links to 20,000 legal and law-related Web sites. URL: <http://www. lexisone.com/legalresearch/legalguide/legal_guide_index.html>. The Directory is organized into topical, resource, and jurisdictional categories. Sites selected by the Lexis editors provide easy access to the most useful and relevant legal, business, and government Web sites available. Another excellent guide available from LexisNexis is Zimmerman's Research Guide created and maintained by librarian Andrew Zimmerman. URL: <http://www.lexisnexis.com/infopro/zimmerman/>. The guide is an extensive listing of legal, business, and other information sources with background and brief explanatory information about specific aspects of legal, business, and factual research. Zimmerman has been updating this guide for more than ten years and it was formally available on another Web site. Zimmerman's is accessible from the LexisNexis Infopro Web site and lexisONE. URLs: <http://www.lexisnexis.com/ infopro> and <http://www.lexisone.com/>.

Other Guides

Other portals or guides to legal research are produced by commercial organizations such as major law firms, policy organizations, and legal research companies. Hieros Gamos (HG), The Comprehensive Legal and Government Portal, is maintained and operated by Lex Mundi, a consortium of law firms. URL: <http://www.hg.org/>. This site is a set of directories to help locate law and related information providing access to virtually all online and many offline published legal information resources. With more than two million links, it provides pointers to locate law-related organizations, continuing education courses, commentary, country sites, and world-wide legal information about a diversity of topics. The creators and editors of Hieros Gamos continue to redesign the site for improved accessibility and navigation. The site is designed for users from the student to the average citizen. The site includes directories containing information on foreign governments, U.S. federal and state governments, more than 6,000 legal organizations, law schools and students, law firms, continuing legal education programs, employment and job listings, law study, practice areas, discussion groups, doing business guides, and electronic law journals and newsletters. Accessible in more than fifty languages, part of Hieros Gamos is a listing service for lawyers and law firms worldwide.

Internet Legal Research from Internet Tools for Lawyers is a guide to primary sources, directories, and interactive legal research assistance. URL: <http://www.netlawtools.com/research/index.html>. The Internet Legal Research Guide is a comprehensive categorized index of more than 4,000 Web sites concerning law and the legal profession from 238 foreign countries. URL: <http://www.ilrg.com/>. Sites are selected and evaluated by the editors according to the value and uniqueness of the provided information to both legal experts and laypersons. The focus of the site is on U.S. legal information with the United States Federal Government Sites page providing a directory to government departments and agencies. URL: <http://www.ilrg.com/gov/us.html>. The American Government Index analyzes information for each state. URL: <http://www.ilrg.com/gov.html>. The site includes information for legal professionals concerning legal education, law reviews and journals, and the industry. There is an e-mail update service for users to receive information when new features are added to the site.

The American Law Sources Online (ALSO) continues to be a popular guide to use when looking for federal and state government information. URL: <http://www.lawsource.com/also>. Each state's listing links to online laws in categories by type, such as statutes or court opinions, and county laws. The pages providing Canadian and Mexican law resources are highly used. ALSO provides links to sources of primary law–cases, statutes, and regulations–then to commentary on the law, such as law reviews and books, and finally to practice aids, such as official forms or court information. Started in 1996 as a personal home page, the Virtual Chase was created and maintained by Genie Tyburski of Ballard Spahr Andrews & Ingersoll, LLP as a way to disseminate legal research teaching materials to law librarians. URL: <http://www. virtualchase.com/>. The site is owned by the law firm and now is a marketing tool for the firm. The Legal Research Guide provides a directory to legal and factual research information. URL: <http://www.virtualchase. com/resources/index.shtml>. The guide includes specialized pages for government resources and other legal subjects. The site also includes legal research presentations and teaching materials for law librarians and research instructors. An early pioneer of customized current awareness for attorneys, the site includes an excellent blog and RSS feed. The newsletter, *Research News*, offers tips on research and information on new Web sites.

Law student Randy Roberts created the Law and Policy Institutions Guide. URL: <http://www.lpig.org/>. The site includes a categorized directory of annotated legal and legislative information sites and resources including domestic and multi-national legal topics, treatises, journals, and legal databases. Each site is selected, reviewed, and evaluated on four criteria: accuracy of content, presentation, uniqueness, and utility. The Law Engine is an index of legal sites organized into major categories organized on a single, fast view page. URL: <http://www. thelawengine.com/>. Created and maintained by the law office of Goldberger & Associates, there is also a search page from which searches can be conducted on a number of major legal and non-legal search engines and indices. Katsuey's Legal Gateway is a directory of legal links to Web sites with substantive, free legal content designed for use by both legal professionals and consumers/lay people to use. URL: <http://www.katsuey.com/index.cfm>. Each site is reviewed before inclusion in the site. Megalaw.com, the Lawyer's Window to the Web, offers a number of useful research features. URL: <http://www.megalaw. com/>. The guide includes current news headlines, interfaces to legal research information, and a directory of legal ready reference resources. URL: <http://www.megalaw.com/research.php>. LawGuru.com offers a unique guide and portal to legal information. URL: <http://www. lawguru.com/>. One of the homes of the former House of Representatives Internet Law Library, LawGuru provides a directory of legal information sites, access to legal news (from various sources via RSS news feed), various chat rooms for discussion of legal issues, an attorney-locator service, and legal forms. The legal questions database provides answers to more than 100,000 previously asked questions about the law.

One of the most unique directories is the Invisible Web Directory maintained by Chris Sherman and Gary Price to update their book, the *Invisible Web: Finding Hidden Internet Resources Search Engines Can't See*. Each entry includes a description of the resource, a specific and home page URL, and if available, related resources. There are directories to Government Information and Data–URL: <http://www. invisible-web.net/database.html?category_selected=Government+ Information+and+Data> and Legal and Criminal Information–URL: <http://www.invisible-web.net/database.html?category_selected=Legal+ and+Criminal+Information>. Librarian Christopher Brown's Virtual Reference Desk includes a guide to Government Documents. URL: <http://www.virtualref.com/govdocs/>. The guide organizes the documents by subject, title, and agency or SuDocs Classification Number. Two other mega directories of legal information are CataLaw and AllLaw.com. The CataLaw mega site organizes sites by topic, jurisdiction, and reference resources. URL: <http://www.catalaw.com/>. This directory aids legal research by arranging all indexes of law and government into a uniform, universal and unique metaindex. The AllLaw.com directory is arranged by jurisdiction and topic. URL: <http://www. alllaw.com/>. The site also provides search interfaces to external sources including a legal glossary.

Guides Developed by Academic Institutions

Academic institutions continue to produce some of the most extensive and reliable legal information sites and specifically guides. The first law site developed on the Internet in 1992, the Legal Information Institute at Cornell University School of Law (LII), is the Granddaddy of legal and government information sites. URL: <http://www.law. cornell.edu/>. The development of Cornell Law School's pioneering Legal Information Institute site established the first legal Web site in 1993. This is one of the oldest and most useful law-related sites online acting as both a gateway to locate other law-related Web resources and a provider of legal content. The LII was one of the first and became the leading Internet site for distribution of Supreme Court opinions and later added the N.Y. Court of Appeals. The hypertext U.S. Code remains its most heavily used feature and one of the best sites to utilize to identify laws in the Code. The LII has also published a host of significant legal documents. Robert J. Ambrogi of *Law Technology News* wrote, "As a lawyer once put it to me, they deserve a lifetime achievement award."[7] The mission of the LII was to experiment with using hypertext to publish legal materials online. In addition to core collections of federal law, New York state legal resources are accessible or downloadable in several formats. There are two searchable indexes to the Web site: Materials Organized by Topic and Materials Organized by Source of Law. URLs: <http://www.law.cornell.edu/topics/index.html> and <http://www.law.cornell.edu>.

Created by the staff of Washburn University School of Law Library, WashLaw–Legal Research on the Web was one of the earliest and most exhaustive indexes to Web-based legal resources. URL: <http://www. washlaw.edu/>. REFLAW offers a directory of links to legal information reference information. URL: <http://www.washlaw.edu/reflaw/ reflaw.html>. DocLaw serves as a gateway to government resources organized according to subject and federal agencies. URL: <http://www. washlaw.edu/doclaw/>. The unique federal organization chart is hyperlinked to the Web sites of departments and agencies. URL: <http:// www.washlaw.edu/doclaw/orgchart/mainog.html>. JURIST is a legal news and real-time legal research Web site powered by a team of over 20 law student reporters, editors, and Web developers. URL: <http:// jurist.law.pitt.edu/>. The Emory University Internet Legal Research Guide is an index to law-related resources. URL: <http://www.law. emory.edu/erd/subject/index.html>. The Emory University-Macmillan Law Library was a leader in providing access to case law and continues to maintain some of the most used and up-to-date sites on the Web including the Federal Courts Finder. URL: <http://www.law.emory.edu/ FEDCTS/>. The Electronic Reference Desk includes links to topical guides, pathfinders, law schools and education sites, legal directories, and career information. URL: <http://www.law.emory.edu/erd/index. html>.

The University of Michigan Library Documents Center presents an excellent guide to online government documents from federal, state, and foreign governments. URL: <http://www.lib.umich.edu/govdocs/>. The Documents Center is a central reference and referral point for government information, providing reference and instructional information on its Web pages for government, political science, statistical data, and news. There are topical guides for all of the types of resources such as federal government, foreign, international, state, and statistics. The Documents in the News feature links to online government documents that are related to current events. URL: <http://www.lib.umich.edu/ govdocs/docnews.html>. There is also an excellent guide to conducting legislative history research.

A few formerly highly used and well-known legal and government information resources continue to house or develop guides or directories, but are not as up to date as other sites. The Villanova University School of Law Library (formerly the Center for Information Law and Policy) produces the Villanova Legal Express, an easy to use index of resources. URL: <http://vls.law.villanova.edu/library/express/>.[8] The Federal Court Locator and Tax Master–the Tax Law Locator continue to be maintained by the staff at Villanova. URLs: <http://www.law.vill.edu/library/researchguides/fedcourtlocator.asp> and <http://www.law.vill.edu/library/researchguides/taxdocuments.asp>. While the Villanova site has updated their guide, the locators from the Illinois Institute of Technology's Chicago-Kent College of Law are still available on the school's site. Among the most popular features from the CILP, the Federal Web Locator and State Web Locator were designed to ease the search process of finding documents. URL:<http://www.infoctr.edu/fwl/> and the State Web Locator–URL: <http://www.infoctr.edu/swl/>. Both pages need updating, but they are still well organized and remain useful starting points for finding government resources. The Indiana University School of Law maintains the World Wide Web Virtual Law Library. URL: <http://www.law.indiana.edu/v-lib/>. Part of the World Wide Web Consortium, this site was chosen by CERN in 1992 to be the host of the Virtual Library–Law. It was one of the earliest collections of Web-based legal resources, but the site has not been kept up to date so is not as useful.

SEARCH ENGINES

Legal and government information search engines provide a second method of accessing the specific subject or topic information that is being researched. These legal search engines are more accurate and provide better precision when searching for resources or documents than is available using general information indexes or search engines such as Yahoo or Google. Meta-indexes and search engines provide comprehensive coverage of legal and government information on the Internet and allow users to search specific Internet resources related to the law, government, or regulatory information. There are currently over 100 legal indexes or search engines that provide databases of resources in exclusively legal and government information domains rather than the entire Internet.

Legal Information Search Engines

FindLaw's LawCrawler search uses the same search engine as Google, but its database is restricted to legal sites. In theory, this should make it better for legal searches. URLs: <http://lawcrawler.findlaw.com/> or <http://www.lawcrawler.com>. LawCrawler provides legal researchers with precision by enabling them to focus their searches on sites with legal information and within specific domains. LawCrawler allows a researcher to select the complete or specific sections of the FindLaw database. The LawCrawler search engine includes special search options for particular legal resources or types or organizations at the international level including limiting to international organizations.

LawGuru.com Multi Resource Legal Research is a meta search engine offering a tool for searching multiple Web sites using a single query. URL: <http://www.lawguru.com/multisearch/multimenu.html>. The Los Angeles law firm Eslamboly & Barlavi maintains LawGuru. com. On the LawGuru-Legal Research Page, searches can be conducted on more than 535 legal search engines, resources, and tools for many of the legal and government research resources across the Web. URL: <http://www.lawguru.com/search/lawsearch.html>. LawGuru allows multiple searches in four categories: state codes and statutes, state court opinions, U.S. circuit court opinions, and federal opinions and codes. There are searchable resources for every state, including cases, court opinions, codes, statutes, and bills. The advantage of this resource is that researchers can search everything from one place. However, you sacrifice the advanced search capability that is available when searching from the actual state. The drop-down menu search form lists the resources, search engines, and tools in alphabetical order and includes federal and state cases, statutes, legislative bills, and administrative regulations. To search state codes, for example, the user checks the states to be searched, types the query, and hits search. For each state selected, a new browser window opens displaying the results for that state. Searchable resources for every state, including cases, court opinions, codes, statutes, and bills are accessible.

Part of the Internet Legal Resource Guide, LawRunner is an intelligent agent-based search engine interface for Google.com and its 3+ billion indexed Web pages that allows researchers to limit their searches to a particular jurisdiction or to Web sites with a specific domain suffix. URL: <http://www.lawrunner.com/>. Searches can also be limited to specific state law through the USA Index or to international law from 238 nations, islands, and territories using the Global Index. URLs:

<http://www.ilrg.com/gov.html> and <http://www.ilrg.com/nations/>. The Law Engine offers access to online law sources in an easy, single-page format organized into a directory listing of federal and state cases, courts, legal newspapers and law reviews, reference sources, government agencies, legal associations, law school and firm directories, forms, and other sites or resources concerning special areas or topics of the law. URL: <http://www.fastsearch.com/law/index.html>.

The Legal.Com search engine offers a meta-index of 400 legal search engines, databases, and tools. URLs: <http://www.legal.com> and <http://www.legal.com/Research/main.html>. From an alphabetically organized drop-down menu, researchers can select the needed federal or state resource. Other meta search pages include Law.com, the Georgia State University Meta Index (GSU), and the Catalaw Meta-Index for U.S. Legal Research. Both the GSU Meta-Index for U.S. Legal Research and the Catalaw Meta-Index incorporate multiple legal search tools on a single search Web page. URLs: <http://gsulaw.gsu.edu/metaindex/> and <http://www.catalaw.com/info/metaindex.shtml>. The site presentation for both is an array of search forms for many law and U.S. government sources such as access to judicial opinions from FindLaw. Each form contains sample search models that can be followed to search for opinions of the U.S. Supreme Court and all federal circuit courts, the U.S. Code, bills, legislative publications, law reviews, and professional directories. An exciting new meta-index is from Surfwax, which launched LawKT, a free service that allows a user to search more than 60,000 law firm publications from over 280 leading law firms. URLs: <http://news.surfwax.com/law/> or <http://law.surfwax.com>. There's also a legal news section that aggregates news on over 1,000 law-related topics.

Government Search Engines

Five years ago there were a number of government search engines, GovBot, SearchGov.com, and SearchGov.mil to retrieve government federal and state sites around the country. These sites are no longer available, but the area of government search engines has been improved with the growth of Firstgov.gov and the stability of Uncle Sam Google. FirstGov is the official gateway to U.S. government information on the Internet. URL: <http://www.firstgov.gov>. FirstGov started with the free loan of search tools from Inktomi to the government. When that gift loan expired, the Fast Search and Transfer system was implemented in 2002. Offering a topical index and search engine, FirstGov connects to more than 51 million pages on more than 20,000 federal, state, territorial, and tribal sites. Most, but not all, links lead to government Web sites. FirstGov allows users to search only for federal government Web sites, eliminating results from state and local governments. Or researchers can select to search only one or all states on the site. Researchers can also browse for legal and government information by branch of government. The site was recently overhauled so that links are now organized by type of user–citizen, business and non-profits, federal employees, and government–as well as by common reference terms, such as forms, laws, and press releases.

Released in 1999, the same year as the Google search engine, Uncle Sam Google is still available without promotion from the parent search engine. URL: <http://www.google.com/unclesam>. Librarians, researchers, and students use this site. Uncle Sam Google is not listed with any of the Google features, services, and tools in Google Help Central, and it is not lurking in the Google Labs.[9] Uncle Sam Google is described on the Google Advanced Search page as a topic-specific search option. This engine searches all .gov and .mil sites. In fact, both SearchGov.com, and SearchGov.mil now forward searches to Uncle Sam Google. One limitation of Uncle Sam Google is that it does not search Web sites using the domain .com or .us but it does search .gov sites that include state government links.

JUDICIAL BRANCH INFORMATION SOURCES: FEDERAL AND STATE CASE LAW

The major focus of American law is case law, the statement of decisions of a court made in settlement of a litigated civil or criminal case. The courts interpret the laws and regulations made by the legislative and executive branches. The judicial system in this country is divided into federal and state levels. The United States judicial system is composed of three types of courts at the federal and state government levels: trial courts, appellate courts, and supreme courts. The trial court, which is the "court of first instance" (i.e., where the case is first heard) in the American system, is where the factual record of the case is made. Generally speaking, appeals courts confine their review of the lower court record to errors of law, not of fact. No new evidence is received on appeal.

In the federal court system, the United States district courts are the trial courts of the federal court system, the "court of first instance."

Within limits set by Congress and the Constitution, the district courts have jurisdiction to hear nearly all categories of federal cases, including both civil and criminal matters. There are 94 federal judicial districts, including at least one district in each state, the District of Columbia, the Virgin Islands, Guam, and the Northern Mariana Islands and Puerto Rico. Each district includes a United States bankruptcy court as a unit of the district court. The judicial districts are organized into 12 regional circuits, each of which has a United States Court of Appeals. The appellate courts hear their appeals from the district courts located within their circuit, as well as appeals from decisions of federal administrative agencies. The Supreme Court is the highest court in the federal judiciary.

The U.S. Courts–Federal Judiciary Home Page published by the Administrative Office of the Courts provides a clearinghouse for information from and about the judicial branch. URL: <http://www.uscourts. gov/>. Historical and current news about the federal court systems, the judicial branch, and its judges are provided. The About U.S. Courts pages provide a description of the court system and explain the role of each court level. URL: <http://www.uscourts.gov/about.html>. There are individual pages explaining each court level on the site. The publication *Understanding the Federal Courts* which was developed by the Administrative Office of the Courts provides an introduction to the federal judicial system, an overview of court operations, its organization and administration, its relationship to the legislative and executive branches, and definitions of common legal terms. URLs: <http://www.uscourts. gov/understand03/> and <http://www.uscourts.gov/UFC99.pdf>. The publication, *Third Branch*–The Newsletter of the Federal Courts, is updated monthly and includes back issues since February 1995. URL: <http://www.uscourts.gov/ttb/index.html>. Information about electronic access to the courts is linked to the PACER system, which is the Federal Judiciary's centralized registration, billing, and technical support center for electronic access to U.S. District, Bankruptcy, and Appellate court records. URL: <http://pacer.psc.uscourts.gov/>.[10] GPO Access has directories of the Web sites and information available from or published by each branch of government including the page–Judicial Branch Resources on GPO Access. URL: <http://www.gpoaccess.gov/judicial. html>. A 1999 issue of the electronic journal *Issues of Democracy* from the U.S. Information Agency is dedicated to information on "How U.S. Courts Work." URL: <http://usinfo.state.gov/journals/itdhr/0999/ijde/ ijde0999.htm>.[11] FindLaw has organized a directory of all of the links to sites providing explanatory information about the courts on the Cases

and Codes: Introductory Materials page. URL: <http://www.findlaw.
com/casecode/intro.html>.

Federal and State Court Opinions

The largest part of a legal information collection that is used by all researchers is the case law or opinions. Thus, a large part of many of the
collections of virtual legal information online is the case law. These
opinions from the federal and state courts are fully accessible from sites
maintained by the courts, government, academic institutions, and commercial organizations. Since the pilot program–Project Hermes from the
Supreme Court–online publication of case law directly to the Internet
has increased. Prior to online access via the Internet, current case law
was only available via the commercial computerized databases of
Lexis and Westlaw. The cost of these databases and access to the systems are cost prohibitive as well as inaccessible to many users of legal
information. The availability of current case law over the Internet is increasing daily, but there are limitations, as most of these databases do
not offer comprehensive or archival coverage of all decisions from the
courts. There are misperceptions that all case law is available on the
Internet. In terms of freely accessible material, the United States Supreme Court is really the only database of case law online where thorough and comprehensive research can be performed, and even all of
those decisions are not available all the way back to the beginning of the
Court. Federal appellate court decisions are available for all circuits
from the courts and a consortium of law schools that provides free access to slip opinions. There has been an increase in state law publication, but federal case law is limited and not as readily available. All fifty
states now provide case law and many local court jurisdictions. The
method of access varies for those courts that publish their recent decisions on their Web sites. Often they are listed chronologically or sometimes through a case number or case name search engine. Some of the
recent opinions may be available to download electronically.

Guides and Directories to Federal and State Case Law

There are a number of guides or directories to case law resources for
all levels of the courts. Many free case law resources can be found on
the Internet including FindLaw, MegaLaw, and lexisONE. Although
these resources are free, the opinions are the raw version of the case
with no editorial enhancements, sophisticated finding aids, tables, or

corrections that are included in the commercially published versions of the decisions from Westlaw and LexisNexis.

Federal Case Law Directories

A number of Internet sites offer access to all of the federal cases. While there are numerous sites on the Internet that provide access to these court decisions, a few sites have the most accessible and explanatory organizational scheme and structure for use. The Courtlinks Web page from the U.S. Courts–Federal Judiciary site provides a graphical map of the country organized by the circuit courts and the Supreme Court. URL: <http://www.uscourts.gov/links.html>. This allows users to retrieve the desired court's home page or opinion site. The All Court Sites–Administrative Office and Federal Judicial Center page is a directory organized according to the Court of Appeals with all of the lower courts listed within their circuit. URL: <http://www.uscourts.gov/allinks. html>. The U.S. Judiciary–Federal Court System and Decisions from the Law Library of Congress provides a directory of links to all federal court sites. URL: <http://www.loc.gov/law/guide/usjudic.html>.

The lexisONE database service offers access to opinions from the Supreme Court, federal circuit courts, and the state courts. URL: <http:// www.lexisone.com/index.html>. Decisions are available from the two highest courts of each state decided within the last five years, all federal circuit court cases for the last five years, and Supreme Court cases from the entire history of cases on the Lexis service from 1790 to the present. There is a fee to access earlier decisions. Cases can be searched by keyword or citation. The FindLaw US Federal Laws and US State Laws pages are a well organized and comprehensive listing of links to federal and state judicial court pages and FindLaw opinions databases for each court. URL: <http://www.findlaw.com/casecode/>. On the Opinion Summaries–Archive page, opinions can be searched since September 2000 from the U.S. Supreme Court, all thirteen Federal Circuit Courts, the California Supreme Court and Court of Appeal, and the New York Court of Appeals. URL: <http://caselaw.lp.findlaw.com/ casesummary/index.html>. American Law Sources On-Line (ALSO)– United States Government-Law Page includes searchable indexes for Supreme Court and Court of Appeals decisions. URL: <http://www. lawsource.com/also/usa.cgi?us1>. Cases can be retrieved by party name, citation, and keyword. Users can also browse the cases by year and volume. The site also provides annotated hypertext listings of other sites for federal case law, court rules, and newsgroups. The U.S. Federal

Courts Finder from the Emory University Law School also provides a graphical map linking to the Supreme Court and the federal courts. URL: <http://www.law.emory.edu/FEDCTS>. There is also a directory of opinions organized in alphabetical order by state so non-lawyers do not need to know in which circuit the court they are looking for is located.

The Federal Court Locator from Villanova School of Law is a gateway to Supreme Court, Circuit, and District court decisions. URL: <http://www.law.villanova.edu/library/researchguides/fedcourtlocator. asp>. The Federal Court Opinions-Georgetown University Federal Judicial Resources, created by the Georgetown University Law Library, provides links to the decisions issued by the federal courts and information concerning the federal judiciary, including slip opinions from both the Supreme Court and the appellate courts. URL: <http://www.ll. georgetown.edu/federal/judicial/index.cfm>. Other directories include the Washlaw Web–Federal Case Law, one of the most comprehensive database indexes. URL: <http://washlaw.edu/searchlaw/federalcaselaw/>. There is a search engine to the federal courts on this site. Other directories include the Internet Legal Resource Guide, MegaLaw–Federal Cases & Courts, Attorney Finder–Legal Resources, Law.com–U.S. Courts, and All Law. URLs: <http://www.ilrg.com/caselaw/>, <http://www.megalaw.com/fed/fedcourts.php>, <http://www.attyfind.com/legalresources.asp>, <http://www11.law.com/nav.asp?h=90>, and <http://www.alllaw.com/law/federal_law/case_law/>.

State Case Law Directories

Access to state case law is primarily done by the West Group's "National Reporter System." This system publishes case reports for all fifty states in a uniform format for all jurisdictions. State case law is published in chronologically numbered volumes called "regional reporters."[12] The units of regional reporters are grouped together geographically based on the country's population during the early twentieth century. The geographic grouping allows for the case reports from neighboring states to be published within the same set of books. The "National Reporter System" is linked by West's editorial treatment and enhancements, which provide for uniform subject access to all cases from each jurisdiction. The full-text databases, LexisNexis and Westlaw, provide full-text searching and coverage for all 50 states from at least 1945 and for many states back to the nineteenth century.

The number of states publishing their court opinions online has greatly increased over the last five years. It is very important that states are making their official decisions available online for access. Historically, state publication of case law has been hindered by long delays in publication, lack of preliminary access to case decisions in advance sheets, and discontinuation of publication of official reports by publishers in many states. Because of this inconsistency in publishing at the state level, the West regional reporter system was the only resource many states had to locate this case information. State case law is available online for many states for the past five years, but there is no consistency among the states concerning how many years of case reports are made available via this technology. Those states that do have case law databases may only publish summaries of decisions, but without the editorial treatments or finding aids that are available from the commercially published print or electronic formats. Some sites do provide full-text search engines, tables of cases or docket numbers, or other indexes.

A number of sites provide access to all fifty states or multiple states from one location and utilize various uses of Web-based technology to present and organize these case law databases. Both major legal publishers provide free access to state case law through the FindLaw State Resources from Westlaw and the Legal Web Site Directory–State Resource Center on lexisONE from LexisNexis. URL: <http://www.findlaw.com/llstategov/>. Both sites provide an alphabetically organized directory of the states linking to the judicial opinion sites for state courts. The Documents Center at the University of Michigan's State Legal Sources on the Web page includes a matrix listing the court opinion publication and coverage for each state. URL: <http://www.lib.umich.edu/govdocs/statelaw.html>. WashLawWEB's StateLaw–State Case Law maintained by the Washburn University School of Law Library and ALSO, American Law Sources Online–United States–all provide a hypertext table of the states linking to individual pages for each state and list court information as well as opinion sites. URLs: <http://www.washlaw.edu/uslaw/states/allstates/> and <http://www.lawsource.com/also/#[United%20States]>. The StateLaw site also includes a search page to search for state information by subject. There are individual directories for state home pages, legislative, and judicial information sites. URL: <http://www.washlaw.edu/uslaw/search.html#judicial>. The Internet Legal Resource Guide–American Government Index also provides individual pages for each state with hypertext links to court sites. URL: <http://www.ilrg.com/gov.html>. A search engine allows users to limit searches to the jurisdictions of any of the states. This site presents the states in an alphabetically-organized directory linking to the judicial opinion sites for state courts. The National Center for State Courts provides judicial branch links for each state, focusing on the administrative office of the courts, the court of last resort, any intermediate appellate courts, and each trial court level. URL: <http://www.ncsconline. org/D_KIS/info_court_web_sites.html>. Other state case law sites include AllLaw, MegaLaw State Cases, Codes, and Resources, State Courts by Jurisdiction from LII, and Hieros Gamos–U.S. State Law. URLs: <http://www.alllaw.com/state_resources/>, <http://www.megalaw. com/states.php>, <http://www.law.cornell.edu/opinions.html>, and <http:// www.hg.org/usstates.html>.

Supreme Court Case Law

As the last resort for people who believe that lower courts have failed them and as arbiter of the Constitution, the Supreme Court will, simply by selecting a case, immediately lift the lives and human situations it contains to national significance. Its rulings will affect not only the two contesting parties, but also may change life for all Americans for generations. The richest database of case law published on the Internet is the judicial opinions from the Supreme Court. These decisions are published in print and electronic format from the earliest rulings made in 1790. The published print reporters are the *U.S. Reports*, officially published by the GPO, *Supreme Court Reporter*, published by Thomson West Group, and *U.S. Supreme Court Reports Lawyers Edition*, published by Lexis Law Publishing. The cases are also published in looseleaf reporters and on both major legal research database systems, Lexis and Westlaw, as well as other systems. An excellent guide to publication of Supreme Court decisions, *Web Guide to U.S. Supreme Court Research* by Gail Partin, law librarian at Dickinson School of Law is available on the Law Library Resource Xchange. URL: <http://www. llrx.com/features/supremectwebguide.htm>.

One of the potential impacts of the Internet was to increase the number of decisions accessible to users who do not have access to the fee-based legal databases. Supreme Court opinions are disseminated to the public via two systems, Project Hermes and the Supreme Court Web site. The problem of inequity of access to case law was addressed by the Court in 1990 with Project Hermes. Through a collaboration of private publishers, academic institutions, and the federal government, this project was designed to experiment with disseminating opinions electronically and to provide public access via Internet technology.[13] On days that opinions are announced by the Court from the bench, the text of each opinion is made available immediately to the public and the press in a printed form called a "bench opinion." The bench opinion is disseminated electronically via Project Hermes, to paying subscribers, who include universities, news media, publishing companies, and other private organizations. A number of these organizations provide online access to the bench opinions via the Internet within minutes after the Court releases them.

The Supreme Court was slower than many other courts to enter the online information age, finally inaugurating the Web site in 2000. URL: <http://www.supremecourtus.gov/index.html>. The site includes weekly orders granting and denying new appeals, the court's schedule and argument calendar, court rules, bar admission forms and instructions, visitor guides, news releases, biographical information on the justices, and general information. The *About the Supreme Court* Web page provides a number of PDF documents providing information about the history, tradition, architecture, photographs, the Justices' workload, and biographies of the Justices. URL: <http://www.supremecourtus.gov/about/about.html>. The *Opinions* page includes links to slip opinions released by the *Supreme Court* since 2001. URL: <http://www.supremecourtus.gov/opinions/opinions.html>. The Court's decisions are made available on the site within hours of the 10 a.m. release as pdf documents through a link to the *GPO Access* Web site run by the Government Printing Office. They are made available directly from the Court's Web site later on the day of release. The U.S. Government Printing Office maintains this site.

Databases providing Supreme Court decisions are available on the GPO Access Judicial Branch Resources page. URL: <http://www.gpoaccess.gov/judicial.html>. This page from GPO Access provides links to two databases of Supreme Court opinions. The "Search Supreme Court Decisions 1937-1975" is a database of the FLITE opinions that is searchable by case name, by case or docket number, and full text. URL: <http://www.access.gpo.gov/su_docs/supcrt/index.html>. This database was created as a project of the U.S. Air Force from its FLITE ("Federal Legal Information Through Electronics") system.[14] The full text of Supreme Court Decisions issued between 1937 and 1975, containing 7,407 decisions from volumes 300 through 422 of U.S. Reports, is in the FLITE database and current case decisions since 1992 are retrievable from the Federal Bulletin Board Online via GPO Access–Supreme Court Opinions Web page which includes decisions released and transmitted by the Court from the Hermes Project. URL: <http://fedbbs.access.gpo.gov/court01.htm>. The addition of the FLITE database of opinions expanded the comprehensiveness and depth of the Supreme Court case law provided via the Internet.

The Legal Information Institute at Cornell University School of Law was the first site to provide access to Supreme Court decisions. URL: <http://supct.law.cornell.edu/supct/>. The Supreme Court Collection provides searchable databases of current opinions issued from May 1990 to the present and the Selected Historic Decisions of the U.S. Supreme Court. The case law included in the Selected Historic Decisions site ranges from Marbury v. Madison (1803) through the most recent term; the Legal Information Institute has assembled a collection with the advice of a panel of educators that includes those decisions that most reflect or have had deepest effect on the country's history. The Collection includes a searchable database of the opinions that allows for searching directly for keywords in either the syllabi or full opinions or to search to retrieve cases by words in a case name (or year or docket number) or opinion author. URL: <http://supct.law.cornell.edu/supct/search/search.html>. There is an archive of both current and historic decisions organized by topic, author, and party.

There are a number of other Web sites that maintain collections of current and historic decisions of the Supreme Court. Access to all decisions since 1790 is provided by lexisONE. URL: <http://www.lexisone.com/>. FindLaw provides a database of Supreme Court decisions since 1893 or Volume 150 of the *U.S. Reports* to the present that can be searched by citation, case name, and volume as well as browsed by volume number and year. URL: <http://www.findlaw.com/casecode/supreme.html>. The FindLaw Resources by Jurisdiction page for the Supreme Court also has links to the opinions and other court information resources. URL: <http://www.findlaw.com/10fedgov/judicial/supreme_court/index.html>. FedWorld sponsored by the National Technical Information Service provides access to the FLITE database of 7,407 U.S. Supreme Court Decisions from 1937 to 1975. URL: <http://www.fedworld.gov/supcourt/index.htm>. The database has two different methods to search and retrieve decisions: full-text searching by keywords or by case and party names.

The Oyez Project (formerly called Oyez, Oyez, Oyez) offers an innovative use of technology to provide access to Supreme Court information with its U.S. Supreme Court Multimedia Database from Northwestern University. URL: <http://www.oyez.org/oyez/frontpage>.[15] This project provides abstracts, audio of oral arguments, information about Supreme Court case history and summaries, and other materials of more than 500 leading constitutional cases. The goal of the OYEZ Project was to create a complete and authoritative archive of audio of Supreme Court oral arguments covering the entire span from October 1955 through the most recently released decisions. Currently, the project provides access to more than 2,000 hours of Supreme Court audio. Before 1995, the audio collection is selective. Recently the project released the first oral arguments in MP3 audio covering court cases from the '50s to the '70s with a description of the case. URL: <http://www.oyez.org/oyez/resource/nitf/273/>. Details about the questions and opinions in the cases are provided, as well as digital recordings of the Court's proceedings, oral arguments, and opinion announcements. Links to the FindLaw database provide the full text of the opinion. There is an index of available cases that can be searched by date, title or party names, citation, and subject. Each case record provides the name of the case, official *U.S. Reports* citation, date argued and decided, names of the attorneys making oral arguments, the facts of the case, a summary of the constitutional question ruled in the decision, the conclusion, and the vote of the judges. *On the Docket* publishes current information about the court and upcoming cases to go before the Supreme Court. Oyez also includes panoramic images of the Supreme Court Building and offers a virtual tour of the courthouse, judges' chambers, and law library. URL: <http://www.oyez.org/oyez/tour/>. The Oyez Project and FindLaw also offer the game, Oyez Baseball. URL: <http://baseball.oyez.org/>.

Supreme Court and Justice Information

Information about the history, procedures, and practices of the Supreme Court and biographies of the justices are also information used by researchers. The background of the Court and its practices can be found on the Supreme Court Historical Society site and in the publication, *How the Court Works*. URLs: <http://www.supremecourthistory. org/index.html> and <http://www.supremecourthistory.org/03_how/03. html>. USSCPlus also publishes a Web version of this information written by the Court. URL: <http://www.usscplus.com/info/>. Biographical information about the justices of the current Court can be found on the Supreme Court Collection–Gallery of the Justices on the LII site and on the USSC Plus–About the Court. URL: <http://supct.law.cornell.edu/supct/justices/fullcourt.html>. The Oyez Project includes a comprehensive database of information about current and past judges on the Justices Page including educational, judicial career, and biographical information for each justice in alphabetical order or in chronological order of appointment. URL: <http://www.oyez.org/oyez/portlet/justices/>.

The LII now has an e-mail subscription for free previews of high-profile Supreme Court cases before they are argued and ruled on. URL: <http://supct.law.cornell.edu/supct/cert/>.

Lower Federal Courts–Federal Court of Appeals, District Court, and Other Courts

There are thirteen federal circuit courts of appeal, including eleven circuit courts geographically dispersed across the country, the District of Columbia Circuit, and the Federal Circuit. These circuit court decisions are published in the sole case reporter for these courts, the *Federal Reporter*, published by the West Group. The Courts Publishing Project from the Emory University School of Law publishes the decisions for a number of circuit courts on the Federal Courts Finder. URL: <http://www.law.emory.edu/caselaw/>. This project began with the distribution of cases from the Eleventh Circuit Court of Appeals in 1994. Today each court has at least one Web site where the decisions of the court are published on the Internet. The Federal Circuit Court Opinions page includes a searchable page for each circuit on the FindLaw database on the Resources by Jurisdiction pages as well as directory listings to links for the specific Web site for each court. URLs: <http://www.findlaw.com/10fedgov/judicial/appeals_courts.html> or <http://www.findlaw.com/casecode/html>. Web sites for each court can be accessed from one of the federal court multi-site directories, such as the U.S. Courts–Court Links or the Federal Court Locator from Villanova. URLs: <http://www.uscourts.gov/links.html> and <http://www.law.villanova.edu/library/researchguides/fedcourtlocator.asp>.

The U.S. district courts hear and adjudicate cases in the 94 district courts in the fifty states, District of Columbia, and all U.S. territories. These cases are published in the print resource, *Federal Supplement* by ThomsonWest Group. While digital publication of circuit court opinions has been implemented successfully in all of the courts, only a small number of the 94 district courts publish their opinions on the Internet. These courts do provide sites to access court and docket information and other court information. The FindLaw–Resources by Jurisdiction page provides a listing of the federal district courts and identifies those courts with opinions available online. URL: <http://www.findlaw.com/10fedgov/judicial/district_courts.html>. A number of other sites provide links to the district court sites including the U.S. Courts–All Court Sites. Emory University Federal Courts Finder, FedLaw from the Center for Regulatory Effectiveness, and AllLaw. URLs: <http://www.uscourts.

gov/links.html>, <http://www.law.emory.edu/FEDCTS>, <http://www.
thecre.com/fedlaw/legal32.htm>, and <http://www.alllaw.com/law/
federal_law/case_law/>.

LEGISLATIVE AND STATUTORY
INFORMATION RESOURCES

The legislative branch makes or writes statutes or laws that are passed by Congress or the jurisdictional law-making branch. Federal and State Legislatures create legislative enactments or statutory law by passing bills, which become law when signed by the executive (president or governor). Legislation includes constitutions, statutes, treaties, municipal charters, ordinances, interstate compacts, and reorganization plans. Federal, state, and local legislative and statutory information is available in print and electronic formats, including on Lexis and Westlaw.

Constitutional Resources

The Constitution of the United States comprises the primary law of the U.S. Federal Government. Law publishes in the U.S. Code and in all state codes the full text of the U.S. Constitution. It is available in digital format at numerous sites on the Internet. The Library of Congress publishes the U.S. Constitution, Text, Commentaries, Historical Texts, and Judicial Decisions, providing a list of information sources available on the Internet about the Constitution. URL: <http://www.loc.gov/law/guide/usconst.html>. This site includes links to historical documents that influenced the content and history of the Constitution, such as the Articles of Confederation and the Iroquois Constitution. Historic documents are published on the Emory University Electronic Reference Desk–U.S. Documents page. URL: <http://www.law.emory.edu/erd/docs.html>. Emory University and FindLaw both publish a searchable database of the Constitution. URLs: <http://www.law.emory.edu/erd/docs/usconst.html> and <http://www.findlaw.com/casecode/constitution/>. The GPO Access Constitution of the U.S. page publishes the document and has full-text searching of the Analysis and Interpretation of the U.S. Constitution database. URL: <http://www.gpoaccess.gov/constitution/index.html>. Digital scanning technology now makes documents accessible and viewable for research and study such as the Constitution from the National Archives and Records Administration–Charters of Freedom page. URL: <http://www.archives. gov/national_archives_experience/charters/constitution.html>. There are hypertext links to information about the history of the Constitutional Convention and the 55 attendees and biographical information about the 39 signers. The Constitution Society on its Founding Documents page also includes scanned copies of the original pages and the Bill of Rights. Other sites offering access to the Constitution include LII Constitutional Law Materials Web page with an overview of the document and source materials such as historic and recent constitutional law decisions. URL: <http://www.law.cornell.edu/topics/constitutional.html>. FindLaw–U.S. Constitution Search and Emory University both publish a searchable database of the Constitution. URLs: <http://www.findlaw. com/casecode/constitution/> and <http://www.law.emory.edu/erd/docs/ usconst.html> or <http://www.law.emory.edu/erd/docs.html>.

The constitutions from all states are published in the state code, usually with annotations and on both the LexisNexis and Westlaw databases. A number of sites provide directories of links to state constitutions including American Law Sources Online–United States and FindLaw–State Constitutions. URL: <http://www.lawsource.com/also/#[United States]> and URL: <http://www.findlaw.com/11stategov/indexconst.html>. The Know Your Rights Web page provides direct links to the Bill of Rights from each state. URL: <http://www.harbornet.com/rights/states.html>.

Congressional Servers

The United States House of Representatives and United States Senate maintain sites to provide information about both bodies. The Web sites for both bodies includes information about the members, organizational structure, legislative procedures, committee structure and membership, leadership and support offices, and active legislation, as well as history of the institutions. URLs: <http://www.senate.gov> and <http:// www.house.gov/>. The Senate Virtual Reference Desk organizes information by subject and links to related materials. URL: <http://www. senate.gov/pagelayout/reference/b_three_sections_with_teasers/virtual. htm>. Senate researchers compile subject bibliographies of resources on the Senate and House, the Capitol and Washington, D.C., and federal and state government. URL: <http://www.senate.gov/pagelayout/reference/ a_three_sections_with_teasers/biblio.htm>. The House of Representatives member directory is searchable by zip code or member name. The House also publishes the U.S. Code from the Office of the Law

Revision Counsel of the House. URL: <http://uscode.house.gov/lawrevisioncounsel.php>.

Legislative Information Sites

The GPO Access Legislative Branch Resources page has a directory of links to congressional information resources available from Government Printing Office and other linked sites. URL: <http://www.gpoaccess.gov/legislative.html>. Resources include the *Congressional Record*, *History of Bills and Resolutions*, *Congressional Directory*, *Congressional Pictorial Directory*, congressional hearings, congressional reports, congressional calendars, public laws, and other legislative resources.

Extensive information about Senate and House legislative activities is available through the Library of Congress' THOMAS service. URL: <http://thomas.loc.gov/>. Acting under the directive of the leadership of the 104th Congress to make Federal legislative information freely available to the Internet public, a Library of Congress team brought the THOMAS World Wide Web system online in January 1995, at the inception of the 104th Congress. Much of the retrospective data included in the Thomas database came from the Library of Congress Information System (LOCIS) Legislative text database. The Library of Congress Information System (LOCIS) service contained summaries, abstracts, chronologies, and status information about legislation (bills and resolutions) introduced in the U.S. Senate and House of Representatives since 1973. The THOMAS database includes legislative information from the 93rd congressional session in 1973 through the current 109th session. THOMAS provides databases of the text of bills, bill summary and status, House and Senate committee information including reports, the full text of the Congressional Record, voting records, public laws, congressional directories, and other historical and legislative reference sources. An improvement for the 109th session is that THOMAS users now can search the text of legislation across multiple congresses from the 101st Congress (1989) to the present.[16] One or more congressional sessions can be searched simultaneously. Word searches can be limited to (1) legislation with floor action or legislation that has been enrolled and sent to the president, and (2) just House or just Senate legislation. Most of the documents in THOMAS originate in the House and Senate, which in turn transmit them to the Government Printing Office (GPO) for printing and further electronic processing. GPO then transmits them to the Library of Congress, which performs some further processing before making them available on THOMAS. THOMAS is updated as soon as new files are received from the GPO. Information about the current Congress is updated within 48 hours of activity. New documents are indexed and made available for searching immediately and the text files of bills are updated several times during the day. Two publications provide in-depth explanatory information on the legislative process. The House of Representatives publication, *How Our Laws Are Made*, and the Senate document, *Enactment of a Law*, describe the steps of the lawmaking process from the origin of a legislative proposal through its publication as a law. URLs: <http://thomas.loc.gov/home/lawsmade.toc.html> and <http://thomas.loc.gov/home/enactment/enactlawtoc.html>. Another guide to the process is accessible on the House of Representatives page. *The Legislative Process, a House of Representatives Guide* provides access to information about bills and resolutions being considered in the Congress and House activities. URL: <http://www.house.gov/Legproc.html>. The guide also includes current information about activities on the House floor. The guide, *The Legislative Process Tying It All Together*, includes explanations of each form of congressional action and each step in the process. URL: <http://www.house.gov/Tying_it_all.html>.

Legislative History

Legislative histories are an official documentary record of the passage of a proposed statute. They provide insight into the legislature's "original" or "legislative intent" in passing a law or for interpreting the meaning of provisions. To identify this intent, all of the information and documents used or created during the legislative process are examined to identify influences on the legislation such as reports that are produced on a topic from the Congressional Research Service. URLs: <http://www.house.gov/rules/crs_reports.htm> or <http://www.llsdc.org/sourcebook/CRS-Congress.htm>. Cheryl Nyberg's *Guide to Congressional Research Service Reports* is a current guide to locate repositories for these CRS products. URL: <http://lib.law.washington.edu/ref/crs.htm>. The courts, Congress, government agencies, and legal scholars consult the legislative history when the meaning of a legislative provision cannot be gleaned from the language of the statue itself. There are a number of guides and tutorials available to assist in conducting this research including Federal Legislative History from the Chicago Kent

College of Law and Researching Legislative History from Harvard Law School. URLs: <http://library.kentlaw.edu/Resources/Leghist%20Tutorial/Intro.htm> and <http://www.law.harvard.edu/library/services/research/guides/grfs/specialized/legislative_history.php>. The LLSDC Legislative Source Book is compiled by Law Librarians' Society of Washington, D.C. URL: <http://www.llsdc.org/sourcebook/index.html>. The Legislative Histories Guide maintained by the University of Michigan Documents Center was created to assist students with legislative history assignments and provides step-by-step directions for identifying bills or new laws and titles of information sources to compile histories. URL: <http://www.lib.umich.edu/govdocs/legishis.html>. The THOMAS database provides access to the documents and resources to compile legislative histories. The THOMAS-Bill Summary and Status database provides searchable summaries of the progress of bills and amendments. URLs: <http://thomas.loc.gov> or <http://thomas.loc.gov/bss/d109query.html>. The database can be searched by type of legislation, stage of the legislative process, sponsor, committee, keyword or phrase, bill or amendment number, date, or any combination of the fields.

Statutory Information Resources–Codification of Federal Statutes

The laws passed by the Congress and signed by the president are published in the U.S. Code. Prior to publication in the Code, the laws are published as public laws in the chronologically organized Statutes at Large. The session or public laws are available at GPO Access, THOMAS, National Archives and Records Administration Public Laws page. URLs: <http://www.gpoaccess.gov/plaws/index.html>, <http://thomas.loc.gov>, and <http://www.archives.gov/federal_register/public_laws/public_laws.html>.

The United States Code is the codification by subject matter of the general and permanent laws of the United States. It is divided into 50 titles or subjects. Two guides to identify information and resources about the U.S. Code are maintained by the Law Library of Congress and the Law Librarians' Society of Washington, D.C. URLs: <http://www.loc.gov/law/guide/uscode.html> and <http://www.llsdc.org/sourcebook/statutes-code.htm>. The Code is available in an individual publication from the Government Printing Office and is published as two annotated code sets, *U.S. Code Annotated* published by Thomson West and *U.S. Code Service* published by Lexis Law Publishing. Both publications provide the codified statutes as well as references to court decisions, regulations, and encyclopedia and law review articles. The full text of the U.S. Code is also searchable on Westlaw and Lexis.

Online versions of the U.S. Code are not as current as what is available on the databases. The U.S. Code is published on the Internet on the House of Representatives Web site and on GPO Access generated from the most recent version of the GPO official code. URLs: <http://uscode.house.gov/lawrevisioncounsel.php> or <http://www.gpoaccess.gov/uscode/about.html>. There is also a browseable version of the Code. URL: <http://www.gpoaccess.gov/uscode/browse.html>. The versions on GPO Access can be searched by keyword or title. The U.S. Code Collection from the Legal Information Institute at Cornell is generated from the most recent version of the Code on the House Web site. URLs: <http://www.law.cornell.edu/uscode/> and <http://assembler.law.cornell.edu/uscode>. The LII version includes a table of all titles and a Popular Names Table. The Code can be searched by keywords or by citation. URLs: <http://assembler.law.cornell.edu/uscode/search/index.html> or <http://assembler.law.cornell.edu/uscode/#SECTIONS>. The American Law Sources Online–ALSO page provides search forms to retrieve code sections. There also are Popular Names of Selected Public Laws and Popular Names of Significant New Laws pages. URLs: <http://www.lawsource.com/also/usa.cgi?usp> and <http://www.lawsource.com/also/usa.cgi?usp0>.

State Laws and Legislative Information

On today's Internet all fifty states have Web sites where legislative and statutory information is published. Every state provides free, official legislative body Web site access to all full-text bills from its current legislative session. The bills are generally available as facsimile image file reproductions of official print versions. Bill tracking information is also generally provided. Other significant legislative history materials, such as hearings and committee reports, are only rarely available online, are frequently not widely disseminated in print, and may not even exist in any full-text, official form. State Legal Sources on the Web maintained by the Documents Center at the University of Michigan provides an excellent matrix identifying publication, coverage, and links for the state constitution, bills, session laws, and codified laws. URL: <http://www.lib.umich.edu/govdocs/statelaw.html>. There are a number of Web sites that provide a directory of the state and links to each state code and legislative site. Useful sites affording direct and sometimes annotated links to bills, bill status reports, and additional legislative information for all states include: FindLaw–State Resources–State Codes and State Law–State Government, Legislative Information from Washburn School of Law Library, the Legal Information Institute Law by Source, and American Sources Online–ALSO. URLs: <http://www.findlaw. com/casecode/#statelaw> or <http://www.findlaw.com/11stategov/ indexcode.html>, <http://www.washlaw.edu/uslaw/states/allstates/> and <http://www.washlaw.edu/uslaw/search.html#legislative>, <http://www. law.cornell.edu/states/listing.html>, and <http://www.lawsource.com/ also/index.htm#[United%20States]>. On the sites there are pages for each state with links to the state code and legislative Web sites. States also provide broadcasts of their proceedings over Internet. The National Conference of State Legislatures maintains the State Legislatures Internet Links database that contains information gleaned from the home pages and Web sites of the fifty state legislatures, the District of Columbia, and the Territories. URL: <http://www.ncsl.org/public/ leglinks.cfm>. The Conference also provides a listing of the 45 states and 74 legislative chambers that have Internet audio or video feeds. URL: <http://www.ncsl.org/programs/press/leglive.htm>. Indiana University School of Law Library maintains the State Legislative History Research Guides on the Web site that provides a table organized alphabetically by state of guides to legislative history in all of the states. URL: <http://www.law.indiana.edu/library/services/sta_leg.shtml>.

Municipal Codes

The city codes, ordinances, and laws of many cities and municipalities are available on the Internet on three sites. The Municipal Code Corporation–Municode site has Codes from more than 1,100 local governments in searchable online databases. URL: <http://www.municode. com/resources/online_codes.asp>. The E-Codes Web site from Municipal Codes on the Internet alphabetically organizes the cities and local areas by state. URL: <http://www.generalcode.com/webcode2.html>. The Seattle Public Library maintains the Municipal Codes Online Web site. This project was begun by the library in an effort to make municipal codes throughout the nation more accessible to the public. URL: <http://www.spl.org/default.asp?pageID=collection_municodes>. The site includes an alphabetically ordered list of links to city and county codes by state.

ADMINISTRATIVE AND EXECUTIVE BRANCH INFORMATION SOURCES

While laws passed by the Congress create programs to address citizen needs, it is the departments and agencies in the executive branch that implement the intent of the Senators and Representatives. The administrative or executive branch is comprised of the regulatory and independent agencies and departments that implement the programs created by legislation from the Congress. The administrative branch is headed by the president and operates through the cabinet departments. The administrators of these agencies write and develop rules and regulations, set procedures, detail technical distinctions, issue opinions, and interpret and apply the governing statute. These regulations are called quasi-legislation or bureaucratic law. Administrative branch information includes the rules and regulations generated by the departments and agencies as well as the independent commissions, establishments, and government corporations. The LII topic guide–Federal Regulations explains the regulatory system and discusses how the rules and regulations can be accessed and updated. URL: <http://www.lawschool.cornell. edu/lawlibrary/Finding_the_Law/Guides_by_Topic/fedregs.htm>. The Library of Congress also publishes a guide to regulatory information, United States Executive–U.S. Executive Agencies and Regulations. URL: <http://www.loc.gov/law/guide/usexec.html>.

Government Directories for Department and Agencies

The *U.S. Government Manual* is the official handbook and directory for information on the agencies and officials of the government. Published annually, the manual is published online on GPO Access as a searchable database and as a browseable table since the 1995 edition. URLs: <http://www.gpoaccess.gov/gmanual/index.html> or <http://www. gpoaccess.gov/gmanual/browse-gm-04.html>. For each agency the *Manual* provides a list of principal officials, the statement of the agency's purpose and role, brief history and legislative/executive authority of the agency, a description of its programs and activities, and a "Sources of Information" section. There are many online directories to the executive branch on the Internet. DocLaw WEB from Washlaw School of Law is a gateway to government Internet resources and other related materials organized by subject, agency, and a graphical organizational chart. URL: <http://www.washlaw.edu/doclaw/>. The Agency has listings of department or agency home pages, publications, electronic forms, and opinions. A number of other Web sites providing directories of the government base their organizational structure on the *U.S. Government Manual* such as the Federal Web Locator from the Chicago-Kent College of Law. URL: <http://www.infoctr.edu/fwl/>. The Louisiana State University Libraries Federal Agencies Directory lists current/active/existing agencies alphabetically and hierarchically and includes an agency keyword searchable directory. URLs: <http://www.lib.lsu.edu/gov/alpha> or <http://www.lib.lsu.edu/gov/tree>. The directory is a partnership of Louisiana State University and the Federal Depository Library Program.

Other guides include the Federal Government Resources on the Web page from the University of Michigan Documents Center and USLinks–U.S. Federal Government Agencies Database from Duke University Public Documents and Maps Department. URLs: <http://www.lib.umich.edu/govdocs/federalnew.html> or <http://www.lib.duke.edu/texis/uslinks/uslinks>. Descriptive information about each agency or site is given and they can be accessed by browsing or searching agency name or acronym. The White House Government page also provides links to cabinet Web sites, agencies and commissions, and the Executive Office of the President. URL: <http://www.whitehouse.gov/government/>. The A-Z Index of Government Agencies on the Firstgov.gov page has an alphabetical listing of the departments. URLs: <http://www.firstgov.gov/Agencies/Federal/All_Agencies/index.shtml> or <http://www.firstgov.gov/Agencies.shtml>. Because government Web sites are constantly changing, the University of North Texas and the U.S. Government Printing Office, as part of the Federal Depository Library Program, created a partnership to provide permanent public access to the electronic Web sites and publications of defunct U.S. government agencies and commissions, creating the "CyberCemetery" so named by early users of the site. URL: <http://govinfo.library.unt.edu/>. Sites are organized both alphabetically and by category.

Administrative agencies–generally those in the executive branch–issue rules and regulations that spell out how laws will be implemented, either because a statute specifies that the agency will do so or because as a practical matter the details are not included in the statute. The regulatory process includes the proposal and final approval of the rules and regulations. On the federal level, such regulations are first published in the Federal Register and are codified in the Code of Federal Regulations. A number of digital publications provide guides and explanatory material about this process and identify Web sites where the federal and state regulations may be accessed on the Internet. These guides have been written and published by government offices, commercial organizations, individuals, and libraries. Regulatory information and documents are accessible from the GPO Access Executive Branch Resources page including links to the documents in the regulatory process, presidential materials, and executive publications. URL: <http://www.gpoaccess. gov/executive.html>.

The Regulatory System—The Federal Register *and the* Code of Federal Regulations

The rules and regulations by the administrative branch departments and independent agencies are published in the *Federal Register* as they are being written, codified, and enacted. The *Federal Register* is a legal newspaper or public bulletin board, published by the U.S. Government every federal business day providing a uniform system for making publicly available the following legislatively mandated government information: proposed and final rules and regulations, legal notices issued by agencies and the President, executive orders, presidential proclamations, agency documents having general applicability and legal effect, congressional documents, Sunshine Act meetings and public announcements, and other Federal agency documents of public interest. The Unified Agenda is also included in the Register twice a year. Published by the Office of the *Federal Register*, National Archives and Records Administration (NARA), it is available on the Lexis and Westlaw databases and via the Internet on the GPO Access Web page from 1994. URL: <http://www.gpoaccess.gov/fr/index.html>. Information can be accessed by full-text searching or by browsing the table of contents of the issues. The NARA and FindLaw provide a portal to the *Federal Register* linking to the GPO Access database. URLs: <http:// www. archives.gov/federal_register/index.html> and <http://www.findlaw.com/ casecode/ cfr.html>.

The NARA also publishes a tutorial on using the *Federal Register—*The Federal Register: What It Is and How to Use It. URL: <http:// www.archives.gov/federal_register/tutorial/about_tutorial.html>. The U.S. government recently launched Regulations.gov to make it easier for the public to participate in federal rulemaking. URL: <http://www. regulations.gov/>. The site allows users to search for, review, and comment on proposed rules that have been published in the *Federal Register*. Users can search for proposed regulations by keyword or by agency name. Regulations can be viewed in either HTML or PDF format.

The *Code of Federal Regulations* is the final repository for the final rules and regulations. They are codified in a subject arrangement of fifty titles, similar to those used for federal statutes in the *U.S. Code*. Each title is divided into chapters, which usually bear the name of the issuing agency. The chapters are further subdivided into parts covering specific regulatory areas. Each title of the CFR is revised once each calendar year and issued on a quarterly basis. The mission of the CFR online is to provide the public with access to this government information. The CFR is officially published on the GPO Access–Code of Federal Regulations site. URL: <http://www.gpoaccess.gov/cfr/index.html>. Regulations from the CFR can be retrieved through searching the entire set or a specific volume by subject or agency or by browsing and retrieving sections by citation. URL: <http://www.access.gpo.gov/nara/cfr/cfr-table-search.html>. Other front-end sites to access the CFR include the LII and FindLaw. URLs: <http://www.law.cornell.edu/cfr/> and <http://www.findlaw.com/casecode/cfr.html>. The *Federal Register* is connected to the CFR by finding aids that are published daily and cumulated in the *List of CFR Sections Affected (LSA)*. The LSA provides a cumulative list of CFR sections that have been changed or amended at any time since each CFR title was last updated. URL: <http://www.gpoaccess.gov/lsa/about.html>. Each LSA issue is cumulative and contains the CFR part and section numbers, a description of its status (e.g., amended, confirmed, revised), and the *Federal Register* page number where the change(s) may be found.

State Administrative Law

Each state's administrative law system parallels that of the federal government. State rules and regulations are also available on a number of sites on the Internet as well as through the Westlaw and Lexis databases. The Administrative Codes and Registers (ACR) Section of the National Association of Secretaries of State (NASS) provides a table listing the regulatory publications for each state. URL: <http://www.nass.org/acr/internet.html>. The Documents Center at Michigan's State Legal Sources on the Web site also lists the publication and provides links to state administrative codes, regulations, and executive orders for all states. URL: <http://www.lib.umich.edu/govdocs/statelaw.html>. The American Bar Association (ABA) Administrative Procedure Database has links to state resources pages on the FindLaw for Legal Professionals–State Resources page. URLs: <http://www.law.fsu.edu/library/admin/admin5.html> and <http://www.findlaw.com/11stategov/index.

html>. The State Web Locator from Chicago–Kent College of Law provides hypertext tables linked to state directory pages listing the Internet sites. URL: <http://www.infoctr.edu/swl/>. The URLs link to sites for administrative law, agency, and state government information. The ALSO American Law Sources Online United States directory pages for each state also provide administrative law sources with links. URL: <http://www.lawsource.com/also/>.

Presidential Information

Presidential documents include executive orders, proclamations or announcements, administrative orders, presidential reorganization plans, messages or communications to Congress, speeches, appointments, and treaties and agreements between other countries. Annually all executive orders and presidential proclamations are cumulated and codified in Title 3 of the *Code of Federal Regulations*. Beginning with the Clinton Administration, the definition of presidential information was changed as radio addresses, speeches, and photos that were posted on the White House Web site were added to the public/published papers, executively controlled papers, official papers, and personal papers that were formerly defined as presidential papers. The White House Web site includes information about all presidential activities, public presentations, and papers of the President as well as information about the history and traditions of the President's home. URL: <http://www.whitehouse.gov>.

The GPO Access Presidential Materials page lists speeches, remarks, executive orders, and other resources for presidential documents. URL: <http://www.gpoaccess.gov/executive.html#presidential>.

The *Weekly Compilation of Presidential Documents*, which began publication with the Presidential papers of Harry S. Truman, contains statements, reprints of speeches, remarks, press conferences, messages, a monthly dateline, lists of laws approved by the President, nominations submitted to the Senate, a checklist of White House releases, and other presidential materials released by the White House during the preceding week. *Weekly Compilation* documents from 1993 to the present can be found by performing keyword searches. This publication is cumulated annually in the *Public Papers of the Presidents* that is published by NARA. Each *Public Papers* volume contains the papers and speeches that were issued by the Office of the Press Secretary during the specified time period, nominations submitted to the Senate, the President's daily schedule and meetings, other items of general interest, and other presidential documents released by the Office of the Press Secretary and published in the *Federal Register*. Both the *Weekly Compilation* and the *Public Papers of the Presidents* are available online since the Presidency of Bill Clinton. URLs: <http://www.gpoaccess.gov/wcomp/index. html> and <http://www.gpoaccess.gov/pubpapers/>. Information about the organization of presidential documents online is explained on the NARA Web site. URL: <http://www.archives.gov/federal_register/ presidential_documents/website_ guide.html>.

LEGAL AND GOVERNMENT REFERENCE SOURCES

Secondary sources play significant roles and are very helpful to researchers in identifying and explaining the law. Legal and regulatory reference tools include citation manuals, dictionaries, encyclopedias, directories, legal periodicals, and news services. The Harvard *Bluebook* is the most used citation manual to properly format legal materials. The Introduction to Basic Legal Citation from the LII written by Peter W. Martin is based on the 17th edition of *The Bluebook: A Uniform System of Citation*, known as the The Harvard *Bluebook* or the *Bluebook*. URL: <http://www.law.cornell.edu/citation/>. The citation primer has an easily searchable table of contents with hyperlinks to material on Cornell's LII Web site. The Boston College Law Library guide for citations, Reading Legal Citations, provides explanatory information for formatting citations. URL: <http://www.bc.edu/schools/law/library/research/ researchguides/citations/>.

There are no authoritative legal dictionaries published on the Internet, but there are a number of sites that provide explanations of thousands of law-related words, terms, and phrases. Legal dictionaries are available from FindLaw and Law.com. URLs: <http://dictionary. lp.findlaw.com/> and <http://dictionary.law.com/>. The Nolo Press, the publisher of the self-help guides, Everybody's Legal Glossary, contains plain-English definitions and explanations for hundreds of legal terms for people with no legal education or training. URL: <http:// www.nolo.com/glossary.cfm>. The Duhaime's Legal Dictionary is also written in plain language by Canadian lawyer Lloyd Duhaime. URL: <http://www.duhaime.org/dictionary/diction.aspx>. Each definition includes hypertext links to terms that are used in the definitions of the legal concepts. The One-L Dictionary was developed by the Harvard Law School faculty to support new law students but it is very useful for the non-lawyer. URL: <http://www.law.harvard.edu/library/services/research/

guides/united_states/basics/one_l_dictionary.php>. JURIST's browseable dictionary of basic U.S. legal terminology focuses on legal procedure. URL: <http://jurist.law.pitt.edu/dictionary.htm>. The Glossary of Legal Terms published on the LexisNexis Lawyers.com site is based on Merriam-Webster's Dictionary of Law. URL: <http://www.lawyers.com/legal_topics/glossary/index.php>.

There are no authoritative legal encyclopedias published online. The law librarians at the Cornell Law Library are creating the Cornell Legal Research Encyclopedia. URL: <http://www.lawschool.cornell.edu/library/encyclopedia/encyclopedia.html>. The compilation of United States and International legal resources is a topical and jurisdictional arrangement of all available formats, including print, microform, CD-ROM, Westlaw, Lexis, and the Internet. Citation to research tools and direct links are provided. The LII also maintains the "Law About" pages providing brief summaries of law topics with links to key primary source material, other Internet resources, and other useful references. URL: <http://www.law.cornell.edu/topics/index.html>. Two topical law Web pages are available from FindLaw. The FindLaw Library from Thomson West provides topical law publications that are available on the Internet. URL: <http://library.lp.findlaw.com/>. The practice area topics publish the latest legal news, case law, and analytical articles. The lawyers.com site from LexisNexis sponsors the Browse by topic site that links to related articles on the topics. URL: <http:// www.lawyers.com/legal_topics/browse_by_topic/index.php?>. Other topical sites include the Law by Subject page from Emory University Law Library. URL: <http://www.law.emory.edu/erd/subject/index.html>.

Legal directories are one of the legal and government resources on the Internet most used by attorneys, judges, businesspersons, and ordinary citizens. They are useful in locating information about a particular lawyer or law firm, court or judge, expert witnesses, law schools, and government agencies. They vary in scope of their coverage listing all lawyers, limited to a region, state, municipality, or specialty. Directories to identify attorneys, elected officials, experts, professors, and legal aid organizations are available on the Internet. The most used legal directory is the Martindale-Hubbell Directory owned by Lexis Law Publishing. The Martindale.com Lawyer Locator provides free online access to the entire Martindale-Hubbell database. URL: <http://www.martindale.com/xp/Martindale/Lawyer_Locator/Search_Lawyer_Locator/lawyer_search.xml>. The site allows consumers to search a database of over one million lawyers and law firms in 160 countries using criteria such as location, lawyer or law firm name, areas of practice, and fluency in a particular language. The site also provides consumer-oriented legal information to help users better understand the law, consumer friendly explanations of 24 major areas of law, articles on current legal topics, links to legal resources on the Web, and a glossary of legal terms. The Martindale database is available from the lawyers.com–Find a Lawyer QuickSearch and from the lexisONE page. URL: <http://www.lawyers. com/> and <http://www.lexisone.com>. The FindLaw West Legal Directory provides search forms to find an individual lawyer or a law firm by practice area, keyword, name, or location. URL: <http://lawyers. findlaw.com/>. The Hieros Gamos Law Firms Worldwide directory lists firms around the world. URL: <http://www.hg.org/lawfirms. html>. The 2004-2005 Chambers USA Guide to America's Leading Business Lawyers is the only legal directory to rank both law firms and individual lawyers. URL:<http://www.chambersandpartners.com/us/>. Published by Chambers and Partners, the London-based publisher of Chambers Global and Chambers UK Leading Lawyers, the guide offers reports on the highest-ranking firms and lawyers for each state in over 20 areas of commercial law.

The Association of American Law Schools (AALS) Member Schools also provides a directory of hypertext links to the Web sites of the 162 member schools and 17 fee-paid schools of the AALS. URL: <http://www.aals.org/members.html>. This nonprofit association is the learned society for law professors and the principal representative of legal education to the federal government and to other national higher education organizations. The Hieros Gamos Law Schools Directory includes the address, telephone number, fax number, and administrative information for over 1,300 law schools linked to their home pages. URL: <http://www.hg.org/schools.html>. Hieros Gamos also makes available Internet directories for foreign countries. The directory listing for each region is organized in alphabetical order by country and school. Both the FindLaw for Students: Law Schools: Full List A-Z Directory and the Jurist Law Schools Directory contain an alphabetical listing of law schools. URLs: <http://stu.findlaw.com/schools/fulllist.html> and <http://jurist.law.pitt.edu/lawschools/>. The Directory of Legal Academia alphabetically lists law schools and gives a link to the faculty and staff directories of the institution. URL: <http://www.law.cornell.edu/ dla/index.htm>.

Congressional and government directories provide contact information for congressional representatives, government administrators, and agencies. The USA Services page from the Federal Citizen Information Center serves as a portal for citizens to contact agencies and find answers from the government. URL: <http://www.info.gov/>. The National Contact Center is a directory of federal telephone directories to congressional and administrative offices as well as toll free numbers. URL: <http://www.pueblo.gsa.gov/call/phone.htm> and <http://www. pueblo.gsa.gov/call/toll-free.htm>. The U.S. Blue Pages gives citizens a standard format for acquiring federal or state agency telephone listings by searching the directory by keyword or agency/service name. URL: <http://www.usbluepages.gov>.

One of the most used government documents is the *Congressional Directory*, published for each Congress every two years by the GPO and linked from GPO Access. Linked from the U.S. Congress page at GPO Access, there are two congressional directories at this site. The Congressional Directory is a searchable online version that is published by the GPO. URL: <http://www.gpoaccess.gov/cdirectory/index.html>. The Congressional Directory presents short biographies of each member of the Senate and House, listed by state or district, and additional data, such as committee memberships, terms of service, administrative assistants and/or secretaries, and room and telephone numbers. It also lists officials of the courts, military establishments, and other Federal departments and agencies, including D.C. government officials, governors of states and territories, foreign diplomats, and members of the press, radio, and television galleries. Directories are available on GPO Access from 1995 and can be searched by keyword or browsed. The Congressional Pictorial Directory provides a black and white photograph of each member of the House of Representatives and the Senate. URL: <http://www.gpoaccess.gov/pictorial/index.html>. It includes information about member's length of service, political party affiliations, and Congressional district. There is also a New Member Pictorial Directory for each session. URL: <http://www.gpoaccess.gov/pictorial/109th/newmems.html>. Other congressional directories include Congress.org and Contacting the Congress. URLs: <http://www.congress.org/congressorg/home/> or <http://www.visi.com/juan/congress/>. The Congressional Directories page from the University of Michigan Documents Center includes leadership positions and e-mail addresses for both houses. URL: <http://www.lib.umich.edu/govdocs/congdir.html>. The Biographical Directory of the United States Congress 1774 to Present is a searchable directory of biographical information about each member, including education, family, professional experience, and government service. URL: <http://bioguide.congress.gov/biosearch/biosearch.asp>.

CURRENT AWARENESS RESOURCES AND BLOGS

A number of Web pages provide current awareness information about the law and new Web sites to access legal information. The Law Library Resource Xchange or llrx.com is an online biweekly newsletter focusing on the newest developments in online legal research and technology-related issues for the legal community. URL: <http://www.llrx. com/>. Published and edited by Sabrina Pacifici, a Washington D.C. private firm law librarian, the newsletter is designed as a resource for legal information professionals, lawyers, law students, librarians, and paralegals to refer to for comprehensive content accompanied by analysis, links, and documentation. Jurist is a daily newspaper for the legal profession providing news, court dockets, and commentary. URL: <http://jurist.law.pitt.edu/cases/>.[17]

ABA Site-tations is a monthly e-newsletter summarizing new or useful Web sites for legal professionals. URL: <http://www.lawtechnology. org/site-tation/>. Site-tation contents have been available either alphabetically or by subject since August 2000. InSITE, maintained by the law librarians of Cornell, is an annotated current awareness service highlighting law-related Web sites. It is issued electronically and in print and has a keyword-searchable database. URL: <http://www. lawschool.cornell.edu/library/Finding_the_Law/insite.html>. Research Buzz is a current awareness tool discussing search engines, databases, and information. Written to meet the needs of lawyers and researchers, it is maintained by Tara Calishain and was formerly published in LLRX. URL: <http:// www.researchbuzz.com>. LawSites, maintained by attorney and author Robert J. Ambrogi, tracks new and intriguing Web sites for legal information. URL: <http://www.legaline.com/ lawsites.html>. The Daily Whirl publishes daily headlines from law-related news and information sites including legal Web logs and displays them on a single page. URL: <http://www.dailywhirl.com/>. Mealey's Online from LexisNexis provides the latest legal news. URL: <http:// www.mealeys.com/>.

The number of Web logs–called "blogs" or, in the legal field, "blawgs"– has grown dramatically. The explosion in blogging has been felt within the legal field, with lawyers, academics, pundits, and even judges introducing blogs. The blog beSpecific maintained by Sabrina Pacifici spotlights news, resources, and law information technology innovations. URL: <http://www.bespacific.com>. To identify the available blogs, Law.com publishes a blog network providing pointers to Web logs on legal topics. URL: <http://blogs.law.com>. Blawg Search and Blawg are directories of law and legal-related Web logs allowing users to search the full text of a variety of blawgs. URLs: <http://blawgs. detod.com/> and <http://www.blawg.org/>. Other legal blogs include The Blawg Ring, Lawblogs.com, Ernie the Attorney, Netlawblog, Law Professor Blog, and Law Librarian Blog.

CONCLUSION

The world of legal information will only move further into electronic publication of legal and regulatory information as we continue into the twenty-first century. The increase in the comprehensiveness of the database will continue to make legal information more accessible for all citizens.

NOTES

1. Mellinkoff's Dictionary of American Legal Usage (1992).

2. "Government Printing Office Electronic Information Access Enhancement Act of 1993 (GPO Access Act), A Public Law 103-40." June 8,1993,107 Stat. 112 (Title 44, Sec. 4101 et seq.).

3. Presidential Memo–The Importance of E-Government, E-Gov, U.S. Office of Management and Budget, <http://www.whitehouse.gov/omb/egov/g-2-memo.html>.

4. Lawson, Jerry, "Web Logs for Lawyers: Lessons from Ernie the Attorney," LLRX.com <http://www.llrx.com/features/lawyerweblogs.htm> (May 23, 2003).

5. <http://www.virtualchase.com/TVCAlert/may03/22may03.html>.

6. Robert J. Ambrogi, "Five Essential Search Sites for Solos," Solo, Winter 2003 vol. 9 Number 2 <http://www.abanet.org/genpractice/solo/winter03/fiveessential.html>.

7. Web Watch: The 10 Best Sites of the Decade By Robert J. Ambrogi Law Technology News <http://www.lawtechnews.com/r5/showkiosk.asp?listing_id=414691& pub_id=5173&category_id=27902Lawsites>, 15 October 2003 <http://www.legaline. com/2003_10_12_lawsites_archive.html#106623379572002954>.

8. The Center for Information Law and Policy (CILP) was a joint effort between the Villanova University School of Law and the Illinois Institute of Technology/Chicago-Kent College of Law. The site began as a research institute and developed sources of legal information from governmental sources, including courts and agencies. After some members of the developing team of the Center moved to other institutions, the joint initiative ended in September 1999. The Chicago-Kent College of Law and Villanova University School of Law discontinued joint operation of the Center for Information Law and Policy and divided the CILP databases and Web sites. The responsibility for continuing portions of the Center's work and housing its archives continues to be administered directly by the library staff of both law schools. The CILP created some well-known publications, such as the Federal Web Locator URL: <http://www. infoctr.edu/fwl/>, the State Web Locator URL: <http://www.infoctr.edu/swl/> main-

tained until 2003 by the Illinois Institute of Technology–Chicago-Kent, and the Federal Court Locator maintained at Villanova University. URL: <http://www.law.villanova.edu/library/researchguides/fedcourtlocator.asp> and Tax Documents URL: <http://www.law.villanova.edu/library/researchguides/taxdocuments.asp>.

9. Garvin, Peggy, "The Government Domain–Why Google Uncle Sam?" Law Library Resource Xchange Published February 13, 2005 <http://www.llrx.com/columns/govdomain2.htm>.

10. Public Access to Court Electronic Records (PACER) is an electronic public access service that allows users to obtain case and docket information from Federal Appellate, District and Bankruptcy courts, and from the U.S. Party/Case Index. Currently most systems must be dialed directly using communication software (such as ProComm Plus, pcAnywhere, or Hyperterminal) and a modem, but the Judiciary is moving toward providing case information on the Internet through PACER-Net sites. The PACER System offers electronic access to case dockets to retrieve information such as: a listing of all parties and participants including judges, attorneys, and trustees; a compilation of case-related information such as cause of action, *nature of suit*, and dollar demand; and a chronology of dates of case events entered in the case record; a claims registry, listing of new cases each day; and Appellate court opinions. Free access to case law varies by court. Many use the PACER (Public Access to Court Electronic Records) system, which requires an account and which has been mandated to charge to recoup costs.

11. *"How U.S. Courts Work"* in 4, *Issues of Democracy* No. 2 (Sept. 1999), published by the U.S. Information Agency.

12. The regional reporters are Pacific Reporter; Northwestern Reporter, Southwestern Reporter, Northeastern Reporter, Atlantic Reporter, Southeastern Reporter; Southern Reporter, California Reporter, and the New York Supplement.

13. The Hermes archive is maintained at Case Western Reserve University, and at the through-streamed conversion, all of the decisions are now available in HTML Supreme Court Collection. URL: <http://supct.law.cornell.edu/supct/cases/historic.htm>. The Legal Information Institute at Cornell has converted the entire Case Western Reserve archive backlist to HTML from Word Perfect 5.1 and ASCII formats and filled gaps in the collection of decisions. Since the October 1997 term, decisions of the Court have been distributed in Adobe Acrobat (PDF) and SGML tagged ASCII format.

14. In 1996, the Office of Information and Regulatory Affairs of the Office of Management and Budget made Supreme Court decisions from 1937 to 1975 available on the Internet. These opinions were created by the U.S. Air Force's Federal Legal Information Through Electronics (FLITE) project, conducted during the seventies to computerize the historic file of decisions. The FLITE database offers a search engine and access to a database of over 7,400 Supreme Court opinions.

15. The OYEZ Project takes its name from the phrase by which the Marshal of the Court calls the courtroom to order. OYEZ is pronounced "o-yay" or "o-yez" or "o-yes." It is used three times in succession to introduce the opening of a court of law. The origin of the word "oyez" is Middle English, from Anglo-Norman, hear ye, the plural imperative of oyer, to hear, which derives from the Latin verb, audire, to hear. The OYEZ Project has been generously supported by grants from the National Endowment for the Humanities, the National Science Foundation, the M.R. Bauer Foundation, Northwestern University, and Mayer Brown & Platt.

16. Peggy Garvin, "The Government Domain–THOMAS: New Congress, A Few Changes," Law Library Resource Xchange, <http://www.llrx.com/columns/govdomain1.htm> (January 17, 2005).

17. The JURIST project is led by law professor Bernard Hibbitts from the University of Pittsburgh School of Law. JURIST was originally launched in 1996 as "Law Professors on the Web," with the name JURIST being officially adopted in 1997. The site was initially designed for law professors as a clearinghouse of online legal materials authored by other law professors.

WEBLIOGRAPHY

GUIDES OR DIRECTORIES TO ACCESS LEGAL AND GOVERNMENT INFORMATION

A Century of Lawmaking for a New Nation: U.S. Congressional Documents
    and Debates, 1774-1873–URL:
    <http://memory.loc.gov/ammem/amlaw/index.html>
AllLaw.com–URL: <http://www.alllaw.com/>
American Law Sources Online–URL: <http://www.lawsource.com/also>
Christopher Brown's Virtual Reference Desk–URL:
    <http://www.virtualref.com/govdocs/>
Catalaw–URL: <http://www.catalaw.com/>
Emory University Internet Legal Research Guide–URL:
    <http://www.law.emory.edu/erd/subject/ilrguide.html>
Federal Courts Finder–URL: <http://www.law.emory.edu/FEDCTS/>
Electronic Reference Desk–URL: <http://www.law.emory.edu/erd/index.html>
Federal Web Locator (Chicago-Kent College of Law)–URL:
    <http://www.infoctr.edu/fwl/>
State Web Locator URL: <http://www.infoctr.edu/swl/>
FindLaw–URL: <http://www.findlaw.com/>
    FindLaw for Business–URL: <http://smallbusiness.findlaw.com/>
    FindLaw for Corporate Counsel–URL: <http://corporate.findlaw.com/>
    FindLaw for Legal–URL: <http://lp.findlaw.com/>
    FindLaw for the Public–URL: <http://public.findlaw.com/>
Global Legal Information Network (GLIN)–URL: <http://www.glin.gov/>
Government Information Online–URL: <http://govtinfo.org/>
GPO Access–U.S. Government Printing Office–URL:<http://www.gpoaccess.gov>
    Core Documents of U.S. Democracy–URL:
        <http://www.gpoaccess.gov/coredocs.html>
    Judicial Branch Resources–URL: <http://www.gpoaccess.gov/judicial.html>
    Legislative Branch Resources–URL:
        <http://www.gpoaccess.gov/legislative.html>
    Executive Branch Resources–URL: <http://www.gpoaccess.gov/executive.html>
Guide to Law Online–URL: <http://www.loc.gov/law/guide/>
    GUIDE: International–URL: <http://www.loc.gov/law/guide/multi.html>

GUIDE: Nations of the World–URL: <http://www.loc.gov/law/guide/nations.html>
GUIDE: United States–URL: <http://www.loc.gov/law/guide/us.html>
Hieros Gamos (HG)–URL: <http://www.hg.org/>
Internet Legal Research from Internet Tools for Lawyers–URL:
　<http://www.netlawtools.com/research/index.html>
　United States Federal Government Sites–URL:
　　<http://www.ilrg.com/gov/us.html>
　American Government Index–URL: <http://www.ilrg.com/gov.html>
Invisible Web Directory–Government Information and Data–URL:
　<http://www.invisible-web.net/database.html?category_selected=Government+
　Information+and+Data>
　Legal and Criminal Information–URL:
　　<http://www.invisible-web.net/database.html?category_selected=Legal+and+
　　Criminal+Information>
JURIST–URL: <http://jurist.law.pitt.edu/>
Katsuey's Legal Gateway–URL: <http://www.katsuey.com/index.cfm>
Law and Policy Institutions Guide–URL: <http://www.lpig.org/>
Law Engine–URL: <http://www.thelawengine.com/>
LawGuru.com–URL: <http://www.lawguru.com/>
Legal Express (Villanova University)–URL:
　<http://vls.law.villanova.edu/library/express/>
　Federal Court Locator–URL:
　　<http://www.law.vill.edu/library/researchguides/fedcourtlocator.asp>
　Tax Master–the Tax Law Locator–URL:
　　<http://vls.law.villanova.edu/prof/maule/taxmaster/taxhome.htm>
Legal Information Institute–URL: <http://www.law.cornell.edu/>
　Materials Organized by Topic and Materials Organized by Source of Law–URL:
　　<http://www.law.cornell.edu/topics/index.html>
lexisONE–URL: <http://www.lexisone.com/>
　lexisONE Legal Web Site Directory–URL:
　　<http://www.lexisone.com/legalresearch/legalguide/legal_guide_index.html>
　LexisNexis Infopro–URL: <http://www.lexisnexis.com/infopro>
　Zimmerman's Research Guide–URL:
　　<http://www.lexisnexis.com/infopro/zimmerman/>
Library of Congress–Multinational Collections Database–URL:
　<http://www.loc.gov/mulp/>
　Bookmarks–Legal Resources on the Internet–URL:
　　<http://www.loc.gov/rr/law/lawresources.html>
Megalaw.com–URLs:
　<http://www.megalaw.com/> or <http://www.megalaw.com/research.php>
University of Michigan Library Documents Center–URL:
　<http://www.lib.umich.edu/govdocs/>
　Documents in the News–URL:
　　<http://www.lib.umich.edu/govdocs/docnews.html>
Virtual Chase–URL: <http://www.virtualchase.com/>
　Legal Research Guide–URL: <http://www.virtualchase.com/resources/index.shtml>

WashLaw–URL: <http://www.washlaw.edu/>
REFLAW–URL: <http://www.washlaw.edu/reflaw/reflaw.html>
DocLaw–URL: <http://www.washlaw.edu/doclaw/>
Federal Organizational Chart–URL:
    <http://www.washlaw.edu/doclaw/orgchart/mainog.html>
World Wide Web Virtual Law Library–URL: <http://www.law.indiana.edu/v-lib/>

LEGAL AND GOVERNMENT SEARCH ENGINES

Law Search Engines

Catalaw Meta-Index for U.S. Legal Research–URL:
    <http://www.catalaw.com/info/metaindex.shtml>
Georgia State University Meta Index (GSU)–URL:
    <http://gsulaw.gsu.edu/metaindex/>
LawCrawler–URLs: <http://lawcrawler.findlaw.com/> or <http://www.lawcrawler.com>
Law Engine–URL: <http://www.fastsearch.com/law/index.html>
LawGuru.com–URL: <http://www.lawguru.com/multisearch/multimenu.html>
    Law Guru–Legal Research Page–URL:
        <http://www.lawguru.com/search/lawsearch.html>
LawKT (Surfwax)–URLs: <http://news.surfwax.com/law/> or <http://law.surfwax.com>
LawRunner (Internet Legal Resource Guide)–URL: <http://www.lawrunner.com/>
    USA Index–URL: <http://www.ilrg.com/gov.html>
    Global Index–URL: <http://www.ilrg.com/nations/>
Legal.Com–URLs:
    <http://www.legal.com> and <http://www.legal.com/Research/main.html>

Government Search Engines

FirstGov–URL: <http://www.firstgov.gov/>
Uncle Sam Google–URL: <http://www.google.com/unclesam>

JUDICIAL BRANCH INFORMATION SOURCES: FEDERAL AND STATE CASE LAW

Information About the Courts

FindLaw–Cases and Codes: Introductory Materials–URL:
    <http://www.findlaw.com/casecode/intro.html>
GPO Access–Judicial Branch Resources–URL:
    <http://www.gpoaccess.gov/judicial.html>
U.S. Courts–URL: <http://www.uscourts.gov/>
    About U.S.–URL: <http://www.uscourts.gov/about.html>
    Understanding the Federal Courts–URLs:
        <http://www.uscourts.gov/understand03/>
        and <http://www.uscourts.gov/UFC99.pdf>

Third Branch–Newsletter of the Federal Courts–URL:
 <http://www.uscourts.gov/ttb/index.html>
PACER System–URL: <http://pacer.psc.uscourts.gov/>
U.S. Information Agency–*Issues of Democracy*–"How U.S. Courts Work"–URLs:
 <http://usinfo.state.gov/journals/itdhr/0999/ijde/ijde0999.htm>
 or <http://usinfo.state.gov/usa/infousa/politics/govtman/getdoc11.pdf>

Federal Case Law Directories

All Law–URL: <http://www.alllaw.com/law/federal_law/case_law/>
American Law Sources On-Line (ALSO)–United States Government–Law Page–URL:
 <http://www.lawsource.com/also/usa.cgi?us1>
Attorney Finder–Legal Resources–URL:
 <http://www.attyfind.com/legalresources.asp>
Courtlinks–URL: <http://www.uscourts.gov/links.html>
 All Court Sites–Administrative Office and Federal Judicial Center–URL:
  <http://www.uscourts.gov/allinks.html>
Emory University Law School–Federal Courts Finder–URL:
 <http://www.law.emory.edu/FEDCTS>
FindLaw–URL: <http://www.findlaw.com/casecode/>
 On the Opinion Summaries–URL:
  <http://caselaw.lp.findlaw.com/casesummary/index.html>
Internet Legal Resource Guide–URL: <http://www.ilrg.com/caselaw/>
Law.com–U.S. Courts–URL: <http://www11.law.com/nav.asp?h=90>
lexisONE–URL: <http://www.lexisone.com/index.html>
Library of Congress U.S. Judiciary–URL:
 <http://www.loc.gov/law/guide/usjudic.html>
MegaLaw–Federal Cases & Courts–URL:
 <http://www.megalaw.com/fed/fedcourts.php>

State Case Law Directories

All Law–URL: <http://www.alllaw.com/state_resources/>
ALSO American Law Sources Online–United States–URL:
 <http://www.lawsource.com/also/index.htm#[United%20States]>
Hieros Gamos–U.S. State Law–URL: <http://www.hg.org/usstates.html>
Internet Legal Resource Guide–American Government Index–URL:
 <http://www.ilrg.com/gov.html>
lexisONE–Legal Web Site Directory–State Resource Center–URL:
 <http://www.findlaw.com/llstategov/>
LII–State Courts by Jurisdiction–URL: <http://www.law.cornell.edu/opinions.html>
MegaLaw State Cases, Codes, and Resources–URL:
 <http://www.megalaw.com/states.php>
National Center for State Courts Court–URL:
 <http://www.ncsconline.org/D_KIS/info_court_web_sites.html>
State Legal Sources on the Web–University of Michigan Documents Center–URL:
 <http://www.lib.umich.edu/govdocs/statelaw.html>

WashLawWEB–StateLaw–State Case Law–URLs:
<http://www.washlaw.edu/uslaw/states/allstates/>
or <http://www.washlaw.edu/uslaw/search.html#judicial>

U.S. Supreme Court Case Law

FedWorld FLITE Database–URL: <http://www.fedworld.gov/supcourt/index.htm>
FindLaw–Supreme Court–URL: <http://www.findlaw.com/casecode/supreme.html>
GPO Access–Supreme Court Decisions 1937-1975–URL:
<http://www.access.gpo.gov/su_docs/supcrt/index.html>
Federal Bulletin Board–URL: <http://fedbbs.access.gpo.gov/court01.htm>
Legal Information Institute at Cornell University–URL:
<http://supct.law.cornell.edu/supct/>
Searchable Database–URL:
<http://supct.law.cornell.edu/supct/search/search.html>
LexisONE–URL: <http://www.lexisone.com/>
OYEZ Project–URL: <http://www.oyez.org/oyez/frontpage>
Virtual Tour–URL: <http://www.oyez.org/oyez/tour/>
Oyez Baseball–URL: <http://baseball.oyez.org/>
U.S. Supreme Court–URL: <http://www.supremecourtus.gov/index.html>
About the Supreme Court–URL:
<http://www.supremecourtus.gov/about/about.html>
Opinions–URL: <http://www.supremecourtus.gov/opinions/opinions.html>

Supreme Court and Justice Information

LII–Supreme Court Collection–Gallery of the Justices–URL:
<http://supct.law.cornell.edu/supct/justices/fullcourt.html>
Liibulletin–URL: <http://supct.law.cornell.edu/supct/cert/>
OYEZ Project–Justices Page–URL: <http://www.oyez.org/oyez/portlet/justices/>
Supreme Court Historical Society–How the Court Works–URLs:
<http://www.supremecourthistory.org/index.html>
and <http://supremecourthistory.org/03_how/03.html>
USSCPlus–About The Court–URL: <http://www.usscplus.com/info/>
Web Guide to U.S. Supreme Court Research (LLRX)–URL:
<http://www.llrx.com/features/supremectwebguide.htm>

Lower Federal Courts–Federal Court of Appeals, District Court, and Other Courts

Federal Courts Finder–URL: <http://www.law.emory.edu/caselaw/>
FindLaw–Resources by Jurisdiction–Federal Circuit Court Opinions–URLs:
<http://www.findlaw.com/10fedgov/judicial/appeals_courts.html>
or <http://www.findlaw.com/casecode/html>
FindLaw–Resources by Jurisdiction–District Court Opinions–URL:
<http://www.findlaw.com/10fedgov/judicial/district_courts.html>
U.S. Courts–Court Links–URL: <http://www.uscourts.gov/links.html>
Federal Court Locator from Villanova–URL:
<http://www.law.villanova.edu/library/researchguides/fedcourtlocator.asp>

LEGISLATIVE AND STATUTORY INFORMATION RESOURCES

Constitutional Resources

American Law Sources Online–United States–URL:
  <http://www.lawsource.com/also/#(United States)>
Constitution Society–Founding Documents–URL:
  <http://www.law.cornell.edu/topics/constitutional.html>
Emory University Electronic Reference Desk–U.S. Documents–URL:
  <http://www.law.emory.edu/erd/docs.html>
  Constitution–Searchable Database–URL:
    <http://www.law.emory.edu/erd/docs/usconst.html>
FindLaw–U.S. Constitution Search–URL:
  <http://www.findlaw.com/casecode/constitution/>
    State Constitutions–URL: <http://www.findlaw.com/11stategov/indexconst.html>
GPO Access–Constitution of the U.S.–URL:
  <http://www.gpoaccess.gov/constitution/index.html>
Know Your Rights–Bill of Rights–URL:
  <http://www.harbornet.com/rights/states.html>
Library of Congress–U.S. Constitution–Text, Commentaries, Historical Texts,
  and Judicial Decisions–URL:
  <http://www.loc.gov/law/guide/usconst.html>
National Archives and Records Administration–Charters of Freedom–URL:
  <http://www.archives.gov/national_archives_experience/charters/constitution.html>

Congressional Servers

United States House of Representatives–URL: <http://www.house.gov/>
  House of Representatives Member Directory–URL:
    <http://uscode.house.gov/lawrevisioncounsel.php>
United States Senate–URL: <http://www.senate.gov>
  Senate Virtual Reference Desk–URL:
    <http://www.senate.gov/pagelayout/reference/b_three_sections_with_
    teasers/virtual.htm>
  Subject Bibliographies–URL:
    <http://www.senate.gov/pagelayout/reference/a_three_sections_with_
    teasers/biblio.htm>

Legislative Information Sites

GPO Access Legislative Branch Resources–URL:
  <http://www.gpoaccess.gov/legislative.html>
THOMAS–URL: <http://thomas.loc.gov/>
  How Our Laws Are Made–URL:
    <http://thomas.loc.gov/home/lawsmade.toc.html>
  Enactment of a Law–URL:
    <http://thomas.loc.gov/home/enactment/enactlawtoc.html>

The Legislative Process, a House of Representatives Guide–URL:
  <http://www.house.gov/Legproc.html>
Legislative Process Tying It All Together–URL:
  <http://www.house.gov/Tying_it_all.html>

Legislative History

Cheryl Nyberg's Guide to Congressional Research Service Reports–URL:
  <http://lib.law.washington.edu/ref/crs.htm>
Congressional Research Service–URLs:
  <http://www.house.gov/rules/crs_reports.htm>
  or <http://www.llsdc.org/sourcebook/CRS-Congress.htm>
Federal Legislative History (Chicago Kent College of Law)–URL:
  <http://library.kentlaw.edu/Resources/Leghist%20Tutorial/Intro.htm>
Law Librarians' Society of Washington, D.C, (LLSDC) Legislative Source Book–URL:
  <http://www.llsdc.org/sourcebook/index.html>
Researching Legislative History (Harvard Law School)–URL:
  <http://www.law.harvard.edu/library/services/research/guides/grfs/specialized/
  legislative_history.php>
THOMAS–Bill Summary and Status–URLs:
  <http://thomas.loc.gov>
  or <http://thomas.loc.gov/bss/d109query.html>
University of Michigan Documents Center Legislative Histories Guide–URL:
  <http://www.lib.umich.edu/govdocs/legishis.html>

Statutory Information Resources–Codification of Federal Statutes

Public Laws

GPO Access–Public Laws–URL: <http://www.gpoaccess.gov/plaws/index.html>
THOMAS–Public Laws–URL: <http://thomas.loc.gov>
National Archives and Records Administration–Public Laws–URL:
  <http://www.archives.gov/federal_register/public_laws/public_laws.html>

United States Code

American Law Sources Online–URL:
  <http://www.lawsource.com/also/usa.cgi?us1#Z3R>
  Popular Names of Selected Public Laws–URL:
    <http://www.lawsource.com/also/usa.cgi?usp>
  Popular Names of Significant New Laws–URL:
    <http://www.lawsource.com/also/usa.cgi?usp0>
Browse the U.S. Code–URL: <http://www.gpoaccess.gov/uscode/browse.html>
GPO Access–URL: <http://www.gpoaccess.gov/uscode/about.html>
House of Representatives–URL: <http://uscode.house.gov/lawrevisioncounsel.php>
Law Library of Congress–United States Code–URL:
  <http://www.loc.gov/law/guide/uscode.html>

Law Librarians' Society of Washington, D.C.–United States Code–URL:
<http://www.llsdc.org/sourcebook/statutes-code.htm>
Legal Information Institute at Cornell–U.S. Code Collection–URLs:
<http://www.law.cornell.edu/uscode/>
and <http://assembler.law.cornell.edu/uscode>
Search Page–URLs: <http://assembler.law.cornell.edu/uscode/search/index.html>
or <http://assembler.law.cornell.edu/uscode/#SECTIONS>

State Laws and Legislative Information

American Sources Online–ALSO–URL:
<http://www.lawsource.com/also/index.htm#[United%20States]>
FindLaw–State Resources–State Codes–URLs:
<http://www.findlaw.com/casecode/#statelaw>
or <http://www.findlaw.com/11stategov/indexcode.html>
Legal Information Institute Law by Source–URL:
<http://www.law.cornell.edu/states/listing.html>
National Conference of State Legislatures–State Legislatures Internet Links–URL:
<http://www.ncsl.org/public/leglinks.cfm>
Internet audio or video feeds–URL:
<http://www.ncsl.org/programs/press/leglive.htm>
State Law–State Government, Legislative Information (Washburn School of Law Library)–URLs:
<http://www.washlaw.edu/uslaw/states/allstates/>
or <http://www.washlaw.edu/uslaw/search.html#legislative>
State Legal Sources on the Web (Documents Center at the University of Michigan)–URL: <http://www.lib.umich.edu/govdocs/statelaw.html>
State Legislative History Research Guides on the Web (Indiana University School of Law Library)–URL: <http://www.law.indiana.edu/library/services/sta_leg.shtml>

Municipal Codes

E-Codes–Municipal Codes on the Internet–URL:
<http://www.generalcode.com/webcode2.html>
Municode–Municipal Code Corporation–URL:
<http://www.municode.com/resources/online_codes.asp>
Municipal Codes Online–Seattle Public Library–URL:
<http://www.spl.org/default.asp?pageID=collection_municodes>

ADMINISTRATIVE AND EXECUTIVE BRANCH INFORMATION SOURCES

Guides

Federal Regulations–Legal Information Institute–URL:
<http://www.lawschool.cornell.edu/lawlibrary/Finding_the_Law/Guides_by_Topic/fedregs.htm>

GPO Access Executive Branch Resources–URL:
   <http://www.gpoaccess.gov/executive.html>

Government Directories for Department and Agencies

Cybercemetery (University of North Texas and the U.S. Government Printing Office)–URL: <http://govinfo.library.unt.edu/>
DocLaw WEB–URL: <http://www.washlaw.edu/doclaw/>
Federal Agencies Directory (Louisiana State University Libraries)–URL:
   <http://www.lib.lsu.edu/gov/alpha> or <http://www.lib.lsu.edu/gov/tree>
Federal Government Resources on the Web (University of Michigan Documents Center)–URL: <http://www.lib.umich.edu/govdocs/federalnew.html>
Federal Web Locator (Chicago-Kent College of Law)–URL:
   <http://www.infoctr.edu/fwl/>
FirstGov–A-Z Index of Government Agencies–URLs:
   <http://www.firstgov.gov/Agencies.shtml>
   or <http://www.firstgov.gov/Agencies/Federal/All_Agencies/index.shtml>
GPO Access–U.S. Government Manual–URLs:
   <http://www.gpoaccess.gov/gmanual/index.html>
   or <http://www.gpoaccess.gov/gmanual/browse-gm-04.html>
USLinks–U.S. Federal Government Agencies Database (Duke University Public Documents and Maps Department)–URL:
   <http://www.lib.duke.edu/texis/uslinks/uslinks>
White House Government–URL: <http://www.whitehouse.gov/government/>
   Citizen's Handbook–URL: <http://www.whitehouse.gov/government/handbook/>
   Executive Office of the President–URL:
      <http://www.whitehouse.gov/government/eop.html>
   Federal Agencies and Commissions–URL:
      <http://www.whitehouse.gov/government/independent-agencies.html>
   President Bush's Cabinet–URL:
      <http://www.whitehouse.gov/government/cabinet.html>

The Regulatory System–The Federal Register and the Code of Federal Regulations

Federal Register

FindLaw–URL: <http://www.findlaw.com/casecode/cfr.html>
GPO Access–URL: <http://www.gpoaccess.gov/fr/index.html>
National Archives and Records Administration–URL:
   <http://www.archives.gov/federal-register/>
   The Federal Register: What It Is and How to Use It.–URL:
      <http://www.archives.gov/federal_register/tutorial/about_tutorial.html>
Regulations.gov–URL: <http://www.regulations.gov/>

Code of Federal Regulations

GPO Access–Code of Federal Regulations–URLs:
   <http://www.gpoaccess.gov/cfr/index.html>
   and <http://www.access.gpo.gov/nara/cfr/cfr-table-search.html>

List of Sections Affected–URL: <http://www.gpoaccess.gov/lsa/about.html>
Legal Information Institute–URL: <http://www.law.cornell.edu/cfr/>
FindLaw–Code of Federal Regulations–URL:
   <http://www.findlaw.com/casecode/cfr.html>

State Administrative Law

Administrative Codes and Registers (ACR) Section of the National Association of Sec-
   retaries of State (NASS)–URL: <http://www.nass.org/acr/internet.html>
American Bar Association (ABA) Administrative Procedure Database–State Re-
   sources–URL: <http://www.law.fsu.edu/library/admin/admin5.html>
ALSO American Law Sources Online–United States–Administrative Law Sources–
   URL: <http://www.lawsource.com/also/#[United%20States]>
FindLaw for Legal Professionals–State Resources–URL:
   <http://www.findlaw.com/11stategov/index.html>
State Legal Sources on the Web (Documents Center at the University of Michi-
   gan)–URL: <http://www.lib.umich.edu/govdocs/statelaw.html>
State Web Locator (Chicago-Kent College of Law)–URL:
   <http://www.infoctr.edu/swl/>

Presidential Information

GPO Access–Presidential Materials–URL:
   <http://www.gpoaccess.gov/executive.html#presidential>
   Weekly Compilation–URL: <http://www.gpoaccess.gov/wcomp/index.html>
   Public Papers of the President–URL: <http://www.gpoaccess.gov/pubpapers/>
National Archives and Records Administration–URL:
   <http://www.archives.gov/federal_register/presidential_documents/website_guide.html>
White House–URL: <http://www.whitehouse.gov>

LEGAL AND GOVERNMENT REFERENCE SOURCES

Citation Manuals

Introduction to Basic Legal Citation from the LII written by Peter W. Martin is based on
   the 17th edition of *The Bluebook: A Uniform System of Citation*, known as the The
   Harvard *Bluebook* or the *Bluebook*. URL: <http://www.law.cornell.edu/citation/>
Boston College Law Library guide for citations, Reading Legal Citations provides explanatory information for formatting citations. URL:
   <http://www.bc.edu/schools/law/library/research/researchguides/citations/>

Legal Dictionaries

Duhaime's Legal Dictionary–URL:
   <http://www.duhaime.org/dictionary/diction.aspx>
Everybody's Legal Glossary (Nolo Press)–URL:
   <http://www.nolo.com/glossary.cfm>

FindLaw–URL: <http://dictionary.lp.findlaw.com/>
Glossary of Legal Terms (LexisNexis Lawyers.com)–URL:
   <http://www.lawyers.com/legal_topics/glossary/index.php>
JURIST–U.S. Legal Terminology–URL: <http://jurist.law.pitt.edu/dictionary.htm>
Law.com–URL: <http://dictionary.law.com/>
One–L Dictionary (Harvard Law School)–URL:
   <http://www.law.harvard.edu/library/services/research/guides/united_states/
   basics/one_l_dictionary.php>

Legal Encyclopedias

Cornell Legal Research Encyclopedia–URL:
   <http://www.lawschool.cornell.edu/library/encyclopedia/encyclopedia.html>
FindLaw Library–Practice Topics–URL: <http://library.lp.findlaw.com/>
Law About (Legal Information Institute at Cornell University)–URL:
   <http://www.law.cornell.edu/topics/index.html>
Law by Subject (Emory University Law Library)–URL:
   <http://www.law.emory.edu/erd/subject/index.html>
lawyers.com–Browse by Topic (LexisNexis)–URL:
   <http://www.lawyers.com/legal_topics/browse_by_topic/index.php?>

Legal Directories

Association of American Law Schools (AALS) Member Schools–URL:
   <http://www.aals.org/members.html>
Chambers USA Guide to America's Leading Business Lawyers–URL:
   <http://www.chambersandpartners.com/us/>
Directory of Legal Academia–URL: <http://www.law.cornell.edu/dla/index.htm>
FindLaw West Legal Directory–URL: <http://lawyers.findlaw.com/>
   FindLaw for Students: Law Schools: Full List A-Z Directory–URL:
      <http://stu.findlaw.com/schools/fulllist.html>
Hieros Gamos Law Firms Worldwide Directory–URL:
   <http://www.hg.org/lawfirms.html>
   Hieros Gamos Law Schools Directory–URL: <http://www.hg.org/schools.html>
Jurist Law Schools Directory–URL: <http://jurist.law.pitt.edu/lawschools/>
Martindale.com Lawyer Locator–URL:
   <http://www.martindale.com/xp/Martindale/Lawyer_Locator/Search_Lawyer_
   Locator/lawyer_search.xml>
   Find A Lawyer QuickSearch–URL: <http://www.lawyers.com/>
   LexisONE–URL: <http://www.lexisone.com>

Congressional and Government Directories

Biographical Directory of the U.S. Congress 1774 to Present–URL:
   <http://bioguide.congress.gov/biosearch/biosearch.asp>
Congress.Org–URL: <http://www.congress.org/congressorg/home/>
Congressional Directories (University of Michigan Documents Center–URL:
   <http://www.lib.umich.edu/govdocs/congdir.html>

Contacting the Congress–URL: <http://www.visi.com/juan/congress/>
GPO Access–Congressional Directory–URL:
  <http://www.gpoaccess.gov/cdirectory/index.html>
  Congressional Pictorial Directory–URL:
    <http://www.gpoaccess.gov/pictorial/index.html>
  New Member Pictorial Directory–URL:
    <http://www.gpoaccess.gov/pictorial/109th/newmems.html>
National Contact Center–URL: <http://www.pueblo.gsa.gov/call/phone.htm>
  Federal Toll-Free Telephone Numbers Commonly Requested at the National Con-
    tact Center–URL: <http://www.pueblo.gsa.gov/call/toll-free.htm>
USA Services from the Federal Citizen Information Center–URL:
  <http://www.info.gov/>
U.S. Blue Pages–URL: <http://www.usbluepages.gov>

CURRENT AWARENESS RESOURCES AND BLOGS

ABA Site-tations–URL: <http://www.lawtechnology.org/site-tation/>
Daily Whirl–URL: <http://www.dailywhirl.com/>
InSITE (Cornell University Law School Library)–URL:
  <http://www.lawschool.cornell.edu/library/Finding_the_Law/insite.html>
Jurist–URL: <http://jurist.law.pitt.edu/cases/>
Law Library Resource Xchange–URL: <http://www.llrx.com/>
LawSites–URL: <http://www.legaline.com/lawsites.html>
Mealey's Online (LexisNexis)–URL: <http://www.mealeys.com/>
Research Buzz–URL: <http://www.researchbuzz.com>

Blogs

beSpacific–URL: <http://www.bespacific.com>
Blawg Ring–URL: <http://www.geocities.com/blawgring/>
Blawg Search–URL: <http://blawgs.detod.com/>
Blawg–URL: <http://www.blawg.org/> or <http://www.blawg.org/index.php>
Ernie the Attorney–URLs: <http://www.ernietheattorney.net/>
  or <http://ernieattorney.typepad.com/>
Lawblogs.com–URL: <http://www.lawblogs.com/>
Law.com–URL: <http://blogs.law.com>
Law Librarian Blog–URL: <http://lawprofessors.typepad.com/law_librarian_blog/>
Law Professor Blog–URL: <http://www.lawprofessorblogs.com/>
Netlawblog–URL: <http://www.netlawblog.com/>

A Guide to Online Map and Mapping Resources

Brenda G. Mathenia

SUMMARY. Quality online maps and mapping resources, while indispensable to library users, can be challenging to locate. The range of available map types continues to expand and includes road maps, historical collections, political and physical atlases as well as maps and images of the moon and certain planets. Interactive mapping sites continue to grow and provide unique opportunities for users to interact with socioeconomic, historic, and physical data while creating unique and personalized maps. This article serves to highlight the best online resources for both map image collections and interactive mapping sites found on the Internet today. *[Article copies available for a fee from The Haworth Document Delivery Service: 1-800-HAWORTH. E-mail address: <docdelivery@haworthpress.com> Website: <http://www.HaworthPress.com> © 2006 by The Haworth Press, Inc. All rights reserved.]*

KEYWORDS. Maps, online maps, electronic maps, map collections, interactive maps

Online map and mapping resources are a valuable resource for libraries both big and small and a boon to information seekers, especially

Brenda G. Mathenia is Assistant Professor/Reference Librarian, The Libraries, Montana State University, PO Box 173320, Bozeman, MT 59717-3320 (E-mail: mathenia@montana.edu).

[Haworth co-indexing entry note]: "A Guide to Online Map and Mapping Resources." Mathenia, Brenda G. Co-published simultaneously in *Journal of Library Administration* (The Haworth Information Press, an imprint of The Haworth Press, Inc.) Vol. 44, No. 1/2, 2006, pp. 325-348; and: *Evolving Internet Reference Resources* (ed: William Miller, and Rita M. Pellen) The Haworth Information Press, an imprint of The Haworth Press, Inc., 2006, pp. 325-348. Single or multiple copies of this article are available for a fee from The Haworth Document Delivery Service [1-800-HAWORTH, 9:00 a.m. - 5:00 p.m. (EST). E-mail address: docdelivery@haworthpress.com].

doi:10.1300/J111v44n01_02

those who lack access to a physical collection or map expert. The challenge, as with most subject areas, lies in locating sites that provide quality content in a readily accessible format that requires little technological know-how. Searching for "maps" in a search engine will get you everything from commercial vendors and distributors hoping to sell you road maps and globes, to major technology firms that provide extensive geographic information system (GIS) services, to map library Web sites detailing the extent of their collections, to actual digital images of maps and interactive map tools. As an exercise in preparing this article, I conducted several searches for different types of maps using the search engine Google. The results of my searches are shown below and include the search terms I used (search terms were typed in as shown using no limits or other methods of refining the search) and the resulting number of hits received:

maps = 266,000,000
weather maps = 16,900,000
topographic maps = 1,460,000
geologic maps = 674,800
historic maps = 9,820,000
atlases = 2,080,000
city maps = 27,300,000
highway maps = 8,860,000
street maps = 25,700,000

No matter how you slice it the above results are huge and while in many instances quality sites can be found within the results list these are still intimidating numbers, especially for non-expert map seekers. To assist information seekers in locating quality resources, I have identified some of the most useful and accessible Web mapping resources available today. The following is by no means a comprehensive list of online map and mapping resources; rather it is a selective set of some of the best available sites in terms of content, quality, accessibility, and ease of use. Having worked with maps in both map libraries and at a general reference desk for many years, I chose to organize the information by map type (historic, world, physical, etc.) as that is often how seekers begin; that is, a user will ask for a "street or highway map" or a "topographic map" or in many cases simply a "map" or "the maps" and so in an attempt to make this collection of sites as useful as possible I have organized the resources by broad type of map or resource.

Freely accessible sites are the primary sources included herein though I have included information on subscription services/sites when there exists clear benefit to the pay service. I consciously chose not to include Internet sites that are strictly dedicated to providing access to data sets and other resources designed to be used with geographic information systems (GIS) due to the fact that to use those types of sites requires a level of skill and expertise above and beyond what the average Internet user possesses. I will save those resources for another article.

The following set of Internet-based map and mapping resources consists primarily of what I like to call virtual collections and interactive maps. The virtual collections consist of scanned, and in some instances constructed (using GIS behind the scenes) images of maps that are basically ready for use once selected from a list of options. The interactive mapping sites vary in their complexity, but all require some level of input from the user beyond selecting the topic or name of a map to view. Most of the resources included herein provide options for printing, e-mailing, and in many cases saving the map to a file. When saving a map to a file, be aware that some finished maps are actually constructed of individual images which may require you to save the map, title, legend, or other auxiliary information associated with that map as individual files. Also, copyright is generally attached to the individual images or collection so the user should carefully read and abide by the rules governing the use of material at each individual site!

The wide range of technologies and resources employed by various Web sites requires that I comment briefly about browsers. The Web resources included in this article were viewed primarily using Mozilla 1.7.1 and in some cases Internet Explorer 6.0. Where one browser or another is obviously needed to access a site I have indicated which browser is preferred. If you experience difficulties with printing, loading of images (either failure to load or incomplete images), sluggish response time, or other oddities with the behavior of the Web site you are using, consider switching browsers as a first attempt at correcting the problems. This is no guarantee and of course browser version, connection speed, computer processing power, and a host of other technological issues may come to bear on your ability to access various resources.

VIRTUAL MAP COLLECTIONS

Virtual map collections include Internet sites that provide access to a wide range of maps requiring minimal interaction between the user and the site beyond selecting subject, type, or title of the map you wish to view. These collections vary in coverage and in technology for delivery of material and often contain digitized images of historic and other paper maps as well as maps constructed using GIS technology to create thematic maps that then are mounted on the Web and ready for use. Output from these sites varies from single page images that fit nicely onto an 8 1/2″ × 11″ sheet of paper to large format maps that can be printed on multiple sheets or converted to more manageable sizes using graphics software such as Photoshop.

World Maps

The CIA World Factbook is the online version of a classic reference resource. Here you will find basic geographic, political, and economic information for individual countries as well as simple, high quality color maps of individual countries and reference maps for regions of the world. A printer-friendly option makes printing the map and associated text clean and easy. Individual maps can be saved as images for use in documents or Web sites. The content is in the public domain and is free of copyright. *Access:* <http://www.cia.gov/cia/publications/factbook>.

United Nations Cartographic Section provides access to more than 100 non-United States general political maps organized by regions and country. A limited number of thematic maps, which change over time and detail topical themes such as new political/cultural boundaries, membership in the United Nations or similar subjects, are available from the main page. These color maps are in PDF format so printing is easy. Unique to this site is the availability of peacekeeping maps showing current location of United Nations peacekeeping operations around the world. Links are provided to further information regarding U.N. activities across the globe. *Access:* <http://www.un.org/Depts/Cartographic/english/>.

National Geographic Map Machine is a project of the National Geographic and Environmental Systems Research Institute or ESRI, the industry leader in geographic information system software and technology, and provides a multitude of mapping products. The Map Machine provides access to very basic maps with the best products being what you expect from National Geographic–specialized thematic maps. The Map Machine is best viewed using Internet Explorer as your browser. Printing is less than optimal due to limited window size, but this remains a useful site for elementary and secondary school level work. From the home page, search for a city and a list of available maps by type is displayed. Users must select the link to open a new window containing the Map Legend, which is simplistic (not necessarily a bad thing) and often lacks clarity in terms of what the map data are showing. There are instances when the legend information just doesn't make any sense. In searching for Lapeer, MI, when one selects "Lapeer, Michigan, United States" and looks at the elevation map–the legend lists the color gray as being "Non-U.S. land." Having spent many years in Lapeer I can attest to the fact that this small city is wholly located within the U.S. Select the printing option and you get a cleaned up screen with the legend below the map. The advertisement for large-format maps available for purchase through this site can be distracting and for some confusing as it is initially unclear that these items are only available for purchase. Maps print reasonably well and the image can be saved to a file for inclusion in a document. *Access:* <http://plasma.nationalgeographic. com/mapmachine/index.html>.

Embassy World Map Search provides access to numerous map resources sorted by country. A drop-down list of country names is provided; select the one you are interested in, then "Launch Map Page." The result is a list of Internet sites containing maps and geographic data about the country. The results page varies from country to country depending on what resources are available. Individual resource pages have a wide range of content varying from regional maps that include the country of interest to detailed street mapping sources. Commercial sites selling travel guides and other merchandise are included. As is all too common, the western countries have the most resources available for browsing. The site can also be used to access information on embassies by using the Embassy Search option instead of Map Search. This site seems to work best in Internet Explorer though that may not be the case for all of the linking options provided from the site. *Access:* <http:// www.embassyworld.com/maps/maps.html>.

WorldAtlas.com is a good site for use by K-12 students and others seeking general information on countries or regions. Maps are accessed most directly by scrolling down the main page to the list of continents/regions found there. Select a continent and then a country to view generalized maps as well as have access to links to other resources (some of which are listed here), both commercial and non-commercial. *Access:* <http://www.graphicmaps.com/aatlas/world.htm>.

Wikipedia List of Sovereign States provides an alphabetical list of countries or sovereign states that includes political, economic, geographic, and social information. Scroll down the page to access a list of countries with links to content pages. A reasonably good site for K-12 users as each entry provides a regional locator map, sections on origin, history, politics, administrative divisions, geography (including a map), culture, economy, and a list of external links. The linking from within the article is at times distracting though often provides definitions or clarifications of terms and concepts from the main entry. This site is best viewed using Internet Explorer. *Access:* <http://en.wikipedia.org/wiki/List_of_countries>.

Historic Maps

The Library of Congress American Memory Map Collections provides access to digital representations of maps found in the Geography and Maps Division of the Library of Congress covering the years 1500-1999. This digital collection is organized into seven (7) categories (Cities & Towns, Conservation & Environment, Discovery & Exploration, Cultural Landscapes, Military Battles & Campaigns, Transportation & Communication, and General Maps) and it is recommended that you search from the main page search option for best results as maps on specific topics or locations can be included in different categories. Search using keywords or browse the subject, title, creator, and geographic indexes to find maps that are focused on Americana and cartographic treasures found in the Library of Congress. *Access:* <http://memory.loc.gov/ammem/gmdhtml/gmdhome.html>.

Library of Congress–Zoom into Maps provides an education access point to a select collection of digitized material from the American Memory Collection of maps from the Library of Congress geared toward K-12 students and educators. This access point to the collection of the LOC includes introductory material including an overview about what maps are, and methods used for analyzing the information they contain as well as information detailing specific types of maps within each subdivision of this site. *Access:* <http://lcweb2.loc.gov/ammem/ndlpedu/features/maps/>.

Perry-Castañeda Library Map Collection is a large, well organized site, created and maintained by the University of Texas at Austin, that provides electronic access to about 5,700 maps for all regions of the world. Maps cover mostly the 19th and 20th centuries though some represent time periods as far back as 980 C.E. Explore the "Online Maps of Current Interest" or use the options in the left hand window to select maps by continent, region, or subject. Map images range from single sheet to multi-sheet images that can be manipulated with graphics software for optimum output. Most maps are copyright free–those that are not are clearly marked and governed by the Materials Usage Guidelines of the University of Texas. Information on viewing and printing maps is provided through a good FAQ located within the Web site. *Access:* <http://www.lib.utexas.edu/maps/>.

The David Rumsey Collection is an ever-growing collection of primarily 18th and 19th century North and South American cartographic materials with approximately 11,000 maps currently available for viewing. High quality digital images showcasing a variety of maps, atlases, globes, and other cartographic items make this an excellent starting point for research and exploration. The collection is relevant for the study of history, genealogy, and family history. Images are easily viewed through the InSight browser and more advanced users can use a one-time download to access the collection using the InSight Java Client. Use the "Help" link to access a general FAQ on the collection as well as to locate technical assistance related to the various browsing options. The Web site was created by David Rumsey, a private map collector and president of Cartographic Associates, as a venue for sharing his expansive collection with map enthusiasts worldwide. *Access:* <http://www.davidrumsey.com>.

Historical Maps of Canada, from the makers of Canadian Geographic Magazine, is home to a set of maps showing the development of Canada over time beginning in the 1700s through the last entry dated 1999. Navigate the site by selecting a time period at the bottom of the viewer window. Brief historical summaries accompany the maps and include links that when selected provide additional information on the topic near the bottom of the viewing window. *Access:* <http://www.canadiangeographic.ca/mapping/mappingcanada/default.html>.

Periodical History Atlas of Europe provides historical images of the make up of the European continent at the end of each century from A.D. 1 to A.D. 2000. The maps are designed and drawn by Christos Nussli with thumbnails provided for online viewing. Full access to the maps is available for a fee and can be handled as a download directly to individual computers or as a CD-ROM, both purchased from the Web page. *Access:* <http://www.euratlas.com/summary.htm>.

Ancient World Mapping Center at the University of North Carolina at Chapel Hill provides an excellent set of maps available freely for educational use. Maps are available in multiple formats from standard .pdf to high-resolution .jpeg. Cartographic and geographic resources focus on material supporting scholarly work in the areas of ancient studies and are suitable for a wide range of users. This site also provides access to information on updates to the *Barrington Atlas of the Greek and Roman World. Access:* <http://www.unc.edu/awmc/>.

Atlases of the U.S. Military Academy Department of History provides online access to a series of atlases and maps detailing America's wars as well as global conflicts. These maps were originally created by the United States Military Academy's Department of History and are the digital versions from the atlases printed by the United States Defense Printing Agency. The site continues to be developed and includes overview maps as well as maps showing detailed military activity related to individual actions and campaigns. The site includes some very large files that can require lengthy download time and image manipulation for maximum usability. *Access:* <http://www.dean.usma.edu/history/web03/atlases/atlas%20home.htm>.

1895 U.S. Atlas provides digitized maps from the *New 11 × 14 Atlas of the World* published in 1895 by Rand McNally and includes all 50 states and the District of Columbia. Access is provided to state level maps (often very large images), county maps, and indexes to select towns and cities. Start by scrolling down the page to the list of states. *Access:* <http://www.livgenmi.com/1895/>.

PHYSICAL MAPS

This section includes a wide range of resources such as topographic maps, air and sea navigation charts, aerial photos, and geologic maps. Use of these types of map resources is wide ranging and they are valuable in support of scholarly research and practical fieldwork as well as for travel or other individual activities. The majority of resources located here are produced by government agencies (or private agencies working for the U.S. Government) and are made available to the public either directly from the responsible agency or through business enterprises that provide at times both free and pay services. North America is best represented in this category and while topographic and navigation map coverage for much of the world exists online access is very limited outside of North America.

The *United States Geological Survey (USGS)* is the original source for the topographic, geologic, hydrogeologic maps, and many other physical mapping and information resources for the United States and in some instances North America. In recent years, USGS has partnered with various private organizations or business entities to make its topographic map products available via the Internet as well as more readily available for purchase in cities across the country. Many additional resources related to the earth sciences are available from the USGS including information on ordering paper and digital map products. This is a large site and contains a significant amount of educational material beyond topographic maps and reports. The USGS does not provide direct access to topographic maps online though some of its reports and subject specific map series are beginning to be made available electronically. *Access:* <http://www.usgs.gov/>.

Map Scales Fact Sheet from the USGS provides overview information on map scale and what that means for map users. This Web site is especially helpful in orienting new users to this important map concept. *Access:* <http://erg.usgs.gov/isb/pubs/factsheets/fs01502.html>.

Topographic Map Symbols from the USGS provides a primer and explanation of the many map symbols found on USGS topographic maps. This is an important tool to have on hand for interpreting map information and is invaluable for beginner or infrequent map users. *Access:* <http://erg.usgs.gov/isb/pubs/booklets/symbols/>.

TopoZone is a commercial site (part of the USGS Digital Cartographic Business Partner program) that provides access to USGS quadrangle maps for personal use. Search by map name, by name of a city or place, or even by entering the name of a geographic feature. The maps have good resolution on screen and you can pan through the four directions from your starting point. Maps print reasonably well though limitations in window size can result in less than optimal usability. You can also pick a new scale on the fly and zoom in or out as you please. *TopoZone Pro*, accessed via TopoZone.com is the subscription service from the makers of TopoZone that provides enhanced access to a wide range of maps and aerial imagery along with free downloads of the original USGS scanned topographic maps and many other features. TopoZone provides a free demonstration of TopoZone Pro features upon completing the free registration on its site. *Access:* <http://www.topozone.com>.

Microsoft's Terra Server provides free public access to maps and aerial photography of the United States. Search for a specific city or click the green areas on the map to zoom into a location of interest. Users can view famous places or explore featured locations directly from the main page. *Access:* <http://terraserver.microsoft.com>.

TerraServer Professional provides access to a wide assortment of digital imagery from around the world via numerous vendors. Users can freely search the site for coverage but must be a subscriber to view images at a resolution of less than 8 meters. Subscription to the service does not include the cost of image download and purchase which varies by size and source of image and ranges from a low of $4.95 to $69.95 depending on the product requested. The search interface works well and includes options for searching by city, by latitude/longitude, zip code, country, and even address. TerraServer Professional includes international imagery, which is unavailable through Microsoft's Terra Server. *Access:* <http://terraserver.com>.

MapTech MapServer is a commercial site that provides access to U.S. topographic maps, nautical charts, and aerial photos, called NavPhotos, which cover coastal regions exclusively. Select "MapTech MapServer" from the online maps page to access the free topographic maps, nautical and aeronautical charts, and the NavPhotos. This site allows the user to search for maps by place name and state. Multiple map scales are available and placing your cursor over the map image will generate coordinates for that point on the map. Maps print well though the size of the image is small with no options for enlarging. This site also provides the option for purchasing data for download to PDAs and or personal computers for a fee. *Access:* <http://www.maptech.com/onlinemaps/>.

USGS Publications Warehouse is a valuable online source for locating a variety of technical publications (map series, bulletins, etc.) of the USGS. Includes 66,000 items including thematic maps, reports, and numbered series dating as far back as 1882. The database is added to regularly with content ranging from citations only to full-text content including maps. Of great benefit to librarians and other library users because it is more current than the latest edition of the invaluable *Guide to USGS Publications* (Andriot, 1998) and provides a single searching point for these types of documents. This is a great index to material found in your local government documents depository library. The multiple searching options and tools for limiting searches within the advanced search screen are your best bet for finding specific material. *Access:* <http://infotrek.er.usgs.gov/pubs/>.

Color Landform Atlas of the United States provides color images for each state in a variety of formats. The links provided for each state bring up a menu of maps and other online information about the state that is available electronically. There are two main types of links on each state page: maps and images local to this Web site, and links to external Web sites. Types of maps provided include topographic maps in shaded relief, county maps, black and white version of the shaded relief map, satellite images, the 1895 map of the state, and a postscript map intended for downloading and printing on a postscript printer. *Access:* <http://fermi.jhuapl.edu/states/states.html>.

National Geologic Map Database is a useful geosciences resource which includes maps and related material in the fields of geology, hazards, earth resources, geophysics, geochemistry, geochronology, paleontology, and marine geology. The USGS in cooperation with State Geological Agencies provides a bibliographic catalog of resources on a wide range of topics from across the U.S. including 2,000+ online images ready for viewing or download. *Access:* <http://ngmdb.usgs.gov/>.

World Geologic Map Search System from the Geologic Survey of Japan Library provides a search mechanism for world geologic map resources (non-Japanese) that are collected by the Library and provides bibliographic citation information for items. Useful when searching for geologic topics for non-industrialized nations and other less well represented areas of the world. Full-text and online images are not available but this is potentially a valuable bibliographic index. Users can search by country, by category (type) of map (topographic, geologic, tectonic, mineral, hydrogeologic, or volcanic), by extent of coverage (global, national, regional, local), by scale, by map name, or map series. *Access:* <http://www.aist.go.jp/RIODB/g-mapi/welcome.html>.

INTERACTIVE MAPPING SITES

Within this category of Internet mapping resources are two basic types of Web sites: those that enable users to map street addresses and city maps and those that permit the mapping of data such as demographic data, health statistics, or earth science data. All of these sites require input (i.e., interaction) on the part of the user, varying from simply selecting map elements to view to choosing specific variables from which to build a multi-layer map. The level of experience and knowledge required of users of these sites varies from basic for most of the street/direction mapping sites to, at times, a need for in-depth understanding of physical and or socio-economic data and rudimentary cartographic concepts. The resources following are not GIS data sites (though some might contain options for downloading information for use in a GIS); rather these resources use Internet-based GIS technology to provide final output data in the form of printable data tables and maps.

Street Mapping Sites

This genre of mapping resource consists of familiar tools that provide easy access to maps of cities, and, typically, driving directions between two (or more) points. This type of online mapping resource may be the most common of the interactive mapping tools found on the Internet today. These sites use geo-referencing within Web-mounted GIS systems to generate maps on the fly with minimal input from users. A best bet for finding additional (or new) online resources of this type is to search for the phrase *"driving directions"* (which helps to limit but not eliminate online sites selling maps, atlases, and paper roadmaps) and the relevant *city* or *country name* in your favorite search engine. There are a wide variety of sites available with varying reliability and usability with the most consistent coverage provided for the United States and Western European nations. Selected resources were chosen because they are generally reliable, easy to use, and provide the best country-level coverage. Some sites are browser-specific from the get-go while others get fussy depending on what you are trying to do–so if something doesn't seem to respond correctly or gives poor graphics, try switching browsers.

MapQuest is an easy to use site with clear instruction for generating a map of a city or acquiring driving directions between two points. Select to search North America or select European nations via links located near the top of the search screen. Output includes clear turn-by-turn directions (based of course on the level of detail provided by the user), basic map showing the route, and options for searching for (and mapping) travel-related amenities for your chosen destinations (such as restaurants, lodging, and banks). The maps are clean and accurate, and a printer-friendly map format is provided. *Access:* <http://www.mapquest.com>.

MapBlast!, a part of the MSN family of Web resources, also maps addresses and cities, and provides driving directions with access to street level mapping for the U.S. and 15 Western European countries. Three graduated sizes for the map-viewing window are offered and changing them is easy. The large window provides plenty of viewing area for most situations. Maps are detailed enough to be useful to travelers while remaining neat and very readable. The results window provides links to online information for traffic (accidents, construction, etc.) in major metropolitan areas, city guides, and weather via weather.com. *Access:* <http://www.mapblast.com>.

Yahoo Maps is Yahoo's contribution to street mapping with an interface and features similar to those of other sites providing street level mapping and driving directions for the United States and Canada. Upon zooming into a location you can select local establishments such as restaurants or ATMs to show on your map (at this point, all the icons look the same). The printable version of the map changes the icons for restaurants or other local features you've added into a numbered list with information on what you will find at that specific location–a nice feature. A link to the Map Legend is provided to help users understand what they are viewing. The large map option is nice, providing clear text and simple useable maps. *Access:* <http://maps.yahoo.com/py/maps.py>.

National Traffic and Road Closure Information provides access via list or interactive map to State Department of Transportation sites that provide traffic and road closure (weather, construction, and other reasons) information. *Access:* <http://www.fhwa.dot.gov/trafficinfo/>.

Great Britain Street & Road Maps provides access to road and street maps of Great Britain. Searching options include street, post code, GB place, latitude/longitude, London street, landranger, tel code, and OS grid (x,y). Search tips provide good information on how to search using the eight different options. Maps are detailed and load quickly with obvious map navigation that works well. Detailed aerial photos are provided for select areas and are viewable when you see the camera icon in the toolbar located below the map window. The Large Map option creates a larger view of the map for printing though no printer friendly version is available. The printed map includes all the advertisements and ancillary information from the online view screen. *Access:* <http://www.streetmap.co.uk/>.

Multimap.com–Online Maps to Everywhere provides some of the best coverage of European countries available online. Maps for some Eastern European countries tend to be less detailed than those for Western Europe (e.g., the largest scale map viewable for Belgrade (Beograd) in Serbia is 1:50,000 with only major highways labeled while Linz, Austria is shown at 1:5,000 with individual street names identified) but given the lack of options for Eastern Europe it remains a good site to locate online city and some street level maps. *Access:* <http://www.multimap.com>.

Mappy–Road Guide, best used in Internet Explorer, provides maps, driving directions, and itinerary planning for a limited number of areas in Western Europe. Navigation tools for zooming, printing, and maximizing map size are visual and easy to find along the left border of the map. This site also allows users to download maps to their handheld computers. *Access:* <http://www.mappy.com/direct/mappy/accueil>.

Drive Alive–Interactive Road Map of Europe is another source for European city maps, driving directions, and travel information. Geographic coverage is limited at this time to Austria, Belgium, Denmark, France, Germany, Italy, Netherlands, Norway, Spain, and Switzerland.

Requires use of Internet Explorer. *Access:* <http://mapping.drive-alive.co.uk/>.

Hot-Maps is a German language site (no English language version) providing detailed maps of select German cities as well as a few non-German cities. A nice feature is that upon loading of the main map for a city, sub-menus appear listing specific streets and in some instances specific business, cultural, or governmental entities that users can use to target their viewing on the map or in some cases to visit a separate Web site with additional information (such as for a theater). These maps are detailed and clear. Maps are printable; just click on the printer icon (below the compass rose) and select Kartendruck to open the print dialogue box. *Access:* <http://www.hot-maps.de/index.html>.

ViaMichelin is one more entry into the European road map and driving direction genre. Some cities such as Rome are available with detailed street level maps while others such as the map for Moscow are much more general and do not allow access to street level information. *Access:* <http://www.viamichelin.com>.

Rand McNally provides online maps of cities, driving directions, and access to the Travel Store where visitors can purchase maps, atlases, travel guides, and other map related products. Paid membership entitles users to discounts (15%) on purchases from the online Travel Store or at retail locations. Members have the option to create customized downloadable maps and to save information such as addresses for faster access to information. Paid membership allows users to create personalized Road Explorer Trip Guides that include directions, information on road work/road construction, airport and city transit maps, plus much more. *Access:* <http://www.randmcnally.com/>.

Japan Map–Tourist Map of Japan is one online source that provides access to maps of major Japanese cities, including Fukuoka, Hiroshima, Kagoshima, Kobe, Kyoto, Nagoya, Nara, Osaka, Sapporo, and Tokyo. These are not true "interactive maps" beyond selecting the map you wish to view. The most direct access to the maps is from the list of city names at the bottom of the page. City names on the map are clickable too; run your mouse over the map to locate those cities that are linked to additional information. Travel guide information is provided for some of the cities when you select them from the map but not for all. *Access:* <http://www.japan-hotel-reservations.net/japan-map.html>.

Maps of Croatia and Bosnia-Herzegovina is a very basic Web site listing in alphabetical order the names of cities, towns, mountains (limited number), islands, and lakes found in the paper resource *New*

Roadmap of Croatia, Slovenia, and B&H published by Naprijed in Zagreb in 1995. *Access:* <http://www.kakarigi.net/maps/>.

Data Mapping Sites

Compared to the street mapping resources these Internet mapping resources provide users with more complex data as well as requiring more input and involvement on the part of the user in order to access or create usable maps or data. Most of these sites allow, and many require, the user to select from multiple options and or data sets that are then used to generate finished maps. Resources listed here are primarily geared toward mapping socio-economic data (such as census data) or mapping physical features such as wetlands or earth science data.

American Fact Finder from the United States Census Bureau is the source for maps and data from the 2000 Decennial Census. The Fact Finder provides access to both Reference Maps (basic boundary information such as cities, counties, census tracts, etc.) and Thematic Maps (population, housing, education, etc.) that displays information at a variety of U.S. geographies using data from the 2000 Census. This is a huge site with multiple avenues for reaching mapping tools.

The most obvious route is via the "Maps and Geography" link found on the left hand side of the homepage which allows the user to select the type of map (reference or thematic), and select the data sets to map, but also requires that users understand the details of census geography and have at least a basic understanding of socio-economic and mapping concepts.

The easiest method for accessing mapped information is to use the "Fast Access to Information" section on the main page. Select from community profiles via "Fact Sheets," data related to "People," to "Housing," or to "Business & Government." Select the geography (United States, State, County, etc.) of the map as well as the "data" to build the map with (such as population less than 18 years of age by state). Once a data set has been chosen for mapping you can easily change the geography to get more or less detail as well as select from other options to manipulate the look of the map. The sheer size of this Web site is challenging so practice makes perfect in terms of getting a handle on creating maps via the Census Bureau.

As one might expect this is *the* site for locating data tables as well as mapping census phenomena. The browser interface for the mapping software at times tends to remember your mapping choices and settings which can be problematic when changing map data or geography and is downright frustrating at times. This is especially noticeable when building maps from scratch via the "Maps and Geography" section of the Web site. To solve this problem users may need to exit the browser in order to reset or lose settings from earlier sessions. *Access:* <http://factfinder.census.gov>.

Demographic Data Viewer (DDViewer) is created by the Center for International Earth Science Information Network (CIESIN) and is an interactive mapping application for data from the 1990 U.S. Census of Population and Housing. It is an easy application to use and provides simple yet effective maps as well as statistical and tabular data for the variables being mapped. Only 1990 data are available for mapping with 2000 Census data available from the American Fact Finder. It is unlikely that CIESIN will provide 2000 data for mapping in this application given the existence of the Fact Finder. Different editions (Java and Non-Java) are provided for different connection speeds. Directions can be cryptic and output options are limited, but screen shots of the maps you create work well in documents. Also available from this site is the US-Mexico DDViewer. *Access:* <http://plue.sedac.ciesin.org/plue/ddviewer/>.

ESRI's Online Hazard Map is a partnership between the Federal Emergency Management Agency (FEMA) and ESRI (Environmental Systems Research Institute) created to support disaster-resistant communities by making multi-hazard maps and information available freely to the public. Users can input a location (city and state), select from a list of possible natural hazards such as earthquakes, flood, wind storms, etc., and generate a basic thematic map of the information. *Access:* <http://www.esri.com/hazards/>.

National Atlas of the United States from the U.S. Geological Survey is an online "cousin" to the original *National Atlas of the United States* produced in the 1970s. From the main page users can learn about the atlas and get answers to their questions by using the buttons on the left side of the page. Select the big oval "Click Here to Make Maps" button on the right to gain access to the atlas. When the viewer opens users can click on the map to zoom into a location, use the drop down menu to zoom to a specific state, or use the "Find" tab on the far right to search for a specific location. Map layer options as well as a brief tutorial on making your first map are located along the right hand side of the screen. After selecting layers to include, users must click the "Redraw Map" button at the top to display their options. Use the "Map Key" tab to view the map legend. A "print map" button at the top of the page lets the user select the orientation of the map (landscape or portrait) and whether or not to include the map legend in the output. *Access:* <http://www.nationalatlas.gov/>.

The National Map from the USGS has been created to provide current public domain-based geographic information for the United States. The data and map content will continue to be updated and improved over time. Users can view The National Map via their Web browser with no special software or downloads required. Once in the "viewer," click on the map to zoom in to a location or use the toolbar on the left to zoom in, find a specific place, or print the map. To the right select layers of data to be displayed on the map. Not all layers will be visible at all scales, and options include elevation, land use, transportation, and hydrography, to name a few. This high-quality, geospatial data and information has been taken from existing sources with future improvements expected to be realized through the involvement of government, private industry, specialists, and locally trained volunteers. *Access:* <http://nationalmap.usgs.gov/index.html>.

Wetlands Interactive Mapper Tool from the National Wetlands Inventory Center of the U.S. Fish and Wildlife Service provides access to National Wetlands Inventory Maps in digital format. This information is also available in The National Map and in fact uses The National Map as a base for generating information. Select "Wetlands Mapper" in the upper left corner or choose an area to search for data in the center of the Web page. Once in the viewer, click the map to zoom into an area and to move around on the map image. Use the right hand menu to select interactive layers and display layers which include topographic maps and digital orthophoto quads via TerraServer when they exist for the area being viewed. While the wetland maps displayed here will not replace the detailed paper maps, the site is a nice place to start for wetlands information. Not all locations in the United States have wetlands maps but as of 2001 more than 90% of the lower 48 states and approximately 35% of Alaska had draft or final maps in place. *Access:* <http://wetlands.fws.gov/mapper_tool.htm>.

ONLINE ATLASES

The Internet resources for this section consist primarily of online versions of traditional atlases or atlas-like products. Some provide for some basic level of interactivity but due to their general nature were more appropriate for a separate section than inclusion in the above sections. Online atlases vary widely in their construction, accessibility, graphics, and inclusion of auxiliary information. They also seem to be created by a wide range of agencies with many being produced by economic interests of the country or region they represent. This collection of Internet atlases represents but a few, though some of the best, of this type of map resource. To locate additional online atlases, try searching for "online atlas" and the relevant country or region name in your favorite search engine.

Australian Natural Resources Atlas is being developed by the *National Land and Water Resources Audit* (the Audit) to provide ready access to information to support natural resource management. The information in the Atlas is organized by topic and geography and includes information on agriculture, coastal environments, land resources, people, rangelands, water resources, vegetation, and biodiversity. This atlas contains a significant amount of text along with color maps and charts. *Access:* <http://audit.ea.gov.au/ANRA/atlas_home.cfm>.

The Atlas of South Australia provides access to a variety of maps relevant to South Australian communities. Best used with Internet Explorer. *Access:* <http://www.atlas.sa.gov.au/menu_flash.cfm>. See also the Western Australian Atlas <http://www.walis.wa.gov.au/walis/content/wa_atlas_popup.html>.

Historical Atlas of Canada Online Learning Project makes the maps and data created for the *Historical Atlas of Canada* (1993) and the *Concise Historical Atlas of Canada* (1998) available to a much wider audience via Internet access. The primary focus is on interactive maps allowing users to zoom in and out as well as manipulate visible layers by turning them on and off. Intended as a learning tool, this site will eventually contain tutorials, learning activities, and exercises for use by students and educators alike. The site was a mere 15% complete as of fall 2004. The information available consists of both maps and text (see the Notes tab at top of map window) related to the historical development of Canada. *Access:* <http://mercator.geog.utoronto.ca/hacddp/imagenew2001_b.htm>.

United Nations Atlas of the Ocean–Maps, Statistics and Online Databases Web page provides access to maps and other online material currently available through the UN Atlas of the Ocean as well as to a selection of other collections related to the world's oceans. Free registration is required in order to access the images. From the main page select the "Maps, Statistics and Online Databases" link in the menu to the left. After login, a menu guides users to locate specific material much of which is from the three volume *Atlas of the Oceans*, published by the Russian Head Department of Navigation and Oceanography (HDNO).

There are some additional images and small maps available in other sections of this Web site but with limits on access, and format usability is limited to content of the textual material. *Access:* <http://www.oceansatlas. org/index.jsp>.

National Atlas of Sweden Web Atlas provides geographical description of Sweden, ranging from population and industry to environmental questions, nature, and culture. The Web Atlas contains over 1,000 images with explanatory text in Swedish and English (ongoing project to provide English versions for all maps). This atlas is partly the result of Sweden's participating in the development of the Eugeo atlas project, the goal of which is the development of a European atlas. *Access:* <http://www.sna.se/webatlas/index.html>.

The Atlas of Canada (L' Atlas du Canada), available in both French and English, provides users access to a collection of maps and information about Canada–similar to the American Fact Finder. Use the left hand menu to explore maps and information on a variety of themes as well as access learning resources. Pre-made maps are provided on a variety of topics and each map includes a text box providing additional information on the topic being displayed in the map window. Zoom in and out of the maps as well as view statistics related to the mapped data. *Access:* <http://atlas.gc.ca/site/index.html>.

Lunar Atlases from the Lunar and Planetary Institute (part of the Center for Advanced Space Studies) provides access to digital images of the lunar surface from the Lunar Orbiter Atlas of the Moon, the Consolidated Lunar Atlas, the Apollo Image Atlas, and the Lunar Map Catalog. Availability of color versus black and white images is atlas-specific. All atlases are organized in a similar fashion with specific options for browsing or searching images. *Access:* <http://www.lpi. usra.edu/research/lunar_atlases/>.

The Electronic Map Library from the Department of Geography, California State University at Northridge contains links to numerous digital atlases created by Dr. William Bowen covering many locations in California as well as major metropolitan areas throughout the United States. *Access:* <http://130.166.124.2/library.html>.

GAZETTEERS

Gazetteers are valuable for historic- and geographic-related research due to their simplicity and breadth. Gazetteers can help users locate basic geographic information on cities, places, mountains, and other geographical features as well as assist in identifying changes in place names over time. The content of gazetteers can vary widely but most entries are brief and provide a physical description of the locale or feature and can include information such as elevation, latitude/longitude, and average temperature/precipitation. Searching for "gazetteer" and a specific country or region is your best bet for locating online gazetteers.

Geographic Names Information System, from the USGS, enables you to query a database containing nearly 2 million physical and cultural geographic features within the United States. To start your GNIS query use the link in the left frame and select to search "U.S. and territories" or "Antarctica," click on the *Query* link, and fill out the form provided. Usually you only need to fill out the *Feature name* box on the form to begin a query. The output will include information such as the feature's official name, the feature type, its elevation (where available), latitude and longitude, population, and the name of the USGS topographic map sheet on which the feature may be found. A nice feature is a link on the output page to access the topographic map containing the feature or place via TopoZone.com, the digital orthophoto or digital raster graphic via TerraServer. *Access:* <http://geonames.usgs.gov/>.

GEOnet Names Server (GNS), from the National Geospatial-Intelligence Agency, provides worldwide coverage *excluding the United States and Antarctica* and contains approximately 4 million features with 5.5 million names. To begin your query click on the "Access GNS" link at the top of the page, then the GNS Search link on the following page. The interface allows you to query a single place name and specify the country, but also enables more sophisticated queries using menus. The reply to a query will verify the feature name (or tell you the appropriate name to search under), supply the feature designation (such as PPL for populated place), and give the place's latitude and longitude. *Access:* <http://earth-info.nga.mil/gns/html/index.html>.

The Columbia Gazetteer of North America 2000 via Bartleby.com provides free electronic access to the 2000 edition of a useful tool containing over 50,000 entries searchable by country and city. Entries include geographical information along with some basic data on major industries, institutions, and prominent individuals associated with the location. The simple search interface brings up multiple listings on the results page so be sure to include both a city and state when possible. *Access:* <http://bartleby.com/69/>.

The Columbia Gazetteer of the World Online is available by subscription and can be an invaluable geographic tool that according to its Web site includes 30,000 new entries with many others substantially revised. Users can search by Place Name, Type of Place, or Word Search (full-text search) and individual entries may include information on many of the following: demography; physical geography; political boundaries; industry, trade, and service activities; agriculture; cultural, historical, and archeological points of interest; transportation lines; longitude, latitude, and elevations; distance to relevant places; pronunciations; official local government place-names; and changed or variant names and spellings. Length of entry varies from a brief notation on a small village to an essay on a country or region. Subscription required. *Access:* <http://www.columbiagazetteer.org/>.

Gazetteer of Australia 2004 Online Place Names Search provides information on the location and spelling of 310,217 geographical names across Australia as of December 2003. *Access:* <http://www.ga.gov. au/map/names/>.

Canadian Geographical Names from Natural Resources Canada provides a simple search form to facilitate queries to the Canadian Geographical Names Database. Type in a geographical feature (city, town, lake, etc.) and hit the Submit Query button. Select specific feature type, province, or territory to limit search results. *Access:* <http://geonames. nrcan.gc.ca/search/search_e.php>.

COMMERCIAL MAP DISTRIBUTORS

USGS Store allows browsing by type of map for individuals interested in ordering map and mapping-related reports and products directly from the USGS. Click the link to "Enter USGS Store"; then browse by coverage area, type of map, or search for a specific product. *Access:* <http://store.usgs.gov>.

Natural Resources Canada is to Canadian map and mapping resources what the USGS is to U.S. resources. While this site provides little in the way of online maps, it is the single best place to look for information on the availability of Canadian natural resources information (including maps.) Users will be taken to the main information page of this large site after they select the English or French version of this Web site. The "Subject Listing" link, located within the top navigation bar, is the best way to locate the wide range of information available through this site. This is a very useful Web site for locating agencies that create, manage, and sell maps and related resources, and for finding links to information sites such as the Atlas of Canada. *Access:* <http:// www.nrcan-rncan.gc.ca/inter/index.html>.

East View Cartographic (EVC) is a producer and distributor of paper and digital cartographic material for a wide range of organizations. Beyond providing access to maps EVC also provides services such as scanning, database design, and consulting. No bargain when searching for U.S. geologic or topographic material (a USGS report sells for $49.95 at EVC versus $7.00 from USGS), this site can be useful for identifying existing maps or map series for non U.S. locations or when searching for custom maps or GIS data. It has recently put into place a customer service representative for academic libraries and is quite responsive to e-mail inquiries. *Access:* <http://www.cartographic.com>.

Omni Resources is a distributor of maps, globes, and other cartographic resources with a focus on paper resources but it does provide some digital material as well. It has an excellent listing for international maps and provides a simple but well organized site with samples of maps available for online viewing. This site is another useful tool when searching for leads on non-U.S. map resources or when in need of unique material such as globes or wall maps. *Access:* <http://www.omnimap.com/maps.htm>.

ITMB International Travel Maps & Books is the licensed retailer for the Canadian Federal Government's topographic maps as well as specializing in Latin American material. This site features online purchasing of travel maps and guides as well as topographic maps and government publications. *Access:* <http://www.itmb.com>.

Maps and Atlases of the World provides access to Treaty Oak Map Distributor's (wholesale) selection of worldwide maps and mapping resources that include travel maps, atlases, and wall maps from major map publishers of the world. Search the catalog of products direct from the Web site. Check out the link to GoneTomorrowMaps, which is Treaty Oak's online retail store. *Access:* <http://www.treatyoak.com/>.

META-SITES

The following resources have been provided to guide interested readers to additional resources. The focus of this article required that many interesting and valuable geographically oriented resources not be included. You will find additional online resources as well as many references to print resources and physical collections.

State Data Centers provides access information for the State Data Centers for each U.S. State. State Data Centers are often the responsible agency for providing data and maps related to socio-economic data or natural resources. This site provides information for state data centers in all 50 states. Note that not all states provide Web sites, data, or maps. It is a good starting point when searching for maps/data of census information for a particular state. *Access:* <http://www.census.gov/sdc/www/>.

Oddens' Bookmarks from the Faculty of Geoscience at the Universiteit Utrecht (Netherlands) is a classic in the world of geography for not only providing links to map resources but also links to the entire world of cartography and geography. Select "Browse" then "Maps & Atlases" and choose the type you want to find. There are 10,412 entries in the "Electronic Atlases" category and 176 in the "On-line Map Creating" category. Many non-English language choices are available and some real gems can be found here depending on the user's needs. *Access:* <http://oddens.geog.uu.nl>.

Maps on Other Web Sites, a subsection of the Perry Castañeda Map Collection at the University of Texas, is a nice listing of maps, organized by categories such as City Map Sites, Historical Map Sites, or Weather Map Sites, that are available on the Web. *Access:* <http://www.lib.utexas.edu/maps/map_sites/map_sites.html>.

Map Resources from the James C. Kirkpatrick Library, Central Missouri State University is a guide to Internet and digital map resources by map type. Not all items listed are available electronically as this resource also directs users to traditional print collections in the J.C. Kirkpatrick Library as well as through other organizations. This site is a good resource to use as a starting point for identifying online map resources. *Access:* <http://library.cmsu.edu/govdocs/maps.htm#geological>.

Online Digital Maps from the Maps Library at The Pennsylvania State University Libraries provides a guide to online map resources including travel and interactive maps. *Access:* <http://www.libraries.psu.edu/maps/digitalmisc.htm>.

Maps and Directions Resources from the Northern Virginia Community College provides links in three basic categories–Driving Directions, Maps & Map Collections, and Topographic Maps. It's concise and includes many of the best online map resources. *Access:* <http://www.nvcc.edu/library/BOW/elecmaps.htm>.

Internet Catalogue: Maps Worldwide (Internet-Katalog: Kartenweltweit) is an excellent site leading to more great sites. Use the link "Worldwide WWW Map Catalogs" to access a detailed list of online map resource sites, links to country and city maps, and links to other geosciences Internet resources. *Access:* <http://www.maps.ethz.ch/map_catalogue.html>.

LANIC Maps from the Latin American Network Information Center (LANIC) at the University of Texas-Austin provides numerous links to high quality maps and related resources about or from Latin America. Provides both regional and country-level maps from a variety of sources in a variety of formats. *Access:* <http://lanic.utexas.edu/la/region/map/>.

CONCLUSION

Internet-based maps and mapping have been developed mainly for the industrialized countries with huge gaps in availability for non-U.S. or Western European locations. The variety of technology in use both from the delivery side (map software, etc.) and from the user's side (browsers and computers) requires explorers of online map resources to be flexible, inventive, and often just plain patient in their quest for advanced mapping tools and resources to view or use. Usability from resource to resource varies such that simply locating online mapping resources or tools is not sufficient. Users must be able to interpret often-cryptic cartographic and computer language as well as understand physical or socio-economic mapping variables not to mention understand issues related to graphical or tabular output. The sites included above were chosen as the most usable and informative of their kind. Internet maps and mapping resources will continue to evolve and grow as technology improves and the demand for anywhere/anytime geographic information continues to grow. We will just need to keep our eyes open and our technology up to date to see it happen.

Searching of Our Surroundings:
Looking at the Environment
from the Internet

Ola C. Riley

SUMMARY. There is a proliferation of Internet sites covering environmental themes. Many of these sites provide reference information in varying degrees. This article highlights environmental Web sites that provide a wide range of pertinent reference sources to a diverse audience. More than 50 highly selective Web sites are included in this paper. Some of these Web sites provide access to library catalogs, full-text articles, and other online resources. The Web sites in this article are in five categories: portals, government sites, special issues, general sites, and databases. *[Article copies available for a fee from The Haworth Document Delivery Service: 1-800-HAWORTH. E-mail address: <docdelivery@haworthpress.com> Website: <http://www.HaworthPress.com> © 2006 by The Haworth Press, Inc. All rights reserved.]*

KEYWORDS. Databases, environmental themes, environmental conditions, environmental resources, environmental Web sites, environmental Web portal resources

Ola C. Riley is Biomedical Librarian, Undergraduate Medical Academy, Prairie View A&M University, Prairie View, TX 77446 (E-mail: ocriley@pvamu.edu).

[Haworth co-indexing entry note]: "Searching of Our Surroundings: Looking at the Environment from the Internet." Riley, Ola C. Co-published simultaneously in *Journal of Library Administration* (The Haworth Information Press, an imprint of The Haworth Press, Inc.) Vol. 44, No. 1/2, 2006, pp. 349-371; and: *Evolving Internet Reference Resources* (ed: William Miller, and Rita M. Pellen) The Haworth Information Press, an imprint of The Haworth Press, Inc., 2006, pp. 349-371. Single or multiple copies of this article are available for a fee from The Haworth Document Delivery Service [1-800-HAWORTH, 9:00 a.m. - 5:00 p.m. (EST). E-mail address: docdelivery@haworthpress.com].

Available online at http://www.haworthpress.com/web/JLA
© 2006 by The Haworth Press, Inc. All rights reserved.
doi:10.1300/J111v44n01_03

INTRODUCTION

There is a proliferation of Web sites on environmental themes on the Internet. A search on Yahoo, Google, AltaVista, or other search engines resulted in an alarming number of hits on environmental issues. Searching the entire Yahoo Web site using the term "environmental issues" resulted in 12,500,000 hits, while using the term "environmental reference" brought an equally alarming 2,560,000 hits. The same search on Google resulted in 17,400,000 and 6,850,000 hits, respectively. A search in Yahoo and Google using the word "environment" yielded an even greater number of hits with each search engine.

The search for environmental reference Web sites yielded hits from a variety of Internet domains. Many of these sites were organizations with limited information: some are sites asking or seeking alliances and others are commercial sites seeking to sell products. There are also many disabled links. There are, on the other hand, informative sites from universities, institutes, government agencies, and organizations that provide reference information on a wide range of environmental topics. In this mix of sites, considering the random arrangement of information on the Internet, there are challenges to finding Web sites that address reference issues. According to Franco, ". . . While these search engines . . . have strengths, their weaknesses are well known: a high percentage of nonauthoritative content mixed with quality content that when indexed together, makes locating relevant information serendipitous at best" (Franco 2003, 229).

In this paper, the Web sites are in five categories: environmental portals, general environmental Web sites, government Web sites, public and proprietary databases, and special issues sites. The portals in this article are "one-stop-shopping" sites for environmental information. Like Yahoo.com, environmental portals arrange Web sites in an organized manner according to themes and related issues. Most of the Web portals are searchable and allow users to link to a wide range of topics.

The General Environmental Web Sites section in this article covers a wide range of topics. Although these Web sites link to many environmental issues, some sites cover one area of the environment with more depth than another does. Many of these sites are arranged by topics.

Most government agencies have a Web page dedicated to environmental issues. The section on Government Web Sites constitutes the largest number of links to reference sources. FirstGov <www.firstgov.gov>, the Web portal for the U.S. government, provides insight into the massive amount of information available on government Web sites in this statement: ". . . you can search millions of web pages from federal and state governments, the District of Columbia and U.S. territories." On many of the government sites, there are databases, statistical information, maps, consumer information, and many downloadable documents.

The databases annotated in this paper are a highly selective representation of environmental databases available. There are numerous public and proprietary databases available on most government and non-profit organizations' Web pages. Many proprietary and public databases that are not specifically environmental databases also provide citations, articles, and reference information on environmental issues. Proprietary and public databases offer a wealth of information through citations, full-text articles, essays, book chapters, and Web links. Although a subscription is needed for proprietary databases, many sales representatives will allow short-term trial access. While some of the databases, proprietary and public, require skills and subject-specific knowledge, other databases are simple, easy to navigate, and offer relevant reference information to a diverse audience.

The Special Issues section covers topics based upon current environmental issues and reoccurring environmental problem areas. The topics selected in this paper are pollution, air quality, global warming, and environmental health. Recently, an annotated review of environmental health Web sites was published (Riley 2002).

ENVIRONMENTAL PORTAL SITES

ClimateArk
<http://www.climateark.org/>

"The ClimateArk is a Climate Change Portal and Search Engine . . ." designed ". . . for non-commercial, educational purposes only . . ." A wealth of climatic issues is available on this Web site through its directory format and eye-catching links. Through keyword searching and relevant links, users can find information on global climate changes, global warming, alternative energy, and landfills. A wealth of information is available through New Links. The information comes through links to Reuters, *Washington Post, National Business Review*, and other news services. Archival news articles are available and date back to 1999.

Environmental Organization Websites
<http://www.webdirectory.com/>

Among the many links on this site are Agriculture, Disasters, Forestry, Health, Pollution, General Environmental Issues, and Recycling. The

General Environmental Issues link provides information to other Web sites such as EnviroLink, National Wildlife Federation, and Natural Resources Defense Council. This site also offers full-text articles on global warming, alternative healing, food, and nutrition from an online magazine entitled *Health Issues Monthly* <http://www.healthissuesmonthly. com/>.

EnviroInfo
<http://www.deb.uminho.pt/fontes/enviroinfo/default.htm>

Themes covering the environment and technology are the major focuses of this site. Topics range from air pollution to conservation and natural resources to wildlife diversity. These topics provide access to datasheets, Web sites, listservs, and laboratories. Other access points to information are the General Section, Other Featured Sites, and Featured Publications. Two significant links from the three access points are Databases and Portals each offering numerous links to other Web sites and resources. This searchable Web site is bilingual and serves users who speak Portuguese and English.

EnviroLink
<http://www.envirolink.org/>

This non-profit organization "unites hundreds of organizations and volunteers around the world . . ." while ". . . providing up-to-date environmental information and news." This site spotlights current environmental issues through links such as News Headlines, Animal Concerns, and EnviroLink US Atlas. EnviroLink US Atlas links to an interactive map of the United States that allows searching by zip code or a city's name. The information from US Atlas addresses issues such as animal rights and wetland habitats. Many of the articles offered in the News Headlines are available through subscription to E-Magazine <www. emagazine.com> and media sources throughout the world. Archival articles are available with a limited life span.

Scientific Information Only (SCIRUS)
<http://www.scirus.com/srsapp/>

SCIRUS offers a wealth of information from scholarly resources and journals. This Web site provides citations from well-known reference databases such as PubMed, Science Direct, and NASA. There are three methods of searching this site: Basic, Advanced Search, and Search Preference. With each search method, the option exists to select journal articles, Web sites, or exact phrase materials. From the Advanced Search module, there is access to material dated as early as 1920. A suggested list of search terms and related Web sites is available with each search.

World Resources Institute (WRI)
<http://www.wri.org>

This searchable Web site updates weekly with news on the environment from around the world. Through keyword searching and numerous links, WRI's Research Topic leads to an abundance of information. There are links to biodiversity and protected areas, climate change and energy, agriculture and food, water resources and freshwater ecosystems, and population, health, and human well-being. A search on this site links to information retrieved in the form of articles, project reports, new releases, and PDF files. When a search in WRI reveals no hits, WRI suggests searching EarthTrends (see below).

EarthTrends
<http://earthtrends.wri.org/gsearch.cfm>

EarthTrends ". . . is a comprehensive online database that focuses on the environmental, social and economic trends that shape our world." This site covers a wide range of topics on the ecosystems, water resources, biodiversity, forest, and grassland. Each of these topics provides a link to a Searchable Database, Maps, Country Profiles, Features, and Data Tables. Combined, these links produce full-text documents of statistical and analytical information, graphs, charts, and articles.

GENERAL ENVIRONMENTAL WEB SITES

Environmental Chemistry
<http://environmentalchemistry.com/yogi/chemistry/dictionary/>

This site is a dictionary of environmental and chemistry terms and articles. Embedded in the textual definitions are hyperlinks to other terms. There are articles on topics related to asbestos, human waste, environmental justice, household waste, and chemicals. There is a link to Environmental Acronyms such as CAA (Clean Air Act), MRF (Municipal Recycle Facility), MSW (Municipal Solid Waste), and RDF (Refuse derived fuel).

Environmental Defense
<http://www.environmentaldefense.org/home2.cfm>

While providing a meaningful tool for concerned citizens to take action on environmental issues, this site also provides a wealth of information on topics that would appeal to the average citizen. Three robust, action-driven links are Campaigns, Take Action, and Programs. Campaigns' link contains information on global warming, endangered species, air pollution, and oceans. The Take Action link provides opportunities to voice concerns to elected officials such as the president, senators, and representatives. The link to Programs provides an abundance of information: interviews with physicians, attorneys, and other environmental experts. Articles are available on various topics such as environmental health, ecosystem restoration, climate and air, local initiatives, and regional news. There are links to other Web sites such as Scorecard, Texas Environmental Profiles, and Oceans Alive. This searchable site has full-text articles on a wide range of topics.

EarthPulse
<http://www.nationalgeographic.com/earthpulse/>

This site combines the efforts of the National Geographic Society <http://www.nationalgeographic.com>, publisher of *National Geographic Magazine* and *National Geographic Kids*, and the Ford Motor Company. According to the National Geographic Society, "Through EarthPulse, our organizations have the opportunity to entertain, engage, and educate people worldwide on environmental issues." The environmental issues on this site address conservation themes such as climate, oceans, energy, fresh water, and wild lands. Some of the links for these topics are interactive maps and excerpts from articles that appear in *National Geographic Magazine* with the bibliography, Webcasts, and educational activities. From the Web site's side bar, there are links to Virtual World, News, WildWorld Sites & Sounds, and EarthPulse Expeditions. Collectively, these links explore Rain Forest at Night, Conservation News that explores many topics, Southeastern U.S. Rivers and Streams, and an expedition to Belize. These links provide access to other Web sites. This is a searchable Web site.

Weather
<http://www.weather.org/>

Access to climatic data around the world is available on this Web site through the World Radar, Snow-Forecast, Earthquakes, Volcano Watch and StormWatch, Aviation, and Global Warming links. The information from these links is current. Access to a city's weather report provides additional information about the city such as surrounding cities and towns, historical weather information that includes a calendar dating back to 1970, and tourist information. Other links that provide reference information are Books, World Newspapers, and Kid Links. The Books' link provides a list of weather publications and a link to an online book entitled *The Revolution in the Understanding of Weather*. The World Newspapers' link provides the names of newspapers from cities and countries both large and small. This site has an extensive list of weather sites.

National Safety Council (NSC)
<http://www.nsc.org/issues/lead/>

This site's mission is "To educate and influence society to adopt safety, health and environmental policies . . . that prevent and mitigate human suffering . . ." The links to News, Products, and Resources contain a wealth of research data. Some of the topics on the Resources' page link users to information on Chemical Backgrounders, farms, first aid, lead, ergonomics, and statistics. The links to the Environmental Protection Agency (EPA) and the Housing and Urban Development (HUD) Department contain data on healthy homes and lead hazards, lead poisoning and water, blood-lead level in children, and pollution. Some of these links are to everyday environmental health topics such as hair dye, miniblinds, lead, and fatalities at the work place. Two Web sites that provide information on work place fatalities are NIOSH's **FACE** <http://www.cdc.gov/niosh/face/> and **Traumatic Occupational Injuries** <http://www.cdc.gov/niosh/injury/trauma.html>. FACE is a research program of the National Institute for Occupational Safety and Health that ". . . concentrates on investigations of fatal occupational injuries." Traumatic Occupational Injuries' Web site offers many links to resources on injuries. There are links to databases, publications, and occupational injury topics that offer statistics, articles, and charts on fatal injuries.

National Library for the Environment (NLE)
<http://www.ncseonline.org/NLE/>

NLE is a component of the NCSE (National Council for Science and Environment) <http://www.ncseonline.org/Site/>. This searchable site has many resources linking to reference information. Links on this site provide information on NCSE Programs such as CRS Reports (Congressional Research Services Reports), Internet Reference Desk, Native Americans and the Environment, and PopEnvironment. Each link allows users to find information through keyword searching or by clicking on a specific topic. Reference Resources' page links to dictionaries, educational information, journals, online bibliographies and catalogs, state and local resources, and government agencies. Environmental Hot Topics, the combined efforts of the National Council for Science and Environment (NCSE) and Cambridge Scientific Abstracts (CSA), accesses over 40 full-text documents. This site has an extensive list of Web links.

People and Planet
<http://www.peopleandplanet.net>

This Web site "... provides a global gateway to the greatest issues of our time . . ." Issues of poverty, agriculture, trade, climate changes, and pollution are the major topics on this site. Most of the links contain full-text articles coupled with picture galleries of environmental concerns. A glossary of unique terms is available for each topic.

Population Reference Bureau (PRB)
<http://www.prb.org/>

PRB provides answers to numerous questions about the world's population and its effect on the environment. Information on topics about aging, education, poverty, rural population, migration, and health is abundant on this site. The data on these subjects are contained in articles, datasheets, and reports. The Highlights' link allows navigation to Web sites and PDF documents that "... explore how shared concern for the environment links people in the United States to people in other parts of the world." The links to Educators, DataFinder, and the PRB Library provide lesson plans, and demographic variables with some information coming from the U.S. Census Bureau and population data. This site is multilingual.

Physicians for Social Responsibility (PSR)
<http://www.psr.org/>

According to this Web site, "Physicians for Social Responsibility is committed to the elimination of nuclear and other weapons of mass destruction, the achievement of a sustainable environment, and the reduction of violence and its causes." Links to Violence, Security, and Environmental and Health are the site's primary focuses. The Environmental and Health page links to two PSR sites: Mercury Action Now and envirohealthaction (see below).

Mercury Action Now
<http://www.mercuryaction.org/fish/>

This site provides information on mercury emission and its effect on public health. Some of the reports on this site are products of the Environmental Protection Agency, Center for Disease Control, Food and Drug Administration, and the National Institutes of Health. An interactive map from the link "Too Close To Home" allows users to locate power plants throughout the United States that contribute to mercury pollution in the environment. The data obtained from the interactive map contain the Power Plant's Name, Owner, Parent Company, and the Initial Year.

envirohealthaction
<http://www.envirohealthaction.org/environment/disease_environment/index.cfm>

Chronic Diseases and Environment, and Climate Change and Health are the major areas of focus on this site that contain numerous topics for a diverse user group. Some of the topics are linked to information on air pollution, climate change, safe drinking water, chronic diseases, land use, public health, and vulnerable population. Security and Violence Prevention's link provides downloadable documents and Web links. Each of PSR's Web sites is searchable.

GOVERNMENT WEB SITES

Center for Disease Control (CDC)
<http://www.cdc.gov/>

"The . . . [CDC] is recognized as the lead federal agency for protecting the health and safety of people–at home and abroad . . . " Some of the major links on this site are Birth Defects, Injury and Violence, Diseases & Conditions, Workplace Safety and Health, Traveler's Health, and Environmental Health. Each major link contains the following items to which information is found: Featured Items, View by Topic, Key Resources, Quick Links, and Programs & Campaigns. These topics provide access to numerous links that open a new Web browser. The link to Traveler's Health provides information on topics such as diseases, safe water, special traveling needs, pets, and vaccinations. There is access to archival issues of the "past features" articles and current health news.

Environmental Health
<http://www.cdc.gov/node.do/id/0900f3ec8000e044>

There is an extensive amount of information on this Web site. Air Quality, Food Safety, Natural Disasters, and Health Disorders and Environment are links to data from tables, reports, and full-text articles. The Featured Items link provides information on hurricanes, floods, asbestos exposure, environmental chemicals, and climate issues. A link to environmental chemicals provides access to the National Report on Human Exposure to Environmental Chemicals <http://www.cdc.gov/exposurereport/>. This report provides an assessment of human exposure to chemicals. From the links to Publications and Products, users can obtain downloadable documents and free software from several government agencies: Agency for Toxic Substances and Disease Registry, National Institute for Occupational Safety and Health, Office of Genomics and Disease Prevention, National Center for Infectious Diseases, and the Epidemiology Program Office.

National Center for Environmental Health (NCEH)
<http://www.cdc.gov/nceh/default.htm>

NCEH is one of CDC's twelve organizations that ". . . promote health and quality of life by preventing or controlling those diseases that result from interactions between people and their environment." This Web site links to numerous subjects: air pollution, cancer, earthquakes, lead poisoning, floods, natural disasters, hurricanes, noise, mold, and sanitation. The information on these links is available for downloading with an Adobe Reader. The link to Environmental Health Services opens a new browser to an extensive list of environmental health topics. These topics contain reports, e-books, and other documents. The links to Spotlights and Emergency Preparedness contain articles on floods, carbon monoxide poisoning, hurricanes, lead and water, and chemical weapons. This searchable site is multilingual.

Environmental Protection Agency (EPA)
<http://www.epa.gov/>

The EPA's Web site is a comprehensive, "one-stop-shopping," government portal of environmental issues. The massive amount of information on this site links to sections such as Laws and Regulations, EPA Topics, Where You Live, Top Stories, and Other News. The link to EPA Topics provides information on major topics such as air, cleanup, compliance and enforcement, economics, ecosystems, human health, pesticide, pollutants/toxics, radiation, waste, and water. Quick Finder's link overlaps some of the EPA Topics, but there is additional data on topics such as acid rain, global warming, oil spills, and radon. Other links provide information on regional and state environmental issues, databases, and related Web sites. This is a searchable, bilingual site.

FireSafety.gov
<http://www.firesafety.gov/index.shtm>

This site has numerous links to information for a diverse user group. Among the links on this site are Projects and Programs, Reference Materials, Latest News, and Product Recall. Product Recall's list is current and only provides the products that relate to fire. Reference Materials' link contains information on interactive databases and statistics. Links to "For the Public" and "For At-Risk Populations" provide free books, fact sheets, forms, reports, and guides to assist users. This bilingual site is searchable.

FirstGov
<http://www.firstgov.gov/index.shtml>

This Web site is "The U.S. Government's Official Web Portal." There is an abundance of information on this site for all users. The Information by Topic link addresses environmental issues such as Consumer Protection, Public Safety, Law, Science, and Technology, and

Environment, Energy, and Agriculture. Some of the issues addressed in Consumer Protections, Public Safety, Law and Science, and Technology are drinking water safety, food-borne illnesses, terrorism, floods, space weather, and plants.

The link to **Environment, Energy, and Agriculture** <http://www.firstgov.gov/index.shtml> focuses on three major areas: General Environment, Environmental Health and Quality, and Environmental Maps, Research, and Statistics. Collectively, these three links contain data from such sources as The Bureau of Land Management, Dictionary of Environmental Terms, Clean Air-Real Time Information, Indoor Air Quality, Geologic Maps Database, and Environmental Statistics.

GrayLIT Network
<http://graylit.osti.gov>

Information from this site represents the collaborative efforts of government agencies such as the EPA, NASA, DOE, and DOD/DTIC. Users may search each of the collaborative agencies simultaneously or individually. A simultaneous search separates the results by agency and provides the results that are available from each agency. Three Web sites that work together retrieving the information received in GrayLIT are Energy Science and Technology Virtual Library, E-Print Network, and Federal R&D Projects Summaries (see below). These Web sites may be searched individually.

Energy Science and Technology Virtual Library <http://www.osti.gov/energyfiles/> provides information from over 500 databases and Web sites on "the effects of any energy-related activity on the environment . . . and on technical aspects of ensuring that energy-related activities are environmentally safe and socially acceptable." **E-Print Network** <http://www.osti.gov/eprints/> provides electronic access to scholarly materials that come from "over 14,800 Web sites and databases world wide." **Federal R&D Projects Summaries** <http://www.osti.gov/fedrnd/> provide "portals of information about Federal research projects."

National Library of Medicine
<http://www.nlm.gov>

NLM, the largest medical library in the world, has an enormous amount of reference information on environment issues. From the many databases available at NLM, there are sources such as journal articles, citations, and databases. Among the list of NLM's databases and resources that offer volumes of information on environmental issues are MedlinePlus, PubMed, and Specialized Information Services (see below).

MedlinePlus <http://medlineplus.gov/> links the user to information from the National Institutes of Health and other valued sources. MedlinePlus provides links to Health Topics, Drug Information, Medical Encyclopedia, Dictionary, News, and Directories and Other Resources. The Health Topics link provides access to broad topics such as disorders and condition, diagnosis and therapy, demographic groups and health, and wellness. One of the more specific links from Health Topics is Poisoning, Toxicology, and Environment which provides information on drinking water, molds, asbestos, anthrax, and food safety. Each of these topic links opens a full Web page with the Latest News, Overviews, Related Issues, Laws and Policy, Treatment, Alternative Therapy, and information that relates to gender factors.

PubMed <http://www.ncbi.nlm.nih.gov/entrez/query.fcgi> offers over 15 million citations from biomedical and molecular biology resources. There are some full-text articles available. PubMed also provides links to other resources such as consumer health information, research tools, and biological sources.

Specialized Information Services (SIS) <http://sis.nlm.nih.gov/index.html>

This site, according to NLM, ". . . is responsible for information resources and services in toxicology, environmental health, chemistry, HIV/AIDS, and specialized topics in minority health." The **Toxicology and Environment Health** <http://sis.nlm.nih.gov/Tox/ToxMain.html> page provides access to consumer health information and databases. Among the databases on this Web page are TOXNET, TOXMAP, WISER, HAZ-MAP, ALTBIB, and Internet Resources. Specific consumer databases are Household Product Database, TOXTOWN, MedlinePlus, and DIRLINE. Among the many other links are chemical information, selected toxicology links, educational and career links, and bibliographies. There is a self-guided tutorial on toxicology <http://sis.nlm.nih.gov/Tox/ToxTutor.html>. Subscribing to the listservs of both NLM-TX-ENVIRO-Health and MedlinePlus Environment keeps one current on environmental issues, new databases, and news.

National Institute for Occupational Safety and Health (NIOSH)
<http://www.cdc.gov/niosh/homepage.html>

NIOSH is responsible for making the environment a safe place to work. Needful information on environmental safety in the workplace is available on this site through links to chemical safety, noise and hearing loss, construction, musculoskeletal disorders, construction, violence, agriculture, and mining. Each topic opens a new Web browser with many links to resources. The Resources link opens to Publications and Products, Databases, and NIOSH eNews. "eNews" provides full text to articles found in the *New England Journal of Medicine*, *Morbidity and Mortality Weekly Report*, Symposiums, and other government agencies reports.

National Oceanic & Atmospheric Administration (NOAA)
<http://www.noaa.gov/index.html>

A wealth of information on many topics that relate to weather, water, and climate is available on this site, including the history of NOAA that began in 1807. Current weather information is available on the link, Today's Weather, by entering the name of a city and state into the search box. Links to Science, Service, and Stewardship yield substantial information on climate, weather, ocean, fisheries, and research from environmental labs. Users have access to Web Cams, Photo Galleries, NOAA's library catalog, and Interlibrary Loan privileges with some restrictions. A primary component of the NOAA site is the Research page that ". . . focuses on enhancing our understanding of environmental phenomena such as tornadoes, hurricanes, climate variability, solar flares, changes in the ozone . . . ocean currents . . . and coastal ecosystem health." Most of the documents on this site are available for downloading with an Adobe Acrobat Reader. The Media Contact's link provides a wealth of links to other NOAA Web sites: NOAA Fisheries, NOAA Ocean Center, NOAA Hurricane Center, and National Centers for Environmental Prediction.

National Centers for Environmental Prediction (NCEP)
<http://www.ncep.noaa.gov/>

NCEP's primary role is providing weather analysis. The National Centers for Environmental Prediction (NCEP) ". . . is the starting point for nearly all weather forecasts in the United States." This site provides considerable amounts of information on current weather issues such as Watches/Warnings, Outlooks, and Current Conditions with additional links to images from satellites and radars. The Education Resources link provides information on tornados including an online document entitled "Frequently Ask Question about Tornados," images, and other unique weather information. There is a link to topics on fire weather, space weather, 6-10 day weather forecast, marine weather, and aviation forecast.

United States Department of Agriculture (USDA)
<http://www.usda.gov/>

The "USDA is the country's largest conservatory agency, encouraging voluntary efforts to protect soil, water and wildlife . . ." Subjects that provide links from the main page are Agriculture, Food and Nutrition, Natural Resources and Environment, Law and Regulations, and Travel and Research. This Web site also accesses issues found on the links Spotlight and In the News. These two links provide documents on current issues of memberships, organizational information, budgets, and links to other Web sites.

Natural Resource and Environment
<http://www.usda.gov/wps/portal/!ut/p/_s.7_0_A/7_0_ 1OB?navtype=SU&navid=NATURAL_RESOURCES>

This USDA Web site provides links from Related Topics on issues such as Backyard Conservation, Disaster and Drought, Recycling and Management, Data and Statistics, Fire and Safety, Homeland Security, Forest and Forestry, and Wildlife. These topics provide access to numerous links that contains fact sheets, reports, charts, statistics, maps, and brochures. These documents are available for downloading with an Adobe Reader. The See Also link directs users to other Web sites such as Clearskies, EarthDay.gov, Forestry Service, and Natural Resources Conservation Science.

Natural Resources Conservation Science (NRCS)
<http://www.nrcs.usda.gov/>

NRSC partners with other agencies and organizations to ". . . help people conserve maintain and improve our natural resources and environment." Three major links on this site are Programs, Technical Resources, and Features. Collectively, these links direct users to topics about farms, ranches, grasslands, watersheds, wetlands, backyard conservation, soil testing, drought, and other Web sites. This searchable site has numerous fact sheets available for downloading.

ENVIRONMENTAL DATABASES

Public Databases

AGRICOLA
<http://agricola.nal.usda.gov/>

This database is the product of the "National Agricultural Library and its cooperators." AGRICOLA consists of citations covering all aspects of agriculture and related disciplines: plants sciences, forestry, farming and farming systems, food and human nutrition, and earth and environmental sciences. This database can be searched through two major links: National Agriculture Library (NAL) and Article Citation Database. These two search modules contain citations to books, serials, audiovisual materials, articles, and reports. The information in AGRICOLA is available from the National Agricultural Library and other libraries. There is a link to "How to Search Both Databases at Once." Although this database is free, it is also available for a fee through some vendors.

EnvironFacts
<http://www.epa.gov/enviro/index.html>

"This website provides access to several EPA databases to provide you with information about environmental activities that may affect air, water, and land anywhere in the United States." Each of the links provides information from three areas: Queries, Maps, and Reports. Another method of retrieving information from these three areas is the Advanced Capabilities search module. From the Advanced Capabilities' links, there is access to databases such as CERCLIS, EMCI, NCOD, and PCS. With a zip code, the name of a city and state, or county and state, users can access information on waste, water, toxicity, land, and radiation.

HazDat
<http://www.atsdr.cdc.gov/hazdat.html>

This database provides information on hazardous substances released from Superfund sites and the effects of hazardous substances on the health of humans. The information that is extracted from HazDat includes many factors: site characteristics, contaminants found, impact on population, contaminants' level of concentration, health concerns of the community, and the impact on the population. Information can be retrieved through several links: Site Activity Query, Site Activity–Sensitive State Map, Site Contaminant Query, ToxFAQ Sheets Text Search, and Public Health Assessment Text Search. This database is a part of the Agency for Toxic Substances and Disease Registry <http://www. atsdr.cdc.gov>.

TOX TOWN
<http://toxtown.nlm.nih.gov/town/main.html>

TOX TOWN, a product of the National Library of Medicine, is available in a text and graphical version. Through its graphical version, users have an interactive guide to toxic substances that affect everyday life. There are two major access points to information in this database: Go to Town and Go to City. The link to "Town" provides an interactive page to locations such as School, Home, Office & Stores, Drinking Water, Factory, and Farms. The link to "City" provides an interactive link to Airplane, Brownfield, Construction, Drinking Water, EMFs, Factory, Parks, and Hair and Nail Salons. Clicking on a location provides a link to Chemical Hot Spots. Scrolling this link highlights the chemical position in the location. Assessing a chemical will provide information such as essays, Web sites, and frequently asked questions.

TOXNET
<http://toxnet.nlm.nih.gov/>

This database is an integrated system of toxicology and environmental health databases offered free of charge through the National Library of Medicine. Among the databases available through TOXNET are HSDB (Hazardous Substances Data Bank), IRIS (Integrated Risk Information System), ITER (International Toxicity Estimates for Risk), TOXLINE (Toxicology Bibliographic Info), and GENE-TOX. Users can search these databases simultaneously or individually. A simultaneous search will result in the displaying of the number of hits found in each database along with the citations. This Web site provides a list of other resources available at NLM and a link to Support Pages. Support Pages provides examples of searches from the databases and a link to a TOXNET training manual. This manual is available in PDF or PPT <http://sis.nlm.nih.gov/Tox/ToxLecture.html>.

Proprietary Databases

Cambridge Scientific Abstracts (CSA)
<http://www.csa.com/csa/>

This privately owned database provides numerous databases on environmental issues and related topics. CSA's Hot Topics link provides full-text articles to current topics on Biomedical, Environmental, and Environmental Policy Issues. These articles are lengthy and include Web sites, a glossary, and a bibliography. The link to "IDS" (Internet Database Services) provides the names of "Databases," "Subfiles," and "Special Collection" that are available in each primary database. Some of the databases in CSA that provide environmental information are NTIS, Environmental Science and Pollution, Aquatic Sciences and Fisheries Abstract with subfiles, and Water Resources Abstracts. A major reference encyclopedic guide in CSA is the *Environmental Route net.* Subscription information is available at the Contact CSA link.

LexisNexis Environmental
<http://www.lexisnexis.com/academic/universe/>

According to this site, "Lexis/Nexis Academic and Library Web services are tailored to meet the needs of researchers and students." *LexisNexis Environmental* <http://web.lexis-nexis.com/envuniv> provides tailored information on environmental issues. Some of the topics in this database are energy, biodiversity, global warming, land use and pollution, toxicology, agriculture, and wildlife. The information in LexisNexis Environmental comes from sources such as conference papers and proceedings, federal and state reports, major newspapers, and over 6,000 journals. LexisNexis Environmental provides a link to the Environmental Protection Agency's Browse Topics <http://www.epa.gov/ebtpages/alphabet.html>. This link provides an abundance of information such as books, environmental programs, reports, and Web sites. Subscription and pricing information can be obtained through contact with a sales representative.

Science Direct
<http://www.sciencedirect.com/>

"ScienceDirect is the world's largest electronic collection of science, technology and medicine full-text and bibliographic information." ScienceDirect, an Elsevier Publishing Company product, provides scholarly information for researchers, educators, and students. The bibliographic databases that are available for environmental issues are BIOTECHNOBASE, Ei Compendex, Elsevier BIOBASE, EMBASE, GEOBASE, and OceanBase. A click on each database will provide a link to the journals available. ScienceDirect has offices located around the world.

SPECIAL ENVIRONMENTAL ISSUES SITES

Environmental Health

National Institute of Environmental Health Sciences
<http://www.niehs.nih.gov/>

The links to environmental health on this Web site are enormous. Some of the site's major links are the Library, "Environmental Health Perspectives," National Toxicology Program, Environmental Genome, and the National Center for Toxicogenomics. The links to Environmental Health Info provide an extensive alphabetical list of topics. These topics provide information on publications, Web sites, and frequently asked questions.

Morbidity and Mortality Weekly Report (MMWR)
<http://www.cdc.gov/mmwr/index.html>

MMWR a product of the Centers for Disease Control, is a weekly online publication. Some of the major links on this site are Top Stories, Reports, Summaries, Disease Trends, Public Health Resources, Continuing Education, and Disease Facts. The link to Disease Facts provides an alphabetical list of diseases that contains fact sheets, lab reports, and the technical and common names for the disease. The Public Health Resources link provides an interactive map to each state's Department of Health Web site. MMWR is available online and can be obtained through subscription free of charge.

World Health Organization (WHO)
<http://www.who.int/en/>

WHO is considered ". . . the United Nations specialized agency for health." There are many links on this site that provide a wealth of information. Health Topics, a major link on this site, contains links to numerous issues with "see also" links. Among the health topics are cancer, drinking water, encephalitis, filariasis, food safety, and uranium. Other links are to Publications, Features, and Research tools. Research tools' link provides access to WHOLIS, the World Health Organization Library database, statistics on diseases and mortality, and geographical information on diseases. This is a searchable multilingual site.

Global Warming

EPA Global Warming Site
<http://yosemite.epa.gov/oar/globalwarming.nsf/content/index.html>

This EPA site provides information on global warming and climate changes for a large user group. Some of the links available are Climate, Emission, Impact, Where You Live, and Resources Center. Collectively, these links contain definitions, interactive maps, essays, events, speeches, publications, and listservs. An interactive map is the source of information for these four links: World, United States, EPA Regions, and Natural Regions. The accumulation of these links provided information to topics such as rangeland, mountains, climate changes, global warming, and greenhouse gas emission. The United States link provided information on each state. This is a searchable site.

Global Warming
<http://www.climatehotmap.org/>

Global warming information on eight regions around the world through an interactive map is the major focus of this Web site. Information gathered from the interactive map is available through two links: Fingerprints and Harbingers. Fingerprints' link contains information on climate change issues: heat waves, glacier melting, ocean warming, and costal flooding. The yellow icons are indicators for Fingerprints' information. Harbingers' link provides information on spreading disease, earlier spring arrival, downpours, heavy snowfalls, droughts, and fires. The blue icons are indicators for Harbingers' topics. Another useful link is the extensive Reference list that includes books, articles, and Web sites. Curriculum information is available for educators.

Air Quality

AIRNOW
<http://www.epa.gov/airnow/index.html>

This database is a partnership effort of many federal, state, and international agencies. There are two major links on this site: National Forecast, and Local Forecasts and Conditions. These links provide users with an interactive map of the United States where information on Current Forecast, Forecast Tables, Web Cams, Air Quality, and Historical Data can be obtained. There are other links to information on ozone, particle pollution, publications, and international information. Users can access essays, reports, and articles. These documents are available for downloading with a PDF Reader.

EHC Air Quality Program
<http://www.nsc.org/ehc/airqual.htm>

This site is a part of The Environmental Health Center and the National Safety Council. The three major links on this Web site: Radon, Mobile Emission, and Indoor Air Quality. Information from these links yields many documents in the form of Facts Sheets, Web sites, educational materials, and reports. Some of the Fact Sheets available are "Background on Air Pollution," "Maintaining Your Car," "Buying a Clean Car," "Radon in Drinking Water," "The Health Effects of Exposure to Indoor Radon," and "Formaldehyde." The education link provides additional links to Kids' Corner, documents on smoking, and outreach activities.

Pollution

healthfinder
<http://www.healthfinder.gov/scripts/SearchContext.asp?topic=672>

This site provides a wealth of information in its Health Library on pollution gathered from " hand-picked . . . government agencies, non-profit organizations, and universities." There are over 20 links to information on pollution ranging from topics such as About Chemicals

Around the House, Combustion Pollutants, and Toxic Waste River Rafting Games. Additional links on this page direct users to organizations and related topics. This searchable site is bilingual.

Noise Pollution Clearinghouse (NPC)
<http://www.nonoise.org/index.htm>

NPC's Web site links to numerous documents on noise pollution. Many of the links are to libraries such as the EPA Noise Library, Hearing Loss and Occupational Noise Library, and NPC Law Library. The libraries' link documents U.S. Federal Codes, State Rules and Regulations, Proposed Legislation and European Laws and Regulations, organizations, news, and other Web sites. This searchable site has full-text documents and provides a newsletter to its users.

Scorecard
<http://www.scorecard.org/>

This Web site can serve as a portal to information on pollution and toxic chemicals. The links on this site provide information on air, water, health hazard, agriculture and many other pollution topics. Other useful links are a glossary of terms related to environmental issues and the latest news on the environmental fronts. This searchable site uses several means of accessing information: keyword, zip code, and hyperlinks.

BIBLIOGRAPHY

Centers for Disease Control. n.d. About CDC. <http://www.cdc.gov/aboutcdc.htm> (accessed August 2004).
_____. National Center for Environmental Health. n.d. <http://www.cdc.gov/nceh/> (accessed August 2004).
ClimateArk. 1999-2004. <http://www.climateark.org/> (accessed October 2004).
E-Print Network. n.d. E-Print Network is . . . <http://www.osti.gov/eprints/> (accessed November 18, 2004).
EarthPulse. 1996-2004. About EarthPulse. <http://www.nationalgeographic.com/earthpulse/#> (accessed September 2004).
Energy Science and Technology Virtual Library. 11/18/2004. Welcome to Energy Files. <http://www.osti.gov/energyfiles/> (accessed November 18, 2004).
EnviroLink. n.d. About the EnviroLink Network. <http://www.envirolink.org/about.html> (accessed October 2004).

Fatality Assessment and Control Evaluation (FACE) Program. n.d. FACE. <http://www.cdc.gov/niosh/face/> (accessed November 21, 2004).

Franco, Adrienne. 2003. "Gateway to the Internet: Finding Quality Information on the Internet." 52, no. 2 (*Library Trends*): 228-246.

Federal R&D Projects Summaries. n.d. About. <http://www.osti.gov/fedrnd/about.html> (accessed November 18, 2004).

FirstGov. n.d. <http://www.firstgov.gov/About.shtml> (accessed November 2004).

————. n.d. <http://www.firstgov.gov/> (accessed November 2004).

healthfinder. n.d. Home> Library. <http://www.healthfinder.gov/Library/> (accessed November 2004).

Lexis/Nexis Environment. 2004. LexisNexis Academic & Library Solutions: Web services. <http://www.lexis-nexis.com/academic/universe/> (accessed October 2004).

National Agricultural Library–Agricola. n.d. What Is AGRICOLA? <http://agricola.nal.usda.gov/help/aboutagricola.html> (accessed September 2004).

National Center for Environmental Prediction. 01-Oct-2004. About NCEP. <http://wwwt.ncep.noaa.gov/about/> (accessed October 2004).

National Library of Medicine–Specialized Information Services. November 16, 2004. About. <http://sis.nlm.nih.gov/index.html> (accessed September 2004).

National Oceanic Atmospheric Administration. n.d. Research. <http://www.noaa.gov/research.html> (accessed October 2004).

National Safety Council. 1995-2004. About Us. <http://www.nsc.org/insidensc.htm> (accessed November 21, 2004).

People & the Planet. 2002-2004. People & the Planet. <http://www.peopleandplanet.net/> (accessed August 2004).

Population Reference Bureau. 2004. The U.S. in the World. <http://www.prb.org/Content/NavigationMenu/PRB/Educators/US_in_the_World/US_in_the_World.htm> (accessed November 21, 2004).

Physicians for Social Responsibility. 2002. About PSR. <http://www.psr.org/home.cfm?id=about> (accessed September 2004).

Riley, Ola Carter. "Environmental Health." *College & Research Libraries News* 63, no. 5 (May 2002): 350-354.

ScienceDirect. 2004. Overview. <http://www.info.sciencedirect.com/licensing_options/index.shtml> (accessed October 2004).

United States Department of Agriculture. n.d. About USDA. <http://www.usda.gov/wps/portal/!ut/p/_s.7_0_A/7_0_1OB?navtype=MA&navid=ABOUT_USDA> (accessed September 2004).

————. n.d. Natural Resources Conservation Science. <http://www.nrcs.usda.gov/> (accessed November 2004).

World Health Organization. n.d. About WHO. <http://www.who.int/about/en/> (accessed September 2004).

World Resources Institute. 2004. EarthTrends: The Environmental Information Portal. <http://earthtrends.wri.org/miscell/aboutus.cfm?theme=0> (accessed December 2, 2004).

Using the Internet to Find Information on Agriculture's Hot Topics

Kathy Fescemyer

SUMMARY. Agriculture is a vital component to the United States economy and is necessary to all our daily needs. This article provides descriptions for the most important Internet sites for agriculture. Sites are described for general resources, statistics and agricultural economics, plant sciences, food sciences, and animal and veterinary sciences. *[Article copies available for a fee from The Haworth Document Delivery Service: 1-800-HAWORTH. E-mail address: <docdelivery@haworthpress.com> Website: <http://www.HaworthPress.com> © 2006 by The Haworth Press, Inc. All rights reserved.]*

KEYWORDS. Agriculture, food science, animal science, veterinary science, horticulture, entomology, agricultural statistics

Agriculture is the backbone of America, and contributes daily to the health, wealth, and security of the American way of life. Agriculture provides the food that is essential for our daily needs. Because agriculture is so important to all, finding answers to reference questions about

Kathy Fescemyer is Life Sciences Librarian, The Pennsylvania State University, Life Sciences Library, 408 Paterno Library, University Park, PA 16802 (E-mail: kaf12@psu.edu).

[Haworth co-indexing entry note]: "Using the Internet to Find Information on Agriculture's Hot Topics." Fescemyer, Kathy. Co-published simultaneously in *Journal of Library Administration* (The Haworth Information Press, an imprint of The Haworth Press, Inc.) Vol. 44, No. 1/2, 2006, pp. 373-394; and: *Evolving Internet Reference Resources* (ed: William Miller, and Rita M. Pellen) The Haworth Information Press, an imprint of The Haworth Press, Inc., 2006, pp. 373-394. Single or multiple copies of this article are available for a fee from The Haworth Document Delivery Service [1-800-HAWORTH, 9:00 a.m. - 5:00 p.m. (EST). E-mail address: docdelivery@haworthpress.com].

doi:10.1300/J111v44n01_04

373

food and nutrition is an important skill. Some of the current hot topics in agriculture include genetic engineering of plants and animals, world hunger, sustainable agriculture, pesticide use, mad cow disease, food irradiation, food safety, food security, avian influenza, and animal rights. The following sites will help to find information on these topics and many other agricultural subjects.

This article emphasizes North American agricultural sites, but important international sites have been included. Two abbreviations used widely in this article are USDA for the United States Department of Agriculture and FAO for the Food and Agriculture Organization of the United Nations.

GENERAL

AgNIC (Agriculture Network Information Center)
<http://www.agnic.org>

AgNIC is an organization that consists of universities, government agencies, and agricultural businesses. The purpose of the group is to provide quality information on agriculture on the Internet. Each institution has created a subject-specific Web site for an agricultural subject. The subjects include such topics as farmland preservation, wildlife damage management, USDA statistics and economics, geospatial information repository, soil health, swine, wildflowers of Kansas, blueberries, maple syrup, cherries, asparagus, aquaculture, food and nutrition, food safety research office, rural information, animal welfare, plant genome, sustainable agriculture, technology transfer, agricultural law, chili peppers, systematic entomology, bison, bees and pollination, rangelands, turf grass, home gardening, Latin American and Caribbean agriculture, viticulture, agribusiness, sub-tropical horticulture, Pacific Island crops, aquaculture, corn, soybeans, agricultural communications, biotechnology, agricultural and applied economics, forestry, plant science, water quality, American cranberry, tree fruits, and winter sowing. The database is searchable or may be browsed by topic.

AGRICOLA
<http://agricola.nal.usda.gov/>

When searching for books, articles, government documents, and other agricultural resources, AGRICOLA is the index to consult. All types of agricultural resources in many formats are included in this database. Each entry includes the citation, language, subject headings, abstract, and other reference information. All aspects of agriculture are included in AGRICOLA and include animal and veterinary sciences, entomology, plant sciences, forestry, aquaculture and fisheries, farming and farming systems, agricultural economics, extension and education, food and human nutrition, and earth and environmental sciences. Many types of literature such as journal articles, books, book chapters, USDA, State Experiment Station, and State Extension service publications are included. AGRICOLA is produced by the National Agricultural Library of the United States Department of Agriculture. The database is accessible to all from the National Agricultural Library's site. Access is also provided from many commercial vendors.

Agricultural Marketing Resource Center (AgMRC)
<http://www.agmrc.org/>

Many farmers are looking for alternatives to traditional crops and livestock to increase the value of their yield. This site provides information and links to information on different crops, livestock, and other agricultural endeavors that build successful value-added agricultural enterprises. These topics include agri-tourism, aquaculture, fruits, grains and oilseeds, livestock such as bison, ostrich and worms, nuts, specialty crops, and forestry. The site helps producers investigate value-added products, explore the available market, analyze the feasibility, devise a business plan, and create and operate a business.

@griculture Online
<http://www.agriculture.com/>

Started in 1995, @griculture Online was created by the editors of *Successful Farming* and was one of the first agricultural Web sites. Articles about current hot topics in agriculture such as the latest disease information on plants and animals, latest political news affecting agriculture, market information, and other topics are provided. Complete market information and future prices are in the markets section. The weather section provides up-to-the minute detailed weather information such as temperature, wind chill, wind speeds, soil moisture, humidity, precipitation likelihood, and other measures of weather. Talk groups provide lively opinionated discussion on over twenty topics from livestock to machinery to ag computing.

Agriculture and Agri-Food Canada Online
<http://www.agr.gc.ca/index_e.phtml>

Comparable to the USDA, Agriculture and Agri-Food Canada provides information, research and technology, and policies and programs to achieve security of the food system, health of the environment, and innovation for growth. Sections include agricultural policy framework, business risk management, environment, finances and economics, food safety and food quality, markets and trade, renewal, rural development, and science and innovation.

AGRIS/CARIS
<http://www.fao.org/AGRIS/>

AGRIS is the international information system for the agricultural sciences and technology which was created by the Food and Agriculture Organization of the United Nations (FAO) in 1974. AGRIS's participating countries input references to the literature that are produced within their boundaries and access information from other participants. The strength of these databases is in the wealth of international agricultural information indexed. Entries in AGRIS provide a basic citation and keyword. Searching is by keyword only and the database is divided into two parts–1975-1996 and 1996 to the present. CARIS is the Current Agricultural Research Information System, created by FAO in 1975 to identify and to facilitate the exchange of information about current agricultural research projects being carried out in, or on behalf of, developing countries. The basic unit in CARIS is a set of data describing a single project, giving such details as the project title, objectives, inception and termination dates, names of researchers and their specializations, contact addresses of individuals, and institutes carrying out the research. Coverage is from 1975-present.

Agrisurf
<http://www.agrisurf.com>

A large database that provides links to many commercial agriculture sites throughout the world. The sections include agritourism, apiculture, aquaculture, catalogs, computing, crops, discussion, environment, extension, farm homepages, farm management, farm safety, farmer's markets, forestry, gardening, general agribuz, government, images, indexes, lifestyle, livestock, machinery, markets and marketing, miscellaneous, organic farming, organizations, publications, real estate, research and education, soil, sustainable agriculture, technology, and weather. The site is searchable by keyword. This site links to many international agricultural business sites as well as to those in the United States and Canada.

AgWeb
<http://www.agweb.com/>

Produced by Farm Journal Media, AgWeb provides four sections of current popular information for agriculturalists. The News section provides current articles on many of agriculture's hottest topics such as soybean rust, market fluctuations, and political influences on agriculture. Weather from the Weather Channel provides a seven day detailed forecast for locations throughout the World. Focusing on the business of agriculture, Money and Markets offers market numbers (agricultural and financial) from all the major exchanges on a 10-minute delay. Discussions is an online meeting place for producers. Discussion categories include Money & Markets, Policy & Politics, Machinery & Technology, and Crop Production and Livestock. The In Focus sections focus on specific crops and livestock such as corn, wheat, soybeans, cotton, cattle, dairy, and hogs.

AgZines
<http://usain.org/agzines.html>

AgZines provides links to full-text electronic journals and magazines which focus on agricultural topics. All journals provide full text and are accessible without charge. Extension publications are not included because they are accessible at E-Answers. AgZines is maintained by Carla Casler at the University of Arizona and is sponsored by the United States Agricultural Information Network (USAIN).

CAB Abstracts
<http://www.cabi.org/>

CAB Abstracts is the foremost index to the agricultural literature, and covers all agricultural subjects from production agriculture to nutrition and economics. The database contains almost 5 million records. It is the best index for searching for articles on international agricultural subjects. Advanced searching allows limiting using over 30 fields, by subject, by year, and by language. Entries provide the citation, an abstract, language, subject heading, and other reference information. *CAB Abstracts* is available from many vendors or directly from CABI Publishing.

CRIS (Current Research Information System)
<http://cris.csrees.usda.gov/>

CRIS is designed by the USDA to describe and report on research projects in agriculture, food and nutrition, and forestry. Over 30,000 descriptions of current, publicly-supported research projects of the USDA agencies, the State Agricultural Experiment Stations, the state land-grant colleges and universities, and USDA grant recipients are in the system. Entries include information on the research project's purpose, the researchers and institutions, progress on projects, and publications produced.

E-answers
<http://e-answers.adec.edu/>

E-answers provides access to publications from the Cooperative Extension Service and Agricultural Experiment Stations from all fifty states. Over 250,000 pages of full-text information are indexed by this site. Articles will be found on all aspects of agriculture, such as agribusiness, horticulture, animal sciences, plant pathology, entomology, food safety, and nutrition.

The Food and Agriculture Organization of the United Nations (FAO)
<http://www.fao.org/>

The Food and Agriculture Organization of the United Nations (FAO) leads international efforts to defeat hunger. FAO helps developing countries and countries in transition modernize and improve agriculture, forestry, and fisheries practices and ensure good nutrition for all. FAO's site provides information on current topics in agriculture, fisheries, forestry, and sustainable development. The site contains technical documents, articles, newsletters, reports, books, and magazines, all available electronically. The Virtual Library provides the full-text electronic documents of FAO and is searchable. This site is an excellent source for international agricultural information.

Farmland Information Center (FIC)
<http://www.farmlandinfo.org/>

The Farmland Information Center is a clearinghouse for information about farmland protection and stewardship. It is a partnership between the USDA Natural Resources Conservation Service and American Farmland Trust. The site provides information and statistics on preserving farmland and preventing it from being developed for non agricultural uses. The site provides a collection of materials on agricultural and land use statistics, laws, literature, and technical resources related to farmland protection and stewardship. The entire site is searchable and has an advanced searching feature.

National Agricultural Law Center
<http://www.nationalaglawcenter.org/>

The National Agricultural Law Center at the University of Arkansas is the gateway to agricultural law resources on the Internet. The Reading Rooms provide links to electronic resources in many subjects. These subjects include administrative law, agriculture and urbanization, agricultural biosecurity, animal feeding operations, animal identification, bankruptcy, biotechnology, checkoff programs, Clean Water Act, Commercial Transactions, cooperatives, country of origin, labeling, estate planning and taxation, farm commodity programs, farm credit, federal crop insurance, food safety, international agricultural law and organizations, international agricultural trade, labor, landowner liability, marketing orders, national organic program, packers and stockyards, perishable agricultural commodities, and pesticides and production contracts. The publications section provides access to full-text research publications created by the Center. The National AgLaw Reporter is a regularly updated electronic newsletter dedicated to reporting to the agricultural and food law communities. Farm Bills provides the text of the most recent farm bill. A glossary and a bibliography covering scholarly articles and books on over 48 topics are also provided.

NASD (National Ag Safety Database)
<http://www.cdc.gov/nasd/>

NASD is an information clearinghouse for agricultural safety-related documents. This database provides links to many online publications from the cooperative extension services and also has links to online videos. Publications may be searched by topic or state. Links for publications in Spanish are included.

WebAgri
<http://www.web-agri.com>

Developed by Hyltel, this site locates agricultural information in over 761,000 agricultural Web pages. Links to all types of agricultural Web sites, United States and internationally, are provided. Searching is by keyword only.

WWW Virtual Library–Agriculture
<http://cipm.ncsu.edu/agVL/>

This site provides links to many types of agricultural information. It is arranged by producer, country, and topic and may be searched by any of these three categories.

The United States Department of Agriculture (USDA)
<http://www.usda.gov>

The USDA is an outstanding source of all types of agricultural information. This site provides current information on all the hot topics in agriculture, agricultural legislation, and agricultural statistics. Subjects include all areas of traditional agriculture and forestry. The many agencies of the USDA provide information in their own sites which are accessible though this site. These agencies include the Agricultural Marketing Service, Agricultural Research Service, Animal and Plant Health Inspection Service (APHIS), Center for Nutrition Policy and Promotion, Cooperative State Research, Education and Extension Service, Economic Research Service, Farm Service Agency, Food and Nutrition Service, Food Safety and Inspection Service, Foreign Agricultural Service, Forest Service, Grain Inspection, Packers and Stockyard Administration, National Agricultural Library, National Agricultural Statistics Service, Natural Resources Conservation Service, Risk Management Agency, and Rural Development.

STATISTICS AND AGRICULTURAL ECONOMICS

AgEcon Search: Research in Agricultural and Applied Economics
<http://agecon.lib.umn.edu/>

AgEcon Search collects, indexes, and electronically distributes full-text copies of scholarly research in the broadly defined field of agricultural economics including sub-disciplines such as agribusiness, food supply, natural resource economics, environmental economics, policy issues, agricultural trade, and economic development. The site is developed and maintained at the University of Minnesota by Magrath Library and the Department of Applied Economics. The database is searchable by any words used in the citations and abstracts, and the full-text papers are available in PDF format.

Agriculture Fact Book 2001-2002
<http://www.usda.gov/factbook/>

The Agriculture Fact Book is a concise view of agricultural issues in the United States. Information and statistics are provided for current topics. The Fact Book is created by the USDA. Chapters include Current Topics, such as homeland security, conservation measures in the 2002 Farm Bill, biotechnology, certified organic, Profiling Food Consumption in America, American Farms, Rural America: Entering the 21st Century, USDA, USDA Rural Development, Farm and Foreign Agricultural Services, Food, Nutrition, and Consumer Services, Food Safety, Natural Resources and Environment, Research, Education and Economics, Marketing, and Regulatory Programs.

Census of Agriculture
<http://www.nass.usda.gov/census/>

The Census of Agriculture provides the most detailed comprehensive statistics on all facets of agriculture from large to small scale operators. Conducted every five years by the U.S. Department of Agriculture's National Agricultural Statistics Service (NASS), the census of agriculture attempts to reach every agricultural operator in America through a mail survey. Detailed information for states and counties in the United States such as number of farms, agricultural acreage, top crop items, market value of production, government payments, and other information is provided. The Census of Agriculture for 2002, 1997, and 1992 are available online.

Census of Horticultural Specialties
Access for 1998: <http://www.nass.usda.gov/census/census97/ horticulture/horticulture.htm>

Access for 1988: <http://www.nass.usda.gov/census/census92/ ag0400.htm>

The Census of Horticultural Specialties provides detailed statistics on the size and structure of the horticulture industry for planning, policy-making, research, and market analysis. The Census is conducted every ten years.

National Agricultural Statistics Service (NASS)
<http://www.usda.gov/nass/>

When looking for agricultural statistics, the NASS site is the best place to begin. NASS conducts hundreds of surveys and prepares reports on almost every aspect of U.S. agriculture from production and supplies of food and fiber, curd prices paid and received by farmers, to farm labor and wages. These statistics are available at this site. NASS also produces publications on a wide range of subjects, from traditional crops, such as corn and wheat, to specialties, such as mushrooms and flowers; from calves born to hogs slaughtered; from agricultural prices to land in farms.

The USDA Economics and Statistics System
<http://usda.mannlib.cornell.edu/>

The USDA Economics and Statistics System contains nearly 300 reports and datasets from the economic agencies of the USDA. These materials cover U.S. and international agriculture and related topics. Most reports are text files that contain time-sensitive information. Most data sets are in spreadsheet format and include time-series data that are updated yearly. Subjects include agricultural baseline projections, Census of Agriculture, farm sector economics, field crops, food, inputs, technology and weather, international agriculture, land, water and conservation, livestock, dairy and poultry, rural affairs, specialty agriculture, and trade issues. The site is searchable by keyword.

FAOSTAT
<http://apps.fao.org/>

This site is the statistical database of the FAO and contains over three million time-series records covering international statistics. Some of the areas covered are production, trade, food balance sheets, producer prices, land use and irrigation, forest products, fishery products, population, codex alimentarius, and fertilizer and pesticides.

State of Food and Agriculture
<http://www.fao.org/es/esa/en/pubs_sofa.htm>

The State of Food and Agriculture provides an overview of agricultural conditions worldwide. The FAO creates this report annually and each issue has a specific theme. The State of Food and Agriculture 2003-04 explores the potential of agricultural biotechnology–especially transgenic crops–to meet the needs of the poor.

PLANT SCIENCES

APSnet–Plant Pathology Online
<http://apsnet.org/>

APSnet provides current information on economically important plant diseases and was created by the American Phytopathological Society. The site includes articles on important and potentially dangerous diseases such as soybean rust, and image resources which consist of pictures of plant pathogens and the damage they cause to plants. The Common Names of Plant Diseases provides a list of diseases found on plants. The list provides scientific and common names of the disease-causing organism.

Aggie Horticulture
<http://aggie-horticulture.tamu.edu/>

Aggie Horticulture is from the Texas Horticulture Program at Texas A&M University and is full of information for the Southwestern horticulturalists. Especially notable are the Sections on Wildflowers, just for KIDS, and Gardening. Sections include Plantanswers, PlantanswersTV, Wildflowers, Plant PicturePages, Texas Superstar, Citrus Web, Ornamentals Web, hortIPM, just for KIDS, floriculture, Gardening, Texas Winegrape Web, vegIPM, and sections specific to geographic regions in Texas. This is a very deep site, full of content on growing many types of fruits, vegetables, herbs, flowers, and ornamentals.

Crop Profiles (USDA)
<http://pestdata.ncsu.edu/cropprofiles/>

Crop Profiles from the USDA provides factual information on major and minor crops of the U.S. Crops included are forages such as alfalfa, and fruits such as apples and blueberries, and also included are Christmas trees, soybeans, cotton, and vegetables such as beans and peppers. The profiles are divided geographically and each entry contains general production information, cultural information, insect pest and disease information, contacts, and references.

Database of IPM Resources
<http://www.ippc.orst.edu/DIR/>

This site is a search engine that will lead to many publications on integrated pest management for insects and diseases affecting a wide variety of crops and ornamentals. It was developed by The Consortium for International Crop Protection, New York Agricultural Experiment Station, Geneva, New York, and the Integrated Plant Protection Center, Oregon State University, Corvallis, Oregon.

Digital Diagnostics @ OSU
<http://www.ento.okstate.edu/ddd/ddd.html>

This site provides images and information on insect pests and diseases on field crops, fruit and nuts, vegetables, turfgrass, ornamentals, and houseplants. The site may be searched in four ways, by subject such as field crops, ornamentals, etc., by plant hosts, by plant disease, or by insects and arthropods. Enties provide photographs of the organism and the damage it causes, a description of the organism, the life cycle of the organism, and the symptoms caused by the organism.

Featured Creatures
<http://creatures.ifas.ufl.edu/>

This site provides information and pictures of many agriculturally important invertebrates. The site may be searched by common name, scientific name, crop, habitat, or classification. Entries include a description of the invertebrate, distribution, life cycle information, photographs, pest status and management, and references. This site is created by the University of Florida's Department of Entomology and Nematology and the Florida Department of Agriculture and Consumer Services' Division of Plant Industry.

Greenbook
<http://www.greenbook.net/>

Greenbook compiles pesticide product information (labels, supplemental labels, and Materials Safety Data Sheets–MSDs) in an unbiased presentation, adding extensive features to help users locate the specific information they need. The information is provided by the manufacturers of the pesticides.

Horticulture and Home Garden
<http://www.extension.uiuc.edu/home/homelawn.html>

The University of Illinois created this large diverse site on all types of horticulture. Hort Corner provides information on lawn care, fruits and vegetables, flowers and ornamentals, trees and shrubs, insects, and seasonal issues. Horticulture Solutions Series provides full-text information on varied topics in horticulture. The Integrated Pest Management section helps identify horticultural pests and how to control them. I PLANT is intended for the use of landscape contractors, commercial nursery and greenhouse operators, and avid plant enthusiasts in the Midwest. Also available for professionals is a section on Pesticide Applicator Training and Pesticide Safety Education.

Iowa State Entomology Index of Internet Resources
<http://www.ent.iastate.edu/list/>

This site provides links to large numbers of entomological sites on the Internet. The site is searchable or may be browsed by content, taxonomic groups, or entomological subdiscipline.

The Maize Page
<http://maize.agron.iastate.edu/>

The Maize Page gives information and links to general, technical, production, and genetic information on corn. This site is provided by Iowa State University's College of Agriculture. The site provides links to information on the history of corn, basic growing information, maize breeding, maize chromosome maps, the National Corn Production Handbook, and many more.

The National Pesticide Information Center
<http://npic.orst.edu/index.html>

This site provides links to all aspects of information on pesticides. The General Section provides links to information for the public on pesticide safety, pesticide risk, pesticide lablels, food and pesticides, environment and pesticides, pets, wildlife and pesticides, waste disposal, and NPIC fact sheets. The technical links provide information on toxicology and active ingredients, health information, environmental and chemical properties databases, product label, and MSDS databases and statistics. The regulatory section provides links to laws and legislative issues for pesticides. The site provides links to pesticides manufacturers' sites. A separate section is for information for identifying and controlling household pests. The Center is a cooperative effort of Oregon State University and the U.S. Environmental Protection Agency.

National Plant Germplasm System (NPGS) and GRIN (Germplasm Resources Information Network) <http://www.ars-grin.gov/npgs/>

NPGS is a cooperative effort by public and private organizations to preserve the genetic diversity of plants. The entries in the GRIN database document information on the germplasm of many economically important plants. More than 450,000 accessions (distinct varieties of plants) are in GRIN and represent more than 10,000 species of plants. This database aids scientists in finding genetic resources to develop new varieties of important food crops.

National Sustainable Agriculture Information Service (ATTRA) <http://attra.ncat.org/>

ATTRA provides the latest information on sustainable agriculture and organic farming news, events, and funding opportunities. In-depth publications on production practices, alternative crop and livestock enterprises, innovative marketing, and organic certification, and highlights of local, regional, USDA, and other federal sustainable agricultural activities are also provided.

NewCROP <http://www.hort.purdue.edu/newcrop/>

Created by the Center for New Crops & Plant Products at Purdue University, NewCROP provides information on lesser known plant species of potential economic importance. The crop index is organized by scientific and common name and provides links to short articles about the plant. CropMap provides information by county on the major and minor crops of the county. Experts are listed in CropEXPERT. The site is searchable.

NRCS Soils Web Site
<http://soils.usda.gov/>

The National Resources Conservation Service (NRCS) provides this site which contains a large amount of excellent information on all types of soils topics. Some of the topics included are the list of published soil surveys and access to the soil surveys available online, the Official Soil Series Descriptions, soil quality information, Soil Science Glossary, and *Keys to Soil Taxonomy*.

PestTracker
<http://ceris.purdue.edu/napis/>

PestTracker provides information on the occurrence and movement of exotic insects, weeds, and plant pathogens in the United States. Links are provided to full-text articles and factsheets for many intro-duced pests. It is produced by the National Agricultural Pest Informa-tion System (NAPIS), the agricultural pest tracking database of the U.S. Department of Agriculture Animal and Plant Health Inspection Service (APHIS), Plant Protection and Quarantine (PPQ), and Cooper-ative Agricultural Pest Survey (CAPS).

Plant Pathology Internet Guide Book
<http://www.pk.uni-bonn.de/ppigb/>

This site provides links to many plant pathology and entomology sites. Included here is the On-Line Glossary of Technical Terms in Plant Pathology which provide definitions for plant pathology terms.

PLANTS Database
<http://plants.usda.gov/>

Information about the vascular plants, mosses, liverworts, horn-worts, and lichens native to the U.S. and its territories is supplied by the USDA's Natural Resource Conservation Service. The site is searchable by common and scientific name. The advanced search allows the searcher to limit by distribution by state, by taxonomy, by life form and native status, and legal status. Fact sheets proved scientific and common names, plant symbols, checklists, distributional data, species abstracts, characteristics, images, plant links, and references. This database provides the most complete distribution information on plants of the United States and its territories.

StratSoy
<http://www.stratsoy.uiuc.edu/welcome.html>

StratSoy provides a large amount of information on soybeans and their products. Sections include answers about soy and human health, varietal information program, soy stats reference guide, commercially available soy products, soy recipes, and soybean history.

Transgenic Plants: An Introduction and Resources Guide
<http://www.colostate.edu/programs/lifesciences/TransgenicCrops/>

This site produced by Colorado State University provides an excellent introduction and overview to the topic of genetically engineered plants. Sections include a history of plant breeding, definitions of transgenic plants, creating transgenic plants, evaluation and regulation, current transgenic plant products, future transgenic products, and risks and concerns. The site includes links to other pertinent pages, a bibliography, and glossary.

WebGarden
<http://webgarden.osu.edu/>

WebGarden from the Ohio State University has extensive databases of horticultural information. The Plant Dictionary (Images) provides photos and basics on ornamental plants, turf, pests, and fruits and vegetables. PlantFacts (Web) searches over 60,000 pages of Cooperative Extension fact sheets and bulletins from 46 different universities and government institutions across the United States and Canada. Over 200 videos provide basic gardening how-to's from landscaping to care of houseplants. Tips answers over 800 frequently asked gardening questions. The PocketGardener provides horticultural images which can be loaded onto handhelds.

Weed Science Society of America
<http://www.wssa.net/>

This site provides information on weeds and herbicides. The Photo Herbarium shows photographs of common weeds. Scientific names and common names are provided. In the Weed Control area, information may be located on herbicides and other methods of weed control.

The Wheat Page
<http://www.oznet.ksu.edu/wheatpage/>

The Wheat Page contains information on organizations, research, varieties, production systems, economics, storage and handling, and links to other Internet sites related to wheat. This site is maintained by Kansas State University.

FOOD AND NUTRITION INFORMATION

Center for Food Safety and Applied Nutrition (CFSAN)
<http://vm.cfsan.fda.gov/>

The Center for Food Safety and Applied Nutrition provides the food information for the Food and Drug Administration (FDA). On the site is an overview of the Center's history and activities, and FDA documents which include FDA dockets, Federal Register and CFR, FOIA Requests, and Laws enforced by FDA. The What's New Section provides links for current news, announcements and press releases, and current topics such as acrylamide, androstenedione, and ephedrine alkaloids. The National Food Safety Programs contain links to all types of food safety sites and bioterrorism information. Program areas include acidified and low acid canned foods, biotechnology, color additives, cosmetics, dietary supplements, food ingredients and packaging, foodborne illness, food labeling and nutrition, hazard analysis and critical control points, imports and exports, infant formula, inspections and compliance, enforcements and recalls, pesticides and chemical contaminants, and seafood. This site provides information on all aspects of food safety and the laws and legislation regulating it.

Food and Nutrition Topics from A-Z
<http://www.nal.usda.gov/fnic/etext/fnic.html>

This site provides links to a complete range of food subjects. It is maintained by the Food and Nutrition Information Center of the National Agricultural Library. Categories include adolescence, aging, allergies and food sensitivities, breastfeeding, cancer, child nutrition and health, community food systems, consumer corner, databases, diabetes, dietary guidelines, dietary supplements, digestive diseases and associated disorders, eating disorders, emergency preparedness, ethnic and cultural resources, fitness, sports and sports nutrition, food composition, food dictionaries and encyclopedias, food guide pyramid, food irradiation, food labeling, food preservation at home, food safety and hazard analysis critical control points, food service, heart health, herbal information, hunger/food security, infant nutrition, kids' sites, legislation and public policy, macronutrients, nutrition assistance programs, osteoporosis, school meals, vegetarian nutrition, vitamins and minerals, and weight control and obesity. Sections contain articles created by professional societies and government agencies.

Food Resource
<http://food.oregonstate.edu/food.html>

Oregon State University provides this site with many links to sites on foods and nutrition. It is focused on food industries and businesses. The Food Information section includes chemicals, color, cultural aspects, flavor, nutrition, pesticides, phytochemicals, plants, fruits, herbs, spices and vegetables, product development, recipes, sensory, starch, safety, and texture. General Information links to culinary schools, education, food online ordering, and restaurants. Comprehensive sites included books, newspapers, journals, libraries, glossary, and government resources. Food and Ingredients links to sites on baked products, beverages, carbohydrates, grains and cereals, dairy products, eggs and egg products, fish and seafood, gums, lipids and fat replacers, meat and poultry, protein, starch, and sugar and sweetners.

HungerWeb
<http://nutrition.tufts.edu/academic/hungerweb/>

HungerWeb is for anyone using the Internet to help find solutions to hunger at the global, national, community, or household level. The site is divided into six sections. The first section provides links to an overview of hunger-related information in the United States and throughout the world. The second section provides links to agencies, associations, and organizations focusing on hunger. News Alerts and Periodicals provide links to current developments in hunger research and links to full-text magazines and journals relating to agriculture and hunger. Links to research centers are the fourth section. Tools provides links to sites that have education and training, statistics and datasets, and maps and mapping tools to support anti-hunger efforts. The last section links to employment opportunities. HungerWeb is produced by the Gerald J. and Dorothy R. Friedman School of Nutrition Science and Policy at Tufts University.

Nutrition.gov
<http://www.nutrition.gov/>

This site is a gateway to information on nutrition, healthy eating, physical activity, and food safety for consumers, educators, and health professionals. Searchers may conduct keyword searches or browse by subject, age group, or audience for the information. Other subjects included are dietary supplements, diseases and disorders, food allergy, food composition, food and nutrition assistance, food safety, nutrition recommendations, shopping, cooking and meal planning, sports and exercise, and weight control.

USDA/FDA Foodborne Illness Education Center
<http://www.nal.usda.gov/foodborne/index.html>

This site provides information about foodborne illness prevention, such as food safety education and training materials, food safety links, and other links for consumers, educators, and professionals. Food Safety Links highlights topic areas such as consumer information, foodborne illness statistics, foodborne pathogens, food safety clip art, retail food safety, seafood, and more.

USDA National Nutrient Database
<http://www.nal.usda.gov/fnic/foodcomp/>

This site, also know as the USDA's Food Composition Data, provides complete nutrition information for a wide variety of foods. The information is provided by the Nutrient Data Laboratory of the USDA. This is the primary entrance to USDA National Nutrient Database for Standard Reference, Release 17 which was published in 2004. The site is searchable by keyword and by specific tables. The entries provide a complete listing of what's in our food products from proximates, vitamins, minerals, lipids, amino acids, and other substances. This site provides useful nutrition information to all from the general public to the research scientist.

www.FoodSafety.gov
<http://www.foodsafety.gov/>

This site provides a complete overview of food safety topics. All government agencies that provide food safety information are included. Sections include News & Safety Alerts, Consumer Advice, Reports of Illness and Product complaints, Foodborne Pathogens, Industry Assistance, National Food Safety Programs, and links to federal and state agencies. The site also provides a search engine to find detailed topics.

ANIMAL SCIENCE INCLUDING VETERINARY SCIENCE

Avian Sciences Net
<http://ag.ansc.purdue.edu/poultry/>

Avain Sciences Net links to all types of information on poultry. The publications link provides access to all types of poultry topics including biosecurity, avian development, broiler production, diseases and pests, egg production, farm management, and waste management.

Breeds of Livestock
<http://www.ansi.okstate.edu/breeds/>

This site is an encyclopedia about all breeds of livestock from throughout the world. Livestock included are cattle, goats, horse, sheep, swine, poultry, and other domesticated animals such as camels and reindeer. Entries provide a description of the breed, information about the breed, pictures of the animals, and references. This site was created by the Animal Science Department at Oklahoma State University.

Consultant
<http://www.vet.cornell.edu/consultant/consult.asp>

Consultant is a diagnostic support system for veterinary medicine. The purpose of this site is to help diagnose disorders in animals based on the visible symptoms. Searches may be done by signs or diagnosis and may be limited by species. Searches may be limited by species such as avian, canine, feline, bovine, equine, and porcine. The entries provide a short description of the disorder, the species it occurs in, and the signs and a short list of references but do not provide pictures of the disorder.

FDA Approved Animal Drug Products
<http://dil.vetmed.vt.edu/>

The FDA Approved Animal Drug Products, also known as the Green Book, provides information on all drugs legally available for veterinary use. Entries include trade names, sponsors, species, routes, dosage information, and the Code of Federal Regulations indications. This searchable database is maintained by the Drug Information Laboratory at Virginia Tech.

Links to Animal Genomics Research Web Sites and Database Resources
<http://www.genome.iastate.edu/resources/other.html>

This site provides links to genomics sites for agricultural animals and domestic animals. Animals included in this site are cattle, pigs, chickens, turkey, sheep, horse, goat, fish and shrimp, rabbit, cat, dog, mouse, rat, human, and fly. Sites provide information on the animal's genetics and genetic maps for the animals.

Merck Veterinary Manual
<http://www.merckvetmanual.com/mvm/index.jsp>

This manual has been a standard authoritative source for veterinary subjects for many years and is sponsored by Merck & Co. Inc. Over 12,000 indexed topics and over 1,200 illustrations are included and may be rapidly searched by topic, species, specialty, disease, and keyword. The table of contents is arranged first by anatomic systems, and specific conditions are located in the system that is primarily affected. Conditions that may affect more than one system are covered in the section Generalized Conditions. The second half of the Manual covers special topics or disciplines. An index locates entries alphabetically. The entries include a detailed description of the disorder with cross references to other articles in the *Merck Manual* that relate to the disorder.

NetVet
<http://netvet.wustl.edu/vet.htm>

NetVet links to many sites on the subjects of animals and veterinary medicine. Some of the sections in NetVet are the Career Information, Education, Specialties, Images, Government and Legal Sources, Specialties, and Organizations. Career Information provides links to resources for those exploring careers in veterinary medicine. Education provides links to Schools of Veterinary Medicine worldwide. Specialties provides links to information and equipment suppliers to veterinary specialists. Images provides links to pictures and videos. A link to the Electronic Zoo is included and this site provides information on all types of animals, domestic and exotic. NetVet and the Electronic Zoo are created and maintained by Ken Boschert, DVM, Washington University.

VetGate
<http://vetgate.ac.uk/>

VetGate offers free access to a searchable catalogue of quality reviewed Internet resources in Animal Health. VetGate entries are evaluated and annotated to provide links to only high quality information. VetGate is created by the University of Nottingham Greenfield Medical Library.

Virtual Livestock Library
<http://www.ansi.okstate.edu/library/>

This site provides links to information on many types of livestock. Beef cattle, dairy cattle, sheep, goats, horses, and swine are all included. Each section contains information about breeds, breed associations, collections of publications, commercial pages, cooperative extension programs, diseases, disorders and pests, genetics and selection, nutrition and feeding, production/husbandry, online magazines, reproduction, and software. Other resources included are academic information, agricultural software, animal welfare, cross species information, fairs and expos, online magazines, and youth information. The WWW Virtual Library for Dairy Production is included in this site.

CONCLUSION

The sites recommended in this article provide an introduction to the vast set of agricultural resources. The resources here represent the many fields of agricultural resources freely available to Internet users. Using these sites, users will find current information on all of agriculture's hot topics.

Health and Medical Resources: Information for the Consumer

Caryl Gray

SUMMARY. The sites reviewed in this article represent only a small fraction of the consumer health information sites available on the Web and are intended to be a starting point for locating authoritative, reliable health information. The first part of this article focuses on evaluation, since this is an important component of using information, particularly information located on the Internet. The second part of the paper reviews consumer-related Web sites arranged by categories: Comprehensive Sites; Directories/Portals; Government Sites; Association Sites; Drug Information; Alternative Medicine; Nutrition and Food Safety; and Other Health Issues. *[Article copies available for a fee from The Haworth Document Delivery Service: 1-800-HAWORTH. E-mail address: <docdelivery@haworthpress.com> Website: <http://www.HaworthPress.com> © 2006 by The Haworth Press, Inc. All rights reserved.]*

KEYWORDS. Consumer health information, Internet resources in consumer health

---

Caryl Gray is College Librarian for Agriculture and Life Sciences, Virginia Tech, University Libraries, PO Box 90001, Blacksburg, VA 24062-9001 (E-mail: cegray@vt.edu).

[Haworth co-indexing entry note]: "Health and Medical Resources: Information for the Consumer." Gray, Caryl. Co-published simultaneously in *Journal of Library Administration* (The Haworth Information Press, an imprint of The Haworth Press, Inc.) Vol. 44, No. 1/2, 2006, pp. 395-428; and: *Evolving Internet Reference Resources* (ed: William Miller, and Rita M. Pellen) The Haworth Information Press, an imprint of The Haworth Press, Inc., 2006, pp. 395-428. Single or multiple copies of this article are available for a fee from The Haworth Document Delivery Service [1-800-HAWORTH, 9:00 a.m. - 5:00 p.m. (EST). E-mail address: docdelivery@haworthpress.com].

INTRODUCTION

The American health care system has undergone rapid change during the last decade. The rising costs of medical care, along with advances in medical technology, have made it increasingly important for consumers to be well informed about their medical choices. Access to current information also facilitates discussion between physician and patient while making decisions concerning treatment options. The Internet provides a unique opportunity for consumers to have access to current medical information so that they can be active partners in their health care.[1] This was the introductory paragraph in my "Medical Resources: Information for the Consumer" article published in 2000. These words still have a ring of truth; however today there is even more information available on the Web and the number of Web sites continues to grow.

An article in the *JAMA* (*Journal of the American Medical Association*) cites several sources indicating that "more than half and as much as 80% of adults with Internet access use it for health care purposes."[2] (One of these sources was the Harris Poll Cyberchondriacs Update for 2002 <http://www.harrisinteractive.com/harris_poll/index.asp?PID=299>). The article also cites sources that indicate that the use of the Internet for health information may be lower. The authors of the article conducted a national survey between December 2001 and January 2002 to "examine the effects that the Internet and e-mail use has on users' knowledge about health care matters and their use of the health care system."[3] The results of the survey indicate that "approximately 40% of the respondents with Internet access reported using the Internet to look for advice or information about health or health care in 2001."[4]

Although the data reported in the article indicate ambiguity concerning the percentage of Internet users, the medical profession has recognized the fact that a significant number of consumers are seeking health information on the Internet. In an effort to help physicians guide their patients to credible Web-based information, the American College of Physicians (ACP) Foundation and the National Library of Medicine (NLM) have joined forces to encourage physicians to direct their patients to MedlinePlus®. This effort, the Information Rx Project, "will provide information and tools to assist physicians in referring their patients to an authoritative, user-friendly and commercial-free Internet site–MedlinePlus®–for patient-oriented information. The project will provide resource material to facilitate referrals to MedlinePlus® and will foster partnerships with libraries, consumer groups, and voluntary agencies to promote awareness of MedlinePlus® and local information sources."[5] The project was piloted in 2003 in Iowa and Georgia and a second pilot program has been launched in Virginia. More information on Information Rx can be found on the project's Web site <http://foundation.acponline.org/healthcom/info_rx.htm>.

Health information located on the Web should not be used in lieu of a consultation with a family physician or other health care provider. These words and other similar phrases will be included as a disclaimer on Web sites offering reliable health information (the lack of a disclaimer should be a cause for concern regarding the credibility of the site). The content of a disclaimer statement will vary from site to site, but the message is the same—**always** consult with your family physician or health care provider concerning the diagnosis and treatment of a specific medical condition or disease.

As an example, here is the disclaimer posted on the Healthfinder® Web site <http://www.healthfinder.gov/>:

All information provided on healthfinder® is general in nature. Please remember that information alone can't take the place of health care or human services you may need.

healthfinder® is an information and referral service only, and does not diagnose medical conditions, offer medical advice, or endorse specific products or services. Do not rely upon any of the information provided on this site for medical diagnosis or treatment. Please consult your primary health care provider about any personal health concerns.

Agencies or organizations listed on healthfinder® are included for informational use only, and inclusion does not imply endorsement by healthfinder® or the U.S. Department of Health and Human Services.

Also, healthfinder® does not control the content of the Internet sites or organizations listed.[6]

EVALUATION OF WEB SITES

Evaluate, Evaluate, Evaluate!

These are or should be the watchwords of all health information users, especially those who extensively use the Web to locate information.

Although one should always critically evaluate Web-based information using the generally accepted list of criteria (authority, coverage, objectivity, accuracy, and currency), it is particularly important to rigorously apply these criteria to Web sites offering medical information. The Medical Library Association (MLA) <http://www.mlanet.org/index.html> offers *Diagnosing Websites* <http://www.mlanet.org/resources/medspeak/meddiag.html>, which lists four criteria (authority, currency, objectivity, and audience) as a quick start to the evaluation process.

A User's Guide to Finding and Evaluating Health Information on the Web <http://www.mlanet.org/resources/userguide.html> "outlines the collective wisdom of medical librarians who surf the Web every day to discover quality information in support of clinical and scientific decision making by doctors, scientists, and other health practitioners."[7] This guide includes basic information on searching the Web for reliable medical information along with a detailed description of the evaluation criteria developed by medical librarians. The MLA site also includes a list of its *Top Ten Most Useful Consumer Health Websites* <http://www.mlanet.org/resources/userguide.html#5>.

In the *Complete Idiot's Guide to Online Medical Resources*, Joan Price presents an evaluation mnemonic that she developed with Shannon Entin. PILOT (**P**urpose, **I**nformation, **L**inks, **O**riginator, **T**imeliness) provides a checklist that can be easily applied as one evaluates a Web site.[8]

The Health on the Net Foundation (HON) <http://www.hon.ch>, based in Geneva, Switzerland, offers an additional "check-up" for reliable health information. The HONCode (Health on the Net Code of Conduct) was developed in response "to concerns expressed to the Foundation by members of the Net community, regarding the varying quality of medical and health information available on the World-Wide Web" and "defines a set of voluntary rules designed to help a Web site developer practice responsible self-regulation and to make sure a reader always knows the source and purpose of the information he or she is reading."[9] A list of the eight HONcode principles with detailed descriptions can be found on the HON Web site <http://www.hon.ch/HONcode/Conduct.html>. This HONcode "seal of approval" is another way for the consumer to verify the credibility of the information provided since the site displaying the icon has been reviewed and has accepted the international code of ethics. Clicking on the HONcode icon links to a page that displays the date of the site's initial review as well as current reviews (if applicable) and certifies that the site meets the principles of the code.

Identifying fraudulent health information can be challenging. The following sites, **Quackwatch** and **Operation Cure-All**, provide consumers with information about health fraud. *Quackwatch* <http://www. quackwatch.com>, a project of Dr. Stephen Barrett, M.D., was launched in December 1996. The purpose of the site is to "combat health-related frauds, myths, fads, and fallacies with a primary focus on quackery-related information that is difficult or impossible to get elsewhere."[10] The site includes an extensive list of articles on topics related to questionable medical practices; however one must scan down the page past information about Quackwatch, Dr. Barrett, and publications for sale before getting to the substance of this Web site. Each article link indicates when the information was posted to the site or updated. A search box at the top of the page facilitates the process of locating information within the site and the *Tips for Navigating Our Sites* <http://www. quackwatch.org/00AboutQuackwatch/navigate.html> provides an overview of the site and a topical index.

The National Council Against Health Fraud (NCAHF) <http://www. ncahf.org/> is also interested in "health fraud, misinformation, and quackery as public health problems."[11] Since NCAHF is a non-profit organization, the primary function of this site focuses on encouraging consumers to become involved in the Council's mission. Although this site includes little content other than position papers, there is a link to the archives of *Consumer Health Digest* (2001-2004), a weekly e-mail newsletter <http://www.ncahf.org/digest04/index.html> edited by Dr. Stephen Barrett.

"The Federal Trade Commission is targeting false and unsubstantiated health claims on the Internet through *Operation Cure-All* <http:// www.ftc.gov/cureall/>, a law enforcement and consumer education campaign."[12] The Consumer Information section of the site includes articles on specific medical fraud topics. Although the articles are not current (for example "Rx for Products that Claim to Prevent SARS? A Healthy Dose of Skepticism" was posted in May 2003), the site includes information of interest to consumers.

COMPREHENSIVE WEB SITES

MedlinePlus®
<http://medlineplus.gov/>

MedlinePlus® is a service of the National Library of Medicine (NLM) and the National Institutes of Health (NIH). The site, also available in Spanish <http://medlineplus.gov/spanish/>, includes information on diseases and conditions from the NIH and other reliable sources. MedlinePlus® is easy to navigate from the home page as well as from secondary pages since the navigation tabs for the primary topic areas appear throughout the site. A search box provides an option to quickly search for information on a specific topic.

Links to primary topic areas: Health Topics; Drug Information; Medical Encyclopedia; Dictionary; News; and Other Resources are listed on the left-hand side of the home page. The center of the home page is devoted to current news and a featured site. The right-hand side of the home page is devoted to links to Interactive Tutorials, Clinical Trials.gov, and NIH Senior Health. The information available on MedlinePlus® is described below.

- Health Topics–an "a to z list" of over "650 topics related to diseases, conditions, and wellness."[13] Each topic page includes a contents list for the page (for ease of navigation), a link to PubMed (a pre-formatted search locates recent articles on the topic), and links to related topic pages as well as links to appropriate Interactive Tutorials.
- Drug Information–"information on thousands of prescription and over-the-counter medications is provided through two drug resources–MedMaster™, a product of the American Society of Health-System Pharmacists (ASHP), and the USP DI® Advice for the Patient®, a product of the United States Pharmacopeia (USP)."[14]
- Directories–information to assist the consumer in the search for a doctor, hospital, dentist, or other health care provider.
- Other Resources–access to libraries and health organizations as well as databases available through NIH or NLM. The libraries link may be of particular interest to a consumer who needs to identify a library that provides service to residents of the community, region, or state.
- Interactive Tutorials–located on the right-hand side of the home page provide access to over "165 slideshows with sound and pictures."[15] These slideshows are arranged by topics: Diseases and Conditions; Tests and Diagnostic Procedures; Surgery and Treatment Procedures; and Prevention and Wellness. A special Flash plug-in is required to view the tutorials. Each tutorial provides a clear explanation of the topic in layman's language. The user can

either choose to work through the entire tutorial or select only the parts of interest. Viewing these tutorials gives the consumer a general understanding of a specific disease or procedure and may help a patient formulate questions to be asked during an appointment.

InteliHealth
<http://www.intelihealth.com/IH/ihtIH/WSIHW000/408/408.html>

InteliHealth is sponsored by Aetna in partnership with Harvard Medical School. The site accepts advertisements; however they are clearly marked and are separate from consumer health content. The site is easy to navigate by browsing one of the main categories or by using one of two search boxes. One search box is devoted to searching for a drug name while the other can be used to search for a specific topic.

An alphabetical list organizes information on specific diseases and conditions. The Healthy Lifestyle category includes information on complementary and alternative medicine, fitness, nutrition, and weight management, as well as health issues related to the work environment. Your Health provides access to information about health issues related to children, men, women, and seniors and Look It Up includes an extensive "A to Z" list of health issues and a medical dictionary. A Drug Resource Center provides information on prescription and over-the-counter medications. The Drug Resource Center also includes a searchable drug database as well as patient advisories, and information on drug interactions.

The site has several interactive tools including illustrations, assessments, quizzes, and a breast self exam video. The Body Mass Index Calculator, Desk Exercises, and nutrition resources will be helpful to those interested in weight loss. The "Ballpark Chow" tool is especially fun and informative since one can calculate the calories of foods typically consumed at a baseball game or other sporting event.

Health A to Z–Your Family Health Site
<http://www.healthatoz.com/healthatoz/Atoz/default.jsp>

This is the consumer health component of the Health A to Z–*Your e-health Solution* <http://www.healthatoz.com/>. The content is arranged under clearly labeled tabs with "roll-over" menus to list specific topics. These tabs also appear at the top of secondary pages for ease of navigation. The only label that does not clearly indicate content is "Channels" but the roll-over menu lists specific topic areas related to women's, men's, children's, and seniors' health, as well as parenting. "The Health A to Z Encyclopedia offers thorough and reader-friendly articles about hundreds of diseases, health issues, and medical developments. Each article is authoritative and specific, with references for further study."[16] In addition to these articles, special centers for cancer, mental health, and the heart provide access to more in-depth information.

Access to the Dashboard, Health Manager, and Personal Health Records sections of the site is restricted to registered users (registration is free). Consumers may find the *Personal Health Record* section a useful place to store personal health information as well as schedule e-mail reminders for medical appointments and prescription refills.

MayoClinic.com
<http://www.mayoclinic.com/index.cfm>

This site is owned by the Mayo Foundation for Medical Education and Research. The guidelines for the site request that the following statement be used to describe the site:

> Mayo Clinic Health Information's award-winning consumer Web site offers health information, and self-improvement and disease management tools. MayoClinic.com's medical experts and editorial professionals bring you access to the knowledge and experience of Mayo Clinic for all of your consumer health information needs, from cancer, diabetes and heart disease to nutrition, exercise and pregnancy.[17]

The content for this well organized site can be viewed with little or no scrolling. The information is organized by categories which are clearly displayed across the top of the page: Diseases and Conditions; Healthy Living; Drugs and Supplements; Health Tools; My Health Interests (registration required); and Books and Newsletters. A "roll-over" displays expanded information for each category. For example, the Diseases and Conditions category includes links to the A to Z list (which also appears on the home page), a list of disease and condition centers, and a list of health decision guides. In addition to these broad topics, a search box is located at the top of the page to facilitate searching. The topic categories and the search box appear on all secondary pages which makes it easy to navigate the site.

There are no advertisements on the home page for MayoClinic.com; however a limited number do appear on secondary pages. All advertisements are clearly marked and a link to the site's advertising and sponsorship policy appears below each ad.

HealthCentral
<http://www.healthcentral.com>

HealthCentral can be easily navigated by using topic tabs (women's health, men's health, diet, kid's health, and seniors' health) located at the top of the page. These tabs do not appear on the secondary pages, making it difficult to move to another section of the site without returning to the home page. However, the search box, the Topic Centers list, and the Consumer Health Information list do appear on each page within the site. HealthCentral, originally co-founded by Dr. Dean Edell, whose name still appears prominently on the site, was acquired by MD Choice, Inc. <http://www.mdchoice.com/> in December 2001. Although it was difficult to locate the "About Us" information for this site, the HONCode logo does appear on the site (latest review by HON is April 2003). Advertisements are clearly marked and located either at the top of the page or along the right side.

Healthlink+Plus
<http://www.healthlinkplus.org/default.asp>

This site was developed by the Public Library of Charlotte & Mecklenburg County (NC) to provide access to the most comprehensive, authoritative, and timely health and medical information through a user-friendly gateway on the Internet (the site is also available in Spanish). The information on the site is arranged under the following headings: Health Topics; Diseases and Conditions; and Reference and Research. An additional category, Piedmont Resources, provides residents of the area with information specific to the Piedmont region of North Carolina.

WebMD Health
<http://my.webmd.com/webmd_today/home/default>

WebMD Health is the consumer health information site from WebMD <http://www.webmd.com/>. Although some scrolling is required to view all the content on the home page, a navigation bar on the left-hand side of the page provides access to specific topics which are similar to the topics available on other comprehensive sites. Most of the information on the site is "free"; however membership provides access to personalized services including newsletters and e-mail alerts.

DIRECTORIES/PORTALS

Web directories bring together sites on a common topic from a variety of domains (.gov, .org, .com, .net). Since these directories usually have a hierarchical subject structure, it is easy to locate numerous Web sites on a specific topic. Most directories include a brief overview of the information included in the major categories and in the sub-categories and in some cases the selected Web sites have been critically evaluated.

About.com–Health and Fitness
<http://www.about.com/health/>

This is an excellent example of a well organized Web directory. The Health and Fitness Channel is subdivided into specific areas of interest (Alternative/Complementary Medicine, Disabilities, Diseases/Conditions, Fitness/Wellness, Medicine/Allied Health, Mental Health, Recovery/Addiction, and Women's Health) and each of these sub-categories is more narrowly focused on specific health topics. Each topic page has been created by a Guide, who has been carefully selected by About.com. The Guide for each topic page is clearly identified and there is always a link to additional information about the guide and his or her credentials.

Internet Public Library (IPL)
<http://www.ipl.org/>

Internet Public Library (IPL) "is a public service organization and learning/teaching environment at the University of Michigan, School of Information."[18] The IPL focuses on several areas as part of its mission. The first area is service and the IPL "provides library services to Internet users by finding, evaluating, selecting, organizing, describing, and creating information resources; and direct assistance to individuals."[19] The Internet Public Library–Health and Medical Sciences <http://www.ipl.org/div/subject/browse/hea00.00.00> is another excellent example of a well organized, topic specific list of evaluated Web resources. The alphabetical arrangement makes it easy to locate information. In addition, the search box (which appears on all pages) provides three search options: search this collection, search all of IPL, and advanced search.

Hardin MD
<http://www.lib.uiowa.edu/hardin/md/index.html>

This site is a service of the University of Iowa Hardin Library of Health Sciences. Hardin Meta Directory of Internet Health Resources is a searchable "directory of directories"[20] and the content is arranged by "Subject Clusters" and an A to Z list of all subjects (cross references and see also references are included). A directory of medical pictures enhances the value to this site.

HealthWeb
<http://www.healthweb.org>

HealthWeb "is a collaborative project of the health sciences libraries of the Greater Midwest Region (GMR) of the National Network of Libraries of Medicine (NN/LM) and those of the Committee for Institutional Cooperation."[21] In addition to providing "access to evaluated non-commercial, health-related, Internet-accessible resources,"[22] the site also includes educational materials for the Internet user. The User Guides <http://www.healthweb.org/userguides.cfm> include articles on accessing Medline, evaluating Web information, and searching the Internet. In addition to the alphabetical list of topics, the site can be searched using either a basic or an advanced search option.

Infomine (Scholarly Internet Resource Collection)
<http://infomine.ucr.edu/>

Infomine "is a virtual library of Internet resources relevant to faculty, students, and research staff at the university level. It contains useful Internet resources such as databases, electronic journals, electronic books, bulletin boards, mailing lists, online library card catalogs, articles, directories of researchers, and many other types of information."[23] This collection of Web resources is arranged by broad topic areas and is searchable. Consumer health information is part of the Biological, Agricultural, and Medical topic area.

Librarian's Index to the Internet
<http://lii.org/search?basic_search=1>

This site "is a searchable, annotated subject directory of more than 14,000 Internet resources selected and evaluated by librarians for their usefulness to users of public libraries. LII is used by both librarians and the general public as a reliable and efficient guide to Internet resources."[24] The general category on Health <http://lii.org/search/file/health> is divided into topics from Air Travel to Women's Health. Several topics such as Death and Dying, Human Body, and Women's Health appear in bold-face type indicating that the topic has been sub-divided into narrower subjects.

NOAH: New York Online Access to Health
<http://www.noah-health.org/>

NOAH is the product of "four New York City library organizations that joined forces to establish a single Web site to provide end-users a place on the World Wide Web to reach reliable consumer health information. The organizations: The City University of New York Office of Library Services (CUNY); the Metropolitan New York Library Council (METRO); The New York Academy of Medicine Library (NYAM); and The New York Public Library (NYPL)–later joined by the Queens Borough Public Library and the Brooklyn Public Library–had as a goal the development of a Web site which would provide health care information easily accessible and understandable to the layperson."[25] The content of this well-organized searchable site is available in English and Spanish. An added enhancement for the visually impaired is an option to change font sizes on all of the secondary pages.

GOVERNMENT SITES

Departments and subordinate units within the Federal government also provide access to health information of interest to the consumer. Many of these sites are linked from comprehensive sites such as MedlinePlus®; however it is worthwhile to highlight a few selected sites.

Agency for Healthcare Research and Quality
<http://www.ahcpr.gov/>

This is a unit of the Department of Health and Human Services with a mission "to improve the quality, safety, efficiency, and effectiveness of health care for all Americans."[26] The Consumer and Patients section of this site includes a series of pathfinders to help consumers make informed decisions about health care. The site also includes a list of selected resources that are available in Spanish.

Centers for Disease Control and Prevention
<http://www.cdc.gov/>

The CDC is another unit of the Department of Health and Human Services. (Information on the CDC site is also available in Spanish.) The Health and Safety Topics section of this site includes links to information of interest to consumers. In addition to the traditional topics related to health care, the site also includes information on:

- *Birth Defects* <http://www.cdc.gov/node.do/id/0900f3ec8000dffe>. Information on current research as well as tips for healthy pregnancy.
- *Disabilities* <http://www.cdc.gov/node.do/id/0900f3ec8000e01a>. Information on developmental disabilities related to birth defects and traumatic brain injuries.
- *Emergency Preparedness and Response* <http://www.bt.cdc.gov>.
- *Environmental Health* <http://www.cdc.gov/node.do/id/0900f3ec8000e044>. Information on environmental conditions that affect health.
- *Genetics and Genomics* <http://www.cdc.gov/node.do/id/0900f3ec8000e2b5>. Information on genetics, family history, and susceptibility to disease.
- *Health Promotion* <http://www.cdc.gov/node.do/id/0900f3ec80059b1a>. Information on changing or adopting lifestyles to promote health.
- *Injury and Violence* <http://www.cdc.gov/node.do/id/0900f3ec8000e539>. Iinformation on preventing injuries.
- *Traveler's Health* <http://www.cdc.gov/travel/>. Information of specific interest to travelers: international health alerts; vaccination requirements; food and water safety; and hints for traveling with children.

- *Vaccines & Immunizations* <http://www.cdc.gov/node.do/id/0900f3ec8000e2f3>. Information on vaccine research and vaccine preventable diseases as well as reports on safety and adverse effects of vaccines.
- *Workplace Safety and Health* <http://www.cdc.gov/node.do/id/0900f3ec8000ec09>. Information about health and safety issues in the workplace and how to create a safe work environment.

ClinicalTrials.gov
<http://clinicaltrials.gov/>

This site "provides regularly updated information about federally and privately supported clinical research in human volunteers. ClinicalTrials. gov gives you information about a trial's purpose, who may participate, locations, and phone numbers for more details."[27] One can either search the database for specific clinical trial or browse by condition, sponsor, or status.

Combined Health Information Database (CHID)
<http://chid.nih.gov/>

CHID is a collaborative effort of several health-related agencies in the Federal Government. The database includes not only bibliographic citations and abstracts for health promotion and education materials, but also information on the availability of the cited references. The database currently includes the following topic areas: AIDS, STD, and TB Education; Alzheimer's Disease; Complementary and Alternative Medicine; Deafness and Communication Disorders; Diabetes; Digestive Diseases; Kidney and Urologic Diseases; Maternal and Child Health; Medical Genetics and Rare Disorders; Oral Health; and Weight Control. The content of the database is updated quarterly.

Healthfinder
<http://www.healthfinder.gov/>

Healthfinder is a well-organized consumer health site developed by the Department of Health and Human Services with the assistance of other agencies of the Federal government. The Health Library includes information on wellness, diseases and conditions, and other health issues, as well as links to medical dictionaries (including one in multiple languages) and drug information. Just for You organizes information by gender, age, race, and ethnic origin, and includes information for caregivers and parents. The Organizations section includes links to selected Federal, state, non-profit, and association Web sites. The link to state agencies is particularly useful since consumers frequently need to locate information about health-related services in their state. The information on this site is available in Spanish.

National Cancer Institute
<http://www.nci.nih.gov/>

This site provides access to a wealth of cancer information in English as well as Spanish. Cancer Topics includes a list of common types of cancer with information about treatment options, clinical trials, and current research, as well as information on prevention and causes and screening and testing and a link to current literature using the PubMed database. In addition to the list of common cancers, there is also an A to Z list of cancers. The Clinical Trials section of the site can be searched to locate information on trials for specific cancers, and the search can also be limited to geographic area.

National Center for Health Statistics (NCHS)
<http://www.cdc.gov/nchs>

NCHS is a unit of the Center for Disease Control and Prevention which collects and disseminates vital health statistical data. Although the data available from the NCHS is of primary interest to researchers, public health policy makers, faculty, and students, consumers will find relevant information including a guide to locating birth, death, marriage, and divorce certificates; information on the prevalence of obesity; and links to a wealth of statistical data. The information on the site is available in Spanish. For an extensive review of this site, read the review by Nancy Allen in *C&RL News* <http://www.bowdoin.edu/~samato/IRA/reviews/issues/feb03/health.html>.

National Institute of Mental Health (NIMH)
<http://www.nimh.nih.gov/>

National Institute of Mental Health (NIMH) is a unit of the National Institutes of Health. The Health Information section provides links to information about specific mental diseases from anxiety disorders to schizophrenia. The specific topic pages for each disease include a brief definition or overview, a list of signs and symptoms, and treatments as well as links to additional information in MedlinePlus® in English and Spanish. There are also links to publications such as booklets and fact sheets published by NIMH. The Clinical Trials section provides information on current trials and research related to mental diseases.

Brad Matthies wrote an extensive review of the site for *C&RL News* <http://www.ala.org/ala/acrlbucket/candrlnews/internetreviews/200407/nimh.htm>.

ASSOCIATION SITES

Association sites including professional medical association Web sites often have a section devoted to consumer health information. Associations and organizations that have been established to support research and awareness of a specific disease also provide sources of information. However, the consumer needs to keep in mind that one of the primary functions of these organizations is to raise funds. A search of the Web using one of several Internet search engines will locate the site for most of these associations. The *Encyclopedia of Associations* (print resource) and *Associations Unlimited* (a subscribed electronic database from Thomson Gale) can also be used to locate information on associations and organizations. In addition to these resources, Healthfinder.gov/Organizations/Professional Organizations <http://www.healthfinder.gov/scripts/SearchOrgType.asp?OrgTypeID=14&show=1> provides access to an extensive list of carefully reviewed professional association and organization sites.

Professional

American Medical Association (AMA)
<*http://www.ama-assn.org/*>

For Patients <http://www.ama-assn.org/ama/pub/category/3158.html> provides information about the AMA, access to patient education information, and links to medical specialty and state medical association sites.

AMA Physician Select <http://dbapps.ama-assn.org/aps/amahg.htm> "provides basic professional information on virtually every licensed physician in the United States and its possessions, including more than 690,000 doctors of medicine (MD) and doctors of osteopathy or osteopathic medicine (DO)."[28]

American Academy of Family Physicians
<http://www.aafp.org/>

   Familydoctor.org <http://familydoctor.org/> includes topic areas with information specifically for men, women, seniors, parents, and children, an A to Z list of diseases and conditions, and a "Health Tip of the Day."

American Academy of Pediatrics
<http://www.aap.org/>

   Parenting Corner <http://www.aap.org/parents.html> provides helpful information for parents including children's mental health, immunization, and car safety seats.
   Health Topics <http://www.aap.org/topics.html> includes information on health development as well as specific childhood diseases and conditions.

American Dental Association
<http://www.ada.org/>

   Your Oral Health <http://www.ada.org/public/index.asp> provides consumer health information and resources to help manage your dental care as well as games and puzzles to help prepare a child for a dental visit.

SPECIFIC DISEASES AND CONDITIONS

   This section includes a selected list of voluntary health organizations which support research on specific diseases. Healthfinder.gov/Organizations/Non-Profit Organizations <http://www.healthfinder.gov/scripts/SearchOrgType.asp?OrgTypeID=2&page=0&show=1> lists over 600 Web sites for a wide variety of associations which support research, provide information about, and advocate for patients with specific diseases or conditions. These association Web sites also encourage individuals to become involved locally and to participate in fundraising events to support continued research.

Alzheimer's Association
<http://www.alz.org/overview.asp>

   This site provides general information about Alzheimer's (warning signs, diagnosis, stages, and treatments) as well as information for those diagnosed with the disease and for their caregivers. The site includes links to information about research and services, and links to local chapters and support groups. The site also includes an index to information available in foreign languages.

American Cancer Association
<http://www.cancer.org/docroot/home/index.asp>

This site provides information for patients and survivors, as well as those interested in prevention and early detection. There are also interactive tools to help one explore and make decisions about treatment options and to search for clinical trials.

American Diabetes Association
<http://www.diabetes.org/home.jsp>

This site provides information of interest to those with or at risk for developing diabetes. About Diabetes includes a general overview of the disease and classifications (Type1 diabetes, Type 2 diabetes, and gestational diabetes), symptoms, and the relationship of diabetes to heart disease and stroke. The Nutrition and Recipes, Weight Loss and Exercise, Diabetes Prevention, and Diabetes Research sections are also of interest.

American Heart Association
<http://www.americanheart.org/presenter.jhtml?identifier=1200000>

The American Heart Association site provides information about warning signs of heart disease and other related diseases and conditions. The Healthy Lifestyle section includes information on diet and nutrition along with fitness and exercise. The Heart and Stroke Encyclopedia provides brief information about topics related to heart disease and stroke with links to related information within the site as well as other sites. The American Stroke Association <http://www.strokeassociation. org/presenter.jhtml?identifier=1200037> is a division of the American Heart Association and the organization of these sites mirrors each other.

American Lung Association
<http://www.lungusa.org/site/pp.asp?c=dvLUK9O0E&b=22542>

The American Lung Association is the oldest voluntary health organization. It was founded in 1904 to fight tuberculosis and it continues to support research for all types of lung diseases as well as advocate against smoking and other environmental health issues.[29] As with other voluntary health organization sites, the American Lung Association site provides information on specific lung diseases and conditions, treatments, and support for patients. The site also provides information on air quality.

DRUG INFORMATION

In addition to locating information on specific diseases and conditions, consumers are also interested in finding reliable information about drugs. In "Drug Information: Where to Look for Drug Information on the Internet" <http://www.ala.org/ala/acrl/acrlpubs/crlnews/backissues2001/julyaugust2/druginformation.htm>, Mignon Adams reviewed several Web sites that provide reliable drug information. Selected sites included in the article are listed below.

Food and Drug Administration
<http://www.fda.gov/>

This is the primary site for information related to public health and the safety of food, drugs, medical devices, cosmetics, and other products. This site is well-organized with links to information about the products that the FDA regulates, current news, as well as information of interest to specific groups (consumers, health professionals, health educators, teens, and an interactive page for children). The Orange Book <http://www.fda.gov/cder/ob/default.htm> is an online resource for the "therapeutic equivalents" (generic drugs that can replace a brand-name drug)."[30] FDA Consumer <http://www.fda.gov/fdac/> is an online magazine that includes articles on new drugs as well as other health and safety issues related to the FDA.

People's Pharmacy
<http://www.healthcentral.com/peoplespharmacy/peoplespharmacy.cfm>

People's Pharmacy includes articles (Drug Library) on frequently prescribed drugs in language that a layperson can easily understand and articles on home remedies (Herb Library). The article also reviewed several sites that provide information on natural products. Since the passage of the Dietary Supplements Act (1994), "the FDA is no longer responsible for assuring the safety of the ingredients in dietary supplements before they are marketed."[31] Since sites that promote natural products are not always reliable sources of information, it can be a challenge to locate reliable information on these products. The following Web sites for information on natural products were included in Ms. Adams' review article.

HerbMed®
<http://herbmed.org>

HerbMed is provided by the Alternative Medicine Foundation and is an "interactive, electronic herbal database–provides hyperlinked access to the scientific data underlying the use of herbs for health. It is an impartial, evidence-based information resource for professionals, researchers, and general public."[32]

National Center for Complementary and Alternative Medicine
<http://nccam.nih.gov/>

This is part of the National Institutes of Health. The Health Information section of this site includes links to information on understanding complementary and alternative medicine as well as treatment options and alerts.

International Bibliographic Information on Dietary Supplements (IBIDS) Database
<http://ods.od.nih.gov/Health_Information/IBIDS.aspx>

The IBIDS Database "provides access to bibliographic citations and abstracts from published, international, and scientific literature on dietary supplements."[33]

Center for Drug Evaluation and Research
<http://www.fda.gov/cder/index.html>

This site also provides access to drug information. The well-organized site includes links to consumer information, a list of recently added information as well as "Quick Links" to Drugs@FDA, the Orange Book, and other FDA sites of interest. For an extensive review of this site, please read the review by Kate Peterson in *C&RL News* <http://www.ala.org/ala/acrlbucket/candrlnews/internetreviews/200406/drug.htm>.

ALTERNATIVE MEDICINE

Complementary and alternative medicine (CAM) is also a topic of interest to consumers. The National Center for Complementary and Alternative Medicine defines complementary and alternative medicine as a group of diverse medical and health care systems, practices, and products that are not presently considered to be part of conventional medicine.[34] Reliable Web resources on this topic were reviewed in an article by Julia Nims, "Complementary and alternative medicine: an overview of nontraditional medicine on the Web" <http://www.ala.org/ala/acrl/acrlpubs/crlnews/backissues2002/september/complementary.htm>. Sites reviewed in the article include the following.

Alternative Medicine: Health Care Information Resources
<http://www-hsl.mcmaster.ca/tomflem/altmed.html>

This is an annotated list of Web sites collected and maintained by the Health Sciences Library at McMaster University.

Alternative Medicine Homepage
<http://www.pitt.edu/~cbw/altm.html>

This site was "created and is maintained by a medical librarian, Charles B. Wessel, M.L.S., Health Sciences Library System, University of Pittsburgh."[35]

Ask NOAH About: Complementary and Alternative Medicine
<http://www.noah-health.org/en/alternative/index.html>

This site is part of the New York Online Access to Health.

Dr. Weil.com
<http://www.drweil.com/u/Home/>

Dr. Weil.com is the creation of Dr. Andrew Weil, a physician and "clinical professor of internal medicine and the founder and director of the Program in Integrative Medicine (PIM) at the University of Arizona in Tucson."[36] The site provides access to information on home remedies and nutrition. There are also discussion forums, electronic newsletters, and daily tips. Although the site includes advertisements, they are clearly marked.

MedlinePlus®–Alternative Medicine
<http://www.nlm.nih.gov/medlineplus/alternativemedicine.html>

This is one of the health topic pages available on MedlinePlus®.

CAM on PubMed
<http://www.nlm.nih.gov/nccam/camonpubmed.html>

CAM on PubMed provides easy access to articles on Complementary and Alternative Medicine in PubMed since a search of this database is automatically limited to the topic.

M. D. Anderson Cancer Center: Complementary/Integrative Medicine (University of Texas)
<http://www.mdanderson.org/departments/cimer/>

This site provides access to educational resources that can assist patients and physicians to integrate appropriate complementary therapies with traditional cancer treatments.

Richard and Hinda Rosenthal Center for Complementary and Alternative Medicine
<http://www.rosenthal.hs.columbia.edu/>

This site is affiliated with Columbia University. The CAM Resources and Information Resources link includes information of interest to consumers.

Alternative Medicine Foundation
<http://www.amfoundation.org/>

The Alternative Medicine Foundation is a non-profit organization established in March of 1998 to provide access to reliable information for consumers and health care professionals on information about alternative medicine. *HerbMed®* is a project of the foundation.

NUTRITION AND FOOD SAFETY

Eating a well-balanced diet is an integral part of a healthy lifestyle. Although many of the sites included in this article link to information on diet and nutrition, the following sites focus on the topic.

Food and Nutrition Information (American Dietetic Association)
<http://www.eatright.org/Public/NutritionInformation/92.cfm>

This site provides links to articles and brochures available through the American Dietetic Association (ADA) as well as links to government resources.

Food and Nutrition Information Center
<http://www.nal.usda.gov/fnic/>

The Food and Nutrition Information Center is a resource of the National Agricultural Library. The site is "a directory to credible, accurate, and practical resources for consumers, nutrition and health professionals, educators and government personnel."[37]

Food Safety
<http://www.foodsafety.gov>

Food Safety is a comprehensive site linking to a wealth of information related to food safety. This well-organized site provides information on the safe handling of food (Consumer Advice) as well as information on food-borne pathogens, food safety programs, and federal and state agencies concerned with food safety.

Nutrition.gov
<http://www.nutrition.gov/>

Nutrition.gov provides access to food and nutrition information. "It serves as a gateway to reliable information on nutrition, healthy eating, physical activity, and food safety for consumers, educators and health professionals."[38] Nutrition.gov was reviewed by Jennifer McKinnell in *C&RL News* <http://www.bowdoin.edu/~samato/IRA/reviews/issues/may03/nutrition.html>.

OTHER HEALTH ISSUES

Health information for specific populations (seniors, men, women, and children) is also of interest to consumers. Although the reviewed comprehensive consumer health sites and the directory sites provide access to information for these populations, the following sites will also be of interest.

NIH SeniorHealth.gov
<http://nihseniorhealth.gov>

The NIH SeniorHealth.gov site was developed by the National Institute on Aging (NIA) and the National Library of Medicine (NLM) to provide reliable health information to seniors, their family and friends, and caregivers. The American Geriatric Society also provided "expert and independent review of the material on the Web site."[39] The site is easy to navigate and to enhance its usability for seniors; there are options to increase the font size, change the contrast, and enable the speech mode for those who are visually impaired. Information for each topic is presented in an easy to read format and includes a general overview of the topic, frequently asked questions, and links to additional information in MedlinePlus®. The site also includes open-captioned videos.

American Association for Retired Persons (AARP)
<http://www.aarp.org/>

AARP provides access to a variety of information for individuals over 50 years of age and serves as an advocate on issues related to the health and welfare of seniors. Two sections of the site, Health and Wellness and Care and Family, provide access to information on keeping active, eating well, caregiving, housing options, as well as Medicare and prescription drug information.

ElderCare Online
<http://www.ec-online.net/>

ElderCare Online serves as a resource for information and support for caregivers. Although the site focuses on Alzheimer's disease and dementia, caregivers will find useful information on providing care for loved ones as well as taking care of themselves. This site was reviewed by Beth Chapman in *C&RL News* <http://www.bowdoin.edu/~samato/IRA/reviews/issues/apr01/elder.html>.

FOR MEN

Not for Men Only: The Male Health Center
<http://www.malehealthcenter.com/>

This site which specializes in men's health, was founded in 1989 by Dr. Kenneth A. Goldberg, a board-certified urologist. The *Not for Men Only* Web site includes overviews on several topics related to men's health, symptoms of diseases and conditions, and health and wellness. The Web site is a good place to begin. MedlinePlus® has an extensive list of resources on Men's Health Issues <http://www.nlm.nih.gov/medlineplus/menshealthissues.html> and one of the centers in the MayoClinic.com site is devoted to men's health.

FOR WOMEN

National Women's Health Information Center
<http://www.4woman.org/>

The National Women's Health Information Center is "a service of the Office on Women's Health in the Department of Health and Human Services."[40] This site is a gateway to a wide variety of women's health information from the Federal government and other sources. Special topic sections are used to organize information on areas such as breast-feeding, body image, girls' health, heart health, HIV/AIDS, mental health, minority women's health, and pregnancy. Another topic area of interest is men's health from the viewpoint of what women should know.

ELECTRONIC JOURNALS

PubMed Central
<http://www.pubmedcentral.nih.gov/>

PubMed Central "is the U.S. National Library of Medicine's free digital archive of biomedical and life sciences journal literature."[41] The archive is managed by the National Center for Biotechnology Information (NCBI). The archive can be searched either by using a basic search or by selecting the advanced search option <http://www.ncbi.nlm.nih.

gov/entrez/query.fcgi?db=PMC> which limits a MEDLINE search to articles available full text in PubMed Central.

Free Medical Journals.com
<http://www.freemedicaljournals.com/>

This is a list of medical journals that provide free access to articles either at the time of publication or after a specified time limit (six months to two years after publication). The list can be sorted by specialty or browsed by journal title. The list also includes foreign language journals including French, German, Spanish, and Portuguese.

NOTES

1. Gray, Caryl. "Medical resources information for the consumer: Helping you make informed decisions." *C&RL News* 61(2000): 995.

2. Baker, Laurence et al. "Use of the Internet and e-mail for health care information: Results from a national survey." *JAMA* 289(2000): 2400.

3. Ibid.

4. Ibid.

5. American College of Physicians: Health Communications: Information Rx Project. <http://foundation.acponline.org/healthcom/info_rx.htm>.

6. Healthfinder: Disclaimer. <http://www.healthfinder.gov/aboutus/disclaimer.asp>.

7. Medical Library Association: A Users' Guide to Finding and Evaluating Information on the Web: Introduction. <http://www.mlanet.org/resources/userguide.html#1>.

8. Price, p. 47.

9. Health on the Net Foundation: Initiatives and Services. <http://www.hon.ch/Project/HONcode.html>.

10. Quackwatch: Mission statement. <http://www.quackwatch.org/00AboutQuackwatch/mission.html>.

11. National Council Against Health Fraud. <http://www.ncahf.org/>.

12. Operation Cure-All. <http://www.ftc.gov/cureall/>.

13. MedlinePlus: About MedlinePlus. <http://www.nlm.nih.gov/medlineplus/aboutmedlineplus.html>.

14. MedlinePlus: Drug Information. <http://www.nlm.nih.gov/medlineplus/druginformation.html>.

15. MedlinePlus: Interactive Tutorials. <http://medlineplus.gov/>.

16. Health A to Z: Encyclopedia. <http://www.healthatoz.com/healthatoz/Atoz/ency/a_encyindex.jsp>.

17. MayoClinic.com: About this site: Our policies. <http://www.mayoclinic.com/agg.cfm?objectid=D926EC6B-C4B1-4492-B83323DECB1A07C9>.

18. Internet Public Library: Mission Statement and Goals. <http://www.ipl.org/div/about/>.

19. Ibid.

20. Hardin MD: About Hardin MD. <http://www.lib.uiowa.edu/hardin/md/about.html>.

21. HealthWeb: About Us. <http://www.healthweb.org>.

22. Ibid.

23. Infomine: About Infomine. <http://infomine.ucr.edu/?view=about>.

24. Librarians' Index to the Internet: About. <http://lii.org/search/file/about>.

25. NOAH: New York Online Access to Health: About NOAH. <http://www.noah-health.org/en/about/#History>.

26. Agency for Health Care Research and Quality: About AHRQ. <http://www.ahcpr.gov/about/>.

27. Clinical Trials.gov. <http://clinicaltrials.gov/>.

28. American Medical Association: AMA Physician Select. <http://dbapps.ama-assn.org/aps/amahg.htm>.

29. American Lung Association: About. <http://www.lungusa.org/site/pp.asp?c=dvLUK9O0E&b=22555>.

30. Adams, p. 701.

31. Ibid., p. 703.

32. HerbMed®. <http://herbmed.org>.

33. International Bibliographic Information on Dietary Supplements (IBIDS) Database. <http://ods.od.nih.gov/Health_Information/IBIDS.aspx>.

34. National Center for Complementary and Alternative Medicine: What is Complementary and Alternative Medicine (CAM)? <http://nccam.nih.gov/health/whatiscam/>.

35. Alternative Medicine Homepage: About. <http://www.pitt.edu/~cbw/about.html>.

36. Dr. Weil.com: About Dr. Weil. <http://www.drweil.com/u/Page/MeetDrWeil/>.

37. Food and Nutrition Information Center. <http://www.nal.usda.gov/fnic/>.

38. Nutrition.gov: About us. <http://www.nutrition.gov/index.php?mode=about>.

39. NIH SeniorHealth.gov: About. <http://nihseniorhealth.gov/about.html>.

40. National Women's Health Information Center: About. <http://www.4woman.org/about/index.htm>.

41. PubMed Central. <http://www.pubmedcentral.nih.gov/>.

WEBLIOGRAPHY

INTRODUCTION

American College of Physicians Foundation. Information Rx Project. <http://foundation.acponline.org/healthcom/info_rx.htm> (accessed on November 14, 2004).

Healthfinder. <http://www.healthfinder.gov/> (accessed on November 14, 2004).

Taylor, Humphrey. Harris Poll Cyberchondriacs Update for May 1, 2002. <http://www.harrisinteractive.com/harris_poll/index.asp?PID=299> (accessed November 30, 2004).

EVALUATION OF CONSUMER HEALTH WEB SITES

Consumer Health Digest. <http://www.ncahf.org/digest04/index.html> (accessed November 29, 2004).

Health Information on the Net Foundation. *Code of Conduct.* <http://www.hon.ch/HONcode/Conduct.html> (accessed on November 7, 2004).

Health Information on the Net Foundation. <http://www.hon.ch> (accessed on November 7, 2004).

Medical Library Association. *Diagnosing Websites.* <http://www.mlanet.org/resources/medspeak/meddiag.html> (accessed on November 7, 2004).

Medical Library Association. MLANET. <http://www.mlanet.org/index.html> (accessed on November 7, 2004).

Medical Library Association. *Top Ten Most Useful Consumer Health Websites.* <http://www.mlanet.org/resources/userguide.html#5> (accessed on November 7, 2004).

Medical Library Association. *A User's Guide to Finding and Evaluating Health Information on the Web.* <http://www.mlanet.org/resources/userguide.html> (accessed on November 7, 2004).

National Council Against Health Fraud. <http://www.ncahf.org/> (accessed on November 7, 2004).

Operation Cure-All. <http://www.ftc.gov/cureall/> (accessed on November 7, 2004).

Quackwatch. <http://www.quackwatch.com> (accessed on November 7, 2004).

Quackwatch. *Tips for Navigating Our Sites.* <http://www.quackwatch.org/00AboutQuackwatch/navigate.html> (accessed on November 7, 2004).

COMPREHENSIVE WEB SITES

HealthCentral. <http://www.healthcentral.com> (accessed on November 14, 2004).

HealthLink+Plus. <http://www.healthlinkplus.org/default.asp> (accessed on November 14, 2004).

Health A to Z: Your e-health Solution. <http://www.healthatoz.com/> (accessed on November 14, 2004).

Health A to Z: Your Family Health Site. <http://www.healthatoz.com/healthatoz/Atoz/default.jsp> (accessed on November 14, 2004).

InteliHealth. <http://www.intelihealth.com/IH/ihtIH/WSIHW000/408/408.html> (accessed on November 14, 2004).

MayoClinic.com. <http://www.mayoclinic.com/index.cfm> (accessed on November 14, 2004).

MD Choice, Inc. <http://www.mdchoice.com> (accessed on November 14, 2004).

MedlinePlus®. <http://www.medlineplus.gov/> (accessed on November 7, 2004).

MedlinePlus®. Spanish version. <http://medlineplus.gov/spanish/> (accessed on November 7, 2004).

WebMD. <http://www.webmd.com/> (accessed on November 14, 2004).

WebMD Health. <http://my.webmd.com/webmd_today/home/default> (accessed on November 14, 2004).

DIRECTORIES/PORTALS

About.com–Health and Fitness. <http://www.about.com/health/> (accessed on November 17, 2004).

Hardin MD. <http://www.lib.uiowa.edu/hardin/md/index.html> (accessed on November 18, 2004).

HealthWeb. <http://www.healthweb.org> (accessed on November 18, 2004).

HealthWeb. User Guides. <http://www.healthweb.org/userguides.cfm> (accessed on November 18, 2004).

Infomine: Scholarly Internet Resource Collection. <http://infomine.ucr.edu/> (accessed on November 18, 2004).

Internet Public Library: Health and Medical Sciences. <http://www.ipl.org/div/subject/browse/hea00.00.00> (accessed on November 18, 2004).

Internet Public Library. <http://www.ipl.org/> (accessed on November 18, 2004).

Librarians' Index to the Internet. <http://lii.org/search?basic_search=1> (accessed on November 18, 2004).

Librarians' Index to the Internet. <http://lii.org/search/file/health> (accessed on November 18, 2004).

NOAH: New York Online Access to Health. <http://www.noah-health.org/> (accessed on November 19, 2004).

GOVERNMENT SITES

Agency for Healthcare Research and Quality. <http://www.ahcpr.gov/> (accessed on November 19, 2004).

Allen, Nancy M. National Center for Health Statistics (review). *C&RL News* 64 (2003) 118. <http://www.bowdoin.edu/~samato/IRA/reviews/issues/feb03/health.html> (accessed on November 20, 2004).

Centers for Disease Control and Prevention. <http://www.cdc.gov/> (accessed on November 19, 2004).

Birth Defects. <http://www.cdc.gov/node.do/id/0900f3ec8000dffe> (accessed on November 19, 2004).

Disabilities. <http://www.cdc.gov/node.do/id/0900f3ec8000e01a> (accessed on November 19, 2004).

Emergency Preparedness and Response. <http://www.bt.cdc.gov> (accessed on November 19, 2004).

Environmental Health. <http://www.cdc.gov/node.do/id/0900f3ec8000e044> (accessed on November 19, 2004).

Genetics and Genomes. <http://www.cdc.gov/node.do/id/0900f3ec8000e2b5> (accessed on November 19, 2004).

Health Promotion. <http://www.cdc.gov/node.do/id/0900f3ec80059b1a> (accessed on November 19, 2004).

Injury and Violence. <http://www.cdc.gov/node.do/id/0900f3ec8000e539> (accessed on November 19, 2004).

Vaccines & Immunizations. <http://www.cdc.gov/node.do/id/0900f3ec8000e2f3> (accessed on November 19, 2004).

Traveler's Health. <http://www.cdc.gov/travel/> (accessed on November 19, 2004).

Workplace Safety and Health. <http://www.cdc.gov/node.do/id/0900f3ec8000ec09> (accessed on November 19, 2004).

Clinical Trials.gov. <http://clinicaltrials.gov/> (accessed on November 20, 2004).

Combined Health Information Database (CHID). <http://chid.nih.gov/> (accessed on November 20, 2004).

Healthfinder. <http://www.healthfinder.gov/> (accessed on November 7, 2004).

Matthies, Brad. National Institute of Mental Health (review). *C&RL News* 65 (2004): 390-391. <http://www.ala.org/ala/acrlbucket/candrlnews/internetreviews/200407/nimh.htm> (accessed on November 29, 2004).

National Center for Health Statistics (NCHS). <http://www.cdc.gov/nchs> (accessed on November 20, 2004).

National Institute of Mental Health. <http://www.nimh.nih.gov> (accessed on November 29, 2004).

ASSOCIATIONS/PROFESSIONAL

AMA Physician Select. <http://dbapps.ama-assn.org/aps/amahg.htm> (accessed on November 20, 2004).

American Academy of Family Physicians. <http://www.aafp.org/> (accessed on November 20, 2004).

American Academy of Pediatrics. Health Topics. <http://www.aap.org/topics.html> (accessed on November 20, 2004).

American Academy of Pediatrics. <http://www.aap.org/> (accessed on November 20, 2004).

American Academy of Pediatrics. Parenting Corner. <http://www.aap.org/parents.html> (accessed on November 20, 2004).

American Dental Association. <http://www.ada.org/> (accessed on November 20, 2004).

American Dental Association. Your Oral Health. <http://www.ada.org/public/index.asp> (accessed on November 20, 2004).

American Medical Association. <http://www.ama-assn.org/> (accessed on November 20, 2004).

American Medical Association. For Patients. <http://www.ama-assn.org/ama/pub/category/3158.html> (accessed on November 20, 2004).

Familydoctor.org. <http://familydoctor.org/> (accessed on November 20, 2004).

Healthfinder.gov/Organizations/Professional Organizations. <http://www.healthfinder.gov/scripts/SearchOrgType.asp?OrgTypeID=14&show=1> (accessed on November 20, 2004).

ASSOCIATIONS/DISEASES AND CONDITIONS

Alzheimer's Association. <http://www.alz.org/overview.asp> (accessed on November 24, 2004).

American Cancer Association. <http://www.cancer.org/docroot/home/index.asp> (accessed on November 24, 2004).

American Diabetes Association. <http://www.diabetes.org/home.jsp> (accessed on November 24, 2004).

American Heart Association. <http://www.americanheart.org/presenter.jhtml?identifier=1200000> (accessed on November 24, 2004).

American Lung Association. <http://www.lungusa.org/site/pp.asp?c=dvLUK9O0E&b=22542> (accessed on November 24, 2004).

American Stroke Association. <http://www.strokeassociation.org/presenter.jhtml?identifier=1200037> (accessed on November 24, 2004).

Healthfinder.gov/Organizations/Non-Profit Organizations. <http://www.healthfinder.gov/scripts/SearchOrgType.asp?OrgTypeID=2&page=0&show=1> (accessed on November 20, 2004).

DRUG INFORMATION

Adams, Mignon. "Drug Information: Where to look for drug information on the Internet." *C&RL News* 62 (2001):701-704. <http://www.ala.org/ala/acrl/acrlpubs/crlnews/backissues2001/julyaugust2/druginformation.htm> (accessed on November 20, 2004).

Center for Drug Evaluation and Research. <http://www.fda.gov/cder/index.html> (accessed on November 22, 2004).

FDA Consumer. <http://www.fda.gov/fdac/> (accessed on November 22, 2004).

Food and Drug Administration. <http://www.fda.gov/> (accessed on November 22, 2004).

Food and Drug Administration. Orange Book. <http://www.fda.gov/cder/ob/default.htm> (accessed on November 22, 2004).

HerbMed®. <http://herbmed.org> (accessed on November 22, 2004).

International Bibliographic Information on Dietary Supplements (IBIDS) Database. <http://ods.od.nih.gov/Health_Information/IBIDS.aspx> (accessed on November 22, 2004).

National Center for Complementary and Alternative Medicine. <http://nccam.nih.gov/> (accessed on November 22, 2004).

People's Pharmacy. <http://www.healthcentral.com/peoplespharmacy/peoplespharmacy.cfm> (accessed on November 22, 2004).

Peterson, Kate. Center for Drug Evaluation and Research (review). *C&RL News* 65 (2004):337. <http://www.ala.org/ala/acrlbucket/candrlnews/internetreviews/200406/drug.htm> (accessed on November 22, 2004).

ALTERNATIVE MEDICINE

Alternative Medicine Foundation. <http://www.amfoundation.org/> (accessed on November 22, 2004).

Alternative Medicine Homepage. <http://www.pitt.edu/~cbw/altm.html> (accessed on November 22, 2004).

Alternative Medicine: Health Care Information Resources. <http://www-hsl.mcmaster.ca/tomflem/altmed.html> (accessed on November 22, 2004).

Ask NOAH About: Complementary and Alternative Medicine. <http://www.noah-health.org/en/alternative/index.html> (accessed on November 22, 2004).

CAM on PubMed. <http://www.nlm.nih.gov/nccam/camonpubmed.html> (accessed on November 22, 2004).

Dr. Weil.com. <http://www.drweil.com/u/Home/> (accessed on November 22, 2004).

MedlinePlus®–Alternative Medicine. <http://www.nlm.nih.gov/medlineplus/alternativemedicine.html> (accessed on November 22, 2004).

M. D. Anderson Cancer Center: Complementary/Integrative Medicine (University of Texas). <http://www.mdanderson.org/departments/cimer/> (accessed on November 22, 2004).

Nims, Julia. "Complementary and alternative medicine: An overview of nontraditional medicine on the Web." *C&RL News* 63 (2002): 576-579, 589, 599 <http://www.ala.org/ala/acrl/acrlpubs/crlnews/backissues2002/september/complementary.htm> (accessed on November 22, 2004).

Richard and Hinda Rosenthal Center for Complementary and Alternative Medicine. <http://www.rosenthal.hs.columbia.edu/> (accessed on November 22, 2004).

NUTRITION AND FOOD SAFETY

American Dietetic Association. Food and Nutrition Information. <http://www.eatright.org/Public/NutritionInformation/92.cfm> (accessed on November 22, 2004).

Food and Nutrition Information Center. <http://www.nal.usda.gov/fnic/> (accessed on November 22, 2004).

Food Safety. <http://www.foodsafety.gov> (accessed on November 22, 2004).

McKinnell, Jennifer. Nutrition.gov (review). *C&RL News* 64 (2003):342-343. <http://www.bowdoin.edu/~samato/IRA/reviews/issues/may03/nutrition.html> (accessed on November 22, 2004).

Nutrition.gov. <http://www.nutrition.gov/> (accessed on November 22, 2004).

OTHER HEALTH ISSUES

For Seniors

American Association for Retired Persons (AARP). <http://www.aarp.org/> (accessed on November 23, 2004).

Chapman, Beth. ElderCare Online (review). *C&RL News* 62 (2001):442. <http://www.bowdoin.edu/~samato/IRA/reviews/issues/apr01/elder.html> (accessed on November 23, 2004).

ElderCare Online. <http://www.ec-online.net/> (accessed November 23, 2004).
NIH SeniorHealth.gov. <http://nihseniorhealth.gov/> (accessed on November 23, 2004).

For Men

MedlinePlus®–Men's Health Issues. <http://www.nlm.nih.gov/medlineplus/menshealthissues.html> (accessed on November 23, 2004).
Not for Men Only: The Male Health Center. <http://www.malehealthcenter.com/> (accessed on November 23, 2004).

For Women

National Women's Health Information Center. <http://www.4woman.org> (accessed on November 23, 2004).

ELECTRONIC JOURNALS

Free Medical Journals.com. <http://www.freemedicaljournals.com/> (accessed on November 23, 2004).
PubMed Central. <http://www.pubmedcentral.nih.gov/> (accessed on November 23, 2004).

BIBLIOGRAPHY

Adams, Mignon. "Drug Information: Where to look for drug information on the Internet." *C&RL News* 62 (2001):701-704. Available at <http://www.ala.org/ala/acrl/acrlpubs/crlnews/backissues2001/julyaugust2/druginformation.htm> (accessed on November 22, 2004).
Allen, Nancy M. National Center for Health Statistics (review). *C&RL News* 64 (2003):118. Available at <http://www.bowdoin.edu/~samato/IRA/reviews/issues/feb03/health.html> (accessed on November 20, 2004).
Baker, Laurence et al. "Use of the Internet and E-mail for Health Care Information: Results of a National Survey." *JAMA* 289 (2003): 2400-2406.
Chapman, Beth. ElderCare Online (review). *C&RL News* 62 (2001): 442. Available at <http://www.bowdoin.edu/~samato/IRA/reviews/issues/apr01/elder.html> (accessed on November 23, 2004).
Gray, Caryl. "Medical resources: information for the consumer (helping you make informed decisions." *C&RL News* 61 (2000):995-1000. Available at <http://www.ala.org/ala/acrl/acrlpubs/crlnews/backissues2000/december3/medicalresources.htm> (accessed on November 22, 2004).
McKinnell, Jennifer. Nutrition.gov (review). *C&RL News* 64 (2003):342-343. Available at <http://www.bowdoin.edu/~samato/IRA/reviews/issues/may03/nutrition.html> (accessed November 22, 2004).
Matthies, Brad. National Institute of Mental Health (review). *C&RL News* 65 (2004):390-391. Available at <http://www.ala.org/ala/acrlbucket/candrlnews/internetreviews/200407/nimh.htm> (accessed on November 22, 2004).

Nims, Julia K. "Complementary and alternative medicine: An overview of nontraditional medicine on the Web." *C&RL News* 63 (2002):576-579, 589, 599. Available at <http://www.ala.org/ala/acrl/acrlpubs/crlnews/backissues2002/september/complementary.htm> (accessed November 22, 2004).

Peterson, Kate. Center for Drug Evaluation and Research (review). *C&RL News* 65 (2004):337. Available at <http://www.ala.org/ala/acrlbucket/candrlnews/internetreviews/200406/drug.htm> (accessed on November 22, 2004).

Price, Joan. *The Complete Idiot's Guide to Online Medical Resources*. Indianapolis: QUE, 2000.

A Virtual Reference Shelf
for Nursing Students and Faculty:
Selected Sources

Eleanor Lomax
Susan K. Setterlund

SUMMARY. A virtual shelf for nursing that closely mirrors what previously was found on a physical reference shelf is now a reasonable goal. Advantages of doing this for nursing students and faculty in an academic setting are enumerated. Overviews of relevant vendor and publisher interfaces and models are included. The authors present a selected list of appropriate electronic reference sources that demonstrate how e-books and Internet sites can be combined to build a virtual reference shelf in this subject area. *[Article copies available for a fee from The Haworth Document Delivery Service: 1-800-HAWORTH. E-mail address: <docdelivery@haworthpress.com> Website: <http://www.HaworthPress.com> © 2006 by The Haworth Press, Inc. All rights reserved.]*

KEYWORDS. Virtual reference shelf, subject guides, nursing reference, e-books, electronic books, bibliography, Webliography, Internet sites

Eleanor Lomax is Electronic Resources Librarian (E-mail: Lomax@fau.edu); and Susan K. Setterlund is Head, Department of Information Literacy and Instructional Services (E-mail: setterlu@fau.edu), both at SE Wimberly Library, Florida Atlantic University, 777 Glades Road, Boca Raton, FL 33431.

[Haworth co-indexing entry note]: "A Virtual Reference Shelf for Nursing Students and Faculty: Selected Sources." Lomax, Eleanor, and Susan K. Setterlund. Co-published simultaneously in *Journal of Library Administration* (The Haworth Information Press, an imprint of The Haworth Press, Inc.) Vol. 44, No. 1/2, 2006, pp. 429-451; and: *Evolving Internet Reference Resources* (ed: William Miller, and Rita M. Pellen) The Haworth Information Press, an imprint of The Haworth Press, Inc., 2006, pp. 429-451. Single or multiple copies of this article are available for a fee from The Haworth Document Delivery Service [1-800-HAWORTH, 9:00 a.m. - 5:00 p.m. (EST). E-mail address: docdelivery@haworthpress.com].

Available online at http://www.haworthpress.com/web/JLA
© 2006 by The Haworth Press, Inc. All rights reserved.
doi:10.1300/J111v44n01_06

INTRODUCTION

Until recently, subject and research guides designed for students and faculty included both online and print resources. Index and abstract services generally accounted for the electronic, with some useful Internet sources included for added value. Most of the other reference sources, however, were in print and located on the physical reference shelves. Today with the continuing presence of electronic books and well-established quality Internet sites, it is quite possible to provide a more than satisfactory virtual reference shelf in many subject areas. In this case, we set out to see if a virtual reference shelf for nursing students and faculty could be put together combining resources that traditionally had been found on a physical reference shelf and quality Internet resources and sites in the field.

There are several reasons why a virtual reference shelf would be more useful to this group in our particular setting. Firstly, this university has a distributed campus structure with the College of Nursing having a presence on four of the seven sites. The College of Nursing also offers online and Web-assisted courses for its students. Having the reference resources readily available to everyone regardless of location is much more desirable and appealing than having them sitting on a shelf in one or more of the libraries. In this way, the resources are also available 24/7 and there is no need for shelving and reshelving. E-books can also be put on a virtual reference shelf and also continue as part of the general collection. Decreasing the need for duplication of reference resources on the various campuses and the subsequent monetary savings are also pluses.

As librarians, we continually struggle to increase awareness of the electronic resources the library has in its collections. This virtual reference shelf for nursing would highlight these resources as well as provide one more access point. We know that many individuals seem to have difficulty locating library materials and perhaps having the resources in one place will alleviate that difficulty to some extent. Building this virtual reference shelf provides an excellent opportunity for comparing the library's electronic reference holdings to what is currently available. In today's educational environment, many institutions will find that the reasons noted here are applicable to their situations also.

As mentioned earlier, bibliographic and journal full-text databases such as CINAHL, MEDLINE, HAPI, etc., are well established and accepted in electronic format. For that reason, these will not be discussed here other than to say that they would necessarily be entries on the virtual reference shelf. Electronic books and their method of delivery, however, are still evolving. The e-book format also has not always been accepted by readers quite as readily as other electronic resource interfaces. But, despite their demise being predicted for several years, electronic books seem to be doing quite well in some niche areas. Textbooks, technical publications, and reference books are examples of successful enterprises in the electronic book market. Additionally, the health professions are frequently identified as appropriate markets for electronic books (Hawkins 2002, 42).

Internet resources freely available in the field of nursing are also well established and accepted. Most continue to evolve, offering new features and access to information that was not as readily available in the print world. New subfields, such as evidence-based nursing, have spawned new Web sites. A virtual reference shelf would not be complete without including these.

Two sources were consulted in order to identify reference titles in nursing that have been designated as essential and/or highly recommended for nursing practice, education, administration, and research: The *2002 Brandon/Hill Selected List of Print Nursing Books and Journals* (Hill and Stickell 2002, 100-113), and *Essential Nursing References* by the Interagency Council on Information Resources for Nursing (Allen et al. 2002, 310-318). The library's physical reference shelf and current electronic collections were also examined to identify nursing and health-related titles for inclusion. Additionally, publisher/vendor and nursing-related Web sites were used to see what more there might be to offer. For electronic resources that require purchase or subscription, only those that provide access by IP authentication and allow for remote access by users have been considered. In searching for and organizing resources for this virtual reference shelf, the traditional approach based on type of resource (directories, dictionaries, encyclopedias, manuals, statistical resources, etc.) has been employed. In each category, nursing-specific resources are listed first followed by more general yet relevant resources.

Today, there is an increasingly multidisciplinary aspect to many fields of study and nursing is no different. For that reason, there are some standard, general reference titles and titles from other disciplines that could find a place on the shelf. The focus here will be nursing, but we are mindful that nurses and nursing students will at times have a need for resources of a general nature or resources in another field. In designing a virtual reference shelf, links to these other resources need to be made accessible in some visible and logical way.

In searching for electronic equivalents to the traditional reference books, it quickly became apparent that several vendors offer electronic versions of print titles included in the sources we consulted. Some offer additional reference titles that are relevant to nursing within their multi-subject collections. Electronic reference works are sometimes only available directly from the publisher. In other cases, publishers might sell their titles directly and also make their titles available electronically through vendor collections. Some titles are also available in formats that can be downloaded to PDAs, allowing for mobility.

Of the vendors that include reference titles of interest here, the purchasing models and user interfaces have both similarities and differences. A discussion of some of the vendor models follows in no particular order of preference.

Books@Ovid
<http://www.ovid.com/site/products/books_landing.jsp?top=2&mid= 3&bottom=7&subsection=11>

Ovid is well established as a provider of e-books in the field of nursing. Titles can be subscribed to individually or as a package. Traditionally, Ovid pricing has used the "number of simultaneous users" model. Ovid allows for searching across the library's entire Books@Ovid or in one or more selected titles. Readers may access a single table of contents for any title owned. Browsing by title and subject are possible with added linking capabilities to the library's other Ovid products. Ovid also offers multiple file searching which allows simultaneous searching of e-books, Ovid databases, and journals.

Gale Virtual Reference Library
<http://www.gale.com/gvrl>

This virtual library includes many of the Gale reference titles and other publisher titles as well. Libraries can purchase one book or an entire collection package. Users only see what their library has purchased. Searching can be conducted across all of that content or in one or more specifically selected titles. Navigation through the e-book mimics the print with hyperlinked tables of content and indexes. Gale uses an unlimited usage model with no checkouts or turnaways. MARC records are available and include embedded InfoMarks that take the reader directly to the selected title. Entries are stored in e-book format allowing for downloading to portable devices. Pricing is on a title basis and once purchased the book is owned. New editions of titles need to be purchased as they are published.

Micromedex
<http://www.micromedex.com>

Micromedex is a division of Thomson Healthcare and offers Internet-based products to researchers, clinicians, and other healthcare professionals. The Healthcare Series includes drug resources, critical and emergency care data, customizable patient education materials, and alternative medicine information. As part of a subscription to the Healthcare Series, information can be downloaded directly to a handheld device. mobileMICROMEDEX is automatically updated on a monthly basis. Products are purchased in the suite although access to some can be purchased individually.

netLibrary
<http://www.netlibrary.com>

netLibrary's general collection of e-books includes some reference titles and, more recently, this vendor has added a Reference Center. netLibrary mimics the library circulation model where users check out an e-book. New users accessing the netLibrary collection must create an account, although e-books may be viewed for a short period of time without one. As check out times expire books are automatically returned to the shelf. No overdue fines are incurred. Searching is available across the titles in the collection. MARC records are available for downloading into library catalogs. The Reference Center includes more than 800 titles. Searching can be accomplished across all content or by subject and section content. A specific reference source can be navigated and browsed. In order to be able to offer the Reference Center, libraries must have a minimum of 50 netLibrary reference titles. These can be chosen individually to meet the specific needs of patrons.

Oxford Reference Online
<http://www.oxfordreference.com>

The *Core Collection* includes more than 100 reference works, all published by Oxford University Press. The resource is updated three times a year with new titles, new editions, and additional features. Only four titles are included in the subject Medicine. The *Premium Collection* enhances the Core Collection with an expanding range of titles. This added content does not, at this time, include any nursing or health related reference works. Searching is possible across all titles, in a subject area or in one specific title. Alphabetical browsing of subject areas and books is also available. MARC records can be downloaded freely for inclusion in the catalog. Although it received the Best Interface award from the Charleston Advisor, this is not a rich source for nursing reference works.

Oxford will be introducing the Oxford Digital Reference Shelf in March 2005. This provides a new purchase option whereby titles are available for a one-time purchase. Libraries can choose one or more of the titles offered to fit their needs. Each work will be available as a fully searchable, stand-alone resource. Libraries that also subscribe to Oxford Reference Online: Premium Collection, will have the option of adding these new titles to the collection while also offering access as individual stand-alones.

Xreferplus
<http://www.xrefer.com>

This reference collection includes the contents of hundreds of reference books from multiple publishers and covers major subject areas. Libraries may choose one of two options; the full collection or a select 100 titles. If the full collection is chosen, access to newly added titles is automatic and at no extra cost. With the *xreferplus100* collection, libraries can change their selections at any time. Purchase of either is by subscription with pricing based on the size and type of institution. Free MARC records are available for download. Searching can be conducted across the collection, by specific subject area, or by individual title. Table of contents browsing is available where applicable.

Depending on the type of library, one or more of these collections may be reasonable choices for providing electronic reference books for nursing. Academic libraries might find the collections that offer titles in various subject areas practical as they could purchase many e-books using the same interface that meet needs across the curriculum. For the medical or hospital library, a vendor that offers title by title purchase from a rich collection of nursing works might be the preferred choice. Several other e-book vendors and publishers such as ebrary, Wiley, and

Elsevier are continually adding to their electronic book collections. Other publishers are just beginning to make their reference collections available electronically. Although the selection of nursing titles from any of these is not extensive at this time, more may be available in the future.

Included below are e-books and Internet resources organized by reference type. This is not an all inclusive list, but rather one that demonstrates the evolution of reference sources from print to electronic and the continued creation and evolution of Internet sites that provide new and original access to information, especially in terms of reference content and currency. In the case of electronic versions of print resources, the vendor/publisher or collection where they can be found is noted. For Web sites, the URL is provided as is a description of the resource. Free resources are designated as such. If the title or Web site was included in one of the source lists consulted, it will be so designated using these symbols:

- ** 2002 Brandon/Hill Selected List of Print Nursing Books and Journals*
- † *Essential Nursing References*

DIRECTORIES

Directories are resources that are very well suited to the online environment, especially with regard to currency. Some online directories without a previous print counterpart have been created as a result of technology using the Internet as a delivery method. Directories are considered below in three traditional areas (research/grants, education/careers, and organizations) and one exclusive to the Web (discussion forums/e-mail lists).

Research/Grants

National Institute of Nursing Research; Research Funding and Programs†
<http://ninr.nih.gov/ninr/index.html>

NINR supports clinical and basic nursing research on health promotion, illness, and chronic and disabling conditions. The site provides listings of areas of research opportunities. Free Access.

Registry of Nursing Research†
<http://www.stti.iupui.edu/VirginiaHendersonLibrary/
RegistryofNursingResearch.aspx>

This electronic directory, from the Virginia Henderson International Library <http://www.stti.iupui.edu/VirginiaHendersonLibrary>, is now provided as a complimentary resource. It is searchable by researcher, study, or keyword. Searching conference abstracts, researcher registration, and study registration functionality are under construction at this time. Individual researchers enter and update their own profiles. Free Access.

Schlachter, Gail A., and R. David Weber. *RSP Funding for Nursing Students and Nurses, 2002-2004.* 3rd ed. El Dorado Hills, CA: Reference Service Press, 2002.

Available in netLibrary.

Catalog of Federal Domestic Assistance†
<http://www.cfda.gov>

The Catalog is a searchable database of federal programs of assistance that are available to state and local governments, profit and non-profit organizations, specialized groups, and individuals. Free Access.

Community of Science (COS)
<http://expertise.cos.com>

This resource currently contains more than 480,000 profiles of scientists and scholars in a wide range of subject fields from more than 1,600 institutions. The coverage is international and it can be searched by member institution, researcher name, keyword, and geographical location. The profiles include contact information, positions held, publications and patents, and funding received. Universities and institutions may purchase subscriptions with fees being based on the size of the institution and the selected package options.

CRISP (Computer Retrieval of Information on Scientific Projects)†
<http://crisp.cit.nih.gov>

This database contains information on federally funded biomedical research projects conducted at universities, hospitals, and other research institutions. It is searchable using multiple criteria such as key terms, institution, principal investigator, and geographic location. Free Access.

The Foundation Directory†
<http://fconline.fdncenter.org>

The database includes both foundation and grant searching, and is available for purchase online directly from the Foundation Center. Direct links to the Web sites of foundations are included. Additionally, the Foundation Center offers a free search function that provides basic, but limited information on foundations and grants.

National Institutes of Health Guide for Grants and Contracts†
<http://grants.nih.gov/grants/guide/index.html>

Published weekly, this official publication of the National Institutes of Health announces funding opportunities in support of basic or clinical biomedical, behavioral, and bioengineering research. Free Access.

National Science Foundation Funding Opportunities†
<http://www.nsf.gov/verity/srchfund.htm>

Through grants, contracts, and cooperative agreements, the NSF funds research and education in science and engineering. Current program announcements are searchable by program area, title, or full text. Free Access.

Education/Careers

American Association of Colleges of Nursing Member Schools†
<http://www.aacn.nche.edu/Membership/membdir.htm>

This site offers a listing of 575 member schools arranged by state, with links to the Web sites of each school of nursing. Free Access.

American Journal of Nursing Career Guide†
<http://www.nursingcenter.com/CareerCenter/CareerGuide.asp>

This resource includes employment opportunities and contact information for facilities and health systems across the United States. Detailed descriptions about benefits and facts about the surrounding communities are provided. The guide is searchable by location or facility. Free Access.

Online Directory of Accredited Nursing Programs†
<*http://www.nlnac.org/Forms/directory_search.htm*>

This online directory from the National League for Nursing Accrediting Commission allows searching for accredited programs by state, country, or institution. Searches can be limited by program type. Direct links to most institutions offering these programs are included. Free Access.

The College Blue Book. 29th ed. New York: Macmillan Reference USA, 2004.

Part of the Gale Virtual Reference Library.

GradSchools.com†
<*http://gradschools.com/*>

This online directory allows searching for programs by subject or the institution's location. Results are comprised of listings which provide a brief description and contact information. Programs which have paid for advertising include longer descriptions and linking directly to the institution's Web site. The directory currently includes more than 58,000 unique graduate programs from around the world. Free Access.

U.S. Department of Labor, Bureau of Labor Statistics. *Occupational Outlook Handbook.* 2004-2005 ed. Washington, DC: U.S. Dept. of Labor, Bureau of Labor Statistics, 2004. <http://www.bls.gov/oco/home.htm> (21 November 2004).

This standard resource from the U.S. Department of Labor is available in e-book format. It is a nationally recognized source of career information, designed to provide valuable assistance to individuals making decisions about their future work lives. Revised every two years, the Handbook describes what workers do on the job, working conditions, and the training and education required. One can search and/or browse the occupations. Free Access.

Thompson Peterson's†
<http://www.petersons.com>

This site provides searching of educational institutions by major, location, size, tuition, name, and keyword. Direct linking to the colleges' and universities' Web sites is provided. Free Access.

Organizations

Nursefriendly.com: Directories: National Nursing Organizations
<http://www.nursefriendly.com/nursing/natlink.htm>

This site lists nursing associations alphabetically as well as categorically by organization topic. A Google-powered search function locates an organization either within its Web site or searches the entire Web. Annotations, contact information, and linkage to organizations' Web sites are provided. Free Access.

VirtualNurse.com: Nursing: Organizations
<http://www.virtualnurse.com/index.php?c=Nursing/Organizations>

This listing of organizations with descriptions is arranged by topic and by geographic location. In addition to browsing, a simple search feature locates the association within the Web site. Links are provided to the external homepages of the organization. Free Access.

DIRLINE
<http://dirline.nlm.nih.gov/>

This directory database from the National Library of Medicine provides a user-friendly resource for locating health and biomedical organizations offering information and support for various diseases and conditions. Free Access.

Discussion Forums, E-Mail Lists

Nursing Discussion Forum†
<http://nursing.buffalo.edu/mccartny/nursing_discussion_forums.html>

This site provides a list of discussion groups and listservs within the nursing profession, including direct links or e-mail addresses for subscription/registration. Free Access.

DICTIONARIES

Dictionaries in nursing and health-related areas are readily available in both online reference collections and on the Internet. Several included in the resources we consulted are listed below with the name of the collection and any other online access available. Also included are Internet sites that provide links to free online dictionaries in the field.

Anderson, Kenneth N. et al., eds. *Mosby's Medical, Nursing & Allied Health Dictionary*. 6th ed. St. Louis: Mosby, 2002.*†

Part of the xreferplus collection. This title is also available (but not for exclusive purchase) in Gale's Health & Wellness Resource Center. Purchase of the print includes a free companion Web site with updates and other Web links.

Booker, Christine. *Churchill Livingstone's Dictionary of Nursing*. 18th ed. Edinburgh: New York: Churchill Livingstone, 2002.†

Part of the xreferplus collection.

McFerran, Tanya A., consultant, Martin, Elizabeth A., ed. *A Dictionary of Nursing*. Oxford; New York: Oxford University Press, 2003.

Part of the Oxford Reference Online collection.

RNstudent.com: Nursing Resources
<http://www.rtstudents.com/rnstudents/rn-dictionary.htm>

This is a portal to general and specialized medical dictionaries relevant to the nursing profession. It also includes a few encyclopedias. Free Access.

American Heritage® Stedman's Medical Dictionary. Boston: Houghton Mifflin, 2002.†

Part of the xreferplus collection.

Dorland's Illustrated Medical Dictionary. 30th ed. Philadelphia: London: W.B. Saunders, 2003.

Part of the xreferplus collection. Merck Source offers a free, online dictionary powered by *Dorland's Illustrated Medical Dictionary*.

<http://www.mercksource.com/pp/us/cns/cns_hl_dorlands.jspzQzpgzE zzSzppdocszSzuszSzcommonzSzdorlandszSzdorlandzSzdmd_a-b_ 00zPzhtm>

Illustrations in this free version are not of the same color quality as found in the print or the xreferplus version. Dorland's in electronic format is now also available directly from the publisher, Elsevier.

Jablonski, Stanley. *Dictionary of Medical Acronyms and Abbreviations.* Philadelphia: Hanley & Belfus, 2001.†

Part of the xreferplus collection.

Multilingual Glossary of Technical and Popular Medical Terms in Eight European Languages †
<http://allserv.rug.ac.be/~rvdstich/eugloss/welcome.html>

This glossary includes more than 1,800 technical and popular medical terms, translated into eight languages: English, Dutch, French, German, Italian, Spanish, Portuguese, and Danish. Free Access.

Stedman's Medical Dictionary
<http://www.stedmans.com>

Many medical terms are not listed in this free, abridged version of Stedman's Medical Dictionary, 27th Edition. Available for purchase at the same site is Stedman's Electronic Medical Dictionary, v6.0 which contains definitions and etymologies for more than 100,000 medical words and nearly 1,500 images.

Thomas, Clayton L., ed. *Taber's Cyclopedic Medical Dictionary* 19th ed. Philadelphia: F.A. Davis Co., 2001.* †
<http://www.tabers.com>

Part of the xreferplus collection. *Taber's* can also be purchased directly from the publisher, F.A. Davis.

ENCYCLOPEDIAS

Encyclopedias in nursing and the medical field are not numerous in print, because they are generally out of date by publication time. Currency is easier to achieve in electronic formats; therefore this reference type may be more obtainable in the future. One title specific to nursing is available online. Several other health-related encyclopedias in e-book format are also appropriate to a nursing reference shelf.

Krapp, Kristine, ed. *Gale Encyclopedia of Nursing and Allied Health.* Detroit: Gale Group, 2002.

Part of the Gale Virtual Reference Library and netLibrary.

Krapp, K. M. and J. L. Longe. *Gale Encyclopedia of Alternative Medicine.* Detroit, MI: Gale Group, 2001.

Part of the Gale Virtual Reference Library and netLibrary.

Longe, J. L., and D. S. Blanchfield. *Gale Encyclopedia of Medicine.* 2nd ed. Detroit, MI: Gale Group, 2002.

Part of the Gale Virtual Reference Library and netLibrary.

DRUGS AND PHARMACOLOGY

Some references in this area of nursing continue only in print or print with PDA compatibility or with an accompanying Web site for updates. Some references are available as e-books. Additionally, online sources for drug information with no print counterpart are now available. Several examples are given below.

Karch, Amy M. *Lippincott's Nursing Drug Guide.* Philadelphia: Lippincott Williams & Wilkens, 2004.*

Available via Books@Ovid.

Skidmore-Roth, Linda. *Mosby's 2005 Nursing Drug Reference.* St. Louis: Mosby, 2004.

Purchase of the print format includes free Internet updates.

Spratto, G. R. and A. L. Woods. *PDR Nurse's Drug Handbook.* New York: Delmar, 2005.*

Individual print purchases include free access to the *Nurse's Drug Database.* However, the institutional version of this database is available at an additional cost based on the number of users.

Springhouse Corporation. *Nursing2004 Herbal Medicine Handbook.* Philadelphia: Lippincott Williams & Wilkens, 2004.

Available via Books@Ovid.

Hawthorn, J. and E. Martin. *An A-Z of Medicinal Drugs.* Oxford: Oxford University Press, 2003.

Part of the Oxford Reference Online collection.

Martindale Complete Drug Reference†

This online resource contains information about drugs used worldwide. It covers 5,800 drug monographs, 70,000 proprietary preparations, 500 herbal monographs, and 5,000 herbal preparations. It is suggested for healthcare professionals with international concerns. Available in the MICROMEDEX Healthcare Series.

Merck Index Online, 13th ed.†
<https://themerckindex.cambridgesoft.com/index.asp?
SubscriptionID=1199335>

This site makes available more than 10,000 monographs on drugs, chemicals, and biologicals. It provides much of the same information as the print encyclopedia, with the exception of drawings of the chemical structure. It is divided into three sections: Compound Search, Organic Name Reactions, and supplemental Tables. Online information is updated before the print. Free Access.

Natural Medicines Comprehensive Database
<http://www.naturaldatabase.com>

This reasonably priced database from the Therapeutic Research Faculty is also available in book and PDA versions. It is an evidence-based resource providing a comprehensive listing of natural medicines, brand name product ingredients, and extensive references. The group now also offers a consumer version.

USP DI Volume I: Drug Information for the Health Care Professional†

Contains complete drug information for prescribing and dispensing. Available through MICROMEDEX Healthcare Series.

HANDBOOKS AND MANUALS

In nursing, some print handbooks and manuals are located in the general circulating collection while others are designated as Reference. In their electronic formats, they can be made available on a virtual reference shelf and continue to be available in the library's electronic holdings.

Diagnosis and Treatments

The Merck Manual of Diagnosis, 17th Ed. Whitehouse Station, N.J.: Merck & Co., 2000. <http://www.merck.com/mrkshared/mmanual/sections.jsp> (19 November 2004).

This manual provides detailed clinical information to health care professionals on topics in internal medicine as well as medical specialties. Free Access.

The Merck Manual of Geriatrics. 3rd ed. Whitehouse Station, N.J.: Merck & Co., 2000. <http://www.merck.com/mrkshared/mm_geriatrics/home.jsp> (19 November 2004).

This online version of the print manual provides descriptions of disorders, symptoms, and treatments with emphasis on the elderly population. Free Access.

University of Iowa Family Practice Handbook. 4th ed. Iowa City, Iowa: University of Iowa. 2001. <http://www.vh.org/adult/provider/familymedicine/FPHandbook/FPContents.html> (22 November 2004).

This handbook contains information on illnesses and therapies necessary for practitioners of family medicine and includes pediatric and adult dosages for commonly prescribed drugs. Free Access.

Laboratory and Diagnostic Tests

Cavanaugh, Bonita M. *Nurse's Manual of Laboratory and Diagnostic Tests.* 4th ed. Philadelphia: F.A. Davis Co. 2003.

Available in netLibrary.

Fischbach, Frances T. *A Manual of Laboratory Diagnostic Tests.* Philadelphia: Lippincott Williams & Wilkens, 2003.*

Available via Books@Ovid.

NCLEX Test Preparation

Beare, Patricia. *Davis's NCLEX-RN Review.* 3rd ed. Philadelphia: F.A. Davis, 2001.*

Available in netLibrary.

Writing and Publishing

Daly, Jeannette M. *Writer's Guide to Nursing Periodicals.* Thousand Oaks, CA: Sage Publications, 2000.†

Available in netLibrary.

Fondiller, Shirley H. *The Writer's Workbook: Health Professionals Guide to Getting Published.* 2nd ed. Sudbury, MA: Jones and Bartlett, 1999.†

Available in netLibrary.

APA Style Helper 3.0†
<http://www.apastyle.org/stylehelper>

This is the electronic companion to the fifth edition of the *APA Publication Manual.* Site licenses are available.

ONLINE Nursing Editors™†
<http://www.nurseauthou.com/ONE/naed.htm>

Provides e-mail contact information for editors of more than 200 nursing journals and books and links to many author guideline Web pages. Free Access.

Instructions to Authors in the Health Sciences†
<http://www.mco.edu/lib/instr/libinsta.html>

This Web site from the Raymon H. Mulford Library of the Medical College of Ohio provides links to author guideline pages from hundreds of health science journals. Free Access.

HISTORY OF NURSING

Although these Web sites could not be considered "reference sources" in the traditional sense, they are included here due to the interest in the evolving role of the nurse.

American Association for the History of Nursing†
<http://www.aahn.org>

The site includes a section on historical methodology, as well as links to archives and research centers, conferences, funding, Internet resources, journals, and more. Free Access.

Center for Nursing Historical Inquiry†
University of Virginia School of Nursing
<http://www.nursing.virginia.edu/centers/cnh>

This center collects and preserves nursing materials such as photographs, textbooks, personal papers, and reports. It includes historical nursing forums and promotes historical scholarship through a yearly fellowship award. Free Access.

Center for the Study of the History of Nursing†
University of Pennsylvania School of Nursing
<http://www.nursing.upenn.edu/history>

This center serves as a resource for research in healthcare history and nursing. Free Access.

STATISTICAL SOURCES

Health statistics are compiled by government agencies and non-governmental organizations. These are included in general statistical reference sources. Additionally, there are sources that specialize in reporting health statistics. Also included in this section are Web sites specific to the profession of nursing.

Nursing Statistics

United States, Health Resources and Services Administration and Division of Nursing. *The Registered Nurse Population, March*

2000 Findings from the National Sample Survey of Registered Nurses, by Ernell Spratley. U.S. Dept. of Health & Human Services, Health Resources and Services Administration, Bureau of Health Professions, Division of Nursing. Rockville, MD, 2001. <http://www.bhpr.hrsa.gov/healthworkforce/reports/rnsurvey/rnss1.htm> (21 November 2004).†

Conducted in 2000, this PDF version of the survey results provides information on the number of registered nurses, their education background and specialty areas; their employment status, including type of employment setting, position level, and salaries; their geographic distribution; and their personal characteristics including gender, racial/ethnic background, age, and family status. Free Access.

Health Statistics

Finding and Using Health Statistics: A Self-Study Course†
<http://www.nlm.nih.gov/nichsr/usestats/index.htm>

This adaptation of Dan Melnick's book *Portrait of Health in the United States* explains how to find methods, sources, and related literature on health statistics using Internet resources. Free Access.

U.S. Department of Health and Human Services. National Center for Health Statistics. *Health, United States, 2003.* <http://www.cdc.gov/nchs/hus.htm> (18 November 2004).

This annual report in electronic format presents statistical trends in health topics such as birth and death rates, infant mortality, life expectancy, morbidity and health status, risk factors, health personnel and facilities, health insurance, and managed care. Free Access.

National Center for Health Statistics
<http://www.cdc.gov/nchs>

This Web site provides links to state and territory health care statistics, national health care surveys, and other data collections of the Centers for Disease Control and Prevention. Free Access.

Brett K. M., and S. G. Hayes. *Women's Health and Mortality Chartbook.* Washington, DC: DHHS Office on Women's Health,

2004. <http://www.cdc.gov/nchs/datawh/statab/chartbook.htm>
(20 November 2004).

This is a collection of current state data on critical issues of relevance to women's health. Each state, the District of Columbia, and Puerto Rico are ranked on such attributes as major causes of death, health risk factors, preventive care, and health insurance coverage. Free Access.

World Health Organization Statistical Information System (WHOSIS)
<http://www3.who.int/whosis/menu.cfm>

The World Health Organization provides health and health-related epidemiological and statistical information. Included are core health indicators, statistics by topic, country or region, and the International Classification of Diseases (ICD-10). Free Access.

General

LexisNexis Statistical
<http://web.lexis-nexis.com/statuniv>

This resource provides indexing and abstracting of statistics produced by the U.S. government, international governments and organizations, state governments, and professional and trade associations. Numerous statistical tables from the publications are included in the database. Available by subscription.

U.S. Census Bureau, Statistical Abstract of the United States, 2003. 123rd ed. Washington, D.C., 2003.
<http://www.census.gov/prod/www/statistical-abstract-03.html>

Published yearly, this ebook contains data on many areas relevant to nursing such as population, vital statistics, health and nutrition, social insurance, and human resources. Free Access.

Data on the Net†
<http://odwin.ucsd.edu/idata>

This portal to statistics from the University of California, San Diego, can be searched or browsed for numerical data, data archives and catalogs, and lists of data pertaining to social sciences. Free Access.

Statistical Resources on the Web†
<http://www.lib.umich.edu/govdocs/stats.html>

This Internet site from the University of Michigan Documents Center is annotated and capable of being searched or browsed. Its Health section contains a comprehensive listing of statistical sources, both national and international. Free Access.

EVIDENCE BASED PRACTICE

Evidence Based Practice is an approach to patient care decisions based on the best available research in combination with clinical expertise and patient values. Emphasis on the validity of research has made databanks of pre-assessed resources particularly valuable. Those listed below are applicable to nursing.

The Cochrane Library†

This library is a collection of databases which promote evidence-based decision making. Included are the Cochrane Database of Systematic Reviews (Cochrane Reviews), Database of Abstracts of Reviews of Effects (DARE), the Cochrane Central Register of Controlled Trials (CENTRAL), the Cochrane Database of Methodology Reviews, the Health Technology Assessment Database, and the NHS Economic Evaluation Database. Available via OVID and Wiley InterScience.

Joanna Briggs Institute
<http://www.joannabriggs.edu.au/services/search.php>

The Joanna Briggs Institute supports international research and dissemination of knowledge in the areas of health care. Searchable at this site are the results of systematic reviews, summarized into Best Practice Information Sheets. Free Access.

National Guideline Clearinghouse
<http://www.guideline.gov>

A searchable database of objective, detailed clinical guidelines sponsored by the Agency for Healthcare Research and Quality (AHRQ), U.S. Department of Health and Human Services. Free Access.

CONCLUSION

As noted previously, there are many advantages to having nursing references in an electronic medium. Twenty-four hour accessibility is a prominent one; neither nursing students nor practicing nurses keep bankers' hours. Unlike a single volume, electronic access allows a resource to have as many simultaneous readers as the subscription allows. And the increasing trend to download information to a PDA or similar device often permits it to be used at the point of need as clinical decisions are made.

On a cautionary note, when working with technology one must be aware of the times when systems fail, glitches occur, and sites disappear. It would be foolhardy to assume that problems never occur–both minor and major ones. As mentioned earlier, people have not accepted the electronic book format as widely as anticipated. For these reasons, a complete dependence on a virtual reference shelf may not be practical or the best choice.

Cost is another consideration when developing a collection. For some of the titles mentioned here, availability is only through purchase of a collection or package. This might not be practical depending on the library's circumstances. On the other hand, some materials freely accessible on the Web do meet reference needs. As an example, many U.S. government documents exist that could supplement any academic collection.

One further observation must be stated. It is impossible to predict what information technologies and strategies may develop in the future. New methods of information transference could make computers obsolete. Open access protocols could revise the current subscription-based systems.

In conclusion, more electronic versions of print reference resources have become available and others have been transformed into a unique blend of print with technological enhancements.

In addition to these, completely new reference resources have been created using the opportunities afforded by digital technologies and the Internet. Using these available resources in combination makes it possible to provide an appropriate and rich collection of reference sources for nursing students and faculty. Therefore, a virtual reference shelf is possible.

REFERENCES

Allen, Margaret et al., "Essential Nursing References." *Nursing Education Perspectives* 23, (6) (2002): 310-318.

Hawkins, Donald T. "Electronic Books: Reports of their Death Have Been Exaggerated." *Online* 26, (4) 2002: 42.

Hill, Dorothy R., and Henry N. Stickell. "Brandon/Hill Selected List of Print Nursing Books and Journals." *Nursing Outlook* 50, (3) 2002: 100-113.

Internet Reference Sources
for Computing and Computer Science:
A Selected Guide

Michael Knee

SUMMARY. Computing and computer science bibliographic databases, bibliographies, dictionaries, encyclopedias, directories, and guides,
along with finding aids for technical reports, online books, and book
reviews are listed and described. Subscription-based sources as well as
free alternatives are covered. Resources are listed for all levels of computing ability including faculty and professionals, graduate students,
undergraduates, and general users. *[Article copies available for a fee from
The Haworth Document Delivery Service: 1-800-HAWORTH. E-mail address:
<docdelivery@haworthpress.com> Website: <http://www.HaworthPress.com>
© 2006 by The Haworth Press, Inc. All rights reserved.]*

KEYWORDS. Computer science, computing, reference resources, Internet
resources, World Wide Web resources, online resources

INTRODUCTION

Computer scientists and computing professionals were early users of
the Internet and related technologies. From electronic mail to gopher
sites to the World Wide Web, as a group, they harnessed the capabilities

Michael Knee is Science Bibliographer and Reference Librarian, University at Albany, SUNY, Science Library, Albany, NY 12222 (E-mail: knee@albany.edu).

[Haworth co-indexing entry note]: "Internet Reference Sources for Computing and Computer Science: A
Selected Guide." Knee, Michael. Co-published simultaneously in *Journal of Library Administration* (The
Haworth Information Press, an imprint of The Haworth Press, Inc.) Vol. 44, No. 1/2, 2006, pp. 453-473; and:
Evolving Internet Reference Resources (ed: William Miller, and Rita M. Pellen) The Haworth Information
Press, an imprint of The Haworth Press, Inc., 2006, pp. 453-473. Single or multiple copies of this article are
available for a fee from The Haworth Document Delivery Service [1-800-HAWORTH, 9:00 a.m. - 5:00 p.m.
(EST). E-mail address: docdelivery@haworthpress.com].

doi:10.1300/J111v44n01_07

of the Internet for communications, information dissemination, cooperative work, and research. Previously, computer science Internet resources were examined and described.[1,2] This article concentrates on reference Internet sources for computing and computer science. It includes a combination of resources cited in the two previous articles, along with new material. The older information has updated URLs and descriptions.

BIBLIOGRAPHIC DATABASES

Bibliographic databases evolved from indexing and abstracting services. In many cases, they are the electronic equivalent paper-based indexing and abstracting services with enhanced search capabilities. The purpose of databases is to assist researchers and students in locating relevant sources of information. Each database is different, but generally, source material covered includes journal and magazine articles, conference papers, master's theses, doctoral dissertations, technical reports, government documents and reports, books, and book chapters.

INSPEC <http://www.iee.org/Publish/INSPEC/> is the most comprehensive bibliographic database for computer science. It is the electronic counterpart of three indexing and abstracting services: *Computer & Control Abstracts*, *Electrical & Electronics Abstracts*, and *Physics Abstracts*. The main database covers from 1969 forward, with an optional archive covering 1898-1968. *INSPEC* is available on CD-ROM, magnetic tape, or online. Online it is hosted by several vendors including Dialog, EBSCO, Ovid, Proquest, and STN, and available by subscription or pay per search. *INSPEC* should be available in most libraries supporting computer science research programs.

The Guide to Computing Literature <http://portal.acm.org/guide.cfm> (11 November 2004) from the Association for Computing Machinery (ACM) is another valuable bibliographic resource. Starting out as the *Comprehensive Bibliography of Computing Literature* in 1960 and becoming the *ACM Guide to Computing Literature* in 1977, it has a long history that evolved from print to CD-ROM to online. Coverage in *The Guide to Computing Literature* dates back as far as 1947 for some publications, and is especially strong for ACM journals, transactions, magazines, and conference proceedings. Basic search and browse functions are freely available. Subscribers and ACM members have access to advanced search features.

Another extensive database, that is fairly new, is *Computer Science Index* <http:www.epnet.com.academic/computersci.asp>. It corresponds to the ceased print index *Computer Literature Index*. However, its publisher EBSCO enhanced the coverage with additional professional and popular computing publications along with citations from numerous scholarly journals including titles from the ACM, IEEE, and other major publishers. Coverage extends back to the mid-1950s for some of the content, and full text is available for some of the citations.

Other noteworthy research level computer science databases are *Computer and Information Systems Abstracts* from Cambridge Scientific Abstracts, *CompuScience* <http://www.zblmath.fiz-karlsruhe.de/COMP/quick.html> (11 November 2004) from FIZ Karlsruhe, *Computer Source*, a full-text database produced by EBSCO, *Computer Abstracts International Database* published by Emerald, and *Computer & Communications Security Abstracts* from Emerald.

Institutions not requiring a research level database may consider subscribing to EBSCO's *Internet & Personal Computing Abstracts* or Wilson's *Applied Science and Technology Index*. Another option is an aggregator database such as EBSCO's *Academic Search Premier* that contains about 450 computing and computer science titles or *InfoTrak OneFile* from Thomson Gale, which covers nearly 350 titles in computing and computer science. Both EBSCO and Thomson Gale offer aggregations with fewer overall and computing and computer science titles.

There are additional options. For a long time, computer scientists have compiled and depended on bibliographies to help organize and control the information for a specialized subject, and advance their research. Bibliographies have appeared in paper format as books, journal articles, as serials, and at the end of articles. Since its rise in popularity, many bibliographies have appeared on the World Wide Web. These bibliographies often have powerful search capabilities. Several are listed below; all are freely accessible.

Annotated Computer Vision Bibliography
<http://iris.usc.edu/Vision-Notes/bibliography/contents.html>
(11 November 2004)

BibFinder: A Computer Science Bibliography Mediator
<http://kilimanjaro.eas.asu.edu/>
(11 November 2004)

BibFinder is a computer science bibliography search engine. It simultaneously searches *The Collection of Computer Science Bibliographies*, the *DBLP Computer Science Bibliography*, the *ACM Digital*

Library, *The Guide to Computing Literature*, the *Network Bibliography*, Elsevier's *ScienceDirect*, *IEEE Xplore*, *CiteSeer*, and *Google*.

Bibliography of Automated Deduction
<http://www.ora.on.ca/biblio/biblio-prover-welcome.html>
(11 November 2004)

The Collection of Computer Science Bibliographies
<http://liinwww.ira.uka.de/bibliography/>
(11 November 2004)

Covering most areas of computer science, this collection of bibliographies contains more than 1,400,000 records from nearly 1,400 bibliographies. It may be searched in its entirety or individual bibliographies may be selected and searched. Technical reports from computer science departments may be searched separately.

CiteSeer: Scientific Literature Digital Library
<http://citeseer.ist.psu.edu/>
(11 November 2004)

CiteSeer is a search system providing access to journal articles, conference papers, and technical reports in computer science and allied sciences. In addition to a list of documents, an author or subject search automatically generates the search context and a list of related documents. The autonomous citation indexing feature executes a citation search similar to *Science Citation Index*.

Computer Graphics Bibliography Database
<http://www.siggraph.org/publications/bibliography/>
(11 November 2004)

Cryptology ePrint Archive
<http://eprint.iacr.org/>
(11 November 2004)

DBLP Computer Science Bibliography
<http://dblp.uni-trier.de/>
(11 November 2004)

DBLP started as a bibliography for database systems and logic programming, but expanded its scope to include other areas of computer science. *DBLP* is currently an acronym for *Digital Bibliography and Library Project*, and contains over 500,000 references.

ECS EPrints Service
<http://eprints.ecs.soton.ac.uk/>
(11 November 2004)

The *ECS EPrints Service* is a publications database for electronics and computer science.

Electronic Colloquium on Computational Complexity (ECCC)
<http://www.eccc.uni-trier.de/eccc/>
(11 November 2004)

The Garbage Collection Bibliography
<http://www.cs.kent.ac.uk/people/staff/rej/gcbib/gcbib.html>
(11 November 2004)

For the purpose of this resource, garbage collection is defined as automatic dynamic memory management.

HCI Bibliography
<http://www.hcibib.org/>
(11 November 2004)

The *HCI Bibliography* is a searchable bibliography on human-computer interaction.

Network Bibliography
<http://www.cs.columbia.edu/~hgs/netbib/>
(11 November 2004)

Containing about 50,000 entries, this bibliography covers the subjects of computer networks, performance evaluation, computer-supported cooperative work, network security, digital signal processing, and related topics.

ÖFAI–IMKAI Library Information System BIBLIO
<http://www.ai.univie.ac.at/biblio.html>
(11 November 2004)

This bibliography lists books, journal articles, conference papers, and research papers on artificial intelligence.

RAND Corporation: Books and Publications: Bibliographies and Abstracts
<http://www.rand.org/publications/bib/>
(11 November 2004)

The RAND Corporation is a nonprofit organization that focuses its efforts on research and analysis of challenges that face the U.S. and the world. RAND produces a variety of publications to communicate and disseminate its research results including briefings, reports, articles, and monographs. This Web page lists subject-oriented bibliographies of RAND publications. A few of the bibliographies have a computing theme. Many of the publications are freely available on the RAND Web site.

Software History Bibliography
<http://www.cbi.umn.edu/shp/bibliography.html>
(11 November 2004)

Compiled by the Charles Babbage Institute, this bibliography lists about 2,500 citations to books, journal articles, magazine articles, conference papers, reports, oral histories, and archival materials on the history of software.

TECHNICAL REPORTS

Academic institutions as well as government, industrial, and corporate research installations issue technical reports. Technical reports are important sources of information in computer science. Sometimes they are revised and published as journal articles or conference papers. However, many are never published, and may be difficult to locate. The resources listed below are useful finding aids for technical reports.

GrayLIT Network: A Science Portal of Technical Reports
<http://graylit.osti.gov/>
(11 November 2004)

GrayLit Network is a portal for technical report information generated through federally funded research and development projects. It is a free database that provides access to full-text scientific and technical reports from the following U.S. government agencies: Defense Technical Information Center, Department of Energy, NASA, and Environmental Protection Agency. Reports are available back to 1960, but most are from the early 1990s forward.

Networked Computer Science Technical Reports Library (NCSTRL)
<http://www.ncstrl.org/>
(11 November 2004)

NCSTRL is a collection of research reports and papers from institutions around the world awarding doctoral degrees in computer science or engineering, and some industrial and government research laboratories. It may be searched by author, title, or abstract keywords, and limited by institution and date. It may also be browsed by institution. Full text is usually available.

NTIS
<http://www.ntis.gov/>
(11 November 2004)

The National Technical Information Service maintains and disseminates a large collection of scientific, technical, engineering, and business-related information produced for and by U.S. government agencies. The freely accessible *NTIS* database contains the records of millions of publications from 1990 forward, along with audiovisual materials, computer data files, and software. All records include an abstract; some of the publications are freely available on the Internet. Other documents and materials may be purchased from NTIS or found in depository libraries.

On-line CS Techreports
<http://www-2.cs.cmu.edu/afs/cs.cmu.edu/user/jblythe/Mosaic/cs-reports.html>
(11 November 2004)

On-line CS Techreports lists and links to over 650 institutions around the world that make their computer science technical reports available online. The institutions are arranged in loose alphabetical order, and can be sorted by country.

TR Archive Sites List
<http://www.eccc.uni-trier.de/eccc/info/ftp_sites.html>
(11 November 2004)

This Web site lists academic and research institutions around the world that distribute online computer science technical reports. The institutions are arranged in alphabetical order.

The Virtual Technical Reports Center
<http://www.lib.umd.edu/ENGIN/TechReports/Virtual-TechReports.html>
(11 November 2004)

The Virtual Technical Reports Center lists and links to institutions or corporations around the world that provide either full text or abstracts of technical reports, preprints, reprints, dissertations, theses, and research reports. The institutions are arranged in alphabetical order.

BOOKS

Even in computing and computer science, online books have not been fully embraced. Perhaps, they have not evolved far enough, or is it we who have not evolved? Maybe when the generation that was born in the digital age become the predominant users, online books will be more accepted. There are several vendors and publishers that offer online computing and computer science books by subscription or pay per title. *Safari Books Online* <http://www.safaribooksonline.com/> (11 November 2004) provides access to numerous up-to-date titles from leading computing and information technology publishers. Its collection contains books from Adobe Press, Addison Wesley Professional, Cisco Press, New Riders, O'Reilly, Peachpit Press, Prentice Hall PTR, Que, and Sams Publishing. Online computer science books from CRC Press can be found via four portals: *ENGnetBASE* <http://www.engnetbase.com/> (11 November 2004), *MATHnetBASE* <http://www.mathnetbase.com/> (11 November 2004), *ITknowledgeBASE* <http://www.itknowledgebase.net> (11 November 2004), and *InfoSECURITY-netBASE* <http://infosecuritynetbase.com/> (11 November 2004). Reference and standard texts are available through these portals. *Ebrary* <http://www.ebrary.com/> (11 November 2004) contains a considerable collection of computing and computer science books from publishers like Kluwer, Idea Group Publishing, Charles River Media, Marcel Dekker, Cambridge University Press, Routledge, Peter Collin Publishing, Johns Hopkins University Press, McGraw-Hill, John Wiley & Sons, and Coriolis Group.

Although mostly standard texts are available, there are a few reference books. Containing mainly texts and a few reference books, *netLibrary* <http://www.netlibrary.com/> (11 November 2004) has a sizable computing and computer science collection. It includes books from MIT Press, Gale, Sams Publishing, O'Reilly, Kluwer, McGraw-Hill, Oxford University Press, Idea Group Publishing, Que, John Wiley & Sons, and Lawrence Erlbaum Associates. *Xreferplus* <http://www.xrefer.com/> (11 November 2004) contains a collection of reference books (dictionaries, encyclopedias, and thesauri) with a cross-reference linking structure. Its technology section has several computing and computer-related dictionaries. Kluwer <http://reference.kluweronline.com/> (11 November 2004) and John Wiley & Sons <http://www3.interscience.wiley.com/cgi-bin/browsebysubject?code=COMP> (11 November 2004), Books24x7 <http://www.books24x7.com> (11 November 2004) also offer online computer science reference books.

In addition to these fee-based services, there are several gateways to collections of free online books. Titles in the public domain as well as copyrighted books are available.

FreeTechBooks
<http://www.freetechbooks.com/>
(11 November 2004)

This site provides links to free online computer books and documentation. There are over 100 books covering programming languages, scripting languages, operating systems, and other computer science topics like data structures, algorithms, object-oriented programming, logic programming, compiler design, software development, and game development.

IBM Redbooks
<http://www.redbooks.ibm.com/>
(11 November 2004)

Developed and published by IBM's International Technical Support Organization, *Redbooks* provide guidance, installation and implementation experiences, solution scenarios, and "how-to" guidelines. Sample code and other support materials are often included. They are accessible by keyword search, publication date, or subject domains.

National Academies Press: Computer Sciences
<http://books.nap.edu/v3/makepage.phtml?val1=subject&val2=co>
(11 November 2004)

The National Academies Press offers free access to numerous books and reports on many subjects. Listing titles in reverse chronological order, this Web page covers the subjects of computing, information technology, and related technologies.

The Online Books Page: Call Numbers Starting with QA
<http://digital.library.upenn.edu/webbin/book/subjectstart?QA>
(11 November 2004)

This Web page from the University of Pennsylvania Libraries lists over 400 books classified in the Library of Congress QAs and covering computer science and mathematics. The titles may be perused; or author and title search and browse functions are available on the main page <http://onlinebooks.library.upenn.edu/lists.html> (11 November 2004).

BOOK REVIEWS

For computing and computer science, there are two subscription-based book review services. *Computing Reviews* <http://reviews.com/> (11 November 2004) is produced through a partnership between the Association of Computing Machinery and reviews.com. It selectively reviews general and specialized books as well as journal articles, conference proceedings, theses, technical reports, and Web resources. *Computing Reviews* is continually updated, and has many browse, search, and customizing options. *Book Review Digest Plus* <http://vnweb.hwwilsonweb.com/hww/> (11 November 2004) from H. W. Wilson is the other source. Covering most academic subjects, it is the online, expanded version of *Book Review Digest*. In addition to the reviews from *Book Review Digest*, it also includes reviews from eleven other Wilson indexes/databases including *Applied Science & Technology Index*, *General Science Index*, and *Business Periodicals Index*. Besides these resources, the following Web sites provide free access to quality reviews for computing and computer science books.

ACCU: Book Reviews
<http://www.accu.org/bookreviews/public/>
(11 November 2004)

The Association of C & C++ Users (ACCU) furnishes access to book reviews that appeared in their journals *C Vu* and *Overload.* The reviews are brief, but cover many computing subjects. They can be browsed by subject, publisher, journal issue, reviewer, title, author, and by the category "highly recommended." A search engine is also available.

Electronic Review of Computer Books (ERCB)
<http://www.ercb.com/>
(11 November 2004)

From the publishers of *Dr. Dobb's Journal, ERCB* contains independent reviews of books about computer hardware, software, and networks. It includes both brief and feature reviews. The "Programmer's Bookshelf" column back to 1990 is also available. A search engine and a catalog provide access to the reviews.

KickstartNews: Computer Book Reviews
<http://www.kickstartnews.com/books.html>
(11 November 2004)

This Web site offers a variety of critical reviews of current computing books. The reviews are arranged alphabetically by title, with new content added regularly. Reviews of software, hardware, and accessories are also available via <http://www.kickstartnews.com/previous.html> (11 November 2004).

TechBookReport
<http://www.techbookreport.com/>
(11 November 2004)

TechBookReport furnishes independent, informative book reviews of computing and computer science books. It covers books on software methodologies, software tools, artificial intelligence, machine learning, programming, Java, and XML. Reviews can be located by browsing one of these subject categories, or by keyword search.

DICTIONARIES AND ENCYCLOPEDIAS

Computing and computer science has an abundance of dictionaries and encyclopedias in print format. There are resources for nearly every level of ability and experience, from home users to researchers and professionals. There are resources that cover the entire discipline and others that address sub-disciplines. It was previously noted in the BOOKS section that CRC Press has four portals that furnish access to online books by subscription or pay-per-title. Many of the titles offered through these portals are encyclopedic handbooks. It was also noted in the same section that the subscription-based *Xreferplus* <http://www.xrefer.com/> (11 November 2004) offers several computing and computer-related dictionaries in its technology section. Other publishers and vendors offer online dictionaries and encyclopedic works. Likewise, there are several free Web-based dictionaries and encyclopedias; they are listed below.

BABEL: A Glossary of Computer Oriented Abbreviations and Acronyms
<http://www.ciw.uni-karlsruhe.de/kopien/babel.html>
(11 November 2004)

Available on the Internet since 1989, *BABEL*, as the sub-title suggests, covers computer-related abbreviations and acronyms. It is updated three times a year.

A Compilation of Software Engineering Terms from Existing Sources
<http://www.computer.org/certification/csdpprep/Glossary.htm>
(11 November 2004)

Based in part on the *IEEE Standard Glossary of Software Engineering Terminology* (*IEEE Std 610.12-1990*), the purpose of this glossary is to provide definitions for the terms used in the specification of the professional exam. There are numerous cross-references, and the exact source of the definition is usually furnished.

Dictionary of Algorithms and Data Structures
<http://www.nist.gov/dads/>
(11 November 2004)

Hosted by the National Institute of Standards and Technology (NIST), this dictionary provides concise definitions of terms related to algorithms, data structures, archetypical problems, and techniques. Some entries have cross-references to further information and links to implementations.

Free On-line Dictionary of Computing
<http://foldoc.doc.ic.ac.uk/>
(11 November 2004)

The *Free On-line Dictionary of Computing* is a searchable dictionary of computing. Containing over 13,000 terms, it provides definitions and detailed explanations. *Computing Reference* <http://www.elook.org/computing/> (11 November 2004) offers another interface and additional features.

IBM Terminology
<http://www-306.ibm.com/ibm/terminology/>
(11 November 2004)

The glossaries of several IBM products have been incorporated to form this dictionary. It includes basic computing definitions along with terminology from the following IBM brands: CICS, iSeries, Lotus, Tivoli, and WebSphere.

Linktionary
<http://www.linktionary.com/>
(11 November 2004)

Based on the *McGraw-Hill Encyclopedia of Networking & Telecommunications* by Thomas Sheldon, *Linktionary* is an online dictionary/encyclopedia of Internet technologies, networking hardware and protocols, and general Web terminology. It provides concise definitions and detailed explanations along with links to additional information.

NetLingo
<http://www.netlingo.com/inframes.cfm>
(11 November 2004)

Based on *NetLingo: The Internet Dictionary* by Vincent James and Erin Jansen, this resource covers terms about the Internet and the World Wide Web, including technology, communication, and business. The definitions are concise and often include cross-references and links to additional information.

Ritter's Crypto Glossary and Dictionary of Technical Cryptography
<http://www.ciphersbyritter.com/GLOSSARY.HTM>
(11 November 2004)

This dictionary explains technical cryptographic terminology. It is arranged alphabetically, with words within entries hyperlinked to other entries for further clarification. It may also be browsed by topic.

TechEncyclopedia
<http://www.techweb.com/encyclopedia/>
(11 November 2004)

Based on an updated and enhanced version of *The Computer Desktop Encyclopedia* by Alan Freedman, *TechEncyclopedia* contains more than 20,000 computing and information technology entries. It includes both brief definitions and in-depth explanations. Most entries have illustrations, photos, charts, or diagrams that help elucidate the terminology.

Usability Glossary
<http://www.usabilityfirst.com/glossary/main.cgi>
(11 November 2004)

The *Usability Glossary* defines over 1,100 usability-related terms.

Webopedia
<http://www.pcwebopaedia.com/>
(11 November 2004)

Webopedia is a searchable dictionary of computing and Internet terms that is continually updated with new terminology. Entries include detailed definitions, pronunciation, cross-references, related terms, and links to additional information.

Wikipedia, the Free Encyclopedia
<http://en.wikipedia.org/>
(11 November 2004)

The *Wikipedia* is a free, collaborative encyclopedia. It contains articles on all academic subjects including computing and the Internet. Using wiki software, users create its contents, which are subject to editing and revision by other users.

DIRECTORIES AND GUIDES

This section contains an assortment of Internet directories, guides, and finding aids for computing and computer science. Reference sources for algorithms, biography, career and employment, colleges and universities, journals, meetings and conferences, standards and specifications, and style guides are described. Although there are a few fee-based services, most provide free access.

Algorithms

Collected Algorithms of the ACM
<http://www.acm.org/pubs/calgo/>
(11 November 2004)

This collection contains the algorithms published in the *ACM Transactions on Mathematical Software* and other ACM journals. The algorithms are refereed for originality, accuracy, robustness, completeness, portability, and lasting value. The site begins with algorithm number 493 (issued in 1975); however, earlier algorithms are also available.

Cryptography: Algorithms
<http://www.ssh.fi/support/cryptography/algorithms/>
(11 November 2004)

This page lists commonly used cryptographic algorithms and methods, and explains their basic concepts. Links are provided to implementations and textbooks.

The Stony Brook Algorithm Repository
<http://www.cs.sunysb.edu/~algorith/>
(11 November 2004)

Based on his book *The Algorithm Design Manual*, Steven S. Skiena has mounted this site containing a collection of algorithm implementations for over seventy of the most fundamental problems in combinatorial algorithms.

Biography

HomePageSearch
<http://hpsearch.uni-trier.de/>
(11 November 2004)

Personal home pages of computer scientists can be located using the search function on this Web page. Using the "author tree" function, names can also be browsed alphabetically. Results include links to home pages and related pages, and direct links to bibliographies that list the scientist's papers and articles.

Career and Employment

ACM Career Resource Centre
<http://campus.acm.org/crc/>
(11 November 2004)

The Association for Computing Machinery developed this Web site to help students and professionals make informed decisions about employment and careers. It contains a searchable jobs database that includes full-time positions, internships, and summer jobs; self-assessment tools; and discussion forums.

Developers.net: Career Index
<http://www.developers.net/careers/>
(11 November 2004)

Developers.net provides a comprehensive employment site for information technology and software development professionals. It contains information on thousands of positions in the U.S. This site is free, but users must register.

Colleges and Universities

Computer Science Departments Across the Web
<http://triluminary.cs.haverford.edu/CS-Departments.html>
(11 November 2004)

Links to the Web sites of academic computer science departments around the world are listed on this Web page.

Graduate Assistantship Directory (GAD)
<http://www.acm.org/gad/>
(11 November 2004)

GAD is a publication of the Association for Computing Machinery; it provides information on graduate programs in computing, including degrees offered and specialties, numbers of faculty and students, faculty interest areas, computer equipment available, types and amounts of financial aid available to qualified students, and admissions requirements and application deadlines.

Journals

All That JAS: Journal Abbreviation Sources: Computer Science
<http://www.public.iastate.edu/~CYBERSTACKS/JAS.htm#Computer>
(11 November 2004)

All That JAS is a listing of Web resources that list or provide access to the full title of journal abbreviations. The computer science section lists two resources.

Computer Science Journals
<http://www.informatik.uni-trier.de/~ley/db/journals/>
(11 November 2004)

Arranged alphabetically by title, this is a directory of selected computer science journals. It provides access to tables-of-contents and the journal's Web page. There are also links to other journal directories.

The Directory of Computing Science Journals
<http://elib.cs.sfu.ca/Collections/CMPT/cs-journals/>
(11 November 2004)

The Directory of Computing Science Journals is a listing and gateway to over 500 computer science and computing journals. Access is provided by an alphabetical list of the titles and a title keyword index. Each journal entry is different but most contain links to its Web page, table-of-contents, abstracts, and full text (for subscribers).

Directory of Open Access Journals: Technology and Engineering: Computer Science
<http://www.doaj.org/ljbs?cpid=114>
(11 November 2004)

Compiled by Lund University Libraries, the *Directory of Open Access Journals* lists free, full-text scholarly journals. There are currently thirty-nine journals in the computer science section. Each journal entry contains ISSN, subject, publisher, language, keywords, start year, and a link to the journal.

Meetings and Conferences

All Conferences: Computers
<http://www.allconferences.com/Computers/>
(11 November 2004)

All Conferences is a directory that focuses on up-coming conferences, conventions, trade shows, exhibits, workshops, events, and meetings. It may be browsed by subject discipline or sub-discipline, or searched by keyword. Each conference record includes event name, dates, place, subject categories, URL, description, and instructions for presenters.

MInd: The Meetings Index
<http://www.interdok.com/mind/>
(11 November 2004)

Created by InterDok, the publisher of the *Directory of Published Proceeding, MInd* lists information on future conferences, congresses, meetings, and symposia. It can be searched by a combination of subject keyword, sponsor, location, and year. Each record includes event name and acronym, dates, location, organizer/sponsor, contacts, keywords, and URL.

Standards and Specifications

Internet-Drafts & RFC Search
<http://mirror.switch.ch/cgi-bin/search/nph-findstd?show_about=yes>
(11 November 2004)

Two types of documents are available through this Web site: Internet-drafts and RFCs (Requests for Comments). RFCs are official documents of the Internet Architecture Board. They are protocols and policies that never change, are permanently archived, and can be updated with a new RFC. An Internet-draft has no formal status, is valid for only six months, and may become an RFC. Using the keyword search facility, either type of document can be located. Once it is found, the full text is freely available.

Internet Requests for Comments (RFC)
<http://www.cse.ohio-state.edu/cs/Services/rfc/index.html>
(11 November 2004)

Maintained by the Department of Computer Science and Engineering at The Ohio State University, the RFCs in this archive deal specifically with the Internet. Access is provided by an index (numerical range listing), keyword search, and numerical listing. Once an RFC is located, the full text is freely available.

Internet RFC/STD/FYI/BCP Archives
<http://www.faqs.org/rfcs/>
(11 November 2004)

This Web site is an archive for the following Internet documents: RFCs (requests for comments), STD (standards), FYI (for your information), and BCP (best current practices). Searchable by keyword or document number, the archives may also be browsed by several indexes. All documents are freely available.

NSSN: A National Resource for Global Standards
<http://www.nssn.org/>
(11 November 2004)

NSSN is a partnership of the American National Standards Institute, government agencies, and international and private sector standards organizations. Its Web site can be used to search for and purchase standards from over 600 global sources.

Standards and Standards Organizations
<http://www.lib.monash.edu.au/vl/standards/stand.html>
(11 November 2004)

After defining standards, this Web page from Monash University Library lists and describes some of the most important international standardization organizations for computing, electronics, and information technologies. The descriptions include links to organizations' Web site, and directions on locating and accessing their standards.

Techstreet
<http://www.techstreet.com/>
(11 November 2004)

Techstreet provides access to standards and codes from over 350 standards organizations. Covering a wide range of industries, including electronics and information technology, this fee-based service delivers documents either by subscription or by individual document. Standards can be searched by keyword, title, ISBN, and document number.

Style Guides

IEEE Computer Society Style Guide
<http://www.computer.org/author/style/>
(11 November 2004)

The purpose of this style guide is to clarify editorial styles and standards used in the IEEE Computer Society's publications. It provides a listing of preferred sources for style and usage, as well as guidance on subjects like abbreviations, capitalization, mathematical expressions, non-English words and phrases, program code, punctuation, and references.

Online! Citation Styles
<http://www.bedfordstmartins.com/online/citex.html>
(11 November 2004)

Developed by Bedford/St. Martin's publishers, this guide covers the elements of citing Internet sources for Modern Language Association (MLA) style, American Psychological Association (APA) style, *Chicago Manual of Style*, and Council of Biological Editors (CBE) style. For each style, the following sources are addressed: WWW site, e-mail message, discussion forum posting, listserv message, newsgroup message, real-time communication, and telnet, FTP, and gopher sites. There are also links to other citation styles.

Submitting Articles to ACM Journals
<http://www.acm.org/pubs/submissions/submission.htm>
(11 November 2004)

This guide contains instructions for submitting articles to ACM journals in the preferred format of LaTeX and in MS Word format. It includes all of the necessary elements for a typical article along with templates to assist the author. The assignment of indexing terms from the *ACM Classification System* is also addressed.

CONCLUDING THOUGHTS

The evolutionary nature of the Internet is apparent in numerous forms and evident by examining the two earlier articles on computer science Internet resources.[1,2] The editors of the first article have attempted to keep it current by inserting up-to-date URLs (uniform resource locators) for sites that are still active but have different URLs, and by removing URLs for sites that have broken links and are no longer available. Of the original 55 Web sites described, 21 (38%) have different URLs and 17 (31%) have disappeared. In nearly eight years, 69% have either migrated or ceased. An analysis of the second article indicates that 25 of 75 Web sites are not available at the original URL; one third either migrated or ceased about four years after publication. The reasons URLs disappear or migrate fall into two categories: (1) the Web site maintainer loses interest and removes the site, or (2) the Web site evolves from a static page to one that is either dynamically generated or uses the latest technologies.

NOTES

1. Knee, Michael. "Guide to Computer Science Internet Resources." *Issues in Science and Technology Librarianship* 15 (Summer 1997), <http://www.library.ucsb.edu/istl/97-summer/internet2.html> (11 November 2004).

2. Knee, Michael. "Computer Science: A Guide to Selected Resources on the Internet." *College & Research Libraries News* 62, no. 6 (June 2001): 609-615, <http://www.ala.org/ala/acrl/acrlpubs/crlnews/backissues2001/june1/computerscience.htm> (11 November 2004).

Web-Based Reference Sources
for Engineering

Thomas W. Conkling

SUMMARY. Engineers and engineering students have an ongoing need for access to reference materials. These might include numerical data, formulas, conversion factors, materials property data, information on components and parts, and information on vendors and their products and services. Many of these information needs can now be satisfied using the Web. Companies, publishers, and government agencies have digitized large quantities of data in the last several years and are making it available on the Web in either free or subscription-based modes. *[Article copies available for a fee from The Haworth Document Delivery Service: 1-800-HAWORTH. E-mail address: <docdelivery@haworthpress.com> Website: <http://www.HaworthPress.com> © 2006 by The Haworth Press, Inc. All rights reserved.]*

KEYWORDS. Engineers, engineering, Web-based reference, reference resources, Internet resources

Thomas W. Conkling is Head, Engineering Library, The Pennsylvania State University, 325 Hammond Building, University Park, PA 16802 (E-mail: twc1@psu.edu).

[Haworth co-indexing entry note]: "Web-Based Reference Sources for Engineering." Conkling, Thomas W. Co-published simultaneously in *Journal of Library Administration* (The Haworth Information Press, an imprint of The Haworth Press, Inc.) Vol. 44, No. 1/2, 2006, pp. 475-495; and: *Evolving Internet Reference Resources* (ed: William Miller, and Rita M. Pellen) The Haworth Information Press, an imprint of The Haworth Press, Inc., 2006, pp. 475-495. Single or multiple copies of this article are available for a fee from The Haworth Document Delivery Service [1-800-HAWORTH, 9:00 a.m. - 5:00 p.m. (EST). E-mail address: docdelivery@haworthpress.com].

doi:10.1300/J111v44n01_08

INTRODUCTION

Engineers are generally not extensive library users. Studies have shown that they rely most heavily on colleagues, internal company materials, and departmental and personal collections of documents to satisfy their information needs (Pinelli, 1997; Shuchman, 1981; Tenopir, 2004). Engineers employed in industry are expected to be self sufficient to a large degree in their quest for job-related information (Rodrigues, 2001). A recent study (Napp, 2004) suggested that this pattern might be a common state of affairs for many engineers–the majority of design firms responding to a survey placed the burden for information searching and retrieval directly on the engineer.

In this environment, the Internet is taking on an important role in the working lives of practicing engineers. It facilitates communications with colleagues, and can be useful in searching internal information resources within the company. It also provides access to millions of Web sites, a number of which have valuable information for engineers, researchers, and engineering students. The actual types of information that can be useful include materials properties, component and product data, developments and news in the field, standards and specifications, units, conversions, handbooks, patents, and bibliographic databases.

This paper explores some of the Web-based information resources in these categories, covering both free and subscription-based sites. This isn't an exhaustive presentation of sources, but rather a selection of some of the major sources in each category. Web resources undergo constant change in content, availability, and structure, so the accuracy of the descriptions presented here may change over time.

READY REFERENCE SOURCES

Ready reference sources offer quick answers to questions that may come up during the course of a work day. An engineer or engineering student may need to look up a definition, a conversion table, units, a technical explanation, or a brief summary of an unfamiliar topic.

Dictionary of Units
<http://www.ex.ac.uk/trol/dictunit/index.htm>
(accessed November 28, 2004)

An extensive collection of units of measurement is presented, with definitions, explanations, formulas, and conversions. It contains a section with online calculators to perform conversions.

Engineers Edge
<http://www.engineersedge.com>
(accessed November 28, 2004)

Tailored to the needs of mechanical design and manufacturing engineers, the site presents a large collection of data and online calculators. Formulas and information on flow, fasteners, bearings, springs, hydraulics, drive belts, gears, heat transfer, dimensioning and tolerancing, corrosion, and mathematics are included.

eFunda
<http://efunda.com>
(accessed November 28, 2004)

The eFunda Web site is intended to serve a broader audience than the Engineers Edge site, which specializes in design and manufacturing. It was developed to answer the daily reference needs of engineers in any discipline. It provides an extensive array of information in these categories: materials, component design, manufacturing processes, unit conversions, formulas, and mathematics. Review and background information is given in all areas, in addition to numerical data.

Acronym Finder
<http://www.acronymfinder.com>
(accessed November 28, 2004)

The site provides definitions of acronyms, with links for searching the terms on Amazon.com.

GATEWAYS TO ENGINEERING INFORMATION

There are a number of Web sites that serve as broad entry points to engineering information. They are valuable in that many have done some evaluation and filtering of contents, and the sites that they list are judged to have quality information, at least to some degree. Most of the gateway services cite both free and subscription-based resources. Google (http://www.google.com) and Yahoo (http://dir.yahoo.com/science/engineering) can also serve as useful tools for locating engineering information on the Web.

EEVL: The Internet Guide to Engineering, Mathematics, and Computing
<http://www.eevl.ac.uk>
(accessed November 28, 2004)

This site was developed by academic information specialists in the U.K. to serve as a national access point to Internet resources in engineering, math, and computer science. EEVL provides descriptions and links to over 10,000 Web sites. A very wide variety of sites has been included in the catalog and includes academic and industrial labs, companies, data sites, tutorials, and various types of publications. Sites can be accessed by keyword searches or through subject compilations.

Infomine
<http://infomine.ucr.edu>
(accessed November 28, 2004)

Infomine is a large collection of Internet resources relevant to engineering faculty, students, and staff. The site is a cooperative effort among librarians, primarily in California. It pulls together resources such as databases, bulletin boards, electronic journals and books, subject guides, online catalogs, and directories. The site contains over 100,000 links (many annotated), covering engineering, science, and many other disciplines. The site can be searched within these disciplines or in its entirety by keyword.

SciTech Resources.gov
<http://scitechresources.gov>
(accessed November 28, 2004)

This is a highly focused entry point to U.S. government-sponsored information resources on the Web. The site describes itself as a catalog of government science and technology Web sites. An advanced option permits searching by topic and limiting by resource type such as software, data, information centers, legislation and regulations, and reports and publications. SciTechResources.gov is managed by NTIS, the National Technical Information Service.

COMPONENTS AND SUPPLIERS

Most engineers deal with equipment and other components on a regular basis. They may need to find out what is available to assist in testing materials or to conduct an experiment, upgrade a facility, or locate items that can be used in design projects. This is one of the areas that the Web excels in–there are a large number of sites to help engineers and others locate all types of specialized products.

Thomas Register
<http://www.thomasregister.com>
(accessed November 28, 2004)

ThomasRegister.com is the online version of the venerable printed catalog of the same name that has been in use for many years. *Thomas Register* is a comprehensive resource for finding companies and the products they manufacture. The focus is on North American industry. The site is free and is searchable by product or service, company name, and brand name. Search results include the name of the company and its address, contact information, a summary of its products, and usually a link to an online product catalog or the company's Web site.

Sweets
<http://sweets.construction.com>
(accessed November 28, 2004)

This is an online version of the *Sweet's Catalog File*, a printed catalog to companies, products, and services in architecture and construction. The site is keyword searchable and results provide company names and contact information as well as a listing of their products and services.

The next three Web sites (Grainger, McMaster-Carr, and MSC) are companies with huge inventories of tools, equipment, components, and parts. There is some overlap in the items that they offer, but there are differences in the varieties and suppliers of many of the products.

Grainger
<http://www.grainger.com>
(accessed November 28, 2004)

The Grainger site provides access to tens of thousands of parts, components, tools, and pieces of equipment of interest to engineers in many disciplines. Searching can be done on keywords, manufacturer, and various identifying numbers. Product search results usually include an image, product description, manufacturer, model number, and unit price. All items can be ordered online from Grainger.

McMaster-Carr
<http://www.mcmaster.com>
(accessed November 28, 2004)

McMaster-Carr is a very large components vendor. The online catalog contains over 400,000 items. Keyword searching is available, or one can browse through an online listing of general product areas such as piping, valves, instrumentation, plumbing, machinery, lighting, electrical, hardware, material handling, and hand tools. Searches return product descriptions, specifications, images, and price. Products can be ordered online from McMaster-Carr.

MSC Industrial Supply Company
<http://mscdirect.com>
(accessed November 28, 2004)

The MSC Industrial Supply Company is one of the country's largest marketers of industrial supplies and equipment. The MSC Web site provides an access point to the half-million tools, components, and other types of equipment that the company offers. An enormous selection of items can be searched and purchased, including fluids, drills, saws, tool bits, fittings, welding supplies, abrasives, measuring instruments, machinery, fasteners, hydraulics, valves, and pumps. Searches retrieve product descriptions, specifications, manufacturer, product number, and price. Search results also link to more detailed display pages in the online catalog.

EngNet
<http://www.engnetglobal.com>
(accessed November 28, 2004)

EngNet brings together a broad range of companies and vendors to assist the engineering community in finding information efficiently on products and services. The site is keyword searchable for products, companies, or brand names. Browsing by broad subject categories is also permitted on the home page.

EE Product Center
<http://eeproductcenter.com>
(accessed November 28, 2004)

This is a good example of a single industry component directory site. EE Product Center is set up to be a comprehensive online information resource for integrated circuits and other electronics products. It provides reviews of new products and can search for components from over 10,000 supplier catalogs. The site also provides new product news.

GlobalSpec: The Engineering Search Engine
<http://www.globalspec.com>
(accessed November 28, 2004)

The search engine on this site can review the contents of millions of engineering Web pages and retrieve product and service information from over 11,000 online catalogs. The home page is divided into broad subject categories, which link to further subdivisions and then to company and product information. Standards, patents, and materials properties are also searchable on GlobalSpec.

Stock Drive Products/Sterling Instruments: SDP/SI
<http://www.sdp-si.com>
(accessed November 28, 2004)

One alternative to searching large Web sites for components and parts information is to go directly to a parts manufacturer's site. Stock Drive Products has been manufacturing and distributing precision grade mechanical and electromechanical parts for years and its Web site provides access to over 60,000 items. Gears, shafts, bearings, motors, pulleys, sprockets, belts, cables, and hardware are among the products offered. The site is free to use and most items are in stock and ready to ship.

MATERIALS PROPERTIES

The need for materials property data spans most areas of engineering and the sciences. Engineering design projects often involve materials, and the selection of materials with optimal properties is crucial for applications. Several of the Web sites mentioned earlier provide this type of data, and there are thousands more on the Web that provide some type of physical, chemical, or thermodynamic properties of materials. This section looks at a few of the more comprehensive properties sites.

MatWeb
<http://www.matweb.com>
(accessed November 28, 2004)

MatWeb contains comprehensive listings of physical and thermodynamic properties of polymers, metals, alloys, ceramics, and other materials such as fibers and semiconductors. Searches can be conducted by material type, manufacturer, composition, UNS number, and trade name. Property ranges can be specified to assist in materials selection. The information provided on each material can include manufacturers and vendors, as well as listings of physical, mechanical, thermal, and electrical properties. Advanced Web site features are available for a subscription fee.

NIST Data Gateway
<http://srdata.nist.gov/gateway>
(accessed November 28, 2004)

The National Institute of Standards and Technology (formerly National Bureau of Standards) has a long and distinguished record of investigating the properties of materials, compiling them, and then making those results broadly available. The NIST Data Gateway provides a portal to a vast collection of material property data in many scientific disciplines contained in over 80 databases. The entire site can be searched by keyword, property, or substance name. The databases can also be searched separately. The "NIST Ceramics Web Book" and the "NIST Property Data Summaries for Advanced Materials" are examples of these databases.

WebElements Periodic Table
<http://www.webelements.com>
(accessed November 28, 2004)

An important resource for engineering and science, the periodic table of the elements is presented in a highly useful format. Selecting any element on the table retrieves a range of basic information: name, CAS registry number, group number, group name, period number, and a description of the element. Links are also provided to numerous physical, electronic, and thermodynamic properties. Some of the more important compounds of the elements are presented, as are means of production. Data are given as text, in graphs, and in tables.

Thermodex
<http://thermodex.lib.utexas.edu>
(accessed November 28, 2004)

Thermodex can be described as a finding guide to thermochemical and thermophysical data. The database is produced at the University of Texas and allows users to search by compound and property, such as the heat capacity of alcohol. The results retrieve the title of a handbook that should contain the data. This will be most useful to engineers and engineering students with access to print or online handbook collections.

ChemFinder.com
<http://chemfinder.cambridgesoft.com>
(accessed November 28, 2004)

A combination of free and subscription-based services are found at this site. Basic searches can be done on a chemical name, CAS number, and molecular formula or weight. Search results provide a wealth of data on the chemical: CAS number, synonyms, structure, density, molecular weight, and other properties. Supplemental links are provided for additional properties, health information, regulations, and miscellaneous other topics. The site also allows searching through the catalogs of 30 chemical suppliers for sourcing and purchasing information. The fee-based components of the site offer more in-depth search capabilities.

CINDAS databases
<http://www.cindasdata.com>
(accessed November 28, 2004)

The Center for Information and Numerical Data Analysis and Synthesis (CINDAS) at Purdue University has produced several well-known databases on materials properties over the years. CINDAS LLC is a small company that is making this materials property data available over the Web on a subscription basis. The "Thermophysical Properties of Matter Database" contains thermophysical properties of over 5,000 materials, and the "Microelectronics Packaging Materials Database" contains data on the thermal, mechanical, electrical, and physical properties of 600 electronics packaging materials. The databases can be searched a number of ways including by name or partial name of the material, and the desired property.

ELECTRONIC HANDBOOKS

Handbooks are indispensable tools for engineers. They provide formulas, data, all types of material properties, and information to either brush up on a topic or explore an unfamiliar one. A number of the Web sites mentioned thus far contain handbook-style information–Engineers Edge, eFunda, MatWeb, and the NIST databases. Many well-known handbooks from major publishers like CRC, Wiley, and McGraw-Hill are now available on the Web on subscription-based sites. This section describes some of these commercial sites as well as a few additional free sites.

ENGnetBASE
<http://www.engnetbase.com>
(accessed November 28, 2004)

CRC handbooks are well-known in engineering. The company has been producing quality publications in print for decades, and is now making these materials available on the Web for a fee. Over 200 handbooks are available online, covering all areas of engineering. Handbooks can be individually selected and browsed, and the entire site can be searched by keyword. Keyword searches return references to sections of chapters which contain the search words.

Knovel
<http://www.knovel.com>
(accessed November 28, 2004)

Knovel is an innovative system that provides a large selection of handbooks and advanced texts from many publishers, including Wiley, McGraw-Hill, Elsevier, and William Andrew Publishing. A number of the online books have been created with interactive features, or "productivity tools." These features include tables in which the data can be manipulated using spreadsheet tools and also plotted in graphs. Chemical structures can be drawn and searched, and various spectra can be viewed for elements and compounds. Book contents can be either browsed or searched. Knovel is a subscription-based product.

ASM Handbooks Online
<http://products.asminternational.org/hbk/index.jsp>
(accessed November 28, 2004)

The *ASM Handbook* (previously known as the *Metals Handbook*) is a twenty-one volume printed set of data and detailed information on thousands of metals and composites. It is now available through subscription on the Web. The American Society for Metals compiles this work and the data it contains is considered comprehensive and authoritative. All aspects of metals are covered by volumes on properties, phase diagrams, heat treating, failure analysis, corrosion, forming, casting, machining, friction, lubrication, fatigue, fracture, and nondestructive evaluation.

The next two sources are representative of the type of free handbook-type Web sites that can be found in all areas of engineering. Such sites tend to be very specific and might appeal to small subgroups of engineers.

Principal Metals Online
<http://www.principalmetals.com>
(accessed November 28, 2004)

This site is maintained by a metals supplier. It offers materials property data on 5,000 ferrous and non-ferrous metals, including information on composition, welding, machining, and forming. A glossary and several conversion tools, as well as a periodic table, are found here. The site is geared to helping customers find the proper metals for applications, but it is also useful for gathering property data.

rf cafe
<http://www.rfcafe.com>
(accessed November 28, 2004)

An example of a very specialized site, the rf cafe bills itself as the "engineering onramp" to electrical engineering information on the Web. It has many of the features expected from an online handbook including numerous formulas, definitions, and conversions. Links to product applications notes, vendors, trade journals, standards organizations, on-line forums, and job postings are provided.

RESEARCH DATABASES

Most of the Web sites discussed thus far were concerned with pro-viding numerical or factual data that could assist engineers in their day-to-day work. Specialized bibliographic databases are available for engineering faculty and research engineers. Searching bibliographic da-tabases permits engineers and scientists to determine what research has been previously done and published on a topic. Most of these databases are available on the Web on a subscription basis from vendors. Some engineering societies with publication programs allow free public ac-cess to their databases. A number of government agencies have exten-sive technical report data available on the Web, and these will be discussed in the "Technical Reports" section.

Compendex
<http://www.engineeringvillage2.org>
(accessed November 28, 2004)

Compendex is the most comprehensive bibliographic database in engineering. It is the online version of *Engineering Index*, a printed abstracting service that has been in business since 1894. Compendex indexes and abstracts approximately 5,000 journals and conference proceedings, on an international basis. The full database contains 9,000,000 records, providing access to the engineering literature back to 1894. A variety of search types can be done (keyword, author, corporate source, serial title, author affiliation), and the retrieved records nor-mally display complete bibliographic information and an abstract. Subscriptions can be ordered from a number of online vendors. The database is produced by Elsevier Engineering Information.

INSPEC
<http://www.iee.org/Publish/INSPEC>
(accessed November 28, 2004)

This is an excellent database covering physics, electrical and elec-tronic engineering, computer engineering, control engineering, and in-formation technology. Both journal articles and conference proceedings are covered on a worldwide basis. The database currently covers from 1969 to the present, and back files for the years 1898 through 1968 are available. Searches on this database retrieve bibliographic data and an abstract. INSPEC is produced by the Institution of Electrical Engineers, and is available by subscription from several vendors.

Web of Science
<http://www.isinet.com/products/citation/wos>
(accessed November 28, 2004)

The most important feature of this database for engineers is the ability to do cited reference searching, to discover which research papers have been cited by other authors. This can be important for determining the quality of a paper and for finding information on elusive topics. Direct subject searching can also be done on this system, but the coverage of the engineering literature is not as extensive as that found in Compendex. The *Science Citation Index* portion of the system now covers back to 1945. This database is produced by ISI and is available on subscription.

IEEE Xplore
<http://ieeexplore.ieee.org/Xplore/DynWel.jsp>
(accessed November 28, 2004)

This is a powerful information system that provides coverage of all IEEE (Institute of Electrical and Electronics Engineers) publications from 1988 to the present. It is limited to IEEE and IEE (Institution of Electrical Engineers) publications only, but these are highly respected organizations in the field. IEEE Xplore contains both the bibliographic records and the full text of the papers. A variety of search modes is available, and searching can be limited to publication type (journals, conferences, standards). IEEE Xplore is a subscription-based product, but non-subscribers can access the bibliographic portions of the system at no cost.

A number of engineering societies provide some level of free public access to their bibliographic records. The ASCE (American Society of Civil Engineers) has a database with records of its publications issued since 1995 <http://www.ascelibrary.org>. Technical papers and standards can be browsed and ordered from the SAE (Society of Automotive Engineers) Web site <http://www.sae.org>. ACI (American Concrete Institute) publication abstracts can be searched at no cost and ordered online <http://www.concrete.org>. Aerospace-related publications can be searched and ordered online from the AIAA (American Institute of Aeronautics and Astronautics) Web site <http://www.aiaa.org>. These sites are only a sampling of the engineering society information on the Web.

TECHNICAL REPORTS

Another important source of information for engineers is the technical report. Though more of a research resource than a reference source, reports can contain valuable data for the engineer. Technical reports are documents that present results from research sponsored by government agencies. The largest sponsors and producers of technical reports in the U.S. include the Department of Energy, Department of Defense, NASA, and the Environmental Protection Agency. A major change has occurred in the last several years in the distribution of technical reports. Until recently, technical reports had been primarily distributed as paper or microfiche copies. Now, however, many agencies are making full-text copies of current reports available from their Web sites.

NTIS Database
<http://www.ntis.gov>
(accessed November 28, 2004)

The National Technical Information Service serves as the main clearinghouse for technical reports produced as a result of government-sponsored research. The NTIS database, covering 1964 through the present, is the single best database to use for accessing the technical report literature. Reports on many engineering topics can be found here, and NTIS also acts as a supplier for copies of these materials. The full database is available on subscription from vendors, but the most recent ten years of the database can be searched for free at the NTIS Web site.

Energy Citations Database
<http://www.osti.gov/energycitations>
(accessed November 28, 2004)

The U.S. Department of Energy has sponsored tens of millions of dollars of research over the years. The agency produced the publication

Nuclear Science Abstracts and its successors to make researchers aware of this work as well as related research activities in other countries around the world. Energy Citations Database has now taken the place of the printed indexes and provides online access to research in nuclear engineering and science and related disciplines. The database includes technical reports, journal articles, and conference proceedings, and covers from 1948 forward. This is an excellent free resource for research in these areas. Full-text copies of many newer Department of Energy technical reports can be found at a companion site–*DOE Information Bridge* <http://www.osti.gov/bridge/>.

DTIC Public STINET
<http://stinet.dtic.mil>
(accessed November 28, 2004)

Public STINET offers bibliographic access to many of the unclassified and unlimited distribution technical reports issued by the U.S. Department of Defense for the last forty years. The site also contains full-text versions of most reports published since 2004. The site is free to all users.

NASA Technical Report Server (NTRS)
<http://ntrs.nasa.gov>
(accessed November 28, 2004)

This database provides bibliographic access to many NACA- and NASA-generated technical reports and other related materials back to the early 1900s. Most of the reports produced by NACA (National Advisory Committee on Aeronautics) have been digitized and are online. Many of the newer NASA reports are also available full text. NTRS is available to the public at no charge.

GrayLIT Network
<http://www.osti.gov/graylit/>
(accessed November 28, 2004)

An alternative to searching each of these sites separately is the GrayLIT Network. This site serves as a portal to full-text reports from DOD, NASA, DOE, and the EPA. It provides one-stop access for engineers interested in publications from these agencies. Searches can be done for materials from all of these agencies, or limited to selected ones. Results link directly to the full-text versions of the reports.

STANDARDS

Engineering standards are documents that provide performance guidelines for materials and equipment, test methods, safety practices, and other information for engineers, designers, researchers, and manufacturers. Standards can be developed by engineering societies, government agencies, industry groups, and the military. Many industrialized nations have produced standards, and there is often one pre-eminent standards issuing body in each country, such as ANSI (American National Standards Institute) in the U.S. Most society and industry standards are not available on the Web for free, although there are numerous free databases available to find out what standards have been issued on a topic. The actual standards can be accessed through online subscriptions or by orders from the developing organization or commercial vendors. U.S. military standards and specifications are available on the Web at no charge to users.

NSSN
<http://www.nssn.org>
(accessed November 28, 2004)

NSSN is a database providing access to information on 270,000 standards produced by over 600 national and international organizations. The site offers "one stop" browsing for the world's standards. NSSN is produced and maintained by the American National Standards Institute (ANSI). Searches can be done by standard number, title word, or keywords in the bibliographic records. Results provide the full document title and number, issuing body, date approved, and ordering information. Companies or individuals can subscribe to the "Standard Tracking and Automated Reporting" service that provides information on changes to crucial standards in a particular area.

ANSI: American National Standards Institute
<http://www.ansi.org>
(accessed November 28, 2004)

ANSI serves as the umbrella organization for the administration and coordination of standards issued by groups within the United States. It is a private, non-profit membership organization supported by over 1,000 companies and institutions. Many of these organizations develop the standards that are issued by ANSI–there are approximately 10,000 active ANSI standards. The ANSI Web site permits searching by keyword and standard number, and for many items, allows online ordering and downloading. The standards listed at this site are included in the NSSN site, but the ANSI site offers more detailed information on its standards activities, related programs, and services.

ISO: International Organization for Standards
<http://www.iso.org>
(accessed November 28, 2004)

The ISO plays a role similar to that of ANSI, but for the international standards community. The body promotes and coordinates the issuing of standards by 146 member groups, the goal of which is to create a system of standards to facilitate and support worldwide manufacturing and commerce. ISO standards are issued for all areas of engineering. The Web site has basic and advanced search interfaces, and permits the online ordering of electronic or print standards. ISO standards are included in NSSN, but the ISO site provides additional information on the ISO, its members, and activities.

ASTM International
<http://www.astm.org>
(accessed November 28, 2004)

The ASTM is an example of a large standards-developing organization. Originally known as the American Society for Testing and Materials, the group produces hundreds of standards for materials, materials testing, products, and services. ASTM standards are held in high regard and are used by engineers and scientists in many applications. The ASTM International Web site offers searching and online ordering of print or electronic copies of documents. The entire set of ASTM standards can be accessed on the Web via subscription.

ASSIST: Acquisition Streamlining and Standardization Information System
<http://assist.daps.dla.mil/quicksearch>
(accessed November 28, 2004)

The U.S. Department of Defense (DOD) produces and adopts many standards of interest to manufacturers and suppliers. The "Assist-Quick Search" Web site permits interested individuals and organizations to search for standards, specifications, and handbooks from the DOD and other agencies. The system lists active, inactive, and cancelled documents, and in many cases a pdf version is available for downloading at no cost.

PATENTS

The patent literature has become very easy to access over the Web during the last several years. Patents used to be sent to depository libraries around the country in either print or microfilmed versions. The U.S. Patent and Trademark Office and similar non-U.S. organizations have now put patents on the Web along with searchable databases for access. Access is usually free to these materials.

United States Patent and Trademark Office
<http://www.uspto.gov>
(accessed November 28, 2004)

This site provides comprehensive access to U.S. patents and trademarks. The patents system has information on all U.S. patents dating back to 1790, as well as recent patent applications. The system is searchable by keyword, patent number, assignee, classification, inventor name, and various other elements. Searches bring back complete identifying information on the patent and a link that retrieves the patent's image. The U.S. PTO site also provides links to the intellectual property offices of many other countries. The "Trademark Electronic Search System" (TESS) provides similar access to several million trademarks.

European Patent Office
<http://ep.espacenet.com>
(accessed November 28, 2004)

This Web site provides access to a collection of over 30,000,000 patents from Europe, the United States, and several other countries. Various types of searches are permitted, retrieving detailed records that provide links to an image of the patent.

MISCELLANEOUS SITES

There are many other types of Web sites that provide useful information to engineers and engineering students. Jobs and career sites can be valuable to those just starting out or contemplating new positions. Professional society sites can help practicing engineers stay current on professional trends. Education-related sites list continuing education courses or online tutorials on relevant topics. Web versions of trade journals give readers news of the industry. This section considers a small sampling of sites like these.

EngineeringJobs.com
<http://engineeringjobs.com>
(accessed November 28, 2004)

This site allows employers to list jobs and those seeking work to post their resumés. It contains a list of headhunters and the jobs that they are trying to fill, and contract recruiters seeking to fill temporary engineering positions.

TrueCareers
<http://www.careercity.com>
(accessed November 28, 2004)

TrueCareers posts jobs in engineering and many other professions. Its job search box allows keyword searching and a number of limiters, including employer's name and geographic distance from a particular zip code. Resumés can be posted at the site.

WWW Information Sources for Short Courses
<http://www.engr.utk.edu/nuclear/TIW/engshort.html>
(accessed November 28, 2004)

This is a straightforward site that lists links to universities and other organizations that offer short courses of interest to engineers and other professionals.

FedBizOpps: Federal Business Opportunities
<http://www.fedbizopps.gov>
(accessed November 28, 2004)

FedBizOpps serves as a single entry point for U.S. government-wide procurement opportunities over $25,000. While more of a business site than an engineering one, many of the products and services that government agencies are seeking would be of interest to engineers and their employers.

Engineers Worldwide
<http://www.engineersworldwide.com>
(accessed November 28, 2004)

Engineers involved in construction can find a wealth of information at this site. There are links to architects, consultants, contractors, construction equipment, building materials, furnishing suppliers, insurance firms, surveyors, job classifieds, and more.

ZDNet
<http://www.zdnet.com>
(accessed November 28, 2004)

ZDNet offers a gateway to information technology data. It provides links to news, blogs, software to download, product reviews, pricing, and technical papers from IT companies. An interesting feature is its listing of the top 50 search terms used on the site during the proceeding 30 days.

Manufacturing.net
<http://manufacturing.net>
(accessed November 28, 2004)

Information on all aspects of industrial and manufacturing engineering, logistics, materials handling, plant engineering, and product design are collected at this site. Links are provided to separate Web sites for each of these topics and more. Manufacturing.net also has industry news, a guide to suppliers, and links to a number of trade journal Web sites.

Circuits Archive
<http://www.ee.washington.edu/circuit_archive>
(accessed November 28, 2004)

The University of Washington Department of Electrical Engineering maintains this large archive of electric circuit information for students and practicing engineers. Circuit diagrams are the primary emphasis of the site, but other items are also presented including data sheets, miscellaneous documentation, and related Web links.

CONCLUSIONS

The Web has made certain information-seeking activities easier for engineers and engineering students. Engineers looking for information have traditionally relied on colleagues and local resources, but Web-based sources can now supply much of the data that was previously only available in printed handbooks and catalogs. Commercial and society publishers and government agencies will continue to develop online resources because of their popularity in the engineering and science communities. More engineering-related sites will also be developed by individuals and small companies, offering combinations of free and subscription services. The best of these sites will prosper and grow, while the others will disappear. The Web sites that can offer the best indexing and consolidation of data and products will probably be the most valuable in the future, since they will present the greatest benefits in time and cost savings to engineers and engineering students.

REFERENCES

Napp, J.B. (2004). "Survey of Library Services at *Engineering News Record's* Top 500 Design Firms: Implications for Engineering Education." *Journal of Engineering Education* 93(3):247-251.

Pinelli, T.E.; R.O. Barclay; J.M. Kennedy; and A.P. Bishop. (1997). *Knowledge Diffusion in the U.S. Aerospace Industry.* Greenwich, CT: Ablex Publishing Corporation.

Rodrigues, R.J. (2001). "Industry Expectations of the New Engineer." *Science & Technology Libraries* 19(3/4):179-185.

Shuchman, H.L. (1981). *Information Transfer in Engineering.* Glastonbury, CT: The Futures Group.

Tenopir, C., and D.W. King. (2004). *Communication Patterns of Engineers.* Piscataway, NJ: IEEE Press.

Index

BOOK ORDER FORM!

Order a copy of this book with this form or online at:
http://www.haworthpress.com/store/product.asp?sku=5728

Evolving Internet Reference Resources

___ in softbound at $49.95 ISBN-13: 978-0-7890-3025-2 / ISBN-10: 0-7890-3025-X.
___ in hardbound at $69.95 ISBN-13: 978-0-7890-3024-5 / ISBN-10: 0-7890-3024-1.

COST OF BOOKS _____

POSTAGE & HANDLING _____
US: $4.00 for first book & $1.50
for each additional book
Outside US: $5.00 for first book
& $2.00 for each additional book.

SUBTOTAL _____

In Canada: add 7% GST. _____

STATE TAX _____
CA, IL, IN, MN, NJ, NY, OH, PA & SD residents
please add appropriate local sales tax.

FINAL TOTAL _____
If paying in Canadian funds, convert
using the current exchange rate,
UNESCO coupons welcome.

❑BILL ME LATER:
Bill-me option is good on US/Canada/
Mexico orders only; not good to jobbers,
wholesalers, or subscription agencies.

❑ Signature _____

❑ Payment Enclosed: $ _____

❑ PLEASE CHARGE TO MY CREDIT CARD:
❑ Visa ❑ MasterCard ❑ AmEx ❑ Discover
❑ Diner's Club ❑ Eurocard ❑ JCB

Account # _____

Exp Date _____

Signature _____
(Prices in US dollars and subject to change without notice.)

PLEASE PRINT ALL INFORMATION OR ATTACH YOUR BUSINESS CARD

Name

Address

City	State/Province	Zip/Postal Code

Country

Tel	Fax

E-Mail

May we use your e-mail address for confirmations and other types of information? ❑Yes ❑No We appreciate receiving
your e-mail address. Haworth would like to e-mail special discount offers to you, as a preferred customer.
We will never share, rent, or exchange your e-mail address. We regard such actions as an invasion of your privacy.

Order from your **local bookstore** or directly from
The Haworth Press, Inc. 10 Alice Street, Binghamton, New York 13904-1580 • USA
Call our toll-free number (1-800-429-6784) / Outside US/Canada: (607) 722-5857
Fax: 1-800-895-0582 / Outside US/Canada: (607) 771-0012
E-mail your order to us: orders@haworthpress.com

For orders outside US and Canada, you may wish to order through your local
sales representative, distributor, or bookseller.
For information, see http://haworthpress.com/distributors

(Discounts are available for individual orders in US and Canada only, not booksellers/distributors.)

Please photocopy this form for your personal use.
www.HaworthPress.com

BOF05